functions and policies of
AMERICAN GOVERNMENT

functions and policies of

contributing authors:

Lewis A. Froman, Jr.
University of California, Irvine

Lawrence J. R. Herson
R. Roger Majak
Ohio State University

James N. Murray
The University of Iowa

Robert H. Salisbury
Washington University

Richard W. Taylor
Coe College

prentice-hall, inc.
englewood cliffs, new jersey

Third Edition

AMERICAN
GOVERNMENT

edited by
J. W. PELTASON
University of California, Irvine

JAMES M. BURNS
Williams College

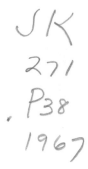
third edition

functions and policies of
AMERICAN GOVERNMENT

edited by PELTASON and BURNS

Current printing (last digit):

10 9 8 7 6 5 4 3 2

Printed in the United States of America

Library of Congress Catalog Card No.: 67–17594

PRENTICE-HALL INTERNATIONAL, INC., *London*
PRENTICE-HALL OF AUSTRALIA, PTY. LTD., *Sydney*
PRENTICE-HALL OF CANADA, LTD., *Toronto*
PRENTICE-HALL OF INDIA (PRIVATE) LTD., *New Delhi*
PRENTICE-HALL OF JAPAN, INC., *Tokyo*

preface

This volume is a presentation of governmental policies, functions, and programs, discussed in greater detail than is possible in standard introductory American government texts. In a context as complete as space permits, specific policies are described against a background of history, politics, and government. The emphasis is on functions, policies, and programs of the national government; but since much of what the national government does is closely intertwined with state activities, there is a good deal of treatment of the latter.

The book is a joint effort in both the full and limited meaning of the words. The authors agreed in advance on the general approach, emphasis, and subject matter; but in the light of the great diversity of the subject, we have not tried to fit each chapter into a narrow, cramping mold. The reader will find, consequently, that the chapters are roughly similar in problems raised and concepts discussed; but the organization, emphasis, and viewpoint may vary somewhat from chapter to chapter.

We wish to thank our colleagues for their suggestions and our students for allowing themselves to be exposed somewhat experimentally to much of the material.

THE AUTHORS

contents

functions and policies of
AMERICAN GOVERNMENT

an approach
to the
study of public policy

J. W. PELTASON

This book is designed for the reader who is acquainted—or is
becoming acquainted with the general organization of American Government as it is taught in the standard introductory
course. In most such courses limitations of time preclude any
extended study of programs and policies: the functions of
government, if discussed at all, are given only cursory treatment.
Here the emphasis is reversed. The focus is on what American
governments do.

The purposes of this book are to provide background for
each major policy area, to describe the broad outlines of existing programs, to identify the interests and organizations most
immediately concerned, to bring to the fore the values that are
in conflict, to point to the interrelations between process and
policy, and to suggest the possible consequences of various
choices.

This study of the functions of government is inevitably also
a study of politics and administration. For questions about what
our governments should do and how they should do it are resolved not through the application of abstract scientific principles but through the policymaking process, in which we all
participate.

THE POLICY PROCESS

To some, politics is a struggle between heroes and villains
—the good guys against the bad guys. Others divide the political
world into two parts, the "government" and the "people." To
others the government is a group of statesmen standing above

1

the clamour of politics and applying predetermined scientific rules to protect the "people" against the "special interests." But the good-guys-versus-the-bad-guys approach is an exercise in conclusions, not in description, nor does it give us precise analytic tools. Similarly, to organize all the "booming-buzzing-confusion" of politics into such broad-gauge moulds as "government" and "people" is an obvious oversimplification. "Government" and "people" are terms of such wide scope that they conceal more than they reveal. Government consists of people, many different kinds of people who have many different kinds of values. And the "people" are not a homogeneous unit, internally united and uniformly hostile to all public officials. We need categories of description more restrictive in their focus.

Politics as Interest Group Conflict

Government programs and politics are fundamentally the products of contests among citizens, both private and official. Within the context of widely shared and deeply held common values, Americans have conflicting political goals—differing ideas about which policies are "in the public interest." Each of us is likely to erect a system of thinking or an ideology in which our own role—manager, professor, inventor, housewife—is the axis on which the world turns. From our differing perspectives we view the world differently. The miner who goes into the earth to dig for coal thinks that he is performing the most essential economic task and his perspective toward government programs that boost wages is likely to be different from that of the harried company treasurer who is worried about meeting the company payrolls.

Because of their varying perspectives, Americans differ concerning the desirability of many public programs. They make various claims on and through the instruments of government. One way to describe this political activity is in terms of *interest groups*. All the kinds of activity—writing, speaking, voting, lobbying, forming organizations—designed to secure a particular political goal may be related to an interest; those engaged in like activities make up a group. It is theoretically possible for a particular interest to consist of the action of only one man. For the most part, however, it is only those programs supported by more than one person that take on enough significance to be of concern to a study of policy-making. We shall consider public policies as essentially the products of interest groups.

The term "interest group" is merely a descriptive category that the observer creates in order to relate diverse events. The term "interest" has the disadvantage of carrying overtones of selfishness, of material and personal gain. No such suggestion is intended here. Differing concepts of ultimate good create conflicts of interest as often as do struggles over the distribution of material rewards. As used here, "interest group" is *not* an evaluating term. There is no implication of either criticism or approval, for example, when it is pointed out that producers of natural gas were an important part of the interest group working to secure passage of a law to free their businesses from regulation by the Federal Power Commission.

People who share common roles and characteristics often have common interests, and they often organize. But an interest group should not be confused either with an organization or with groups of people having certain attributes in common. Workers, farmers, veterans, fathers, and Negroes, for example, are labels used to group people by common characteristics or roles. The United Mine Workers, General Motors, and National Association for Advancement of Calendar Reform are organizations. Proponents of compulsory health insurance and opponents of federal civil rights legislation, for example, are interest groups. Although organization is, as we shall presently note, a characteristic activity of an interest group, the organization and interest group should be kept distinct. Not all members of the American Legion, for example, belong to the interest group working for pensions for veterans. On the other hand, some who are not members of the American Legion do work for veterans' pensions.

The Role of Government in the Policy Process

Government consists of public officials. In a democracy what they do is related to what those who are not public officials want done. These officials are not outside the group struggle, but very much in it. When a congressman votes, a President vetoes, a judge decides, or a civil servant issues an order, his actions constitute interest group activity and he becomes a member of an interest group. A congressman may resent our description of his votes as interest activity: he may insist that he is supporting the "public interest." We do not deny that the vote may be in the "public interest"— but that is a conclusion, not a description. Some people think, for example, that civil rights legislation is in "the public interest"; others deny this. When a congressman casts his vote he supports one view and rejects the other. The very function of public officials makes them participants in the group struggles. In fact, victory in our democracy goes to the group able to recruit the support of the largest number of public officials.

To describe the action of public officials as interest activity is not to suggest that they have "sold out to the special interests." Rather it is an attempt to give a three-dimensional scope to our study of public policy so that what public officials do can be seen in relation to the political community of which they are part. Hence, the debating, voting, decision-making, speechmaking, and conflicts in Congress, the White House, the courts, and the state agencies may be seen not as isolated events, but as part of the competition among the overlapping interest groups, which these officials reflect and represent.

Politicians—the Vital Link

Even in nondemocratic countries it is likely that the government, through force and suppression, does gain some support among the citizenry. But in a democracy, where all interests are allowed to use peaceful procedures to secure their goals, the connections between public programs and private wishes is more direct and immediate.

Frequently pleas are made to "keep politics" out of policy-making. If keeping politics out of governmental decision-making and administration means restricting political-party partisan advantage, conceivably this could be done in some areas without undermining democratic procedures. But to suppress interest conflict, that is politics, is to suppress democracy. In a police state a small group of rulers can make policy and imprison all who would oppose it. The policy reflects only the claims and concepts of the rulers. But in a democracy the dependence of public officials on approval at the polls is the ultimate assurance that they will be responsive to the larger rather than the smaller segments of the community.

Voters do not directly determine the nature of governmental programs and do not administer them. Government is always the special responsibility of a few. But the voters select the officials who make the decisions, and the officials are subject to criticism and possible defeat at the polls. Moreover, voters do not mark their ballots and then retire abjectly to their homes unconcerned and uninterested. Some of them, the group leaders, have many devices to influence policy. Congressmen, presidents, governors, civil servants, and judges make decisions, but in a free society these decisions reflect and are part of the group struggle.

It is the politicians who provide the vital link. And "politicians" is used here in the broadest sense to include all those who are active in making and applying policies. They sponsor programs and provide the means of access to the decision-making arenas. Because they desire and need to win votes, the political system operates in a democratic fashion and public officials promote the interests of majority groups. Unless they please more voters than they displease, they will be replaced by other politicians.

Our political system, like our economic system, harnesses private goals. It is not necessary for either the politicians or the businessmen to be angels, willing to sacrifice their own aims for those of others. Both are expected to work within accepted channels, and they have other roles and values besides business and politics. But their own goals can be satisfied by providing the goods that the voters or customers will buy; in short, their desires to win votes and make money are put to social use.

The socially useful role of the businessman's desire for profit is widely recognized. Not much energy is spent in determining whether a businessman is "sincere." Seldom is he condemned because he sells his customers the kind of shoes they ask for rather than those he feels are best for them. No one is disturbed by the fact that the businessman's personal motive may be to make money rather than to provide people with shoes. And few would argue that profit-making should be "kept out of business."

But the indispensable and socially useful role of the politician is less widely recognized. Often he is accused of not really being interested in farmers when he votes for farm supports but rather of playing politics in order to get votes. (This is about as profound as saying that a businessman is playing business in order to make money.) The politician is criticized because he lacks courage to support programs the voters do not like, and he is urged to operate without regard to the political repercussions of his actions. It is, however, the decision-makers' dependence on the voters that makes our system democratic.

This democratic fusion of politics and policy growing out of the dependence of decision-makers on popular approval does not turn politicians into mere puppets responding to the commands of the electorate. The electorate is not a unit but represents many interests. Even if the politician were content to do what his constituents wanted, he would not find his constituents in agreement. On many issues most of the voters would be unconcerned and content to leave the choice to others, subject only to approval of the ultimate consequences. The criss-cross and push-pull of the interest struggle give policy-makers ample room for maneuver and for playing a dominant role. They are leaders as well as followers. They do what a majority of their constituents want done, but in part, the constituents want what their political leaders tell them they should want.[1]

The Ground Rules of Policy-Making in a Democracy

So far we have stressed the element of conflict, but we must remember that these conflicts take place within the context of agreement on fundamental questions. Despite their many differences over immediate issues, Americans are strongly committed to certain basic values. In a sense, there is an interest group supporting our constitutional and democratic system, and this interest group includes almost all Americans. All unite in believing that the preservation of our free system and the use of democratic procedures are more important than winning any political victory.

Without this basic agreement it would be impossible for political conflicts to be resolved by peaceful procedure. If any group of significant

---

[1] The analogy between customers and voters breaks down in at least one major respect. When one man wants brown shoes, he can achieve his desires without denying his neighbor the chance to buy black shoes. But all the voters cannot be pleased. Some wanted Johnson to be President and some wanted Goldwater. Through politics we decide which group will be disappointed. Since ours is democratic politics, this group is ordinarily the group with the least votes.

size were to become convinced that attaining its goals was more important than abiding by the ground rules, we would have a civil war or would cease to be a single political community. This is not likely to happen, however, because Americans have so many overlapping and conflicting interests that no single dominant conflict divides the public into permanent camps. Today's political allies are tomorrow's enemies. A businessman, besides belonging to that large and indefinable grouping of consumers, may also be a member of a church, a fraternal society, the American Legion, and a trade association. One of his employees may belong to the same church and American Legion post, but may be associated with a trade union and a different political party. On some issues, the worker and his boss may belong to the same interest group, on others to a different group. A single individual may even participate in conflicting interest groups. As a veteran, he may write to his Senator urging support for a bonus bill, but as a businessman he may contribute to an organization that is writing to the same Senator urging him to vote against the bonus bill.

This pluralism of American society with its overlapping allegiances— this basic social check and balance—tempers and moderates the intensity of interest conflicts. It makes public decisions highly tentative. Few laws, court decisions, regulatory orders, or elections make any drastic alteration in governmental policy. Rather there is a continuous stream of action in which the group that gains a small advantage at one moment will lose the next round. No one group feels that it has been forced to sacrifice basic values; hence groups are willing to accept their defeats gracefully and hope for a victory tomorrow.

Tactics

Our political battles thus take place according to the rules of the game upon which all agree. Everybody is free to argue, cajole, propagandize, nominate candidates, and campaign. Nobody may use bribery, intimidation, suppression, or violence to achieve his goals. Those who get the most support through peaceful persuasion get their way, for the moment. Those disappointed by the immediate decision must abide by it, but they are free to work for its reversal, provided they work through democratic and legal channels.

Participation includes more than merely marking a ballot. Although some people are more active than others, even those who do nothing participate in the battle because their apathy aids the group which at the moment is strongest. As Paul H. Appleby pointed out, "Citizens vote by adding their names and energies to membership rolls. They vote by swelling, or failing to swell, the circulations of particular newspapers or periodicals. They vote by contributing to the popularity of particular radio or newspaper commentators. They vote by writing 'letters to the editor.'

They vote in every contribution they make to the climate of opinion in a thoroughly political society."[2]

Following are some characteristic kinds of political action:

Organization. A small number of well-organized persons who work hard may be victorious over a large number of unorganized people whose political action is passive and undirected. As a result, persons who share a common interest or set of interests frequently create an organization to promote their goals or work through existing organizations.

Lobbying. A direct approach to public officials is of course an ancient and important political tactic. Lobbying is not restricted to pressures on legislators. Attempts are also made to influence judges, administrators, political leaders, and all others who make significant decisions. The procedures vary. Legislators may be appealed to by promises of help in the next election, or by threats of opposition. Evidence may be presented to them to persuade them that a certain position is sound. Judges are approached through lawyer's briefs and appeals to law and logic.

Propaganda (or Persuasion). As the word is used here, "propaganda" refers to the use of symbols to secure a desired response and reaction from certain persons or groups. Interest groups attempt to persuade those who matter, and in the United States those who matter amount to millions of people. These groups try, however, to make a special appeal to opinion leaders. With the development of public relations experts, considerable skill and even science has been marshalled to mould opinion. Voters are approached through a variety of media and with a variety of arguments, which are channelled through many organizations and tied into existing loyalties. Organization leaders usually insist that they are carrying on "an educational campaign," but they are just as sure that their opponents are engaged in "propaganda." Organizations often develop ideologies that by their abstractness and generality seek to appeal beyond the goals of one group and provide a broader basis for support.

Electioneering. Interest groups not only are active in campaigns for the selection of elected officials but also attempt to influence the selection of *appointed* officials as well. Those who are subject to governmental regulation are especially concerned with the administrators who regulate them, and they can be expected to work for the appointment of men whose concepts of policy jibe with their own.

These tactics are obviously interrelated. Interest groups are much more likely to be successful in winning the support of a congressman if they have persuaded a large number of voters to join their cause. And if they have the support of a large number of voters, they will have more influence over the selection of public officials. Nevertheless, groups stress those tactics that are most suitable to their nature. Large membership organizations

---

2 Paul H. Appleby, *Policy and Administration* (University, Ala.: University of Alabama Press, 1949), p. 168.

such as trade unions are likely to promote their interests through election-eering for candidates, and they devote most of their political energies to mobilizing the political strength of their own members. On the other hand, the American Medical Association, which has relatively few members but which enjoys prestige and influence, is not likely to endorse candidates or to ring doorbells but is likely to use propaganda and lobbying tactics.

Interest groups are active in all branches, and at all levels, of government. Watching the American political process is harder than keeping an eye on all rings of a big circus. Congress may enact a law, but opponents of the measure may nullify it by blocking the necessary appropriations to carry out the program. Or they may alter its nature by securing the appointment of men to administer the program whose concepts of policy are favorable to their position. Policy conflicts suffuse the entire stream of governmental activity. Politics are everywhere.

THE POLICY CONSEQUENCES OF ORGANIZATION

The emphasis in this volume is on substance rather than instruments; nevertheless, the shape of the machinery of government cannot be ignored. Congressional procedures, the role of judges, relations between national and state agencies are some of the features of our governmental system that set the frame, establish the rules, and provide the arenas for battles over policy.

Disputes about the organization and procedures of government are not uncommon and these disputes are closely related to policy and programs. *To change the procedures of government is to affect the kinds of policies that will be adopted and the services that will be performed.* For when procedures are altered, the accessibility of the decision-makers to the influence of various groups is altered. Thus decisions about the forms of government have an impact on policy decisions.

The merits and demerits of a particular form of organization are sometimes judged by what purport to be nonpolitical scientific standards divorced from considerations of immediate group advantage. There are, of course, standards for measuring procedures other than their impact upon the strengthening or weakening of particular interests. However, procedure and policy are so interrelated that conflict over which procedures should be adopted is frequently merely another dimension of a conflict over which public policies should be pursued.

Groups with different values and different assessments of the policy consequences that may flow from a particular change come to different conclusions about its desirability. Judgments, for example, about changing the electoral college, limiting the jurisdiction of the courts, shortening the ballot, and adopting the manager form of government are influenced by expectations about how these changes will enhance or diminish the strength of particular interests. Perhaps we can see the relation between process and policy by considering the politics of some recent organizational discussions.

National-State Relations

Within the last few decades many commissions have been composed of members of both political parties, instructed to make impartial and objective studies and to present recommendations about the "proper" distribution of functions between the national and state governments. (Incidentally, it is worth noting that this device of appointing "high level commissions" has been adopted frequently in an attempt to take issues "out of politics.") Apparently it is thought that these commissions can find some nonpolitical standards to determine which functions are "proper" for each level. But it is not long before it is apparent that the criteria to determine the "propriety" of vesting a function in the national government rather than the states are, whoever applies them, *political* judgments.

Those who anticipate that they will have influence with state officials and who believe that state agencies are likely to adopt programs in accord with their own values favor vesting functions in state governments. On the other hand, those who believe that a state legislature may not support programs they want and who anticipate that they will find national officials representative of their values champion national action. For example, segregationists have rightly recognized that their values are likely to be the values of those who dominate southern state and local governments. They fear that national officials, responsive to different political majorities, are likely to oppose segregation. Naturally, segregationists sing of the virtues of local government close to the "people," they talk of the dangers of "over-centralization," and they do not believe that the protection of civil rights is a "proper" function of the national government.

In recent decades, employers have discovered that state legislatures and state courts are more likely than their national counterparts to make decisions favored by employers. They recognize that pressures for regulation of employer activity are more apt to be felt through national rather than state agencies. On the other hand, labor leaders find national agencies more responsive to their claims. It is not surprising, therefore, to find that businessmen's organizations are quick to defend the states against what they characterize as the "federal octopus," while labor leaders emphasize the need for national action and charge the states with being dominated by "special interests." Although the debates over national-state relations are couched in constitutional language, and appeals are made to general principles, the words are symbols used to debate more immediate and specific policy goals.

The Policy Consequences of Congressional Reform

Attitudes toward reforming congressional procedures furnish another example of the "seamless web" between procedure and policy. Chairmen of congressional committees are important: they have much to say about what kinds of laws Congress enacts. Under the rule of seniority these positions go to the member of the majority party (in the chamber) with the longest continuous service on the committee. This means that congressmen from one-party states and districts, which tend to be rural areas, dominate Congress.

Proposals to abolish the rule of seniority are debated in terms of experience versus competence, accountability to the congressional majority versus accountability to local constituents. Those whose influence in Congress would be decreased by abolishing the rule—southern states and rural and small town regions in the North—generally support the rule. Groups whose geographic strength is in areas where congressmen are less likely to acquire seniority, favor new techniques of selection.

The "Proper" Scope of Judicial Review

Until recent decades federal judges usually made decisions more apt to win the applause of political conservatives and employers than of liberals and union leaders. The courts frequently dismissed as unconstitutional social legislation supported by trade union and liberal organizations and opposed by businessmen and conservative groups. They narrowly interpreted laws regulating business and closely supervised the establishment of rates and other regulations imposed by administrative agencies.

Those who did not like the decisions charged the judges with being biased and usurping authority. They argued that the scope of judicial review of administrative agencies should be limited since administrators were trained experts dealing with technical issues and should be allowed some measure of flexibility in the procedures they used. Liberal lawyers, of whom there were a few and liberal political scientists and historians, of whom there were many, wrote articles and books emphasizing the policy-making role of the judiciary, the significance of the judge's personal values, and the desirability of imposing political checks upon the judiciary. They emphasized the undemocratic connotations of judicial review as a check on the people's elected representatives.

On the other hand, those who liked the decisions argued that judicial review of administrative regulation of business was an essential check on biased administrators who used unfair procedures. Conservative lawyers, of whom there were many, and conservative political scientists and historians, of whom there were a few, wrote articles and books denying that the judges made policy or that the judges' values had anything to do with the decisions they made. Judges, they insisted, merely *discovered* the law by applying the established rules to the facts. They emphasized the value of checks and balances and insisted that critics of the courts were really attacking the Constitution and the rule of law.

Then, perhaps for the first time in American history—beginning in 1937 and especially in the 1950s—the Supreme Court was more "liberal" than the Congress. The Court supported generous construction of national laws regulating business and protecting labor, championed the civil rights of Negroes, struck down state laws regulating civil liberties, and gave narrow interpretations to federal legislation touching on the First Amendment.

Coincident with this liberal domination of the Supreme Court was a shift in the nature of old as well as new regulatory agencies. Administrative agencies responsible for the regulation of businessmen came to be headed by men less inclined to vigorous action than their predecessors had been. But perhaps even more significant, whereas administrators had in the past regulated only businessmen, by the 1940s they were being given discretion to determine which government employees were loyal, which books were "obscene," which immigrants were "deportable," and other matters affecting civil rather than property rights.

In this new situation, many who had previously insisted on broad judicial review of administrative decisions began to argue that determinations of loyalty, obscenity, and deportability required administrative expertness and special procedures and that judges should not interfere or require the use of established legal procedures. Conservatives began to write articles and publish books accusing the judges of being "biased." They began to agitate for legislation to curb "judicial usurpations." On the other hand, liberals began to use the arguments of their former opponents. They began to find new virtues in the doctrine of separation of powers and checks and balances. They insisted that the judges were merely applying the clear commands of the Constitution.

What then is the "proper" role of judges? In part it depends upon whose values the judges are supporting. It is another illustration of how organizational issues are related to policy conflicts.

TECHNIQUES OF GOVERNMENTAL ACTION

Conflicts over *how* the government, that is how public officials, should do something are frequently as serious as controversies about whether the government should do anything at all. In the chapters that

follow we shall describe various kinds of governmental programs. We shall
see that all the following techniques are used:

Public ownership and operation.   Our governments provide police and
fire protection; recruit, operate, equip, and direct the military services;
carry the mails, build some dams, build highways either through public
employees or private contractors; build and operate many hospitals, and in
many other fields provide the services that are paid for from taxes or fees
charged. Many of these "socialized" activities are old and widely supported. Others such as building dams, generating and selling electricity, are
hotly opposed by certain groups. These programs are authorized by the
legislatures, and the actual tasks are carried out by administrators.

Imposition of criminal sanctions.   The legislature makes certain kinds
of conduct illegal and provides for punishment of those who commit these
acts. The police are charged with apprehending the law-breakers, and
public officials prosecute them before the judges. The function of protecting life, liberty, and property is largely effected by the government through
the imposition of criminal sanctions.

Imposition of civil sanctions.   The legislature, by statute, and judges,
through the common law, define the rules governing many areas of human
relations. But the government merely provides the courts to adjudicate
disputes and establishes sheriffs and others to help enforce the courts'
decisions. It is up to the aggrieved persons to invoke judicial authority to
defend their rights.

Taxation.   Governments do not exist to collect taxes, but they collect
taxes in order to exist. However, through taxation the flow of money from
some people to others can be affected, and in these days of large-scale
budgets, the kinds and amounts of taxes influence the general level of
economic activity, as later pages will show. Moreover, by imposing heavy
taxes on some goods and some kinds of activity, the government can
discourage or even prohibit them.

Expenditures.   Governments may give money in order to encourage
certain activities. For example, in the nineteenth century, railroad builders
were given subsidies; today airlines are subsidized. Governments also spend
money to provide pensions for veterans and relief for the needy.

A very important technique is the intergovernmental grant by which
the Congress grants money to the states and the state legislature grants it
to municipalities. These grants are usually conditional, the "giving government" requiring that the "receiving government" do certain things and do
them in certain ways.

In addition to capital grants, governments make loans and use their
control over credit institutions to encourage them to make loans for certain
purposes.

Publicity and investigations.   In these days of mass communication
this technique has become increasingly significant. It is used by congres-

sional committees and administrative agencies. In the 1930s a Senate subcommittee investigated and publicized certain sabotage practices used by some employers against unions; in 1957 a Senate Committee investigated and exposed the unethical use of labor union funds by certain prominent labor leaders. Both these investigations resulted in corrective action. The impact of adverse publicity is often so great and has such a punitive effect that there are growing demands for procedural safeguards for those who stand "accused."

Licenses and franchises. Individuals and corporations are permitted to do certain things only with a license or franchise. The corporate charter is a franchise, as are permits to corporations to lay tracks on streets or to run gas, water, electricity, or telephone lines under, by, or over streets. By requiring a license for engaging in certain activities—operating a utility, practicing medicine, selling eye glasses, and selling alcoholic beverages—public agencies exercise regulatory supervision.

Inspection. A technique dating back to medieval times is the municipal inspection to insure the quality, price, and weight of commodities sold on local markets. Modern uses are to insure safety of working conditions, sanitation of food, protection against fire. Inspection is supported by a variety of sanctions for violations such as revocation of licenses, fines, imprisonment, publicity.

CONCLUSION

The chapters that follow describe the policies and programs of our governments in important fields. The authors know that complete objectivity is impossible. As citizens each of us has strong convictions. Certainly our commitment to democratic procedures is evident. But it is our intention to be as objective as possible and to attempt to correct for our own biases. It is not our purpose to take sides, instruct the reader as to merits or demerits of particular programs, or to pronounce judgments about which programs we believe are, or are not, in the national interest.

In a democracy no group has any special claim to having the purest insights into what programs should be adopted. Political scientists are no exception, and our functions should not be confused with those of politicians, partisans, or public officials. True, as citizens we participate in politics. And it may be that some give special weight to our pronouncements, but such pronouncements are more likely to reflect our values as men rather than the dictates of our discipline.

government finance
and
economic policy

RICHARD W. TAYLOR

Of every dollar spent in the United States thirty cents is spent by government—nineteen cents by the national government and eleven cents by the states and municipalities. Before expressing alarm or approval we should note that this money purchases public services: roads, defense, education, welfare, law enforcement, recreational opportunity, and foreign policy. Indeed, a major portion is military appropriations; the Johnson budget for 1967 proposed $64 billion in payment for past and future wars out of a total administrative budget of $113 billion. These large public expenditures should also be related both to the increase of population and to the expanding output of the economic system. In terms of 1961 currency, public spending in 1902 approximated $84 for each person residing within the United States; in 1962 it was $933 per person. In 1900 total public spending by the national government was 2 per cent of the Gross National Product (GNP), and in 1966 it was 19 per cent. These increases are substantial, and so also are the increases in public services. However, not all citizens would agree with Justice Holmes who said, "When I pay taxes, I buy civilization."

Public expenditures are a significant measure of government involvement in the economic affairs of the nation. The fact that national expenditures are above $145 billion each year has a considerable impact on the national economy. No private business has a similar impact, nor do state or local governments, either separately or in combination. The taxing, borrowing, and spending activities of the nation are important devices by which the flow of the national economy can be influenced. Moreover, the national government controls the money and credit of the nation.

Public finance is the label given to the study of these issues. It includes *fiscal* and *monetary* policy, as well as the *means* by which the government arrives at its policy decisions. *Fiscal* policy, although originally synonymous with public finance, has come to signify the financial tools (taxation, expenditure, and borrowing) available to government to control the development and stability of the economy. *Monetary* policy relates to public control of the currency, credit, and banking. Obviously there is a close relation between *fiscal* and *monetary* policy. Debt management has significant impact upon *monetary* controls, and loan programs and spending policies influence each other as well. Although these definitions may appear abstract and detached, *fiscal* and *monetary* decisions translate public financial resources into civic purposes. The *means* by which these decisions are reached provide the institutional framework for public finance.

THE PROCESS OF PUBLIC BUDGETING

The principal means of fiscal planning is the *budget*; but financial planning within the United States is much more complex than this suggests. First, budget decisions reflect the competition of a variety of group interests; second, there is within this country great diffusion of responsibility for public financial policy. One way to illustrate the competing interests is to describe the process by which fiscal planning decisions are reached. The diffusion of responsibility is evident principally in the fact that there are many budgets instead of one. Local governments, the states, and the national government plan their financial courses somewhat independently of one another; and within each governmental level there is further division of responsibility. Both the President and Congress are zealous guardians of their respective jurisdictions, but in many respects both the executive and legislative branches are also houses divided within themselves. Although the President may significantly control the appropriations process through the Bureau of the Budget, the various agency programs must be carried through in an economic environment that is partly controlled by monetary policies of the Federal Reserve Board, which is often out of sympathy with and out of the control of the President. When Congress deals with budget proposals, the many stages of the legislative course lend themselves also to an attenuation of responsibility. Authorization legislation is handled by substantive committees in both Houses; the appropriation stage is handled by appropriations committees. Revenue measures follow a different course, starting with House Ways and Means Committee and progressing through the House to the powerful Senate Finance Committee and Senate action.

National Budgeting

The annual budget message has several significant uses. Initially, it is the President's plan for meeting national objectives; it is an instrument of economic policy, since budget policies influence the economy; it is the major financial report by the President as to how he has utilized previous years' appropriations; it is a request for legislation, since approval by Congress is required before the tax and spending proposals can be carried into effect; and finally, it brings together many of the facts and figures that are so essential for both executive and legislative appraisal of national goals.

Accomplishing these objectives entails a lengthy process, which is well described in *The Budget in Brief: Fiscal Year 1967*:

> The budget is the culmination of many months of planning and analysis. For example, the formulation of the 1967 budget began in March 1965. Ten months later, in January 1966, the budget was sent to Congress—nearly six months before the beginning of the new fiscal year. When the fiscal year comes to a close on June 30, 1967 over two years will have elapsed since the start of the budget cycle. These intervals of approximately ten months, six months, and twelve months correspond roughly to three basic steps of budgeting—executive formulation, congressional deliberation and enactment, and administrative program performance.[1]

Within this cycle, the claims of various interests, of different government agencies, and of the politically important legislators are adjudicated principally by the Bureau of the Budget (BOB). This is the agency, which since the Budget and Accounting Act of 1921 has had the responsibility both to prepare and to supervise the administration of the budget.

To carry through its responsibilities BOB can depend for help upon many sources. The President has a program by which BOB can measure the competing claims. The Treasury, the Council of Economic Advisers (CEA), the Federal Reserve Board, and the Joint Economic Committee all make economic projections that predict the environment in which the budget must function. Bureau chiefs and department heads have their aspirations and consequently their pet projects, which are funneled to BOB in budget estimates. The recommendations from various sources must be evaluated and pruned; unimaginative agencies must be prodded to contribute to the total public effort. Manifestly, the budget-making process is not an entirely scientific piece of accounting; it is, in fact, thoroughly political, in that choices must be made among competing interests within the policy proposals of the President.

---

[1] *The Budget in Brief*, which students can procure at the end of each January from the Bureau of the Budget, is a useful device for familiarizing oneself regarding the major financial policies of the government for the forthcoming fiscal year.

The politics of the budget-making process gives rise to budget strategies—strategies by individuals responsible for agencies and strategies by those responsible for adjudicating among competing agency requests. As an agency formulates its proposals for departmental submission to BOB, a basic question arises: Should it provide each year specific line-by-line justification for each proposed expenditure; or should the agency start with the assumption that what was received in last year's allocations provides the appropriate base for incremental rises in the level of expenditures? Some agencies have experimented with the "zero based budget"; usually the budget strategy is closer to the incremental approach. As Professor Wildavsky has remarked, the "largest determining factor of the size and content of this year's budget is last year's budget. Most of the budget is a product of previous decisions."[2]

The variety of possible budget strategies suggests that those responsible for preparing the budget to Congress in January may desire some way of judging among the competing claims. The old line-by-line budget, no matter how rationalized, tended to mitigate conflict among agencies and between various possible programs, since the previous year's decisions provided the base for the current decisions, and it limited the capacity of department heads and BOB and Congress to judge conflicting claims. The first Hoover Commission recommended in 1949 that "The whole budgetary concept of the federal government be refashioned by the adoption of a budget based upon functions, activities, and projects": this was designated as the performance budget. This recommendation has been implemented in the intervening period to a considerable extent, but it has been followed by an even more radical change called Planning-Program-Budgeting (PPB) which has been pioneered in the Department of Defense since 1960. All major agencies were requested to follow the PPB method for the 1967 Budget.

Under PPB, each agency must first decide its specific goals and priorities for the following five years, and then find a way to measure its operations "objectively." Each program must be evaluated in terms of its current and proposed costs. Finally a determination must be made as to whether or not the objectives are worth the costs in terms of the priorities.

Modern computer technology makes this systematic approach a genuine possibility; however, a number of years will be required before the actual pattern of many departmental budgetary decisions will be altered to conform completely to the new system. As this takes place, the objectives of centralized appraisal of departmental programs will become more nearly realized, and the political conflict among agencies and between programs will probably become more intense.

---

[2] Aaron Wildavsky, *The Politics of the Budgetary Process* (Boston: Little, Brown & Co., 1964), p. 13.

Some Fiscal Myths

When President Kennedy spoke to the 1962 Yale Graduating Class he challenged some widely held economic illusions. He said:

> . . . the myths are legion and the truth hard to find. But let me take . . . the problem of the Federal budget. We persist in measuring our Federal fiscal integrity today by the conventional, or administrative, budget with results which would be regarded as absurd in any business firm . . . or in any careful assessment of the reality of our national finances. The administrative budget has sound administrative uses. But for wider purposes it is less helpful. It omits our special trust funds and the effect they have on our economy. It neglects changes in assets or inventories. It cannot tell a loan from a straight expenditure. And worst of all it cannot distinguish between operating expenditures and long-term investments:[3]

The *administrative* budget is largely an estimate of revenue and expenditure, and a request by the President to Congress for new obligational authority in the form of appropriations acts. Because the administrative budget provides such a partial picture, the annual budget message also includes a consolidated *cash* budget which estimates the flow of cash in the form of revenue and expenditures between the government and the public. The cash budget also includes such segregated tax revenues as the Social Security Tax and the Federal Gas Tax, which go into the Social Security and Highway trust funds respectively, and from which nonbudgeted expenditures are made in accordance with separate acts of Congress. The cash budget is often descriptively referred to as Receipts from and Payments to the Public, and the differences between this statement and the Administrative Budget are well illustrated in Figures 2.1 and 2.2.

Both budgets fail to distinguish between current operating costs and long-term investments. A payment out of the Social Security Trust Fund, for example, represents a present benefit that has been prepaid in large part through payroll taxes; a payment in one fiscal year for a highway represents a long-term investment; a government loan program may involve a present fiscal year expenditure but a repayment in a fiscal year in the future. In other words, not all governmental expenditures as reflected in a budget in a single year are of the same nature, and consequently, a budget is not a complete statement of government finance.

The administrative budget is not an entirely reliable guide even for what the government will do. The months between budget preparation and its execution often bring unanticipated changes in the economic environment. For fiscal 1959, for example, President Eisenhower proposed in January of 1958 a budget to be balanced at $74 billion. An unanticipated

---

[3] John F. Kennedy, "The Myth and Reality in Our National Economy," *Vital Speeches of the Day,* XXVIII (July 15, 1962), 578–81.

FIGURE 2.1

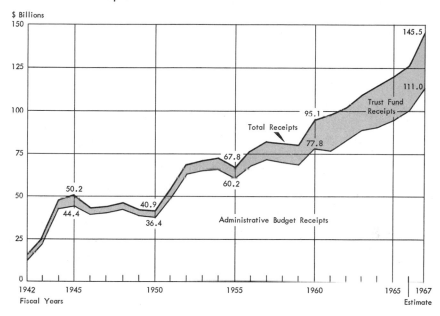

Federal Receipts

Source. The Budget for 1967.

recession resulted in a decline in public revenues and an increase in expenditures, resulting in a $12 billion deficit.

Deficits and debts were the subject of two more "myths" in President Kennedy's Yale graduation address:

> The myth persists that Federal deficits create inflation, and budget surpluses prevent it. Yet sizable budget surpluses after the war did not prevent inflation, and persistent deficits for the last several years have not upset our basic price stability. Obviously, deficits are sometimes dangerous—and so are surpluses. But honest assessment plainly requires a more sophisticated view than the old and automatic cliché that deficits automatically bring inflation.
>
> There are myths also about our public debt. It is widely supposed that this debt is growing at a dangerously rapid rate. In fact, both the debt per person and the debt as a proportion of our Gross National Products have declined sharply since the end of the Second World War . . . There is no single simple slogan in this field that we can trust.

The relation between the national debt and GNP is graphed in Figure 2.3.

The central point of the late President's message is that the budget-making process is more than a simple accounting of income and expense.

FIGURE 2.2

Composition of Federal Payments

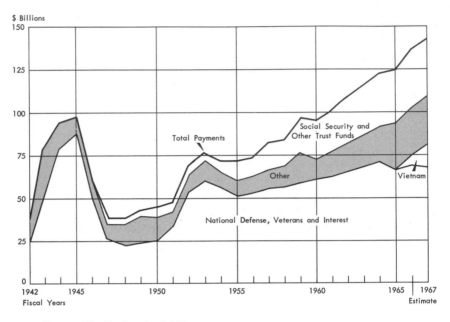

Source: The Budget for 1967.

The sum of the foregoing figures exceeds the net total of Federal payments to the public, largely because some transactions, which take place wholly between Government agencies, have not been deducted.

The budget-making process must have regard to the total economic impact. There is little difference of opinion about this question among most Democrats and most Republicans, no matter how they may differ regarding the details.

Congressional Acceptance of the Budget

Responsibility for the enactment of the budget lies in Congress. As has been suggested, congressional action is fragmented and responsibility is diffused through many committees and subcommittees. This has led to serious criticisms. The widely respected Committee for Economic Development (CED) said:

> Dissatisfaction with present congressional budgetary procedure is shared by most observers and by many members [of Congress]. Among the criti-

FIGURE 2.3

Public Dept as a Per Cent of Gross National product

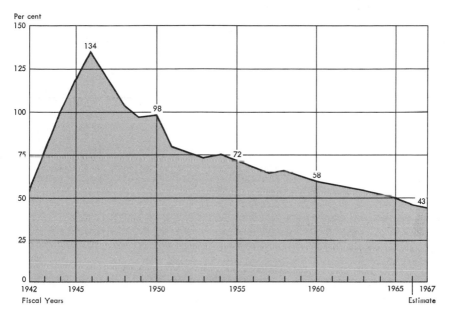

Source: The Budget for 1967.

cisms are these: 1) failure to debate and decide national fiscal policy on broad, over-all terms, 2) a piecemeal approach to appropriations, 3) undue attention to short-term authorizations rather than longer range considerations, 4) emphasis on things and services to be purchased rather than on functions performed or purposes served, 5) excessive delegation of authority to subcommittees and to their chairmen, and 6) improper interference with administrative operations.[4]

The history of efforts by Congress to reform its budgetary procedure does not support CED's optimistic statement that the "ground for such criticisms can be overcome without fundamental changes in the functions or basic structure of Congress."

Fragmented congressional consideration of the budget is the consequence of divided congressional power, which in turn serves the purposes of many senior legislators. Congressional creation of the executive budget

---

[4] Committee for Economic Development, *Budgeting for National Objectives* (Washington: CED, 1966), p. 42.

in the Budget and Accounting Act of 1921 brought with it reforms of the legislative process. Under this law, appropriations were to be handled by one committee in each chamber instead of many, and tax legislation was also given to one committee in each chamber. However, appropriations that were previously dealt with by many committees in both chambers were subsequently divided among many subcommittees of the two appropriations committees. At present each appropriations committee has twelve subcommittees, each handling one major appropriations act. The Congressional Reorganizations Act of 1946 tried another approach to this problem by establishing a Joint Budget Committee, which included the members of the two appropriations committees, the Finance Committee of the Senate, and the House Ways and Means Committee. This effort to exert congressional control over the budget proved unavailing. House members were jealous of their constitutional prerogatives to initiate tax legislation; some other committees with important financial powers, such as the Banking and Currency Committee, were ignored in this plan; and there was a lack of political desire in Congress to realize the purported benefits of coordinated budgetary supervision.

The hearings of the appropriations subcommittees, which in the Senate are public, provide additional evidence for the controversial character of many aspects of the budget process. These hearings often provide the most significant examination of departmental organization or interdepartmental politics. Bureau chiefs and department heads occasionally testify against the budget recommendations of the BOB; sometimes chiefs of bureaus within departments undermine the political front loyally adopted by the department head, in support of the presidential program. Occasionally, evidence of maladministration and misappropriation are uncovered at this level. Such evidence often provides fuel for the traditional political cross fire between Congress and the Executive.

Significant changes in the legislative consideration of the budget would probably require or result in significant changes in the congressional power structure or in the power relations between Congress and the President. The most significant CED recommendation for reform, namely that "the House Appropriations Committee and the Ways and Means Committee meet together each January to examine the over-all fiscal implications of the President's plans, and subsequently to adopt revenue and expenditure targets related to each other and to the needs of the economy," meets only the constitutional problem of House priority in the process. It is true that they suggest that "key Senators" should be "invited to attend the House joint committee hearings . . . to improve communications and mutual understanding on fundamental issues." However, changes are more likely to come by providing long-term authorizations for two, three, or possibly five years than through tinkering with congressional organization; these changes are likely to result in additional shifts of power from Congress to the President.

Implementation of the National Budget

The President has the principal responsibility for administering the budget, although some of his powers intermingle with Congress, as some of the previous paragraphs suggest. Although President Eisenhower felt he needed the *item veto* of appropriations acts in order to maintain control over policy and administration, Presidents Truman, Kennedy, and Johnson have demonstrated that Presidents can prevent the expenditure of funds they consider unwarranted.

The President's principal means of exercising administrative budgetary control is again through the Bureau of the Budget. This agency may require periodic reports from the agencies, and it has the power to order the agencies to keep within their allotted appropriations. One means by which Congress exercises some control in addition to the hearings of the appropriations committees is through the General Accounting Office, an agency of Congress. Created by the Budget and Accounting Act of 1921, this office is headed by the Comptroller General. Its primary function is the postaudit, designed to guarantee that all funds have been spent in accordance with legislative intent and that they have been properly accounted for. The Comptroller is appointed for fifteen years; he is required to report to Congress and he may be removed either by joint resolution or by impeachment.

State and Local Budgeting

Budgeting at state and local levels differs in several significant respects from national budgeting. The more significant impact of the national budget on our economy has already been demonstrated; there are also important differences between state budgetary processes and those of the national government. In forty states the governors have an *item veto*. This *veto* gives governors more formal authority over the budgetary procedures than the President, although whether it has this significance in practical fact is questionable. Probably of more significance is the fact that most state legislatures meet only a few months each two years, operate under constitutional restrictions, and often do not present the governor with the same kind of political rival as Congress does the President. On the other side, the governor usually does not have the same formal constitutional authority over the state executive departments that the President has over the national executive. The governor is only one of the elected members of the executive branch; in most states, he shares administrative powers with a number of other elective officials and commissions.

Among local units of government (especially in counties), budgetary responsibility is often dispersed among a large number of elective officials, although many municipalities have this process firmly centralized in the office of the mayor or city manager. In "strong-mayor" cities the responsibility for presenting the budget belongs to the mayor, who often has also an *item veto* over council appropriations. In a few cities, the council is not even permitted to add to the appropriations requests of the mayor; here its responsibility is largely review, although it must give final approval before expenditures may be made. In the council-manager plan, the city manager frequently acts as a director of the local budget, although he must maintain good political relations with his council. Under the commission plan of municipal government there is always a commissioner of finance.

In "weak-mayor" cities, annual budgets, insofar as they are orderly plans, are generally the product of efforts of the council finance committees; however, financial planning in this type of city is most likely to resemble national budgetary practice prior to 1921. County government in the United States has been labeled the "dark continent" of our political institutions; the multitude of elective officers who are not responsible to any central authority reflects itself in unintegrated budgetary practice. The fact that counties are primarily administrative subdivisions of the state, are confined to administering laws, and are without legislative authority of their own suggests that coordination of budgetary practice in counties is largely the work of state legislation and not of local planning. The county-manager plan is in part an effort to alter this legal and budgetary situation by reposing more authority in one county official. But this form of county government has not been extensively adopted.

THE POLITICS OF TAXATION

Each year the different levels of government collect more than $190 billion in taxes. More than 28 per cent of GNP is taxed from private individuals to pay what Justice Holmes referred to as the cost of civilization. As Figure 2.4 suggests, different levels of government depend primarily on different sources of revenue for their support. What the taxpayer *earns* determines his national tax bill through the personal income tax; what he *spends* determines his major state taxes through the sales tax; and what he *owns* determines his local tax bill through the property taxes. State and local governments both receive considerable support from the higher levels of government through the systems of grants-in-aids, and each level of government secures some support through income from services performed. Miscellaneous income will not be examined here, and public borrowing is treated later in this chapter; the politics of taxation requires careful examination here.

The imagination of legislatures has been fertile in devising means for taxation, and this, in addition to the pressure of a multitude of interests searching for economic advantage over other interests, accounts for the bewildering variety of taxes levied in the United States. This variety often obscures the fact that in one sense taxes are simply compulsory contributions made by persons or corporations from their wealth to be used for public purposes. It also frequently renders indistinct the economic impact of taxation, although it is undoubtedly this impact that makes the political and legislative mind so fecund when this sensitive topic must be dealt with. Grievances over taxes can quickly be converted into votes. Perhaps an ideal tax system would focus on income and real property alone. By manipulating taxes on each, needed revenues would be secured with the desired regulatory effect in such a way that the voters could be sure precisely what the taxes were doing for and to them. However, the citizen is not always interested in having these unpleasant matters made clear to him, and the politician who dwells on them overlong may not be reelected. Public desire to avoid the distasteful makes taxation a complicated and painful topic.

Adam Smith's *Wealth of Nations* (1776)[5] provides the conventional standards by which the fairness of a tax is judged. Taxes to be fair should: 1. Be *equitable*—they should fall upon individuals in accordance with their economic capacity to pay; 2. They should be *certain* and not *arbitrary*— the taxpayer should be aware of the fact that he is paying a tax or he may be subject to excessive levies, or on the other hand, he may avoid payment; 3. They should be *convenient*—they should not require the taxpayer to make inappropriate payments at seasons when he is unprepared to make them; and 4. They should be *economical*—they should be inexpensive to collect. To these four criteria is usually added a fifth, namely that taxes should be *stable*—they should provide a steady and predictable source of revenue. The standards established by Smith are still very useful, especially for state and local governments. But they tend to overemphasize the revenue aspect of taxation and to underemphasize the impact of taxation on the economy.

---

[5] *An Inquiry into the Nature and Causes of the Wealth of Nations* (Homewood, Ill.: Richard D. Irwin, Inc., 1963), II, 321–23.

FIGURE 2.4

Government Revenue by Source, 1965

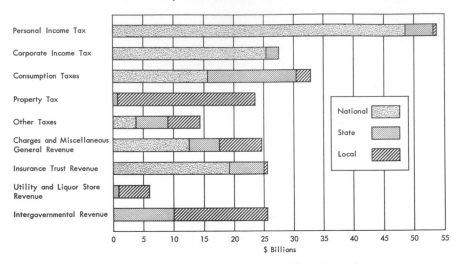

Source: Table 4, *Government Finances in 1964–65*, 1966, p. 20.

The Federal Income Tax

Following the adoption of the Sixteenth Amendment in 1913, the income tax rapidly became the chief revenue producer for the national government. In the fiscal year of 1966 the personal income tax yielded nearly $50 billion, and the corporate income tax yielded over $25 billion more. These taxes have not lost their controversial character. The main conflict surrounding the personal income tax concerns its incidence. Some contend that the "progressive" rates—that is, the higher rates on higher incomes— burdens the enterprising and stunts private initiative. Others argue that ability to pay principle requires that the affluent should pay a larger share of their wealth in taxes; they maintain that the "progressive" graduated rates are justified, and that "loopholes" that prevent the consistent application of these principles should be closed.

Some groups have organized a campaign to repeal the Sixteenth Amendment. Others like the United States Chamber of Commerce have urged the establishment of an upper limit on the rate of the tax. Senator Barry Goldwater condemned the progressive features of the income tax prior to his involvement in the 1964 presidential campaign in the following words:

> *Government has a right to claim an equal percentage of each man's wealth, and no more.* Property taxes are typically levied on this basis.

Excise and sales taxes are based on the same principle—although the tax is levied on a transaction rather than on property. *The principle is equally valid with regard to incomes,* inheritances and gifts. The idea that a man who makes $100,000 a year should be forced to contribute 90 per cent of his income to the cost of government, while the man who makes $10,000 is made to pay 20 per cent is repugnant to my notions of justice. I do not believe in punishing success.[6]

Supporters of the repeal of the Sixteenth Amendment secured petitions from twenty-seven State legislatures to Congress urging a constitutional convention to achieve their object, but Congress has shown little interest in their efforts.[7] Supporters for the principle of the "progressive" tax have had their spokesman in Senator Paul Douglas and occasionally in the different Presidents. Both Republican and Democratic administrations have appreciated the revenue-producing capacity of the income tax. However, differences of emphasis can be detected without regard to partisan lines concerning the tax base and the differential treatment of different kinds of income.

The actual incidence of the income tax remains highly controversial. Computers have made possible a careful examination of tax returns, and some studies by the Brookings Institution show that the present progressive tax rates do not in fact yield in accordance with the "ability to pay" principle. Under the 1954 Revenue Act, with its many exemptions and the special treatment of capital gains, those with large incomes may not have paid income taxes at as high a rate as many people with low incomes. A summary of Dr. Joseph Pechman's study, based on a sample of 100,000 income tax returns, shows a gradual rise of the effective tax rate to incomes of $125,000 and then a slow decline of the effective rate to $1 million. In order to compare the effective rates of the 1954 act with the 1964 tax revision, Dr. Pechman applied the new rates to another sample of 1962 income tax returns, and his study demonstrated that the large reduction in rates in the 1964 law actually improved the graduation of effective income tax rates. This fact is illustrated in Figure 2.6. The reason for this anomaly is that there was no change in the way that capital gains were calculated under the new law. Other studies have shown that the federal income tax laws result in remarkably little shift of wealth from rich to poor, and they demonstrate also that there is little justification for Senator Barry Gold-

---

[6] Barry Goldwater, *The Conscience of a Conservative* (New York: Hillman Periodical, Inc., 1960), pp. 63f. The Senator's figures are designed to illustrate his opposition to the principle of graduation of tax rates. They do not have factual reference to the 1954 Revenue Act applicable in 1960. As Figure 2.5 suggests the nominal rates on incomes of $10,000 and $100,000 were approximately 24 per cent and 60 per cent respectively; these same figures also demonstrate that it is doubtful that many paid at the nominal rate.

[7] The constitutional question regarding the effect of legislative petitions, which have continued during the 1960s on this issue, are examined in C. F. Brickfield, *Problems Relating to a Federal Constitutional Convention* (Washington: U.S. Government Printing Office, 1957).

water's complaints; serious complaints on the part of advocates of a progressive rate structure are, however, justified.

Discussion of the incidence of the tax laws by proponents and opponents of the Sixteenth Amendment had remarkably little impact on the Revenue Act of 1964. President Kennedy's 1963 Tax Message did express some concern on this question. He said that one of the purposes of tax reform was to

> . . . provide greater equity in a broader tax base, to encourage the full efficient flow of capital, to remove unwarranted special privileges and hardships, to simplify tax administration and compliance and to release for more productive endeavors the energy devoted to avoiding taxes.

However, these reforms were deleted in order to achieve another objective, tax reduction. According to a widely held view, tax reduction would stimulate the economy sufficiently to bring down the level of unemployment; the tax reductions, which amounted to $10 billion, certainly supported this objective. There was no broadening of the tax base, nor was there in the law an attack on the special privileges represented by the depletion allowances. The only major contribution of the 1964 act toward equity was, as has been suggested, in simply not changing the formula with regard to capital gains.

FIGURE 2.5

Influence of Various Provisions on Effective Rates, Taxable, Returns, 1960.

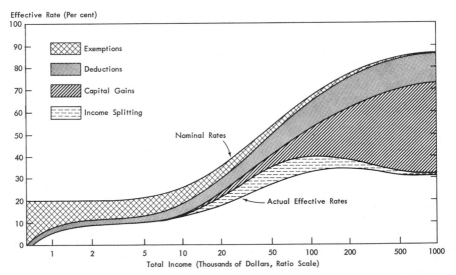

Source: Special file of about 100,000 Federal Tax Returns for 1960. Joseph A. Pechman, "Individual Income Tax Provisions of the Revenue Act of 1964," *Studies in Governmental Finance* (Washington: Brookings Institute, 1965). Used with permission of the author.

FIGURE 2.6

Influence of Various Provisions on Effective Rates, Taxable Returns, 1964 Act.*

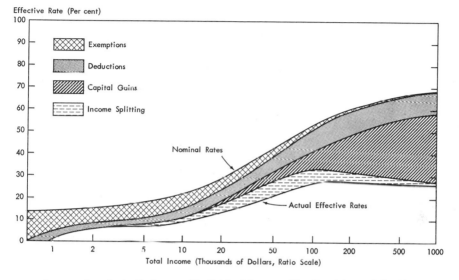

Source: Joseph A. Pechman, "Individual Income Tax Provisions of the Revenue Act of 1964," *Studies in Government Finance* (Washington: Brookings Institute, 1965). Used with permission of the author.

* Based on 1962 incomes, with rates applicable beginning Jan. 1, 1965, using special file of 100,000 Federal Tax Returns for 1962.

In theory the income tax is a simple device by which the government may collect revenue. It is made complex by the multitude of social and political purposes which lawmakers feel they must accomplish while they also try to raise money. Experts demonstrate that the present income tax is steeply graduated on an eroding base, and moralists point to the erosion as "tax avoidance." Experts also demonstrate that there is a considerable disparity between the nominal legal tax rate and the effective tax rate, and that this disparity is the consequence of legislative and administrative decisions that provide for differential treatment of different types of income, for exemptions and exclusions, and for deductions and allowances for business expense. The problems of the corporate income tax are not different in principle, although there is the additional complaint that this tax amounts to double taxation. It is double taxation; but the corporate form of organization has such advantages as permanence and limited liability for which it may be expected to pay.

Over three-fourths of the national revenues, but only 15 per cent of all
state income, are derived from individual and corporate income taxes.
Although thirty-three states have some form of income tax, for several
reasons states have not relied heavily on this revenue source. The national
government has occupied this field. Income tax is a "fair weather" tax,
which can result in serious financial embarrassment to states. This is
because during times of high unemployment state expenditures increase;
should this happen while state revenues decline because of decreased
income tax collections, the state budgets would become seriously unbal-
anced and serious political repercussions would ensue. Another reason that
states have not used the income tax as a primary revenue source is that
politically potent interests opposed to this form of taxation, especially in its
graduated form, find protection in rigid state constitutional provisions that
either forbid this kind of tax or its graduated form. In the past the income
tax has also been viewed as a discouragement to the bringing of new
industry into the states, but increased interstate and federal cooperation of
tax officials has made this a much less important factor.[8]

Consumption Taxes

Consumption taxes such as the sales and use taxes, excises, and the tariff
constitute an important source of revenue. In 1963 the sales tax raised
almost 60 per cent of all state tax revenue and a little more than 5 per cent
of local tax revenue. During the same year the national government received 13 per cent of its revenue from excises and tariffs; at the national
level this has been a gradually declining source, and with the repeal of
World War II emergency excises in 1965, this decline has become more
marked.

National excises on liquor, tobacco, transportation, entertainment, and
luxuries are a major source of revenue. The excise taxes are designed mainly
for the purpose of securing money from special classes of consumers, but
occasionally excise taxes have been used to prevent the sale of certain
products. A 1911 tax on phosphorous matches destroyed a dangerous
business and had no revenue intent; on the other hand, periodic efforts by
the national and many state governments to protect the butter industry by
taxing the sale of oleomargarine has often been a fruitful source of revenue
while quite ineffective in preventing competition of margarine with butter.

More often the excise tax is used because it is an effective money
producer. One should carefully examine the moralistic arguments fre-

---

[8] Dixwell L. Pierce, "State Taxes not Business Barriers," *National Tax Journal,*
xiii (September 1960), 232–42.

quently advanced in favor of liquor and tobacco taxes. It is interesting to note that the advocates of prohibition, for example, are generally opposed to liquor taxes because they do not wish governments to become dependent on this lucrative source of revenue.[9]

Local Property Taxes

Property taxes constitute almost 90 per cent of all local tax revenues. Some states continue to use the property tax as a minor source of their revenues, but the national government raises no revenue from this source. The emphasis on this tax for securing local revenue cannot be explained on the basis of any inherent virtue; the units of local government have been creatures of a rural culture and the property tax in part is a carry-over from early rural conditions. Furthermore, as other governmental units—such as the states and the nation—have become aware of the political and administrative difficulties of this type of tax, local government has increasingly been allowed to occupy this field; hence cities, villages, counties, townships, and school districts have a major source of otherwise untapped revenue that is at least relatively flexible and sure.

It is difficult to administer the property tax. Indeed, some have facetiously suggested that the chief virtue of the property tax is the difficulty in applying it. Although real estate is easily found, its value is not apparent and is subject to great debate. Items of personal property are not easily identified, and the assessor is likely to be instructed to give them arbitrary valuation. Intangibles present a notorious difficulty; these same difficulties lend themselves to hiding and dishonest manipulation.

Much of the present tax controversy in the states concerns the question of whether or not they should retreat from property taxes to sales or income taxes. During this century some states have met the issue by shifting some of their fiscal burden exclusively from property to sales or income taxes, and some have compromised and tried both (or all three). More generally, the states have shifted substantial burdens, particularly in the welfare field, to the national taxpayer because the federal income tax has proven such an excellent source of revenue for the national government.

Another issue involves the twin problems of making the property taxes both financially bearable and administratively fair. The gradual exclusion of intangibles and personal property from the tax rolls either through administrative lethargy or by explicit law has tended to throw the burden of this tax on land and improvements. This has simplified some problems

---

[9] The Prohibition Party in 1961 retreated from its firm stand against liquor taxes and public regulation of the consumption of liquor. Perhaps scenes such as in the 1961 Iowa legislature when prohibitionists joined in coalition with sellers of illegal liquor to prevent passage of a law regulating and taxing bars influenced the Party to re-examine its traditional position.

of administration, but ownership of land has not been found a sure guide to ability to pay. In the first place, such a focus (unless it provides exceptions—for example, forest lands) tends to encourage the exhaustion of natural resources. Secondly, agricultural properties around cities have a tendency to rise in price and force farmers off the land prematurely, thereby encouraging land speculation. Finally, assessors usually under-assess large landholdings and valuable improvements to the disadvantage of small landholders. States have sometimes tried to provide for equalization of assessments between districts and within districts by providing state boards of equalization and by increasing the professional qualifications of the assessor, a job traditionally subject to local election. These efforts, besides improving revenue potentialities of the property tax, have run into obstructions because again they inevitably result in shifting tax burdens from one class of property holder to another.

Despite all these difficulties, the property tax can be an important tool for land-use planning; however, these possibilities have been only partially exploited in the U.S. in isolated communities. And this tax also has its articulate champions like Republican Representative Thomas Curtis who declared that the:

> . . . most efficient tax economically to collect is the real estate property tax. All it requires is an assessment every ten years or so and a yearly billing —no accounting, no time on the part of the tax payer, and little time on the part of the tax collector. It is almost all done by mail.[10]

Representative Curtis was protesting against the campaign to shift the costs of local and state government to "the Federal income tax which has created the economic damage to our society."

Revenue Sharing Proposals

The large increases in the costs of state and local government and the strident complaints against the property tax have led to a variety of proposals which in one way or another would tap the U.S. Treasury for the support of local services. Each of these proposals alters the past practice whereby federal grants are assigned to other governmental bodies to achieve specific purposes. The most significant proposals are the Heller-Pechman plan for block grants, a Republican alternative to the Heller-Pechman approach, and a proposal for a guaranty of minimum income by the President's Commission on Technology, Automation, and Economic Progress in 1966.

Walter Heller, former CEA chairman under Kennedy, and Joseph Pechman, who chaired the President's Task Force on Intergovernmental Fiscal Cooperation, proposed a system of block grants to be distributed to

---

[10] "Supplementary Views of Representative Curtis," *1966 Joint Economic Report* (Washington: U.S. Government Printing Office, 1966), p. 77.

the states largely on the basis of population. These grants would be equal to 1 per cent of the individual income tax base in the first year and increase in equal stages for five years until there would be a 2 per cent redistribution to the states yielding an estimated $5 billion. The plan was first broached during the 1964 Presidential campaign, but President Johnson has subsequently lost interest in it, although Republicans have shown increased interest in the idea. A 1965 Republican task force under the leadership of Robert Taft, Jr. recommended "initial block grants [which] should start at 2 per cent of Federal income tax collections and be stepped up annually to a figure of no more than 10 per cent." The Republican Coordinating Committee in 1966 advocated the replacement of the entire grants-in-aid system with a system of block grants that would start at 2 per cent of individual and corporate income tax revenues, and increase in a period of eight years to 10 per cent. The redistribution in the Republican formula would return 50 per cent to the states on the basis of income tax revenues from those states and the remainder on the basis of population and other factors. Although the Heller-Pechman formula would provide the states with money in addition to the existing grants-in-aid programs, the Republican proposal would be in the form of functional grants, without federal controls, in broad areas such as mental health, education, water pollution control, and highways with the purpose of gradually replacing the existing grants-in-aid programs. Opposition to both these plans has come from organized labor, racial minorities, and advocates of current programs, who feel that the national government is more sensitive to their political pressures. State governments as well as opponents of the welfare state have been attracted to these revenue-sharing plans. A national government guaranty of private income to each person might serve the same function economically in that welfare costs, which are a major cost of state and local government, would be shifted, releasing local and state resources to support other functions; such a proposal has been attractive both to some conservative and liberal economists and to the President's Commission on Technology, Automation, and Economic Progress.

Other Taxes

A large variety of other types of taxes render a substantial amount of revenue to national, state, and local government treasuries. Licenses, franchises, and private utility taxes are one form. Revenues derived from these sources are in exchange for permission to exercise some kind of profession, or to use the public right of way, and may even involve the right of eminent domain or the right to occupy some monopolistic position under explicit state grant.[11] Another form of tax is represented by the motor vehicle fuel taxes, which are generally segregated as revenue for highway purposes only, under the pressure of the automotive industry,

---

[11] See Chapter 7.

trucking interests, and automobile clubs. Tax authorities generally frown on this type of segregation of revenues; some claim that it simply uses the tax laws to subsidize a particular group of interests to the disadvantage of good budgetary and administrative control. The alliance of road-using pressure groups claim that this segregation is justified as a fee for highway use. A third form of tax is exemplified by the social security taxes that are intended to pay for Old Age and Survivors Insurance and Unemployment Compensation. Since this type of tax has a specific nonrevenue purpose, it is explained in the chapter on social insurance in this volume.[12] The issue of grants-in-aid, which constitute over 20 per cent of state and local revenue, is dealt with in terms of the particular purposes such as highways and welfare, which these grants propose to advance.

Taxes—Conclusions

The system of taxation that has been devised in the United States reflects the institutions of government, the political process, and the ideas and interests that find expression in that process. The system of national taxation is much more a mirror of tax politics and tax-writing processes in Congress than a realization of the criteria according to which Adam Smith thought taxes should be levied. Consequently, one should not be surprised that the tax system is only partially designed to help the government pay its bills; in recent years there have been few occasions when the budget has in fact been balanced. Taxes are likely to be applied where political repercussions are the least hostile. Once applied, a tax is unlikely to be lifted when it has proved a fruitful source of revenue. Hidden and uncertain taxes have not been unknown, and much effort has been applied to the question of making taxes more tolerable by such methods as grafting the installment feature of the withholding tax on to the income tax. These factors make the study of taxation difficult; they make our revenue measures more complicated than theoretically would be necessary; and they conceal from the voter the significance of a wide variety of tax measures.

THE PUBLIC DEBT

Annual pleas for a balanced budget and for fiscal responsibility reflect a widespread concern for the national debt, which now exceeds $1600 per capita. Figure 2.7 and Table 2.1 demonstrate that the long-term trend is for increased reliance by public bodies at all levels on borrowing to finance their functions. Although liberals tend to be concerned with the cost of servicing the debt, conservatives emphasize the size of the national debt.

With the national debt at the $320 billion level, two questions arise.

---

[12] See Chapter 9. Much of the foregoing discussion of taxation depends on the very careful study of this subject by Harold M. Groves, *Financing Government* (New York: Holt, Rinehart & Winston, Inc., 1964).

FIGURE 2.7

Total Public Debt by Level of Government for Selected Years
(logarithmic scale)

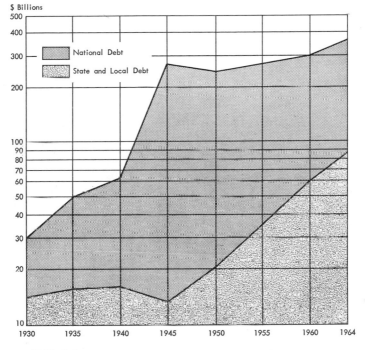

Source: Table 2.1.

What functions does this debt perform, and what are its consequences? Two-thirds of the national debt was acquired during World War II, when borrowing provided a politically tolerable way of paying for the war and of withdrawing money from circulation to dampen inflationary pressures. Combined with the tax increases of the period, public borrowing supported the system of price control and the increased allocation of resources to war production. During times of depression and recession the national government also borrows to pay for increased welfare expenses. Although war-induced borrowing has a dampening effect on consumer spending, depression-induced borrowing should be economically stimulating because it utilizes resources that would otherwise be idle and because it bolsters consumer spending power through welfare payments. In normal times governments go into debt because revenues are not adequate to pay for expenditures. State governments often have serious constitutional obstructions to borrowing, but local governments generally pay for long-term capital improvements such as schools and highways through the issuance of bonds.

Total Public Debt by Level of Government for Selected Years, 1930–1964

Year	All governments	National	State & Local
		(Amount in billions of dollars)	
1930	30.6	16.5	14.1
1935	50.5	34.4	16.0
1940	61.3	44.8	16.5
1945	266.4	252.7	13.7
1950	239.4	218.7	20.7
1955	269.8	231.5	38.4
1960	301.0	241.0	60.0
1964	352.4	267.2	85.2

Source: *Statistical Abstract of the United States, 1965*, Table 549, p. 407.

A number of the effects of the national debt deserve mention. Public borrowing at all levels provides a source of relatively secure investment for financial institutions like insurance companies and for private individuals. (The intimate relation of the national debt to the currency in circulation is described in the next section.) The existence of a large national debt imposes an annual obligation on the national government to pay the interest, and it imposes upon the Treasury rather complicated financial management to service the debt. For example, in 1963 the Treasury found itself in a situation in which $85 billion was to be repaid within a year and an additional $143 billion within five years. Repayment of these obligations from revenues within this period would have required almost a doubling of the income tax, which was politically impossible; repayment had to come from additional borrowing. The Treasury has a constant battle to lengthen the maturity structure of the debt. Borrowing also has its consequences; long-term bonds during periods of prosperity generally have high interest rates, which adds to the cost of the debt, and long-term bonds which are issued during a recession and carry a low interest rate serve to deplete some of the scarce private venture capital, which might also be used in activating business. In spite of these difficulties, the Treasury has sought to follow a policy of lengthening the maturity structure, which requires the cooperation of the Federal Reserve System.

Citizens in the U.S. are not accustomed to applying the same standards to determine the propriety of public and private borrowing. Figure 2.8 shows that private debt has increased at a more rapid rate than public debt. Figure 2.3 demonstrates that since World War II the national debt has declined as a proportion of GNP. It should be recalled that the policy of post-Civil War debt retirement resulted in a constraint on the money

FIGURE 2.8

Net Public and Private Debt

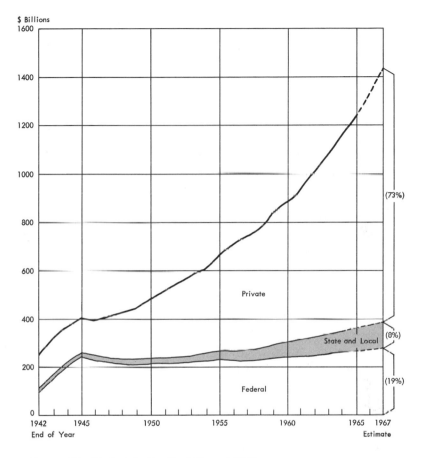

Source: The Budget for the fiscal Year of 1967.

supply and an increase in political conflict and "funny money" theories. The political agitation of this conflict led to the establishment of the Federal Reserve System.

MONETARY POLICY

The principal monetary institutions of the national government are the Treasury Department and the Federal Reserve System. Divided responsibility and the diverse interests reflected in the Treasury and the

Federal Reserve System frequently result in conflict.[13] The Department of Treasury is directly subordinate to the President, and its Secretary is a political appointee in the President's cabinet. The Treasury, consequently, is likely to reflect the views of the dominant interest groups having access to the President. In contrast, the organization of the Federal Reserve System is designed to limit presidential influence. The primary device for this insulation is the use of long overlapping fourteen-year terms for members of the Board of Governors of the Federal Reserve System. In addition, the Chairman of the Board of Governors has a four-year term, which concludes two years after the quadrennial Presidential elections. The Board of Governors (FRB) has seven members, who are appointed by the President with the advice and consent of the Senate, and one term ends in January of every even-numbered year. They are supposed to come from separate Federal Reserve Districts, of which there are twelve, and they are supposed to reflect interests in finance, agriculture, industry and commerce; in practice they represent finance and predominant business interests, and members of the FRB are often promoted from within the system. Furthermore, the Federal Reserve Banks are owned by privately controlled member banks, which elect six of nine directors for each of the twelve District Reserve Banks; the other three are appointed by the FRB, and all officers of the District Reserve Banks must be approved by the FRB.

Powers of the Federal Reserve System

Within the Federal Reserve System, the three major tools of monetary policy are formally located in different agencies. The most important monetary instrument is the capacity of the system to purchase government securities on the open market, and this policy is set by the Open Market Committee, which includes not only FRB members but the Presidents of five of the District Reserve Banks as well. The effect of purchases of government securities on the open market is to expand the currency; conversely, by selling government securities, the currency is contracted.

The setting of reserve requirements for member banks and the rediscount rate charged by Reserve Banks to borrowing by member banks constitute the additional monetary tools. Reserve requirements are set by FRB, and the rediscount rate is fixed every fourteen days by the separate district banks, subject to consultation and review by the FRB. The amount of bank credit that may be extended is determined by the level of reserves a member bank is required to maintain against bank deposits. (Banks which are members of the Federal Reserve System hold over 85 per cent of all bank deposits.) When FRB increases the reserve requirement, credit

---

[13] See Michael D. Reagan, "The Political Structure of the Federal Reserve System," *The American Political Science Review*, LV (March 1961), 64, on which much of the following depends.

may be contracted and money is said to be "tight." When reserve requirements are reduced, credit may be expanded and money is said to be "easy." To a considerable extent, a corresponding effect is created by raising or lowering the rediscount rate. When this rate is high, borrowing by large commercial banks becomes expensive and credit is tight. When this rate is low, commercial interest rates tend to decline as well and private borrowing is encouraged. These latter tools influence credit conditions, but their general economic impact is a matter of controversy. However, Federal Reserve policies have a notable effect on the cost of Treasury security issues and the national debt; treasury policies are directly influenced by Federal Reserve policies. Tight money and high interest rates increase the cost of Treasury borrowing and increase the cost to the taxpayer of servicing the public debt; corresponding ramifications are felt in the costs of state and local debts.

Practically speaking, the issue is not whether to control the economy or not, but rather to *whose advantage* the economy should be controlled. Although the Federal Reserve Act provides little guidance for monetary policy makers, The Employment Act of 1946[14] suggests some general purposes for economic policy-makers. According to this law, "it is the continuing policy and responsibility of the Federal Government to use all practicable means . . . to promote maximum employment, production, and purchasing power." Should a conflict develop between these stated values or the presumed value of economic stability the law provides no priorities. In short, the government is really given a flexible mandate about which a variety of conflicting interests contest. The different economic agencies that this act is designed to guide become the foci of these conflicts; it is not surprising that there are occasional differences between the President, the Bureau of the Budget, the Treasury, and the Federal Reserve System. Significantly, Congress did not feel that these agencies would adequately inform policy-makers, so a three-man Council of Economic Advisors to the President was also created to provide the principal policy-maker with superior economic advice. Congress provided its own check on this diffuse organization for economic policy by constituting a Joint Committee on the Economic Report. This Joint Committee and occasionally the Council of Economic Advisors have provided some articulate criticism of economic policy, which has occasionally been followed by the agencies with substantive responsibility. The Federal Reserve System arose from political conflict over monetary policy, and has been the center of continued political controversy since its creation. The national banking system created in 1863 was designed to stabilize currency and assist in the sale of government bonds. To this end the paper money issued by state

---

[14] See Stephen K. Bailey, *Congress Makes a Law* (New York: Columbia University Press, 1950) for an instructive examination of the variety of group pressures which are concerned with this issue and helped or hindered in the passage of this act.

banks was taxed out of existence, and national banks enjoyed a monopoly over the issuance of paper currency. The national banks were limited in this regard, only by the requirement that note currency could be issued only to the extent that the national banks were holders of national government bonds. A gradual reduction of the national debt during the late nineteenth and early twentieth centuries resulted in a reduction of currency that severely hampered small business transactions. Part of the political cry for free coinage of silver was an effort to expand the currency to meet the needs of small and new business establishments as well as agriculture. Senator Carter Glass, the author of the Federal Reserve legislation of 1913, described in forceful terms the national banking system that his legislation replaced as "the Siamese twins" of an "inelastic currency and a fictitious reserve system."

The monetary powers given the new reserve system, although extensive, were only gradually and cautiously used. Only during the late depression years and the period of World War II did some plausible theories develop for their use in relation to the whole economic system, and most of these theories followed the theoretical studies of Lord Keynes. Recent controversy has involved the respective merits of monetary, fiscal, and direct methods of economic control, and they have revolved around the proper policies to deal with recessions or to encourage economic growth. Keynes was quite skeptical of the monetary approach.

FISCAL OR MONETARY POLICY

An examination of post-World War II economic policy clearly demonstrates conflict both in and out of government regarding the wisdom of particular fiscal or monetary policies. According to modern fiscal theory, the economy can be stimulated and unemployment reduced by tax reduction and increased public spending; and growth can be curtailed and inflationary pressures may be dampened by reverse policies. According to economic theory the same results can be achieved by monetary policies. Tight money is caused by high interest rates, which reduce the currency in circulation; the reverse policies may encourage economic expansion. However, institutionally there is a major difference, because monetary decisions can be made by FRB and the Treasury in large part without any congressional action, whereas congressional action is required for major fiscal decisions. Monetary policy is said to be more flexible, and many advocates of fiscal policy have urged congressional delegation of power to the President to raise and lower tax rates to make fiscal policy more flexible and more effective.

Since bankers have great influence over monetary decisions, businessmen tend to approve monetary approaches against the "more political" fiscal decisions. This difference tends to be reflected in the political parties as well. As Professor Harris explains:

> Though this is no black and white matter, Democrats tend to stress fiscal policy more and monetary policy less; the [Republican] administration, monetary policy more and fiscal policy less. In part, this difference of emphasis is based on the theory that fiscal policy means government activity and intervention through debt policy, through variations of the amount and structure of taxes and expenditures. Hence Republicans tend to look with disfavor on the use of these weapons. They prefer monetary policy because to them this reflects the operations of the free market.[15]

Meeting the Economic Emergencies of 1958 and 1961

The 1959 budget proposals of President Eisenhower exemplified the means by which the Republican administration proposed to deal with the four major financial problems of 1958. First it was necessary to find additional money to pay for the administration's augmented space age defense program to meet the challenge of the Soviet Sputnik. Second, the budget had to cope with increasing signs of a depression, such as declines in production, in national income, and on the stock market, as well as increases in the number of unemployed workers, to over six million. Third, in spite of business decline, the administration also faced a continued inflation in prices. Finally, the administration was under severe pressure from Republican congressmen to provide a program that would enhance their chances of re-election. The last pressure was particularly urgent since the success of the Eisenhower proposals depended so much on Republican congressional support.

To cope with the defense, economic, and political difficulties, the President submitted a $73.9 billion budget. To meet the immediate military problem this budget included $3.8 billion additional for missile development and $1 billion for educational assistance, primarily for the training of scientists and engineers. To cope with the recession the administration asked for an extension of unemployment benefits and eliminated many previously proposed plans to retrench civilian projects. The budget even provided advance planning for public works to the amount of approximately $8 billion, in case some of its other policies did not succeed in halting the business decline. In spite of the billion-dollar increase budgeted, a surplus of almost $.5 billion was projected on the basis of an expected increase in tax revenues because of business improvement, higher taxes on aviation fuel, and increased postal rates. These expectations were not realized and the administration found itself with a $12 billion deficit.

---

[15] Seymour E. Harris, "Effectiveness and Relationship of Fiscal and Monetary Policy," *Hearings on the 1957 Economic Report of the President,* Joint Committee on the Economic Report, 85th Cong., 1st Sess. (1957), pp. 484 ff.

The Republican administration relied upon both fiscal and monetary devices to cure the recession. The fiscal tools were largely embedded in the existing tax laws, which provided *automatic stabilizers*. Fiscal theory holds that during bad times tax collections should be reduced and government spending should be increased. The lowering of revenue reduces the government claim upon active currency and this, in addition to increased public spending, tends to stimulate economic activity. During good times tax collections should increase, according to this theory, and public spending should decline; consequently, depression-induced debts may be reduced and inflationary pressures moderated. During the 1958 recessions, revenues from the corporate and personal income taxes declined by $8 billion, and the rate of unemployment increased so that unemployment compensation by government put an additional $2.3 billion into the economy. These *automatic stabilizers* cushioned the recession against a more drastic decline and helped stimulate a recovery. They were, however, not the only fiscal tools upon which President Eisenhower relied. He announced a willingness to entertain deficit financing, and he secured an increase by $5 billion in the national debt limit to "give the Treasury some much needed flexibility." The Republicans placed greater reliance on monetary policy, and it was during this difficult time that the FRB changed its tight money approach. In November 1957 the discount rate was reduced from 3.5 per cent to 3 per cent; in January it was reduced to 2.75 per cent, and in March to 2.25 per cent. Banks were thus permitted to lower interest rates on their loans, making it easier to borrow. In February, 1958, the Treasury announced a thirty-two year 3.5 per cent bond issue to refund almost $17 billion of government securities; this was a dramatic retreat from previous Treasury policy of issuing 4 per cent long-term maturities. These monetary adjustments, along with a $10 billion increase in civilian spending (not proposed in the budget), proved to be the principal devices by which the recession was halted. Whether or not the recovery proved adequate became a controversial issue of the 1960 Presidential campaign.

In the 1960–61 recession there were some old and some new factors at work. The downturn emphasized the problems of chronically depressed areas and growing technological unemployment due to automation; these factors manifested themselves in increasing unemployment rates (exceeding seven million jobless and also in much "hidden" unemployment. At the same time there was a serious drain of gold reserves along with U.S. capital to central Europe where short-term bank rates were comparatively high. Significantly, the incoming Kennedy administration focused its attention on particular trouble spots and sought to deal with various questions individually. To alleviate domestic economic distress, the administration asked Congress to extend unemployment benefits up to thirteen weeks since over one million unemployed workers had exhausted these benefits. Increases in the minimum wage and social security were also requested, and Congress also passed legislation to deal with the distressed area and agricultural depression. Administratively, the President ordered the Director of Internal Revenue to speed the payment of income tax refunds; he allocated a large portion of the proposed highway funds for the interstate highway system; and he directed the Secretary of Agriculture to commence, on a trial basis, a food stamp plan in certain particularly hard-hit areas. Reduction of the interest rate on FHA loans from 5.75 per cent to 5.5 per cent was designed to increase consumer buying on the flagging housing market. To deal with the gold question, the administration sought to keep short-term U.S. obligations at a relatively high rate of interest, a measure which to some extent conflicted with another policy to increase the sale at lower interest of long-term government obligations. Increased military spending as well as increased procurement also had a substantial effect in halting the economic decline.

Economic Growth and Stability: The Long Term

While the new Administration mixed short-term fiscal and monetary decisions to deal with the immediate recession, President Kennedy also sought to deal with the long-term problem of economic growth. During the Presidential campaign, he had promised to "get America moving again" in an inconclusive debate with Vice President Nixon. Both candidates had agreed that economic development had been unsatisfactory, but they disagreed about the cure. President Kennedy submitted a much more sophisticated statement of his concern in his February, 1961 "Message to Congress on Economic Recovery and Growth," an analysis that continued to have vitality in the 1966 Report of the Council of Economic Advisors. In his message to Congress Kennedy pointed out that there was an annual increase of the labor force of 1.5 per cent and an annual increase in productivity of 2 per cent. These figures suggest an annual potential economic growth rate of 3.5 per cent, which Kennedy regarded as insufficient. He pointed out, however, that the economy had not been living up to this modest potential, having grown "From the peak of the business cycle in the second quarter of 1953 to the top of the anaemic recovery seven years later . . . at an annual rate of 2.5 per cent." This disparity between actual and potential growth has lead to what the president referred to as a "gap" and this gap is exemplified in Figure 2.9. To overcome this "gap" Kennedy argued that the administrative "budget can and should be made an instrument of prosperity and stability, not a deterrent to recovery."

Having defined the twin problems as slow economic growth and high unemployment, the Administration had to reach a decision regarding the causes and possible cures. Some conservatives argued that the causes were to be found in the loss of business confidence brought on by inflation and

FIGURE 2.9

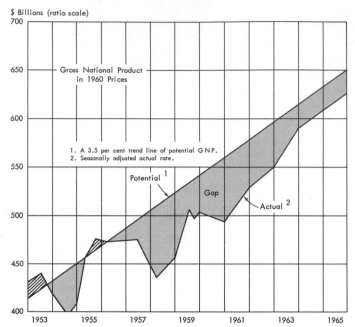

Gross National Product, Actual and Potential

Sources: Joint Economic Committee, *House Report 328*, 87th Congress, 1st Session, and *1966 Annual Report of Council of Economic Advisers.*

the gold drain as well as in high rates of taxation. A second approach emphasizing new structural conditions in American industry was supported in a one-year study by Senator Joseph Clark's (D. Pa.) manpower sub-committee. The Clark committee report in early 1964 found that the accelerated automation of industry, the low level of education on the part of large segments of labor, racial discrimination, and the expansion of urban blight and unemployment suggested structural problems in the economy that required specific remedial legislation in addition to general policies to support economic growth. The CEA argued in 1963 that the major source of unemployment and the sluggish growth rate were the result of inadequate aggregate demand; the CEA position was supported in February 1966 by the President's Commission on Technology, Automation, and Economic Progress, which also supported many of the Clark committee arguments as well.

Public policies following 1963 tended to reflect with differential emphases all three views. Presidential prestige was involved in the largely voluntary efforts to develop and enforce labor and industry wage-price guidelines; and these voluntary efforts were occasionally supported by threats to use anti-trust laws to hold down prices in basic industries like steel and aluminum. Although these actions may have disturbed business confidence, tax reductions did not. Poverty, civil rights, and education legislation (all treated later in this volume) sought to remedy some of the structural problems. Income and excise tax reductions of 1964 and 1965 increased aggregate demand and were profoundly stimulating. Tax reduction during these years proved to be a principal reason for reduced unemployment (to the 4 per cent level) and to the narrowed gap between actual and potential growth (illustrated in Figure 2.9). These policies, however, were adopted in an atmosphere of increasing involvement in the international arena, especially in Vietnam; and their joint effect, by early 1966, was to create a threat of inflation. FRB responded predictably by raising discount rates over token opposition by the Johnson administration, which urged on Congress some revision upward of the excise taxes for the same effect.

Economic problems are continuous and require continuous policy adaptations. Fiscal and monetary policies must be considered in terms of the economic environment which they seek to control; they are not adopted in a vacuum of economic theory. They must be considered in terms of the other values involved in other public policies. It is apparent that both Democrats and Republicans are committed to the use of both fiscal and monetary tools to achieve their goals no matter what their rhetoric; differences are of nuance in large part, and they reflect the aspirations of the different groups that support these two parties. Technical as well as political considerations determine the policies. The wide support for the Johnson administration during 1964 and 1965 was partially caused by the fact that Democratic policies tended to reflect the entire range of concerns found in the political spectrum—from moderately conservative to strongly liberal.

BIBLIOGRAPHICAL NOTE

An excellent discussion of increasing government involvement in the economy is found in Frederick C. Moscher and Orville F. Poland, *The Costs of American Governments: Facts, Trends, Myths* (1964). *The Statistical Abstracts of the U.S.* annually provides the most recent data of public finance, although state and local government statistics are generally outdated by three or four years. To some extent these deficiencies are remedied by *Compendium of State Government Finances* and *Compendium of City and Government Finances*, which are annual publications of the Census Bureau.

Jesse Burkhead, *Government Budgeting* (1956), and Aaron Wildavsky, *The Politics of the Budgetary Process* (1964), provide the most useful discussions of this topic for the general student. *The Budget in Brief* provides each year the easiest way to glean the essence of the annual budget message; it can be secured from the Bureau of the Budget each January.

Harold M. Groves, *Financing Government*, 6th ed., (1964), continues to be the most useful general treatment of public finance. H. C. Simmons, *Personal Income Taxation* (1938), provides a careful examination of the theory of this tax from the point of view of a strong defender of *laissez faire*. A. P. Lerner, *The Economics of Control* (1944), provides a strongly contrasting view; and J. K. Galbraith, *The Affluent Society* (1958), includes a provocative treatment of the relations between public financial policies and other public policies. On detailed problems the Brookings Institution, "Studies in Public Finance" are most helpful; Clara Penniman and Walter W. Heller, *State Income Tax Administration* (1959), and John F. Due, *Sales Taxation* (1957), are most helpful on these particular issues.

Michael Reagan, "The Political Structure of the Federal Reserve System," *The American Political Science Review*, Vol. 55, pp. 64 ff (1961), provides a useful supplement to the FRB's own *The Federal Reserve System*, which is periodically updated.

For the economics of the subject, students might well start with Otto Eckstein, *Public Finance* (1965).

foreign policy

JAMES N. MURRAY, JR.

It has become commonplace to say that the position of the United States in world affairs has undergone a revolutionary transformation. For almost 150 years the American people felt insulated politically as well as geographically from the major centers of international politics, and could turn to the task of shaping their common destiny in the New World free from the influence of important international commitments and responsibilities. Although we sometimes negotiated treaties and even fought an occasional war, before the First World War neither the treaties nor the wars with foreign powers made much of an impact on the average citizen. And even as late as the 1920s it was our tradition of insulation that in part led to a policy of retreat from international commitments following that war. What the "return to normalcy" meant in the area of foreign policy was a return to the tradition of noninvolvement in the affairs of Europe and Asia.

Today, of course, the situation is very different. Not only is the United States at the center of the whirlpool of international politics, where our very existence as a nation may well be at stake, but the life of almost every American is closely affected by our attempt to cope with the problems of foreign policy. The situation is strikingly illustrated by noting that only thirty-five years ago our total expenditures on matters relating to foreign affairs were about $2.65 billion—a not inconsiderable sum. Yet in 1966 the corresponding figure was well over twenty times that amount.[1]

---

[1] Based on figures in James L. McCamy, *The Administration of American Foreign Affairs* (New York: Alfred A. Knopf, Inc., 1952), p. 5, and U.S. Bureau of the Census, *Statistical Abstract of the United States,* 1965, (Washington, D.C., 1965).

Nor can we find clear-cut, well-defined solutions to the problems we face. The United States has interests, commitments, and responsibilities that are today literally global. Although at present the headlines direct almost all our attention to the war in Viet Nam, to the virtual exclusion of problems in other parts of the world, any one of numerous other smoldering crisis areas could erupt at any moment: Cuba, West Berlin, Israel, for example. Clearly, then, these responsibilities are unavoidable, interwoven, and exceedingly complex. In attempting to grasp this tremendous complexity of issues facing those responsible for formulating American foreign policy, it is useful to remember the story of Alexander and the Gordian Knot. The application is greatly complicated, however, by the fact that the United States faces simultaneously a multitude of Gordian knots. Further, a successful attempt to untie any one of them may make the others that much more difficult to unravel. Finally— and this is especially important—not all these Gordian knots are ours to untie; witness the recent revolution in Indonesia. And the decision as to *whether* to make the attempt may be more significant than when or how.

Obviously one of the crucial problems facing America as a nation is the formation of effective, coherent foreign policies. This is necessary because the stakes include the very existence of our society, and also because of the extraordinary complexity and fluidity of international relations today. Given the most efficient, well-organized system for forming policy, the problems would be staggering enough. But this question arises: Is our society organized to promote the formation of intelligent foreign policy? Implicit in this question is the important consideration that the process by which policy is formed may have great bearing on the substance of policy. The suddenness with which the American people were thrust into the role of leader of the free world raises not only misgivings about our experience in dealing with the substantive issues of international affairs, but also questions as to the adequacy of our institutions to produce intelligent policy.

And there is more to the problem. The goals and methods of policy formation cannot be stated in terms of efficiency alone, at least in a democratic society. We are committed to the idea that in some way the government should reflect the demands of the governed. It is not enough, in other words, to achieve efficient, intelligent foreign policy if the price is the destruction of the institutions of democratic government.

In sum, our problems include both the substantive issues of foreign affairs and our capacity for dealing with those issues in terms of the organization of our government. Further, any attempt to create an efficient system of foreign policy formation must be attempted within the context of democratic values, lest in attempting to meet the challenges from outside we destroy the very things we are trying to preserve.

A BRIEF HISTORICAL SURVEY

Broadly speaking the history of the United States as a power in world affairs may be divided into two periods: pre- and post-Spanish-American War. Prior to 1900 our two underlying foreign policies were 1) isolation of the New World from the affairs of the Old, as manifested in the Monroe Doctrine, and 2) expansion in the New World about as far as our relative power position could carry us. This meant, with respect to the second point, territorial acquisitions westward across the continent and southward as far as Mexico would permit. It did not mean northward because the nation in control of the territory to the north, Great Britain, was too powerful for us.

This twofold basis of foreign policy—isolation from Europe, expansion in the New World—obviously does not account for all our activities on the international scene until 1900. There were, of course, occasional departures from these principles, but they do represent the essential aims. In these aims we were fortunate in facing a dying empire (Spain) in the West and South, a state anxious to liquidate its New World assets (France, with reference to the Louisiana Territory), and a state which, though it could have given us considerable trouble in pursuing either or both of these aims (Great Britain), viewed it as complementary to her interests to have the United States emerge as the dominant force in the New World.

The Spanish-American War marks a turning point in our diplomatic history because its conclusion saw American commitments now stretched far beyond our continental limits—for example, controlling the Philippines —and it saw an industrialized America capable of sustaining the national power necessary to defend those overseas commitments. At that time it might have still been possible to turn back—to withdraw from the Philippines and remain aloof from the developing maelstrom in Europe. We chose not to. We remained in the Philippines, thus establishing ourselves as a Pacific power, and became inextricably intertwined in the fate of Europe with our entry into World War I. Viewed with hindsight, the "return to normalcy" of the 1920s and early 1930s in the arena of international politics seems little more than an emotional reaction against the responsibilities that our ever increasing national power and our chosen overseas commitments inevitably brought on.

World War I sapped the strength of the once major powers of Western Europe, and left the United States potentially more powerful than any state in the world. Any expansionist country, whether in Europe (where our ties with England had been increasingly strengthened since the middle of the nineteenth century), or in Asia (where we were committed to the defense of the Philippines), had to—and did—take the United States into account, whether Americans liked it or not. Without attempting to argue the immediate responsibilities for American entry into World

War II, it seems obvious—again from the vantage point of historical hindsight—that given the relative decline in British and French power, given our economic and emotional ties with Europe, and given our commitments in the Pacific, such entry was inevitable. The only questions were those of time and place.

For almost twenty years following the end of the Second World War the international scene was characterized by the existence of the two super-powers, the United States and the Soviet Union. Subordinate, though related, developments of this period were 1) the relative decline of our two traditional West European allies, Britain and France, and 2) the revolutionary transformation of vast colonial areas of the world into independent states. The first brought the withdrawal of the British and French from their overseas commitments and presented the United States with the hard choice of assuming responsibilities in many of those areas or risking the possible consequences of Communist domination of the areas. From this point of view, Greece in 1946 and Viet Nam in 1966 are merely two different examples of the same phenomenon. The second led to a re-evaluation of the importance of the developing world, especially in its relationship to the Cold War.

Our response to these fundamental challenges was initially one of containing the Soviet Union, and more recently—as the policy of *containment* seemed not so much incorrect as incomplete—an attempt to elaborate a policy of *competitive coexistence*.

Yet, essentially, whether containment or competitive coexistence, the United States has continued to view the world largely through the lenses of bipolarity. The world is still that of East *versus* West to many, if not most, Americans, and the central challenge remains that of Communist imperialism. In recent years, however, the implications of three developments—China, polycentrism, and the potential cold war between North and South—have cast considerable doubt about the continued existence of the post-World War II era as we have come to view it. At present all three are incipient, related, and capable of completely revolutionizing the world as we know it.

By "China" we mean of course the growing power and prestige of the Communist government in that country, along with the continuing militantly hostile policies of that government toward the West and its increasingly independent and hostile attitude toward the Soviet Union. Polycentrism refers in part to the obvious schism within the Communist world, exemplified by current Sino-Soviet relations, but including centrifugal forces within Eastern Europe as well. It also refers to the challenge to Western unity implicit in the policies of de Gaulle, and the refusal of much of the developing world to succumb to the blandishments of either East or West.

The last point brings up the distinct possibilities of ever increasing friction between North and South—the former representing the industrialized, economically secure countries of the Northern hemisphere, including the Soviet Union, the latter a large part of the Afro-Asian and Latin American areas of the world. The gap between North and South in economic terms is growing rather than lessening: it is a gap, which although primarily economic has potentially very ugly racial overtones, and it is a gap about which it makes little sense—least of all to the "Southerners"—to talk in cold war terms.

As we proceed to discuss current problems and policies, we must not lose sight of these developments, for individually and collectively they are potentially of the most profound importance.

CURRENT PROBLEMS AND POLICIES

Faced with the initial challenge of the Soviet Union just after World War II, the basic decision facing the United States was whether to liquidate our commitments in Europe and Asia and attempt to create an impregnable position in the New World, or to support non Communist states in Asia, Europe, and Africa in an effort to contain Soviet expansion before it threatened the New World directly.

Containment and Its Problems

Although there were some who argued for what was known as the Gibraltar Approach—which would confine our defense commitments to the New World and the oceans separating us from Europe and Asia[2]—these were comparatively few in number, and the American response to the challenge of Soviet expansionism developed along the lines of containment. This meant a commitment to support non Communist countries on both the Asiatic and European continents, and should the need arise, in Africa as well.[3] Making this commitment, however, did not relieve us from several other hard questions.

One such question is: Just where should the line of containment be drawn? Is our national power together with that of our allies sufficient to contain the Communists along the present borders of the cold war? If not,

---

[2] The clearest statement of this approach was made by former President Herbert Hoover. See his "Our National Policies in This Crisis," broadcast over the Mutual Broadcasting System in December, 1950. Quoted in *Vital Speeches*, XVII (1950–51), p. 164.

[3] The first official statement of this doctrine was that of President Truman in requesting aid for Greece and Turkey in 1947. Although the remarks of the President applied specifically only to those two countries there was implicit in them an argument for similar action in other parts of the world should the occasion necessitate it. See R. J. Bartlett, *The Record of American Diplomacy*, 2nd ed. (New York: Alfred A. Knopf, Inc., 1950), p. 728.

where should we concentrate our efforts? If we decide we cannot possibly hope to defend every bit of territory not now in Communist hands, should we make clear just what we will defend and what we will not? If we do make this clear, we are in effect writing off those territories for which we make no commitment. If we do not, even assuming our policies are enough to avert direct Communist imperialism, how do we know that the Communists won't guess wrong and precipitate a conflict by attacking a territory about which our position is unclear? Such might well have been the case in Korea, where prior to the invasion from the North, it was an open question whether or not the United States would in fact aid South Korea.

Even if we can decide where to draw the line of containment, there remains the question of how to draw that line. If we were capable of arming every non-Communist country in the world to the teeth, what is to prevent an internal Communist coup? Hence it can be argued that military aid must be buttressed by economic aid, lest in our concern with potential overt military aggression we forget that the same end might be achieved by internal coup, economic penetration, or even through successful campaigning in free elections. The latter point brings up the question of what military and economic aid will achieve without a proper information program that can spell out our objectives in various parts of the world in order to combat Communist charges of imperialism against us. We must face the fact that providing arms, economic aid, and troops may well be insufficient if the people of the country do not support containment.

Implicit in all these questions is the very fundamental one of whether our national strength is or is not sufficient to sustain our international commitments. This, in many respects, is what underlies much of the criticism of containment by those who preferred the Gibraltar approach in our struggle with Communism. If there is a limit to what we can do, and if that limit is something short of what we would like to be able to do, then the very complicated question arises of just how much strength should be expended to support any particular aspect of containment. Concretely, if we want to prevent the communization of South Viet Nam, and if our capacities are not unlimited, to what extent should we expend wealth for arms, for economic aid, or for propaganda purposes? A related choice is whether it would be better to concentrate our wealth in an attempt to support one country, or to spread the same amount more thinly in an attempt to support another as well. None of these questions has an easy or precise answer; yet we are forced to provide answers to them in any decision we make to carry out the general policy of containment.

More recently two other questions have asserted themselves: 1) against whom or what is containment to be applied, and 2) for how long? The answer to the first was, of course, very simple—as long as the notion of a monolithic Communist world dominated by the Soviet Union had any relation to reality. But given the Sino-Soviet split, it is a fair question as to whether the policy used against the Soviet Union in Europe is feasible for China in Asia. Is, for example, Viet Nam as strategically or politically important to the West as Greece and Turkey were in 1947? Does, for further example, the Viet Cong in fact represent Chinese expansionism, or is it an indigenous revolution against an unpopular government—or both? If it does represent Chinese expansionism, does a policy of containing China necessitate an alliance with the Soviet Union in order to have any real chance of effectiveness? And, if that is true, how can we seek that alliance in view of Soviet support of the Viet Cong? Merely to ask these questions —and they are by no means all that could be asked—indicates the tremendous complexity of the problem.

The second question has been raised implicitly by France's increasingly independent policies in Europe. From de Gaulle's point of view the time may well be ripe to inter the bones of NATO—the major manifestation of containment in Europe—in favor of a European settlement reached by the countries of Europe exclusively. If NATO was designed to blunt possible Soviet military expansion in Europe, hasn't it served its purpose? If there is no longer any real danger of a Soviet attack, isn't it now time to attempt a negotiated settlement in Europe, which may well involve the dissolution of NATO? On the other hand, one of the Soviets' primary goals in Europe has been that very dissolution, and if we agree to withdraw the American presence from Europe and destroy the Alliance, might not the Soviets obtain through diplomacy what they have been prevented from doing militarily: predominance on the European continent? Finally, it should be noted that it is not enough to face these problems. We must be aware that their resolution does not lie solely in our hands. If we decide to continue NATO and Europe does not, there is not a great deal we can do about it. And even if the rest of Europe, because of American opposition, does not follow de Gaulle's lead, there remains the question of which better serves American interests: an Alliance in disarray or a European negotiated detente with the Soviet Union.

The Third World

The situation facing Americans would be worthy of our best efforts even if it were confined to relations between Communist and non-Communist systems. But there is a whole range of problems stemming from a situation that is intrinsically distinct from these relations, although they have become increasingly intertwined. Since the end of World War II, approximately three-quarters of a billion people have achieved their political independence. Colonialism is almost dead in Asia and dying rapidly in Africa. Nor are expectations confined to political emancipation. Older nonwhite states plus Latin American countries and the newly independent countries face great economic problems in the attempt to raise the abysmally poor levels of living among their peoples. Our tradition as an independent, largely anticolonial country and our interest in seeing economically viable, democratically oriented states emerge in Asia and Africa force us to be concerned with these areas. At the same time this "third world" offered opportunities to the Soviets to extend their influence. Based on a posture of adamant anticolonialism, the Russians were in a position to aid and perhaps influence new states through economic assistance, and to tar western activities with the brush of neocolonialism.

In this situation many Americans became increasingly convinced that the containment policy formulated for the problems of the late 1940s is not adequate for the 1960s, and there have been attempts to reformulate the basic premises of American foreign policy. Although such reformulations have not been made explicit—at least officially—it is possible to sketch some possibilities along these lines.

Toward Competitive Coexistence?

One of the more striking manifestations of the fact that we live in a truly revolutionary age is the simple, but fundamentally important, truth that the categories of yesterday's analysis are no longer relevant for today. Although a good deal of the discussion concerning the grand design of American foreign policy is still couched in terms of bi-polarity, the non-Communist coalition, and winning the cold war, Americans have been forced, more and more, to rethink the underlying assumptions of containment in the light of the changed international situation.

Implicit in the policy of containment, as originally conceived, were the assumptions of the military superiority of the West, the aversion of all non-Communist societies to Communism, and the vaguer notion that by standing firm, by building an anti-Communist coalition we could in some way win the cold war. These assumptions have had to give way to the reality of nuclear parity, the development of the psychology of the third camp (or uncommitted nations) among many non-Communist states, and the realization that our efforts against the Soviets showed little likelihood of rolling back the iron curtain—at least in the form of substituting liberal democratic for Communist regimes.

By mutual agreement, especially since the Cuban missile crisis of 1962, direct confrontation of the United States and the Soviet Union seems to have given way to a more long range competition between them concerning the ultimate nature of the societies in the "uncommitted" countries of the world. This results from our present day situation of nuclear parity and the tremendous political, economic, and social transformations in Afro-Asia and Latin America.

Reservations on this point are in order. First, such an image largely ignores the role of China, which, at least verbally, has shown no indication of its acceptance of coexistence, of whatever variety. Second, competitive coexistence does not guarantee that war can be avoided, nor that once started it can be contained. The Viet Nam conflict illustrates that. Third, by no means would all Americans accept this version of contemporary international affairs. More than one political leader has called upon Americans to redouble their energies in the task of winning the cold war and in so doing to overcome our fears of the risks of nuclear warfare.[4] Despite these reservations, however, it seems fair to say that American policy—in its broadest outlines—has changed from the notion of a comparatively short run, crisis-necessitated containment of the Soviet imperialism to one of acceptance of the long range, quite conceivably only paramilitary, struggle with the Communists concerning the ultimate fate of the Afro-Asian and perhaps even the Latin American societies.

Within the general context of containment and/or competitive coexistence, then, what have been our major policies with regard to various regions of the world?

Europe

The central fact of post-World War II Europe has been its division between East and West, reflecting essentially the military distribution of power at the end of the fighting. The development of the cold war was given formal recognition in the Truman Doctrine, which in effect put the United States on record as ready to oppose any further Communist advances in Europe or, potentially, anywhere else in the world. The specific problems that had to be faced included: economic disequilibrium, military weakness, and the physical split of Germany. The very success in meeting the first two has created new challenges, and raises serious questions about our approach to the—still unresolved—third.

After World War II the economies of the major West European powers were in bad shape. The economic dislocation caused by the war might have been remedied over a long period of time, but in the interim the Communist parties—particularly in France and Italy—might have made sufficient gains to capture control of the governments. Faced with this possibility, and the general desire not to see any Western democracy sink into economic chaos, the United States responded with the boldly conceived Marshall Plan, which in essence was a proposal to furnish the necessary American capital to enable Western European countries to get on their feet economically, provided they in turn worked cooperatively toward the same end.

As the various European economies became increasingly stabilized, and

---

[4] See, for example, Barry Goldwater, *The Conscience of a Conservative* (New York: Hillman Periodical Inc., 1960), especially Chap. Ten.

as the Korean fighting seemed to indicate the possibility of overt Soviet military action in Europe, American aid became increasingly military rather than economic, so that by 1953 by far the most amount of dollars were allotted for arms. The two most crucial questions rising out of the aid program have been 1) to what degree could the European states sustain a shift from economic to military aid, since our aid is dependent on their making sacrifices; and 2) to what extent could the United States, by reducing its trade restrictions, promote continued European economic recovery and stability through trade rather than aid? Although there has been considerable discussion concerning the promotion of trade, not aid, not very much actually has been done to promote the increase of European exports to this country. Nevertheless, the countries of Western Europe— and in particular West Germany—demonstrated marvelous recuperative powers during the 1950s. Further impetus to economic development was given by the creation of the common market, originally among West Germany, France, Italy, and the Benelux countries, but potentially embracing all Western Europe including the United Kingdom. In recent years the United States has supported such efforts at economic integration and has begun to indicate a willingness to share the burden of economic aid to non-European areas with our European allies. This applies especially to West Germany, which unlike France, the United Kingdom, and others does not have overseas responsibilities.

A second fundamental aspect of American policy with respect to Europe has been the development of the North Atlantic Treaty Organization, in essence a military alliance of some fifteen states in which the participants have agreed that an attack on any one of them will be considered an attack on all. Perhaps more than anything else NATO symbolizes the revolutionary character of America's post-World War II foreign policy, for it is graphic evidence that the United States is committed to maintaining the defense of free Europe. It is the first peacetime "entangling alliance" since the period of the Revolutionary War. It is important also as a tacit recognition by the United States that the peace and security provisions of the United Nations Charter had become inoperative due to the breakdown of East-West (that is, Soviet-American) relations. Regardless of how one strains to reconcile NATO with commitments under the Charter, the fact remains that the U.N. was designed to be the peace-keeping agency following World War II, and the creation of the North Atlantic alliance indicated that its members feel the basic assumption underlying effective U.N. operation as a peace-keeping agency—amicable relations among the Big Five—has not materialized.

Although the treaty establishing NATO speaks of an Atlantic community and provides for increasing economic as well as military cooperation, to date practically all efforts have been directed toward the second of these considerations. What is unique about NATO in this respect is that a continuing international agency has been created with a standing international army in constant readiness. That is, where traditional alliances call for aiding an attacked state, NATO provides for military cooperation before such an attack occurs, in order to be more certain of preventing that attack or meeting it should it occur. Thus under one Supreme Commander, NATO army, naval, and air forces are stationed throughout Europe on constant guard against attack. What this means for Americans is that should an attack come, American personnel will be immediately involved, and there is little doubt we would be in the middle of the conflagration immediately. This has the effect of removing any discretion concerning entering a war in Europe—as was the case in 1914 and 1939— but it also has the effect of making it clear to any would-be aggressor that he cannot move against a NATO country without facing the opposition of the United States. The defenders of NATO often argue that had Hitler known this as clearly as the Russians do, World War II might well have been avoided.

Given the success of these two policies in the sense of an economically rejuvenated Europe and a situation in which a Soviet military attack in Europe seems increasingly improbable, new questions arise. How can economic relationships between Europe and the United States best be arranged on a basis of equality rather than dependence? The answer to this is being sought through detailed negotiations concerning trade agreements. The more difficult question concerns possible new relationships between East and West in Europe. One aspect of this was discussed in the preceding section. Another way of understanding this new challenge is to review the situation with regard to the still unresolved problem of divided Germany.

Given the de facto division of Germany following the close of World War II, two broad policy alternatives were discernible: we could attempt to negotiate a united Germany, neutralized and with strictly limited armaments, along the lines of what eventually was agreed to in the case of Austria. This policy was rejected, in part because of the opposition to it from the ruling Christian Democratic Party in West Germany, and (later) because it was deemed absolutely essential to the military feasibility of NATO to incorporate a rearmed West Germany into its defense posture. This meant that the Western position on unification of Germany necessitated Soviet acceptance of a unified, rearmed Germany, free to join any military alliances it desired. Not only were the Russians unlikely to accept such a settlement, the East European states had historical reasons to fear such an outcome. But the military requirements for the defense of Western Europe were seen as more important in the long run than a possible detente with the Soviet Union on the basis of a neutralized and unified Germany—if such indeed was possible.

As the threat of Soviet military intervention in Western Europe appeared to recede, however, and as the East European states themselves began to hope for an existence less closely related to the Soviet Union, many Europeans—President de Gaulle, is a notable example—have begun to voice the idea of a European settlement, divorced from the cold war, permitting the reunification of Germany within the context of that settlement, and European guarantees (including the prohibition of atomic weaponry to Germany) of the safety of East European countries.

These notions cannot be said to dominate in the chanceries of all European states. But they are an indication of the axiom that as policies succeed they will almost inevitably create new challenges; and that there can be real danger in a devotion to policies to the point of giving them the status of fundamental principles, in which change must never be considered. This is not to say that the Atlantic Alliance, involving the recognition of the interdependence of the United States and Europe, must be sacrificed on the altar of German reunification or Gaullist ambition. It is to suggest, however, that an alliance conceived in the first instance as necessarily military must be prepared to shift the emphasis of its policies to meet the challenges of a different age.

China and Japan

The basic fact concerning contemporary China is of course the successful revolution staged by the Communists and their ultimate control over the mainland. The question of what kind of response should be made to this involves two distinct, though related, levels of relationship. The first of these—and the one which has until very recently been controlling—resulted from the fact that with the expulsion of the Nationalists from the mainland, American policy has consistently supported Chiang against the Communists, although the fervor of that support has varied. Whatever antipathy there was between the United States and the Communist government of China was of course greatly intensified once the Chinese had entered the Korean fighting. At present American policy includes continued aid to Chiang Kai Shek of Formosa, refusal to recognize the Communist government of China, refusal to vote for its admission to the United Nations, and an almost complete severance of private intercourse—commercial or even informational.

The basic dilemma facing American policy-makers in China and Formosa is that continued support of Chiang to the point of nonrecognition of the Communists flies in the face of 1) our allies' attitude on the matter, 2) what at least many responsible observers see as a fact of life—Communist control of the Chinese mainland, and 3) growing sentiment, reflected in the annual General Assembly votes on the issue, that Communist China should be represented in the United Nations. The most salient argument in opposition to recognition is that it might tend to destroy the will to resist Communism among the free areas of Southeast Asia.

One suggestion to meet this difficulty, offered by a number of close students of the Far East, is the doctrine of the "two Chinas"—we would recognize the fact that Communists are in control of the mainland, but we would continue to support the Nationalists, on Formosa. This implicitly would mean admission of both the Red Government and Formosa to the United Nations. Whether this is feasible in the face of the avowed Communist goal of "integrating" Formosa into China, not to mention the violent opposition to any move toward recognition of Red China in this country, is a matter of conjecture.

Our involvement in Viet Nam has recently forced a consideration of Chinese-American relationships on a more fundamental level. Like it or not, the United States has had to accept the continued existence of Communist China for the indefinite future. This, added to the virtual withdrawal of the British and French in the areas of South Asia adjoining the Chinese mainland, has necessitated an examination of our general posture with regard to China. Is American presence—military as well as civilian—on the mainland of South and Southeast Asia a requirement for stability in the area? Is it feasible? What is the over-all nature of the Chinese threat? Can an Asian equivalent of NATO succeed, given the entirely different political and economic systems and structures of the two regions? It is fair to say that at this level we are now only beginning to formulate a policy, although it may be brewing, at least implicitly, in the cauldron of Viet Nam.

Following the Second World War our original policy of substituting China for Japan as the major power in East Asia had to be reversed in view of the victory of the Communists on the mainland. This entailed considerable economic aid to help revitalize the Japanese economy; but it meant also an alliance of Japan and the United States in the cold war.

Although still facing a slightly unfavorable balance of trade with the United States, Japanese trade—and the economy along with it—has expanded markedly in recent years,[5] to the point where it is no longer significantly dependent upon the United States for aid to sustain its economy. This has led, naturally enough, to a desire for greater independence. Though the present Japanese government has evinced no desire to revoke the alliance, it does view Japan as one of the three pillars of the "West"—(the other two being Europe and the United States), desires to increase trade with Communist China, and more broadly to pursue policies independently of Washington with a view to acting as a bridge between East and West in the geographic sense.

In a word, Japan has emerged from a status of dependent to that of partner. Upon our willingness to accept it as such and to recognize that our

[5] During the period 1960–1964, Japanese total exports and imports increased by 50 per cent; its trade with the United States increased by the same percentage; its trade with Communist China, though still amounting to only about 2.5 per cent of its total trade, increased by a factor of fifteen. Figures based on information in *United Nations Statistical Yearbook*.

policies might necessarily differ—Japanese refusal to commit troops to Viet Nam is a case in point—will depend the future degree of amity between the two countries.

Southern Asia and Africa

From Viet Nam to Morocco, from the Mediterranean to the Union of South Africa, hundreds of millions of people are in political, economic, and social turmoil—for it is in this tremendous area that a revolution against the past proceeds apace. Actually this revolution has at least three distinct though entwined strands, the individual importance of which will vary depending on the historical situation in the specific area. There is first of all a revolt against imperial control—and with it a revolt against white western peoples, for in this area are the yellow, brown, and black-skinned peoples whose traditional overlords have been white westerners. There is also a revolution in the ownership of the means of production and distribution of goods and services; and in many if not most of the areas, socialism rather than free enterprise appears to many people as the most promising solution to their economic problems. There is, finally, in many areas (particularly the Middle East) a revolt against the old indigenous ruling classes with the attendant struggle for support of the masses.

America's policies in the face of this threefold revolution have been 1) economic aid for newly independent states, 2) support for legitimate nationalistic aspirations, 3) attempts to induce the independent states in the areas to join in anti-Communist military coalitions—SEATO (Southeast Asia Treaty Organization) and CENTO (Central Treaty Organization). The primary problems of these policies concern 1) the type of aid given to these underdeveloped territories—whether or not a larger initial investment would pay off to a greater degree than comparatively small annual appropriations; 2) the dilemma brought on by the fact of nationalistic aspirations, mainly at the expense of our important allies in Western Europe; and 3) the understandable neutralism of many newly independent countries, for whom one main objective is to stay out of the cold war. At least until recently, it is probably fair to say that to date we have attempted to steer a middle course on all three policies: economic aid—but not a great deal of it; support of nationalism—but not to the point of engendering French, British, or Belgian enmity; promotion of military alliances—but not to the point of cutting off all aid for those nations not joining the alliances.

With the advent of the Kennedy administration, however, there developed three important changes in approach to these areas. First the United States assumed a more decidedly anticolonial posture—manifested in our support of Angolan nationalism against Portugal, our wholehearted cooperation with the United Nations in crushing the Katanga secession in the Congo, and our recognition of the revolutionary regime in Yemen. Second, with respect to foreign aid, both the Kennedy and Johnson administrations have attempted—without much success—to put aid on a long-term basis for the purpose of allowing development planning that would not be dependent on the annual Congressional battle for funds.

Third, there is some indication that—especially in the face of local as opposed to external Communist inspired rebellion—the United States cannot attempt to defend profitably all parts of the non-Communist world. Thus President Kennedy was willing to accept a neutral Laos with Communist participation in the government, and more than once indicated that although the United States could render military as well as economic aid to South Viet Nam, in the last analysis it "was their fight." Given the fact that President Johnson has stated that he is carrying on the policies of the prior administration, many Americans, most notably Senator Fulbright, have viewed our present military involvement in Viet Nam as an aberration. And the situation is often painted in such terms, even by members of the administration, who imply that what we seek is a settlement so that we may withdraw.

Such may be the case. It may also be the case that underlying our actions in Viet Nam is a much more basic policy development involving a long range commitment of American presence on the Asian mainland; not so much to quash indigenous revolutions as to contain Communist China. Whether such a policy is in fact taking shape, and if so, whether such a policy is feasible in a world of revolution are perhaps the most critical questions of American foreign policy today.

"Backing down" in the face of Communist pressure may be distasteful to Americans. But where the pressure is local—that is, where rebellion is indigenous—where the terrain is unsuited for anything but guerrilla warfare, and where the non-Communist elements show little enthusiasm for their government and less disposition to fight for it, it is easily conceivable that a commitment may amount to more than it is worth. This is especially true over a long period of time.

Latin America

Perhaps even more than Sputnik I, the rise of the Castro regime in Cuba and the subsequent missile crisis have caused Americans to shake off complacent attitudes concerning the allegiance of our neighbors to the South as well as our military invulnerability. Not only has the Cuban revolution enlisted widespread sympathy if not support throughout Latin America, but Castro's success in Cuba, the failure of the U.S. backed counter-revolution, and the socialization of the society on that island have served to emphasize, as little else, the changing nature of the world confronting us.

What the lessons of Cuba may teach us above all are that the revolutionary demand for change is by no means confined to Asia and Africa, that authoritarian socialist systems can engender widespread popular support as alternatives to military dictatorships (no matter how anti-Communist), and finally, that Communism may be more effectively fought through social and economic reform than suppression. Even the "successful" intervention in the Dominican Republic, designed to prevent another Castro in the Caribbean, does not guarantee that revolutionary fervor has been quelled; especially if the present regime fails to promote economic development and social reform.

United States attempts to help effect such policies has been centered in the Alliance for Progress, a potential Marshall Plan for Latin America. To date, however, appropriations for the Alliance have nowhere near approximated those for the Marshall Plan, and the too easily assumed notion that money would solve the problem has so far foundered on the rocks of political instability, economic dislocation, and social unrest.

But it cannot be over-emphasized that it is one thing to play Monday-morning quarterback about the feasibility or desirability of American foreign policy and quite another to be responsible for making the actual decisions; and it also bears re-emphasis that these decisions cannot be avoided—failure to act is action itself in the area of foreign policy, and action that may have the most profound consequences.

THE EXECUTIVE AND FOREIGN POLICY

In making foreign policy, almost from the beginning of our nation's history, it has been the President rather than Congress who has been looked to for leadership. Of course Congress plays an important role. Indeed, as Professor Corwin has pointed out, the constitutional provisions concerning responsibility for foreign affairs are "an invitation to struggle for the privilege of directing American foreign policy."[6] Yet for a number of reasons, constitutional and otherwise, the executive branch generally and the President in particular have assumed primary responsibility for the formation as well as the execution of foreign policy.

Reasons for Executive Supremacy

The Constitution itself is characteristically brief in its delegation of authority in this area. In general, presidential powers in foreign affairs are confined to three matters: 1) the President is Commander-in-Chief of the Armed Forces; 2) he may receive and, with the consent of the Senate, appoint ambassadors; and 3) he may, with the consent of two-thirds of the

---

[6] Edward S. Corwin, *The President, Office and Powers*, 4th ed. (New York: New York University Press, 1957), p. 171.

Senate, make treaties with foreign powers. At first glance this constitutional delegation of authority may not seem sufficient to uphold presidential supremacy in the field. If the President can command the armed forces, only Congress can declare war. The Senate must consent to appointments and the ratification of treaties. And the reception of ambassadors is after all largely a formal act. It would seem, then, that the Constitution envisaged cooperation between the executive and Congress rather than executive supremacy in the foreign field.

Yet a moment's reflection will reveal that even in the constitutional provisions, implicitly at least, the initiative lies with the President. The Congress may refuse to declare war, the Senate may refuse to consent to an appointment or a treaty, but the responsibility for proposing clearly lies with the President. Further, although Congress itself can, and on occasion has attempted to, take the initiative in foreign affairs, its organization is such that, compared to the President, it operates at a tremendous disadvantage. Thus, although the Constitution in one sense divides authority in the area of foreign policy between the President and Congress, at the very least it implicitly places the responsibility for initiation in the hands of the executive. But in addition to the Constitutional provisions, presidential supremacy has been buttressed by three other sets of factors relating to control over foreign affairs: traditional, representational, and informational.

Traditional Factors

Traditional factors buttressing presidential supremacy are those notions either accepted at the outset of our history or developed through custom that have served to center control over foreign affairs in the executive. Four such may be mentioned.

In the first place it is customary in almost all countries that the executive assume primary responsibility in this field. This idea dates back to the beginnings of the Western state system, when dynastic diplomacy among the monarchial heads of state was the order of the day and remained even after the various dynasties were replaced by republics. Thus when the framers of our Constitution assembled at Philadelphia they accepted the view that over and above any explicit provisions in the Constitution, the President, by the very fact of his position as chief executive, would preeminently represent the new nation in its intercourse with other states. This did not mean, of course, that the President was in sole control of foreign policy, but it did mean that in the words of John Marshall, "The President is the sole organ of the nation in its external relations, and its sole representative with foreign nations."[7]

---

[7] Quoted in Corwin, *The President, Office and Powers,* p. 177. The author after citing numerous instances in which this doctrine was challenged, concludes on page 184: ". . . there is no more securely established principle of constitutional practice than the exclusive right of the President to be the nation's intermediary in its dealing with other nations."

Closely related to this idea of the President being the sole intermediary in our foreign relations is his exclusive power to recognize new states or governments, usually through the device of receiving their ambassadors. Again, potential congressional hostility may in fact limit his discretion, but ultimately the President, and he alone, decides if and when to extend recognition.

Still another traditional factor leading to presidential supremacy in the field of foreign policy is the gradual emasculation of the constitutional injunction that the President shall seek the "advice" as well as the consent of the Senate in the negotiation of treaties. Again, this does not mean that the President can afford to ignore the Senate in his negotiation of treaties. Certainly the classic episode of Wilson and the League of Nations illustrates that point. But it does mean at best that he will seek the advice of senatorial leaders, sometimes confined to his own party, and that so far as initiative is concerned, what may have been the constitutional intent of coordinate authority has developed through custom into the normal practice of presidential action. And even when the President feels constrained to seek the support of Congress for a statement of policy, many Congressmen will feel they should give him that support even if they have some misgivings about the policy; for to do otherwise might weaken the stature of the President internationally and thus undermine our foreign policy generally. This was the case at the time of the Tonkin Bay incident in August, 1964. Following two alleged attacks by North Viet Namese patrol craft on American destroyers, President Johnson requested a Congressional Resolution that would, among other things, indicate legislative approval and support of the President's determination "to take all necessary steps including the use of armed force to assist [South Viet Nam or any other territory covered by] the Southeast Asia Collective Defense Treaty," which requested assistance. Although Congress approved the resolution overwhelmingly, many legislators felt it was far too broad a grant of support, but hesitated to vote "No" because that could be taken as a sign of American disunity.[8]

Finally, the treaty-making provisions of the Constitution themselves may be circumvented to a degree by the use of executive agreements. These may be defined as legally binding agreements between the heads of two or more states. There is some disagreement as to whether or not such an agreement is binding on the United States after the administration of the President who made it, but it has long been accepted that at least while the President involved remains in office, he may commit the United States to international obligations equally as binding and important as those involved in treaties. The reasoning behind the practice of executive agreements is itself an aspect of the pre-eminence of the President in

---

[8] See *The New York Times*, August 3, 5, 6, 8, 1964. The vote was unanimous in the House, 88–2 in the Senate.

international affairs. Because of the need for secrecy and speed, very often the debate and delay associated with the treaty-making process cannot be safely brooked. It is customary during war, for example, for the President to make military agreements with our allies, which by their very nature could not be openly debated. Yet, as the Yalta Conference demonstrated, such agreements may not be confined to military matters but may include political commitments as well. Although some people, particularly Congressmen, have deplored this extra-constitutional aspect of presidential power, usually with reference to some specific executive agreement, attempts to limit it by constitutional amendment have failed so far.

Representational Factors

If there is one genuinely national officer elected by the people in this country it is the President. Congress as a collective whole represents all the people, but only the President centers in one person the notion of national representation. From this it follows that only the President, or someone he allows to speak for him, may make foreign policy pronouncements for the nation as a whole. Congress may pass a resolution declaring our opposition to recognizing the government of Red China, but no single Congressman can authoritatively make such a policy pronouncement. The President can. As our nation must act as a unit in international affairs, so the nature of our government has placed responsibility for that action in one office—the Presidency. This point has been accepted to the degree that it is a federal offense for a private person to speak abroad claiming to express United States policy, but lacking presidential authorization. Further, even Cabinet members have got themselves into difficulty by speaking out on foreign affairs without the full approval of the President.

Another aspect of this representational factor is this: Since the President represents the people nationally, they tend to look to him for leadership in areas in which our nation acts as a single unit. Thus the President becomes the chief governmental molder of public opinion in the area of foreign affairs. When international crises face the United States, it is to the President that the people turn for initiative. It is significant that important policies in the domestic area are often named for the originators of the bills spelling out those policies: the Taft-Hartley Act, the Wagner Act, the Smith Act, and so on. Yet in the area of foreign policy it is the Eisenhower or Truman Doctrine, Roosevelt's interventionist policy, the Monroe Doctrine, and so on, even though the Congress ultimately might have just as much to say about the policy as the President.

In sum, because our nation must act as a single unit in international affairs, because the President is our one important policy-maker elected by all the voters, it is natural that the people will look to him for leadership and initiative in foreign affairs.

Informational Factors

Finally, the executive's position of supremacy in foreign policy results from his exclusive access to all sources of information on which foreign policy is based. Any policy quite obviously will be affected tremendously by the policy-makers' view of the factual situation—their picture of reality. And while the normal channels of communication are open just as much to Congress as to the President, the latter has at least three sources not always available to anyone but himself. These are 1) the diplomatic reports of our ambassadors; 2) military intelligence; and 3) the information gathered by the Central Intelligence Agency, whose duties include the collecting of accurate and largely secret information about other states. It has long been established that not only is the information gathered by these sources intended primarily for the President's ears, but also that Congress has no right to compel the President to reveal any information that he deems would jeopardize the national security. Further, the activities of the Central Intelligence Agency are so secret that Congress has thus far refrained from attempting to supervise its activities through the device of legislative investigation, although there were rumblings that this might be done following the Cuban fiasco. Under these circumstances even the most hard-working and sincere Congressman, when concerned with foreign policy issues, might well feel constrained to go along with the President on the grounds that the latter may know more about the situation.

In sum, although the President is by no means in sole control of foreign policy he, and that part of the executive branch concerned with foreign policy, normally takes the initiative in such matters and in any case assumes primary responsibility for the effective formation as well as the execution of foreign policy.

So far we have been using the words President and executive almost interchangeably. There is of course an important distinction between the President himself and the executive branch under him, but this distinction should not cloud the fact that only the President, under our system of government, is responsible for the acts of his administration. Yet the nature of his multitudinous tasks means that he must operate with and through his administration. If he is chief foreign policy formulator, he must nevertheless rely on the advice, abilities, and wisdom of his subordinates. The organization of the executive branch for developing foreign policy, then, takes on extreme importance—for the President is physically unable to make every decision on foreign policy, and even if he attempts to make all the important ones, his decisions will be no better than the information supplied to him or than the effectiveness with which they are carried out.

The Department of State

Every department, agency, bureau, or division within the executive branch is in some way connected with foreign policy, since any action taken in any field may have international repercussions. Currently, as well as historically however, the Department of State plays the role of chief assistant to the President in both formulating and executing policy. Broadly speaking, the chief question in the internal organization of the department is whether to organize around functions performed—political, economic, cultural—or areas dealt with—Western Europe, the Soviet Union, Latin America. Essentially, procedure has been based on the principle that one can have his cake and eat it too—although the core of the department is organized on a geographic-area basis, there are also important functional offices. Although logically this may not seem very tidy, it does make sense to create a functional division whenever such function—say economic policy— becomes sufficiently important to require overall rather than area-by-area policy.

By far the most important aspect of the department's role in foreign policy formation for our purposes, however, is the twofold problem of the relations between the Secretary of State and the President, on the one hand, and between the Secretary and other Cabinet officers, particularly the Secretary of Defense, on the other. What is meant by the first is the degree to which the President is guided by the Secretary of State, ignores him, or permits him in fact to be the chief executive in matters of foreign policy. Chart lovers may draw lines of responsibility from the Secretary of State to the White House ad infinitum, but the fact remains that even though the President is constitutionally and politically responsible for foreign policy, the Secretary of State may have a great deal to say about its actual development. This appears to have been the case during much of Dwight Eisenhower's administration when the President, though retaining overall responsibility for foreign policy, delegated considerable discretion to John Foster Dulles. On the other hand, President Kennedy is reported to have become discouraged by the bureaucratic inertia of the Department and the unwillingness of its Secretary to take a positive stand on issues. As a consequence he turned increasingly to members of his White House staff, most notably McGeorge Bundy, and to other members of his administration for policy-making advice. There is no hard and fast rule about this relationship. The point is that at all times the Secretary of State is a man ordinarily of significant, potentially of decisive, influence on the development of policy. How much influence will depend upon the talents and personalities of the individuals involved in foreign policy making. His position as Secretary gives him an inside track, but it is still necessary for him to generate his own steam. Nor is there any institutional gimmick that will provide a foolproof method of assuring the "proper" relationship between the Secretary of State and the President—whatever that may be.

AID and USIA

Over and above the functional units within the State Department, two semi-autonomous agencies have been created since the end of World War II that reflect the increasing importance placed on two aspects of foreign policy and that deserve special mention.

Beginning with the Marshall Plan, the United States has spent many billions of dollars in both economic and military aid to countries all over the world. A new agency had to be created; what was its relation to be to the Department of State? Many different arrangements were tried, culminating in the Agency for International Development, which has charge of virtually all overseas aid, and is semi-autonomous, although its head reports to the Secretary of State. Under the Kennedy proposals, all foreign aid programs (Development Loan Fund, Food-for-Peace Program, the Peace Corps, donations of agricultural surpluses, and local currency-lending activities of the Export-Import Bank) were integrated into AID, whose head reports to the Secretary of State and the President.

A similar development has occurred in the area of our overseas information program. To explain ourselves and our policies effectively to other peoples, it was felt that a separate agency should be created. This body, the United States Information Agency, was for a while autonomous in the sense that its director was not directly responsible to the Secretary of State. Later, however, this status was changed so that the agency now occupies a position similar to that of AID.

Before leaving the subjects of economic aid and overseas information programs, we might note that for the most part neither of these has been traditionally considered a permanent major element of American foreign policy—comparable to diplomatic and military components. Yet it seems clear that given the long-term and potentially extra-military nature of our foreign policy commitments, each of these will necessarily assume, if it hasn't already, an importance comparable to the traditional elements of foreign policy. From this point of view the proposals to put foreign aid on a long range basis are a recognition of this fact. To date, however, the American information program has remained essentially the stepchild of foreign policy formation.[9]

---

[9] Two very useful books on these subjects are George Liska, *The New Statecraft: Foreign Aid in American Foreign Policy* (Chicago: University of Chicago Press, 1960), and Robert Holt and Robert W. van de Velde, *Strategic Psychological Operations and American Foreign Policy* (Chicago: University of Chicago Press, 1960).

The Defense Department

Although all the other major departments are in one way or another concerned with foreign policy—Treasury with international monetary policy, Labor with the International Labor Organization, Commerce and Agriculture with economic policy, and so on—other than the State Department, the Defense Department is most crucially concerned with foreign affairs. Strictly speaking, the military arm of government is one of execution rather than formation of policy. But it is easy to see that as long as the United States is faced with a clear threat of involvement in a third world war, the military implications of any proposed policy cannot be ignored. Further, the policy itself may result at least in part from military rather than political or economic considerations. Illustrative of both these points is our policy toward Franco Spain. Omitting here the arguments concerning the merits of the case for the military necessity of bases in Spain, it was clear that military experts considered the bases very important. Thus even though for other reasons it might have been desirable to refuse to have anything to do with the Franco dictatorship, military requirements led to a policy of reconciliation. However undesirable it may be to base foreign policy on military requirements—and admitting that in any given case a mistake in the direction of overemphasizing the military elements may be made—we ignore these requirements only at the risk of jeopardizing our national security.

That military considerations have become inextricably bound up with foreign policy is, then, obvious. A result is the not quite so obvious yet crucial problem of how to coordinate the military with the economic and political aspects of policy—or in institutional terms how to coordinate State and Defense—and perhaps more important, how to control these enormous agencies of policy formation to keep them responsible to the people whom they serve.

Largely in response to this challenge, Congress in 1947 created the National Security Council, whose functions include the assessment and appraisal of the

> "objectives, commitments, and risks of the United States in relation to its actual and potential military power in the interest of national security . . . and to advise the President with respect to the integration of domestic, foreign, and military policies relating to the national security so as to enable the military services and the other departments and agencies of the Government to cooperate more effectively in matters involving the national security."[10]

The National Security Council represents a top level attempt to mesh all aspects of public policy involving the security of the United States. Since

---

[10] *U.S. Government Organization Manual*, 1961–62, p. 63.

the emphasis is on security, detailed discussion of that body and subsidiary agencies will be deferred to the chapter on military policy.

Coordination and Control

Broadly speaking there are three general ways by which coordination of the various agencies concerned with foreign policy formation may be effected: 1) by the President himself, 2) by agencies in the executive office of the President, or 3) by interdepartmental or agency cooperation.

All the agencies participating in the executive's formulation of foreign policy should also be considered as organs of coordination. For although it is theoretically possible to separate the functions of policy formation from coordination, in practice most agencies do both. Even the State Department, which has traditionally held that its job was to make foreign policy and the job of others to execute it, is faced with the problem of coordinating the activities of its own internal division as well as cooperating with other major agencies that take part in the foreign policy process. And the National Security Council is both the formulator of long range security policy suggestions and the coordinator of agencies charged with carrying out that policy. But despite this welter of staff agencies and interdepartmental committees, ultimately the President, and he alone, is responsible for foreign policy.

This has important implications for both coordination and control. For coordination it means that although some integration of policy can take place below the level of the President, if two major departments—say State and Defense—cannot agree, it is the President himself who must make the ultimate decision. In this sense foreign policy making within the executive branch can be viewed as the clash of competing interests both within and between departments. As long as the clash stays within a department, the Secretary concerned can resolve the issue; when it develops between departments, only the President can ultimately decide. Even the National Security Council cannot perform this function, for as President Truman has written:

> . . . the Council does not make decisions. The policy itself has to come down from the President, as all final decisions have to be made by him. A "vote" in the National Security Council is merely a procedural step. It never decides policy. That can be done only with the President's approval . . .[11]

In terms of control it means that the President is the one popularly elected official who can be held accountable for policy making in the executive branch. It is true that the Vice President is popularly elected, and under Presidents Eisenhower and Kennedy, has participated in top

---

[11] Harry S. Truman, *Years of Trial and Hope* (New York: Doubleday and Company, 1955), p. 59.

level policy decisions, but any control he exerts is derived from the authority of the President, who alone is responsible.

Both the process and the problems involved in the executive determination of foreign policy are perhaps best illustrated by a case study. The issue itself was not of monumental importance, but the process involved in reaching a decision resembles that used for more vital questions.

A Case Study: Strategic Trusts

In the years immediately preceding the end of the Second World War, the United States sought, as part of its general planning for postwar international organization, to develop policies for the future status of colonial territories. Initially, the responsibility for formulating proposals on this subject was in the hands of the State Department. The original plans called for international supervision of all colonies. However, largely as the result of unfavorable reactions by the British and French, under the Secretary of State's direction the types of dependent territories to be placed under international supervision were confined to: 1) those that had been under League of Nations supervision (in what was called the Mandates System); 2) those to be detached from enemy states at the end of the war; and 3) those that might be voluntarily placed under the new system (to be called the Trusteeship System of the United Nations) by the mother countries.

To this point the policy developed as we might think it ordinarily would—within the State Department, modified by reactions of our allies. But the former mandates that were to be placed under the Trusteeship System included many of the islands, specifically in the Carolines, Marshalls, and Gilberts, which we had wrested from Japan only at heavy cost. And it could be argued that American retention of those islands was vital to our security in the Pacific, as the terrible days of early 1942 demonstrated. This is precisely what the military leaders argued when they saw the State Department proposals. Admiral King asserted, for example, that "American possession of the bases in the Pacific islands which have been taken from Japan was essential to the United States and world security after the war."[12] Earlier, Henry L. Stimson, then Secretary of War, had sent a memorandum to the Secretary of State in which he argued that the islands were "not colonies; they are outposts, and their acquisition is appropriate under the general doctrine of self-defense by the power which guarantees the safety of that area of the world."[13]

The State Department offered the counter-argument that exempting the former Japanese mandates from the new Trusteeship System would

---

[12] Quoted in *The New York Times*, April 19, 1945.

[13] Quoted in Henry L. Stimson and McGeorge Bundy, *On Active Service in Peace and War* (New York: Harper & Row, Publishers, 1948), p. 600.

lead "to reservations of other territory by other nations until the non-aggrandizement plan of the Atlantic Charter would become a mockery."[14] Implicit in this policy difference between the State Department and the military was a fundamentally different view of the world situation as it would exist after the war. The State Department's proposals reflected the general position that America's best interests lay in wholehearted support of the United Nations, and that any reservations to such a commitment meant subverting the chances of maintaining peace through that organization. The military leaders, on the other hand, took the view that we had to preserve our own security position, whether in the Pacific or elsewhere, irrespective of commitments in the direction of promoting international organization for peace.

It is idle now to speculate on which side was "right." The point is rather that the case shows how two important agencies within the executive branch can fundamentally disagree on policy; how each in a sense acts as a pressure group—a public pressure group—for the policy to which it adheres. In such a situation either a compromise or presidential decision was necessary. Actually, it involved both. At a meeting of the President, the Secretaries of State, War, and Navy, and advisers, it was decided to introduce the notion of strategic territories in the Trusteeship System. These strategic territories would be placed formally under the system, although the administering state could prevent direct international supervision of the territories should the interests of security so require.

It should be noted that opposition to the State Department plan was not confined to the military leaders. Congressmen also voiced disapproval of proposals that would entail anything other than unhampered control of the islands by the United States. And this congressional opposition doubtless played a part in the willingness of the State Department to compromise and the President's decision to approve it.

Certainly one can see from this case that the executive branch is not a monolithic institution composed of nicely integrated parts, all working smoothly with the same means toward the same goal. In the largest sense, of course, all Americans want to pursue the national interest of the United States; but what that national interest is and how best to pursue it may be subject to honest disagreement among honest men. The struggle over foreign policy, that is to say, is a struggle within the executive as well as between the executive and Congress, for example, or between political parties.

It deserves re-emphasis that the President, though constitutionally and electorally responsible for executive foreign policy making, cannot possibly oversee even all the important aspects of foreign policy, much less personally coordinate agencies within that branch. And this problem—the discrepancy between the legal and political responsibilities of the President

---

[14] Article by Arthur Krock in *The New York Times*, April 3, 1945.

and the physical impossibility of personally carrying out that responsibility
—is one of the crucial problems of contemporary American government;
crucial, that is, as long as Americans feel that effective policy is not enough,
but that those who decide what in fact is effective policy be held
accountable to the people. In the case just discussed, time was not a critical
factor nor was military conflict imminent. In crisis situations, although the
process involved may be remarkably similar to that described, the presence
of these two additional elements make the pressures on the President almost overwhelming. We shall examine such a crisis situation in connection
with the discussion of the National Security Council in the next chapter.

The mention of Congressmen in the case study, however, raises the
general question of Congress' role in foreign policy making and the more
particular question of the degree to which Congress can reinforce popular
control of foreign policy, either through direct participation or by controlling the executive branch.

CONGRESS AND FOREIGN POLICY

Implicit in the constitutional provisions concerning foreign policy is
the notion that Congress has a twofold role to play: 1) in part as the
initiator of policy; 2) in part as the single most important device for
popular control over the executive agencies that carry out foreign policy.
Because of constitutional provisions and the structure of Congress, however, that body plays its major role in control rather than initiation.

Until comparatively recently, even though the House was necessarily a
participant in any foreign policy involving appropriations, the Senate had
the main part in congressional foreign policy making. One striking bit of
evidence of this was the difference in prestige of membership between the
Senate's Foreign Relations Committee and the House Committee on
Foreign Affairs. The former has always been a much sought after assignment, while the latter was viewed, in the words of one Congressman, as "a
dump heap, where service was a chore rather than a privilege."[15] Since the
end of World War II, however, the House has come to play a crucial role
in congressional participation in foreign affairs. This is undoubtedly due in
the first instance to the increased importance of appropriations necessary to
underwrite American foreign policy. For example, our fundamental program of military and economic aid to countries all over the world necessitates House as well as Senate acquiescence. Second, much of our foreign
policy is dependent not on treaties but on legislation passed by both
houses. Finally, the increased use of executive agreements that, more often

---

[15] Quoted in Robert A. Dahl, *Congress and Foreign Policy* (New York: Harcourt, Brace and World, Inc., 1950), p. 147.

than not, are based on congressional authorization has enhanced the position of the House as participant in foreign policy making.[16]

Congress as Participant

Broadly speaking both the House and the Senate are organized to participate in foreign policy making in about the same way as for the consideration of other aspects of public policy. As already indicated, each house has a permanent committee on foreign relations. In addition, from time to time temporary investigatory committees have been created to look into some aspect of foreign policy. Thus the House appointed a temporary committee on foreign aid that toured Europe to gain information on the actual conditions in various countries to whom it was proposed Marshall Plan aid be extended. Further, individual Congressmen may travel to various parts of the world to make a firsthand assessment of conditions—as the virtually continuous coming and going of Congressmen in Viet Nam exemplifies.

To aid the various committees in research and analysis on various foreign policy questions Congress in its *Legislative Reorganization of 1946* and subsequent acts authorized each committee to employ experts. The primary purpose of these professional staffs is to remove some of the otherwise impossible burden on Congressmen of becoming fully informed on every relevant question concerning a proposed policy. The implications of appointing a professional staff for Congress will be discussed later.

Other important standing committees in both the House and Senate include the appropriations committee of each house, and since military and foreign policies have become so closely interwoven, the military affairs committees of the two houses.

Yet, as we have already noted, executive initiative is the rule in foreign policy formation; and even those Congressmen who have made foreign policy their special concern have been the first to admit this. As the chairman of the Senate Foreign Relations Committee, Senator Fulbright of Arkansas, has testified:

> In other words the function of the Senate, and of the Foreign Relations Committee in particular, is to try to be the conscience of the executive— without in any way indulging in the frivolous delusion of coequality.[17]

Whether that same Senator's Committee hearings on Viet Nam some seven years later were designed to prick that conscience or were in fact an attempted step toward coequality will be discussed presently.

---

[16] See Holbert N. Carroll, *The House of Representatives and Foreign Affairs* (Pittsburgh: University of Pittsburgh Press, 1958).

[17] Quoted in S. Hyman "Advice and Consent of J. William Fulbright," *The Reporter*, XXI, Sept. 17, 1959, pp. 23–25.

One other point about the general role of Congress as participant in foreign policy making should be noted. Congress collectively represents a microcosm of the American people, at least to the degree that it is a genuinely representative body. In this sense it mirrors the views of the people on all issues, foreign as well as domestic. But Congress, and especially leaders of Congress, not only reflect but help to mold public attitudes on various issues. Thus the executive branch, even when no one would doubt its authority to make decisions, may well hesitate to pursue a particular policy in the face of known and intensive opposition by congressional leaders. This appears to be the case, for example, in the hesitancy of the executive concerning our policy toward the Communist government of China. Under both the Eisenhower and Kennedy administrations, there was evidence that many members of the executive including both the secretary of State and the President had serious doubts about the advisability of continuing support for the Nationalist government on Formosa and refusing to consider recognition of Communist China. Yet in the face of known opposition of congressional leaders, both Republican and Democratic, any administration might well feel the necessity of caution concerning a marked change in our China policy. Even though at first a majority of the American people might be opposed to such change, in the absence of marked congressional opposition it might be "sold" to the people. But as long as Senators of opposing parties and eminent positions such as Russell of Georgia and Dirksen of Illinois manifest antipathy toward such a change, the administration would find it difficult indeed to muster public support for any radical shift in policy. This, again, because individual Congressmen doubtless lead as well as reflect current public attitude. The degree to which Congress will be influential in foreign policy determination in this regard is, of course, dependent upon the Congressmen involved, the popularity of the President, and the specific issue. But that Congress in this informal way can and does materially affect executive discretion, even in those matters constitutionally under executive control, is an important aspect of the foreign policy process. To use the same example, China, for the converse point, other Senators (especially Fulbright and Morse) have taken the lead in the Foreign Relations Committee to expand the hearings on Viet Nam to a consideration of China policy generally, with a view to engendering public support for a reconsideration of that policy.

Power of the Purse

Except for the Senate's role in consenting to treaties (and the much less important power of approving ambassadors), by and large most congressional participation in foreign policy, especially in the contemporary era, involves the funds requested by the executive to implement its policies of military and economic aid to foreign nations. The crucial committees involved here are the foreign relations and appropriations committees in each house. Because the Constitution itself distinguishes between legislation on the one hand and appropriations on the other, the appropriations process is a two-stage transaction: 1) authorization, providing the legal basis for executive expenditure of funds; 2) appropriation, providing the necessary funds to carry out the authorization. This explains why many times the executive in defending its budget before Congress will emphasize that the actual appropriations called for will not be nearly as much as the total figure in the budget (funds authorized in previous years, but not expended, can be, with congressional approval, used for the current program).

Essentially, the foreign relations committees consider the authorization requests while the appropriations committees of each house pass on the actual appropriation of funds. Because the foreign relations committees are for all practical purposes exclusively concerned with foreign policy, while the appropriations committees must consider domestic needs for funds as well as those for foreign policy, there is sometimes disagreement over the total amount to be authorized and appropriated. Again, with a ceiling on the national debt and an economy-minded Congress, not only the appropriations committee, but also the Ways and Means Committee of the House may well play an important role; if money cannot be borrowed it must be forthcoming through taxes before it can be spent.

This over-all power of the purse gives Congress its most effective tool in the foreign policy formation process. Obviously executive initiative would be meaningless if Congress chose not to furnish the necessary financial support. But the importance of this power of the purse can be overstated. After all, Congressmen no more want to see the United States suffer diplomatic, economic, or ultimate military defeat than does the executive. And, for information on which it will base its consideration of executive requests for funds, Congress must depend primarily on the executive branch itself.

Despite these reservations the congressional power of the purse remains an important aspect of the foreign policy process. And, together with other types of participation mentioned above, it means that Congress remains a vital part of that process. Still, congressional participation, even when the purse is involved, and especially when it is not, remains intermittent at best. American foreign policy is a continuing, literally day-by-day process—it is the day-by-day relations with other states, both friends and enemies, that ultimately produce the "big situation" in which Congress is called upon to approve and support executive action at the very time when the pressure of events is such as to coerce Congress into accepting the President's proposals. Hardly any Senator who has expressed himself on Viet Nam has failed to indicate puzzlement and concern as to how the United

States became so entangled on the mainland of Asia. Yet the vast majority feel constrained to support the President now that we are entangled. Further, any attempt to limit future escalation by cutting back present funds subjects the Congressman to the charge of "not supporting our boys at the front." In effect the power of the purse is circumscribed by the power of the President to order troops to Viet Nam, then present Congress with the "alternative" of financially supporting the commitment or turning its collective back on American troops engaged in battle. The point is that while Congress can and does play an important part in foreign policy, its role is essentially of an intermittent rather than a continuing nature. And this intermittency itself may lead to a situation in which the choice left to Congress is more formal than real.

Other Congressional Weaknesses

From the foregoing it may be summarized that with respect to the Constitution, representation, organization, and information, the executive is naturally in a much stronger position than Congress to be the effective formulator of foreign policy. In addition to these comparative weaknesses of Congress, two others are important. The first concerns the nature of the legislative process itself. Implicit in that process is the notion of discussion, with a view toward pointing up rather than obscuring issues, compromising among various interests, and assuring sufficient deliberation so that all interests may be heard. Yet by its nature foreign policy is the more effective when based on unified support; compromise may well mean disaster, and many times speed in action precludes the delay associated with deliberation. It is these considerations that underlie the phrase "politics should stop at the water's edge." To have an effective foreign policy, it can be argued, we cannot afford to have the deliberation, delay, and compromise usually associated with the legislative process. Hence the tendency of even the most conscientious Congressmen to "go along" with the President rather than risk the dangers of delay and compromise.

It is essential to remember that a Congressman, in addition to his responsibility to think and vote intelligently on matters of foreign affairs, must also concern himself with all other aspects of public policy. He must also worry about his political fences back home and perform all varieties of services for constituents. It is easy to see, then, the physical impossibility for any Congressman, let alone every Congressman, to keep fully informed on every aspect of foreign affairs. Both houses of Congress have, of course, attempted to meet this situation in a number of ways. The committee system itself is designed in part to allow some degree of specialization so that Congressmen can become expert in certain areas; funds for the committees to hire experts to help provide informational and analytical ability as noted above, have been provided; the committees have subdivided themselves to provide for greater specialization within the general area of foreign relations. But all these are improvements rather than remedial measures. Comparing the vast numbers of people in the State Department whose sole concern is with some area or function of foreign policy, not to mention the large numbers of persons in CIA, Congress is at a tremendous disadvantage when confronted by the executive.

One example of this problem illustrates the point nicely. The following is an exchange between the former Staff Director of the Republican Senate Policy Committee and ex-Senator Ferguson of Michigan:

> MR. SMITH. Now, Senators, for your amusement as well as to bear out my point on the impossible work load put upon Members of Congress, I have gathered here a group of the books and reports, limited solely to an official character, you should be reading right now on the Marshall plan.
> (Mr. Smith here presented a stack of material eighteen inches high.)
> You are going to take the most momentous step in the history of this country when you pass upon the Marshall plan. . . . That is what you ought to be studying. It contains the Krug report, the Harriman report, the State Department report, the reports of the Herter committee, the Foreign Relations Committee digest, it includes part of the hearings just completed on the Foreign Relations Committee. It does not include hearings yet to be held by the Appropriations Committees. This is one work load you have now on a single problem out of the many problems you have to decide.
>
> SENATOR FERGUSON. How long would it take in your opinion . . . for a person to read it?
>
> MR. SMITH. Well, Senator, I have been reading for the last thirty-five years, nearly all of my life, in the field of research; and if I could do an intelligent job on that in two months of solid reading, excluding myself from everything else . . . I would credit myself with great efficiency.
>
> SENATOR FERGUSON. A normal person would probably take four to five months.[18]

What has been discussed so far may be summed up as follows: 1) Despite the general proposition that the legislature is the primary agency for policy formation, in the area of foreign relations initiative lies largely in the hands of the executive, with Congress playing its most important role as the agency of control over the executive. 2) In this control function Congress is handicapped in a number of ways, so that control is intermittent, at best, and may introduce ignorance and shortsightedness into the foreign policy process. The question arises: What has been and could be done to provide a more effective role for Congress?

---

[18] Quoted in Dahl, *Congress and Foreign Policy*, pp. 129–30.

A More Effective Role for Congress?

One conceivable answer to this question is to recognize the necessity for centralized direction and control of foreign policy, to recognize that the President is best equipped to provide this direction and control and to remove Congress as much as possible from the foreign policy process—in short, to develop a kind of constitutional dictatorship in the field of foreign affairs. The case for this cannot be dismissed lightly. Given all the natural handicaps faced by Congress in its attempts to play a meaningful role in the development of foreign policy, and the converse advantages of the executive, and given the perhaps crucial need of effective, coherent, and consistent policy based on expert analysis of the exigencies of the world situation, it can be argued that the executive should not only be the supreme, but the sole, formulator and executor of contemporary American foreign policy. The stakes, it can be argued, are too high (ultimately the very existence of the country) to permit congressional interference by men without adequate information, training, or time to participate intelligently in foreign policy making. This general line of argument is relevant to perhaps the most basic problem facing us today, for this argument is an attack on democratic government generally. But in one sense the answer is too easy—for it ignores the fact that one of the things our foreign policy is designed to preserve is American values—values that include a commitment to democratic government. And if, in order to promote more effective foreign policy, we remove democratic controls on the foreign policy makers, are we not subverting those very institutions that our foreign policy is ostensibly trying to protect? It may well be that democratic government cannot cope successfully with the problems of a crisis age; but until such time as we are prepared to admit this, any discussion of foreign policy formation in the United States must include the promotion and not the abolition of democratic controls.

Congress and the Expert

Congress itself has attempted to meet this problem in at least two general ways. First, it has tried to develop expertise concerning foreign relations through the devices of subcommittees of the major committees and the hiring of experts on the substantive questions faced by the committees. The essential problem concerning the development of congressional expertise is that if one or two members of a subcommittee of the Senate Foreign

Relations Committee become expert on a given problem or area, and the rest of the Senate relies on their judgment concerning executive proposals in this area or function, democratic controls are not advanced very much. The same thing applies to the committee experts. Yet it is the latter who offer the hope that real progress can be made in developing a more effective role for Congress.

As Professor Robert Dahl has pointed out, there are at least three different roles that the expert may play for the committee. The committee may in fact abdicate its responsibility for making decisions and merely follow the advice of the expert—a situation that may make for good decisions but one that does not solve the problem of control. Or the committee may confine the expert to a role of providing information that committee members do not have the time to absorb for themselves. This is obviously helpful, but it does not take full advantage of the expert's ability to suggest intelligent courses of action that the limitations of training and study may cause the Congressmen to overlook. Third, the expert may, in addition to providing information, suggest possible alternative courses of action indicating the implications of each, but leave the ultimate decision as to what course is chosen to the Congressmen. This arrangement combines greatest utilization of expertise with meaningful congressional participation in decision-making.

Bi-Partisanship

Another way Congress has attempted to overcome some of the obstacles in the road to effective participation in foreign policy is through bipartisanship. As this word is used popularly it involves two assumptions: 1) that party leaders in Congress should consult among themselves and with the executive in order to develop an executive-legislative consensus of foreign policy issues, and as an aspect of this 2) that opposition to foreign policy proposals should not be based on "political" considerations, that is, embarrassment to the administration, emotional appeals to constituents, or aggrandizement of personal political power. In terms of the second assumption, a better word would probably be nonpartisanship. While bipartisanship has had considerable appeal in recent American history, there are a number of things that limit its possibilities.

In the first place congressional leaders do not have the time to engage in intra-Congressional consultations as well as Congressional-Presidential consultations on a systematic enough basis to develop consensus on all matters of foreign policy. Second, even if they did, the lack of party discipline characteristic of the American Congress would not assure congressional agreement with that consensus. Third, what may seem to be an irresponsible disagreement with administration proposals on the part of some Congressmen may actually be based on very serious considerations. Consider, for example, the possibility that the executive and legislative leaders agree that "trade not aid" should underlie American economic relations with Western Europe; that from this it follows that there should be a general reduction of tariff barriers on the flow of European goods to the United States; that Swiss watches be included in tariff reductions. If a Massachusetts Congressman violently objects to such reductions because they would have an adverse effect on the watchmakers in his district, is he playing "politics" with foreign policy? And if all other Congressmen similarly object to tariff reductions on commodities produced in their districts or states, are they too playing politics? The point is, simply, that foreign policy cannot be separated from domestic considerations, and to ask Congressmen to support bipartisanship at the expense of the immediate economic interests of their constituents is to ask them to sacrifice concrete local demands for comparatively vague national advantages.

Finally, there is implicit in the notion of bipartisanship—at least in the way the word is often used—the idea that disagreement should stop at the water's edge; that, at the extreme, severe criticism of an administration's policies weakens America's dealings with foreign powers. Yet democratic government means the right, not to say duty, of legislators to criticize as constructively as they can any public policy, foreign or domestic. To argue the dangers of criticism is to argue the dangers of democracy. Certainly it is hoped that the criticism will in fact be constructive; but to view criticism itself as by definition a hindrance to the pursuit of foreign policy goals is to challenge one of the basic functions of the legislature.

The Viet Nam Dilemma

All that has been said about Congress and foreign policy is subject to the reservation that in time of war criticism stops, unity prevails and the executive assumes virtually sole responsibility for foreign policy. This idea of a temporary constitutional dictatorship is based on the premise that war is an aberration in international affairs, necessitating a temporary reliance on a unified direction of policy, best left in the hands of the President.

The practice has much merit. Once Congress has declared war, the degree to which it was a "mistake" to get involved is an argument more suitable for postwar scholarship than partisan debate when the war is on. Military success in large part is based on morale, at home as well as at the front, and argument concerning the justice, utility, or legality of a war effort may serve primarily to undermine that morale. This line of thought was almost universally accepted during the first and second world wars— both of which were assumed to be temporary, after which our political institutions could return to their normal processes.

But with the Korean and, especially, the Viet Namese conflicts this traditional attitude has come under increasing question. Neither of these brought in a declaration of war; both meant a tremendous outlay of national wealth and the sacrifice of thousands of lives. And both may be examples of frequently recurring possibilities rather than abnormal crises. In this case, is Congress still to adopt the attitude of deference to presidential monopoly of the control of policy-making?

It is to this fundamental question that such Senators as Fulbright and Morse, along with others, have begun to address themselves, with particular reference to Viet Nam. The Senate hearings, from this point of view, did not represent a desire to embarrass the President or undermine the morale of our fighting men, but were an attempt to assert the right of Congress to participate in the decision-making process with regard to foreign policy even after the fighting has started.

Those opposed to their criticism have relied on the traditional demands for unity in time of crisis, and have castigated these critics as "nervous nellies." Yet, if Viet Nam is open-ended in the sense of the absence of any clear indication as to the limits of our commitment, and if at the same time it is not an aberration, but an example of increasingly common situations involving the use of force, then it is a fair—and an extraordinarily difficult—question as to whether Congress should abdicate its responsibilities once the shooting has started.

The many proposals for closer collaboration suggested by students of Congress and the Presidency are all relevant to this question. Professor Corwin's suggestion for a joint legislative-executive Cabinet, Senator Kefauver's proposal for a question period in Congress similar to that used by the English parliament in which executive leaders are called upon to account for their policies to the legislature, and Professor Dahl's contention that even the Central Intelligence Agency, however necessarily secret its activities must be, should not be immune from congressional oversight, are all to the point.[19]

In the absence of any marked institutional change, however, perhaps the most effective device for developing close executive-legislative collaboration is the informal consultation between the White House and congressional leaders, including their participation in decision-making, combined with the use of experts as policy advisers to Congress. Certainly no institutional changes will accomplish any more than a desire on the part of Congressmen and the executive to cooperate effectively in the development of foreign policy. This reliance on the desires of the people involved rather than institutional "gimmicks" may seem a weak recommendation for improvement in Congress' role—until it is remembered that it is not institutions, but people, who make foreign policy.

THE ROLE OF PUBLIC OPINION

When Senator Snodgrass stands up in Congress and declares "The public wants this foreign policy," to what public is he referring? He cannot

---

[19] See also, Carroll, *The House of Representatives and Foreign Affairs*, especially chapter 15.

mean everybody, for there is bound to be some difference of opinion among seventy million voting Americans. But he probably cannot mean even a majority because polls have shown that only 25 per cent of the people consistently show knowledge of foreign problems,[20] and even fewer have an articulate opinion on them. When we speak of the "public" in public opinion on foreign affairs, then, we are usually speaking of a much smaller group than the total public—what have aptly been called the "attentive publics."

Who composes these attentive publics? Generally speaking, their membership may be divided into two broad categories: 1) articulate leaders of opinion (newspaper editors, commentators, columnists, educators, and the like) who, although they have a concern for the formation of effective, intelligent foreign policy, have no direct or immediate interest that will be affected thereby; 2) organized interest groups, whose concern will ordinarily be with the effects of a policy on their particular interests. The latter, although concerned with promoting America's international position, are more immediately involved in the domestic implications of any foreign policy and are likely to view the national interest in terms of their particular interest.

When the Senator used the words ". . . wants this policy," what did he mean? Did he mean that certain people interested in the policy banded together and attempted to influence Congress and the President in behalf of it? Or did he mean that a proposed policy, formed largely in the executive branch, is acceptable to that segment of the total public that knows and cares about it? Whether an attentive public is attempting to influence government or whether the executive is essentially trying to "sell" policy proposals depends largely on the issue involved, but in any case it is rarely completely either one or the other.

The Executive Reaches Down

In the attempt to "sell" policy proposals, the executive has a number of devices at its disposal. One technique is that of cloaking highly debatable specific proposals in the mantle of unimpeachable generalities. The decision to attack North Viet Nam directly was justified by the President on the general support of his policy to assist South Viet Nam in its resistance to aggression. When some Congressmen criticized this escalation the President could, as he did, refer them to the Tonkin Bay resolution that the Congress had almost unanimously supported.

Another technique, used a good deal by President Franklin Roosevelt, is the trial balloon, launched either at a press conference or during fireside chats. This device is the practice of indicating that a proposed policy is

---

[20] Martin Kriesberg, "Dark Areas of Ignorance," in *Public Opinion and Foreign Policy*, ed. Lester Markel, p. 51. Cited in Gabriel Almond, *The American People and Foreign Policy* (New York: Harcourt, Brace & World, Inc., 1950), p. 82.

under consideration and awaiting popular reaction to it. If such reaction, in the form of letters, editorials, and commentators' remarks, is favorable—the policy may then be formally proposed.

Still a third technique is that of the weighted announcement. While informing the public of an important international event the executive may, by his choice of words, hope to build up support for his policy. Thus President Kennedy's discussion of the Berlin crisis of 1961 was largely dedicated to engendering popular and congressional support for a general revision of policy in the direction of increasing our conventional striking forces.

The process works both ways, for the executive does make some systematic attempts to collect and analyze at least some manifestations of articulate opinion. The State Department's Public Opinion Studies Staff, for example, reads editorials, columns, and feature stories in the press as well as the *Congressional Record*, analyzes findings of public opinion polls, and covers radio broadcasts and pressure group policy announcements. Based on these sources, a daily two or three page summary is circulated to officials in the department and every month a nine to eleven page summary is sent to our representatives abroad as well. Finally, a digest of outstanding articles on foreign affairs is distributed to department officials.[21] But in practice these devices for bringing public opinion directly into policy formation apparently do not count for very much. In the first place, the measurements of popular views do not always reveal intensity of opinion, which may be a decisive factor in the minds of the policy-makers. Secondly, members of the State Department, or other governmental officials, are probably more influenced by their individual reading and thinking about a problem than by scanning the office mimeographed reports on public opinion. Finally, in many cases policy cannot await the initiative of a public outside the government or, especially, the executive branch.[22]

The Attentive Publics Push Up

The question of the extent to which attentive publics participate actively in the formation of foreign policy is a deceptive one. This is true in part because of the tradition of executive supremacy in foreign affairs and in part because of the distinction between foreign and domestic policy.

One of the first things the student of American politics learns is that the how and why of policy formation cannot be completely explained solely by reference to the formal institutions of government. To get a clear picture of just why Congress passes one law rather than another or of how the executive goes about "faithfully executing" the laws, it is necessary to

---

21 Robert E. Elder, *The Policy Machine: The Department of State and American Foreign Policy* (Syracuse: Syracuse University Press, 1960), pp. 140–44.

22 See McCamy, *The Administration of American Foreign Affairs*, pp. 329–32.

identify the groups that are actively interested in any policy question and to attempt to measure their relative influence on the ultimate policy decision. Put briefly: look behind the Medicare Act and you would have found not 435 Representatives and 100 Senators sagely stroking their metaphorical beards, while deciding on a suitable policy, but whole congeries of individuals and groups both in and out of government attempting to influence the direction of policy in a way they deemed favorable to their particular interests or ideas.

When the student turns to foreign policy, however, he may well look in vain for identifiable interest groups whose complex of activities will explain the emergence of a policy. By and large, every major area of concern of our government has its counterpart in one or more identifiable interest groups. When we think of labor questions we may expect that the AFL-CIO, the National Association of Manufacturers, and the United States Chamber of Commerce will, along with other groups whose interests may be somewhat less directly affected, take an active part in the attempt to steer public policy in the direction they want it to go. The same is true for agricultural questions, civil liberties problems, transportation policy, and so on. When we turn to foreign policy, however, such easily spotted groups may seem notable by their absence.

The second reason that the role of attentive publics in the formation of foreign policy is obscured is a matter of historical tradition. Throughout most of our history, matters of foreign policy were of secondary concern to the vast majority of Americans because of our geographic isolation from the vortex of international affairs. Throughout the nineteenth and even the early twentieth century, American interests and efforts were directed toward carving out and developing our own nation; what happened in Europe or Asia or even South of the Rio Grande seemed of little consequence to us. It was thus not unnatural that governmental foreign policy makers, particularly the executive, were left comparatively free to exercise their initiative. And while the exigencies of our present status as a major world power have made foreign policy issues of immediate concern to all Americans, the tradition of executive initiative in foreign affairs is still very much with us.

Yet, no matter how obscured their activities may be, an attentive public may have an important influence on foreign policy. In the first place, there are a number of highly articulate individuals and groups, concerned with America's general international position, that take stands on public issues. An incisive analysis by a man like Walter Lippmann may have considerable influence on any one of a number of important governmental officials, though how much or on whom is difficult to ascertain.

Groups such as the League of Women Voters and the Council on Foreign Relations spend a considerable amount of energy and funds on foreign policy. But the primary function of such groups is education, and there is little evidence that the groups as groups have had a great impact on

the formation of any particular policy. They may, however, act as inter-
mediaries in bringing together important governmental officials and
thoughtful students of international affairs—an activity carried on by the
Council on Foreign Relations.

Turning to those groups with specific domestic interests on which
foreign policy will impinge, we can discern a much more immediate impact
on the formation of that policy. This impact may take the form of direct
influence on the executive, or it may be revealed through congressional
representation of the interest. As interests manifest themselves in Congress
they may be immediate, in the sense of a congressional threat not to
approve a presidential proposal, or long range; for example, when the
President, having discretionary authority based on annual or biennial
legislation, is threatened with a limitation on that authority. And the very
fact that many people tend to assume that, although "special interests"
participate in the formation of domestic policy, the "government" makes
foreign policy unhindered by such interests, gives those groups that much
greater leverage. This is further buttressed by the fact that foreign policy
will ordinarily be defended in terms of America's international interests,
almost never with reference to the domestic considerations involved.

To illustrate some of these points, two examples may be cited. During
1956 the United States first offered, and then withdrew the offer, to aid the
Egyptian government under Colonel Nasser in the construction of the
Aswan Dam on the Nile River. The withdrawal was defended in terms of
the failure of the riparian states to make the necessary agreements concerning the dam, and Egypt's apparent inability to make her necessary financial
contribution to the project. Another, and very important, factor in the
decision, however, was the known opposition of Congress. This congressional opposition was based primarily on the fear that a "big investment in
Egypt would offend Zionist sympathies and on the fear of southern
legislators that Egypt might raise more cotton than the U.S."[23] Here, both
ethnic-religious and economically oriented interest groups were influential
in determining policy.

A second example illustrates both how a broad policy may be agreed to
in principle, but opposed in its specific, and—very interestingly—how the
perspective of a policy-maker may change depending upon his constituency. In 1956, President Eisenhower as part of his general policy of
promoting "trade not aid," turned down requests of several twine and
cordage companies to increase our tariffs on those products, imported
largely from Canada and Mexico. Appearing for one of the cordage
companies was Senator John F. Kennedy who, while agreeing in principle
with the trade promotion policy of the President, nevertheless felt constrained to support an affected firm (the Plymouth Cordage Co.) in his
state. Five years later, President John F. Kennedy rejected appeals of twine

---

[23] *The New York Times,* July 20, 1956.

and cordage companies to raise tariffs on these products. The point is not that Mr. Kennedy was some sort of a turncoat; it is rather that as a Senator he certainly had to be concerned with the economy of his state, but as President he had to take a "broader view in the national interest," to quote *The New York Times*. Further, it is one thing to elicit agreement on broad statements of principle and quite another to get approval for the detailed implementation of that principle.[24]

Interest groups do, then, play a significant role in many aspects of policy formation. In general, those organized around economic, religious, or ethnic interests appear to be the most active and influential. The degree to which they do impinge on foreign policy will be, other things being equal, roughly proportionate to the degree in which the proposed policy affects their concerns. Thus if we look at the development of the treaty establishing NATO we find that identifiable interest groups did not play a role comparable to that with regard to the Aswan Dam decision—in large part because, although no one would dispute the importance of NATO, the proposed treaty did not have immediate effects on any interest groups as did the Aswan Dam Project. One other situation in which private interest groups would not exert direct influence on the decision-making process is a crisis situation, such as the invasion of South Korea, when speed and secrecy are both imperatives, and the stakes are too momentous to be reduced to interest group calculation.

We have said that insofar as public opinion impinges directly on foreign policy formation, the public by no means consists of all Americans, nor on most specific issues, even of most Americans. It is, rather, a comparatively small number of people—the attentive public. We have also said that the role of interest groups, as the attentive public, is an important role for many, though not all, aspects of foreign policy. This leads to two further questions: 1) Is there any sense in which the public—the "at-large public"—affects foreign policy? and 2) How does public opinion at large impinge on foreign policy indirectly through the electoral process?

Opinion and Mood

The answer to the first question is necessarily speculative, but it seems fair to say that the at-large public sets the outside limits within which initiative may be exercised. Put another way, the at-large public has moods rather than specific opinions; moods that provide thresholds over which foreign policy makers cannot step. Of course moods are themselves subject to change and to a certain extent can be altered by the effective use of the devices the executive has to mold opinion. But in any given period, certain

---

[24] See *The New York Times*, February 7, 1961 and an editorial on February 10, 1961.

alternatives would appear to be closed to foreign policy makers because the American people generally would be overwhelmingly opposed to them.

Perhaps even more important than setting the outside limits of policy formation, mood will affect the terms in which our policies are articulated. So long as our mood was one of bitter hostility toward the Soviet Communists, any projected negotiated settlement with the Soviets in any part of the world ran the risk of being viewed as appeasement. Thus any concession our government made had to be disguised and any public position taken by an American official had to be couched in "tough" language. This in turn tended to minimize or restrict the possibilities of negotiation with the Soviets. An example of how shifts in mood may occur is the fact that China now appears to be our public enemy number one, and though the Russians have not exactly become our closest allies, it is not considered treason to suggest increased trade relations or even joint moon shots with the Soviet Union.

Elections as Measurements of Opinion

Turning to the question of the public's influence on foreign policy through the devices of representative government, the classic formulation of the public's role is stated in terms of the two major political parties taking stands on foreign policy issues and the public—that is, the electorate—choosing between alternatives proposed by the parties. But the United States is noted for its absence of party discipline and responsibility. It is traditional in American politics that party positions on major issues as spelled out in the national platforms are vague rather than clear cut, and this is especially true of foreign policy issues.

On the other hand, meaningful alternative domestic policies are often presented to the voters in the individual congressional, senatorial, or presidential campaigns. Here, again, it is by way of exception that foreign as opposed to domestic issues are posed in terms of clear alternatives. In most congressional and senatorial races, domestic questions are almost always of first concern (to the extent that policy issues enter at all). At the presidential level, campaigns are marked by vagueness rather than specific proposals in the area of foreign affairs. In the television debates during the campaign of 1960, for example, each candidate at one time indicated a fairly definite stand on one aspect of foreign policy: Nixon on Quemoy and Matsu, Kennedy on Cuba. In the face of mutual criticism, however, each rapidly modified his proposals to the point where the positions of the two men were virtually indistinguishable.

The campaign of 1964 appeared to many to be different. Two distinct sets of foreign policy alternatives were represented by the candidates—especially with regard to Viet Nam. Yet the victor has carried out a good many of the proposals of the vanquished, proposals he rejected during the campaign. This isn't, necessarily, to accuse President Johnson of being a hawk in doves' feathers. It is simply to point out that foreign affairs may develop in such a way that what was rejected in October seems critically necessary in February, campaign oratory to the contrary notwithstanding.

This whole question of campaigns and elections as devices by which public opinion can play a role in the shaping of foreign policy is illustrated by the election that perhaps more than any other is viewed as a solemn referendum on an issue of foreign policy—the presidential election of 1920. Yet a close examination of that election shows that, however solemn it may have been, the election was something less than a referendum on the League of Nations. Given statements by candidate Harding and other leading Republicans during the campaign, it would have been perfectly logical for a voter to have believed that Harding's election would not constitute a rejection of the League. More important, it would have been perfectly possible for a voter to have viewed the election as a referendum on the League, to have been in favor of American entry, yet to have voted for Harding, because he felt other issues to be more crucial. In short, what we are saying here is that even at election time when the public is called upon to express direct preferences on issues, the results very rarely, perhaps never, give a clear indication of the public's view on any one issue. And in the interim between elections, of course, concrete manifestations of the public's desires are still less in evidence.

In sum, if we mean by the public the American people, generally it is more realistic to talk of moods rather than opinion—moods that at any given time set the outside limits for initiative in the making of foreign policy. Articulate opinion based on some knowledge of a foreign policy issue is ordinarily confined to a small part of the total public and here its role is often, though not always, confined to the comparatively passive role of accepting, rejecting, or perhaps causing the modification of proposals emanating from the government, particularly the executive branch. And, finally, our elections—the means by which the total public may directly impinge on foreign policy—are intermittent in time and inconclusive in results.

FOREIGN POLICY AND THE DEMOCRATIC PROCESS

This discussion of the major groups of participants in the foreign policy process brings to light four important points that often tend to be obscured in our concern with developing effective foreign policy, and deserve special emphasis.

Domestic Necessities and International Responsibilities

No matter how much, for purposes of discussion, we differentiate foreign and domestic policies, it should never be forgotten that the two in practice are very much related. Regardless of how beautifully thought out and constructed any foreign policy is, if it does not take into consideration the domestic needs and desires of the American people as manifested primarily through Congress, its adoption will be jeopardized. Nor is this a one-way street. Our international responsibilities may, and do, have important repercussions on domestic policy as well. We cannot spend fifty billion a year to build up our own and our allies' military might without sacrificing a considerable amount of domestic goods and services. Any attempt to understand American foreign policy, then, must take into account the total picture of American public policy, with foreign policy viewed as an important, but still only one, aspect of that total picture.

Relation of Substance and Process

Another point that may well be obscured in our concern for effective foreign policy is that the substance of that policy is related in at least two significant ways to the process of arriving at it. First, it does make an important difference as to who in fact makes policy—whose picture of reality will serve as the basis for action. We have seen an example of this in the case study on strategic trust territories. On a broader screen, the degree to which we will feel constrained to commit ever more troops to Viet Nam will be largely conditioned by the questions of whose analysis of the nature of the Chinese threat is used as the basis for policy development. Second, regardless of who in fact does make policy, the question arises as to whether or not they are in fact controlled by the American people, either directly or through their elected representatives. If we are not to throw out the baby with the bathwater, democratic controls over policy-making— foreign or domestic—must be retained.

Continuing Control Versus Elective Aristocracy

We have seen that these controls are by and large incomplete and inter-mittent. Necessity has led to considerable independence of the executive branch in the formation of foreign as compared to domestic policy. Does this mean that in fact about all we can do is elect a President every four years and turn over foreign policy decision-making to him, and the executive departments under him, in the hope that we have selected a wise man and able administrator? Perhaps so—certainly a case can be made that the tendency in that direction is present, if indeed the end has not already been reached. But if so, there is no use in beclouding the fact that a vital aspect of democratic government has been vitiated. To the extent that in our quest for security we are willing to sacrifice democratic institutions, to that extent we destroy what we hope to preserve. Again, the exigencies of crisis may necessitate such a sacrifice—just as most of us accept the need for less democracy in wartime. But where does crisis stop and the "normal" pattern of international affairs begin? In a world which knows no peace, but in which the almost constant warfare is confined in scope and limited in intensity, it is perhaps more understandable that we should tend to overlook the more gradual accretion of decision-making authority into the hands of appointed rather than popularly elected officials. But this tendency favors what may be called an elective aristocracy as against continuing control, without our even being aware of it.

Institutional Change Versus Responsible Citizenship

But is the tendency irreversible? Must we of necessity turn our backs on the question of continuing control in order to achieve effective foreign policy? What might be done to promote more, rather than less, democracy without sacrificing intelligence and flexibility in our foreign relations at the same time? Several suggestions have been made on this point, some of which have already been discussed. In addition, one might mention the oft-repeated assertion that the development of disciplined, responsible, political parties would make our elections more meaningful in terms of popular choices among alternative policies while promoting greater congressional effectiveness in controlling the executive. None of these proposals should be disparaged, but the possibility of developing responsible political parties itself indicates the real nature of the problem: that democratic government is after all a belief system as well as a structure of formal institutions. As students of political parties have pointed out, although institutional changes may affect the structure of parties, we will get responsible parties only when we want them. Similarly, no institutional change—reorganization of the executive branch, question periods in Congress, joint legislative-executive Cabinet meetings—will, however useful, in and of itself assure effective popular control of foreign policy. However trite it has become, the statement that in democracies people get the kind of government they want is still very much the case.

In the last analysis, then, democratic controls on foreign policy making depend not so much on institutional change as on responsible citizenship. In a very real sense one of the great challenges of our age is whether in our concern with earning a living, going to parties, and achieving equal status with the Joneses, we are to turn over the responsibilities of decision-making to a kind of elective aristocracy; or whether American citizens can effectively cope with the problems of foreign policy themselves. Can we overcome the tempting but disastrous tendency to think, if at all, with the slogans of yesterday? Or can we instead become sufficiently educated and interested to make thoughtful judgments on important issues and demand that our government be responsive and responsible to us? Responsive government calls for responsible citizens.

BIBLIOGRAPHICAL NOTE

An excellent general work, dealing with both the substance and the process of American foreign policy, is Richard C. Snyder and Edgar S. Furniss, Jr., *American Foreign Policy: Formulation, Principles, and Programs*, 1954.

A number of very good monographs on various aspects of foreign policy formations have been published, their titles indicating the subject matter with which they are concerned. Included among these are Gabriel A. Almond, *The American People and Foreign Policy*, 1950; James N. Rosenau, *Public Opinion and Foreign Policy*, 1961; Robert A. Dahl, *Congress and Foreign Policy*, 1950; James A. Robinson, *Congress and Foreign Policy-Making*, 1962; James L. McCamy, *The Administration of American Foreign Affairs*, 1952; H. Bradford Westerfield, *Foreign Policy and Party Politics: Pearl Harbor to Korea*, 1955; Robert E. Elder, *The Policy Machine: The Department of State and American Foreign Policy*, 1960; and Holbert N. Carroll, *The House of Representatives and Foreign Affairs*, 1958.

Dexter Perkins, *The Evolution of American Foreign Policy*, 1948, provides a fine brief summary of the historical development of American foreign relations. Recent surveys include Cecil V. Crabb, *American Foreign Policy in the Nuclear Age*. 2nd ed., 1965. A critical assessment is Edmund Stillman and William Pfaff, *Power and Impotence: The Failure of America's Foreign Policy*, 1966.

Useful collections of readings and documents may be found in Ruhl J. Bartlett, ed., *The Record of American Diplomacy*, 2nd ed., 1950.

military policy

JAMES N. MURRAY, JR.

As noted in the preceding chapter, the problems of foreign policy can be adequately understood only in the context of the revolutionary transformation of the position of the United States in world affairs. Yet this change in the international role of the United States has had, if possible, even greater implications for military policy. It was something less than fifty years ago that a President directed the War Department to cease all war planning because, in addition to its inconsistency with America's position as a peace-loving nation, our security did not require it.[1] A similar directive today, or for the foreseeable future, would be unthinkable.

BACKGROUND FACTORS

To appreciate the significance of this change, and the implications of it, it is necessary to recall the traditional position of the military in public affairs. Essentially, the role of the military was that of an agency of policy execution, whenever the civilian formulators of foreign policy, in trying to preserve our security, so directed. And because during the eighteenth and nineteenth centuries our geographic isolation from Europe and Asia meant our military isolation as well, we had no need of a large standing army and felt little necessity for a sizeable navy. Traditionally, the assumptions underlying America's relations with other states were that peaceful intercourse was the rule, armed conflict the temporary aberration. In this sense Clausewitz' famous statement that war is an extension of diplomacy by other means was modified in the United States to include the notion that these "other means" were at most temporary,

---

[1] Townsend Hoopes, "Civilian-Military Balance," *Yale Review*, XLIII (Winter, 1954), 219.

to be discarded immediately after having fulfilled their purpose. It has been as much a boast as a complaint to assert that America has never been prepared for a war. And our uninterrupted record of very rapid disarmament at the conclusion of wars bears this out further. Underlying this tradition of the abnormality of war was the fact that for over a century before World War II the physical security of the United States itself was never directly threatened.

Consider, then, the implications of the modern era for this tradition. The Soviet Union is not only a state whose interests conflict with those of the United States; it is also a nation capable of inflicting untold damage, if not total destruction, on us. At present there is little doubt that the threat to American security posed by the Communists includes not just strategically located countries and territories overseas, but the United States proper as well. In addition to these considerations, technological developments have tremendously enhanced the importance of actual rather than potential military might. That is to say, the fact that the United States can out-produce any nation in the world does not mean it can, as it has in the past, wait until the outbreak of war to develop military striking power sufficient to win the war. Ballistic missiles with nuclear warheads no longer permit any nation that luxury. Although it is an overstatement, there is an element of truth in rephrasing Clausewitz' dictum to read for our own times: diplomacy is the extension of war by other means.

What the revolutionary transformation in America's role in world politics means, as much as anything else, is the revolutionary transformation of the military in the shaping of that role. Today it is fair to ask whether or not the traditional roles of the diplomat and soldier should be reversed—whether in view of the tremendous threat to our national security, strategic-military considerations ought not to govern our foreign policy.

Military-Civil Relations

The Gargantuan growth of military considerations in all aspects of public policy raises a further fundamental problem: the relations between the military and civilian participants in policy-making. It has long been recognized that one of the greatest threats to democratic government is the emergence of a strong military organization not easily susceptible to control by civilian officials. The framers of our Constitution were acutely aware of this, and it was not by accident that the President was made Commander-in-Chief of the Armed Forces, that Congress was empowered to raise and maintain an army and navy, that congressional appropriations for the military were limited to a period not to exceed two years, and that army and navy officers were excluded from nonmilitary governmental positions. Indeed, one of the arguments used to support the adoption of the Constitution was that congressional power to raise and maintain an army and navy provided safeguards against possible military dominance.[2] This attitude was further buttressed by the very fact that throughout most of our history we did not need a large military establishment. Until recently, civilian-military relationships did not cause grave concern, because the problem simply did not arise to any significant degree.

Now, however, the problem is very much with us. With our tremendous military establishment, with the clear necessity of including the professional military in the highest councils of policy-making, and with the apparent necessity of viewing the world through the lenses of military strategy, we are faced with the danger not only of the dominance of military considerations in forming public policy, but also of the dominance of military men. It is highly significant that in President Eisenhower's farewell talk to the American people, he felt it incumbent to stress the necessity of guarding "against the acquisition of unwarranted influence, whether sought or unsought, by the military-industrial complex. The potential for the disastrous rise of misplaced power exists and will persist."[3] Any discussion of the problems concerning the development of adequate military policy must, then, include the basic question of control of the military by the civil. Nor is it enough to say, "If the military is getting too powerful, then let us remove them from the councils of policy-making." For military men participate in policy-making precisely because they are indispensable. The real problem concerns the development of a governmental system that can make use of the necessary military expertise in the formation of policy, and at the same time provide for authoritative, effective civilian control. We ignore the problem of control at the peril of our democratic institutions; we ignore military considerations at the risk of our security; we can afford to do neither.

A Word about Words

Before proceeding to a discussion of these problems, it will be useful to distinguish between three phrases with overlapping connotations: foreign policy, military policy, and security. Traditionally foreign policy has meant that collection of activities—largely political and economic—used to pursue our goals with respect to other states. Military policy has been concerned with the ways in which specific objectives should be pursued using military means—the objectives themselves being defined ostensibly by those in control of foreign policy. It is obvious that given our present position in the world, the line between foreign and military policy will be vague at best. But in an age when the physical security of the nation is

---

[2] *The Federalist Papers*, No. 26.
[3] Quoted in the *Department of State Bulletin*, XLIV, (February 6, 1961), 179–82.

threatened with total war, attention must be paid to the potential mobilization of all the domestic resources we have for the maintenance of our security. In this sense security policy may be viewed as a three-dimensional composite for foreign, military, and domestic policies.

To take a concrete example, consider the decision to rearm West Germany and include its forces in NATO's military structure. Such a decision obviously was of a military nature, justified on the basis of troop requirements of NATO. But at the same time it had important implications for what has been traditionally thought of as the separate area of foreign policy. The State Department could not ignore the implications of this decision for 1) relations with our allies, 2) the potential unification of Germany or 3) what might be called the general climate of East-West relations.

But this is not all; the capacity of the American economy, or more accurately, the willingness of the American people, to underwrite increased American mobilization if West Germany remained unarmed was certainly a crucial factor in the decision. Thus our total policy on the rearming of West Germany necessarily included foreign political, military, and domestic considerations. This total policy we may call security policy. To generalize, we have security—rather than merely foreign or military—policies today because superimposed on our relations with any given area of the world is the East-West conflict—a conflict that can become both total and nuclear at any time. Potential total war calls for total planning both for its prevention and for its outbreak, and this in turn necessitates consideration of domestic capabilities, in addition to foreign and military policies. Finally, those domestic capabilities themselves include the degree to which American people are willing to make the necessary sacrifices to pursue any tactic, policy, or grand strategy. Problems of military policy, then, must be discussed in terms of the more general question of security.

ORGANIZING FOR SECURITY

The attempt to develop security policy, as distinct from the more specialized foreign or military policy, is essentially a product of the post-World War II era. As a consequence, the hallmark of American efforts in this direction has been change—trial and error, reorganization, shift of function. And, although under the Eisenhower administration some attempt was made at the regularization of security policy formation, it is unlikely that there could ever be a set, patterned, policy formation process in this area. This is true for the simple reason of the overriding importance of security affairs in any administration; which in turn means that each President will bring to the subject his own distinctive style and methods of operation.

The basic legislation underlying our present arrangements is the National Security Act of 1947. In general, two considerations are behind this law. The first, already alluded to, was the growing realization that it was impossible to separate rigidly the functions of the State Department and the military services. Even during the last world war, when the military was theoretically running most of the show, it became obvious 1) that military-strategic decisions might have grave political implications—for example, bringing the Soviet Union into the war in the Far East or deciding not to invade Europe through the Balkans—and 2) that the problems of occupying defeated countries would call for close cooperation between the civil and military agencies of our government. In response to this, a joint State, War, Navy Coordinating Committee (SWNCC) was created, in the hope that our foreign and military policies could be effectively coordinated. When, after the end of the war, it became apparent that "peace" was giving way to the cold war, there was obvious utility in continuing this kind of joint policy-making agency.

The second reason for enacting the National Security Act was the increasing acknowledgment though not without bitter controversy, that the traditional distinction of functions between the military services made less and less sense. At one time technological limitations on military power provided the basis for this distinction in fact as well as principle. Throughout most of our history the Army was pretty much confined to the ground—the Navy to the sea. Aircraft, upon their invention, were confined to tactical roles in connections with the other Armed Forces. But with aircraft able to journey thousand of miles, with land-based rocket launchers capable of sending airborne missiles hundreds of miles, with carrier-based aircraft able to penetrate far inland, and with any of these capable of delivering tremendous nuclear explosives, this military separation of powers needed reassessment.

With these considerations in mind Congress did two things in the National Security Act: 1) provided for the unification of the Armed Forces—now including a separate air force as a concession to the fact that air power could be strategic as well as tactical—under a single Secretary of Defense; 2) created a National Security Council whose job it is to formulate and review basic policies of the United States relating to our national security. Thus the act dealt with developing more unified military policies in the more confined sense and with promoting comprehensive security policies in the broadest meaning of the term.

The National Security Council

As presently constituted, the NSC consists of the President, the Vice-President, the Secretaries of State and Defense, and the Director of the Office of Emergency Planning. In addition to this formal membership, the

President may invite other officials to participate without vote in its deliberations. Often the Director of the Central Intelligence Agency, the Chairman of the Joint Chiefs of Staff, the Secretary of the Treasury, and the Director of the Bureau of the Budget attend meetings.

The *Central Intelligence Agency* was created by the National Security Act "to coordinate the intelligence activities of the several Government departments" and to advise the NSC "in matters concerning such intelligence activities . . . as related to national security."[4] During the course of its operations it has also collected and evaluated intelligence on its own, and particularly since the Korean War, has engaged in covert operations of a paramilitary nature.

This agency provides a good example of the uncertainty regarding organization for security policy. On the one hand, the need for an organization engaged in secret operations is clear. On the other hand, controlling such an organization—making certain that its activities are consistent with the overall purposes and the specific goals of policy—is another problem. If Congress is handicapped by the fact that its control of the executive is based largely on information supplied by the latter, the President faces a similar situation with regard to the Central Intelligence Agency. For example, although President Kennedy assumed full responsibility for the fiasco at the Bay of Pigs, there is evidence to show that to a large degree his decisions were based on inaccurate information given to him by the CIA.[5] And more than once in the past has the CIA been accused of conducting its own foreign policy in the field, often at cross purposes with the State Department.[6]

Both Presidents Kennedy and Johnson have been aware of this problem, and each has experimented with attempts at managing it. The most recent Presidential directive in this regard provided that the Secretary of State henceforth would:

> assume responsibility . . . for the over-all direction, coordination and supervision of interdepartmental activities . . . overseas (less exempted military activities) . . .
>
> To assist the Secretary of State in this new role, there will be a permanent interdepartmental committee, called the Senior Interdepartmental Group (SIG) with the Under Secretary of State as its "Executive Chairman." [SIG is to be] an incisive, decision-making body.
>
> The other regular members of the Senior Interdepartmental Group are: the Deputy Secretary of Defense, the Administrator of AID, the Director of CIA, the Chairman of the Joint Chiefs of Staff, the Director

---

[4] *United States Government Organization Manual*, 1966–67, p. 60.

[5] See, for example, Arthur M. Schlesinger, Jr., *A Thousand Days* (Boston: Houghton Mifflin Co., 1965), Chapter XI, especially, p. 290.

[6] For example, see an article by Arthur Krock in the *New York Times*, October 3, 1963, which quotes Scripps-Howard reporter Richard Starnes as asserting "according to a high United States source here [Saigon*], twice the CIA flatly refused to carry out instructions from Ambassador Henry Cabot Lodge . . . ."

of USIA, and the Special Assistant to the President for National Security Affairs.[7]

Yet it is doubtful if any institutional reforms can in and of themselves assure effective integration of the CIA and other agencies of American security policy. Two other alternatives open to the President are: 1) appoint a close and trusted associate to the directorship,[8] or 2) appoint a professional as Director, on the assumption that what is needed is expertise —expertise that will look exclusively to the President for policy direction. President Johnson has followed the latter course with the promotion of Mr. Richard Helms, formerly Deputy Director, to head the Agency.

In addition to the Central Intelligence Agency, the NSC has a small staff under the direction of the Special Assistant to the President for National Security Affairs,[9] which acts as a liaison between the President and various departments concerned with security policy.

So much for the machinery. The question is: does it work? And if so, how?

NSC in Action

Essentially the function of the NSC is twofold: 1) to deal with the immediate problems of security as they confront the nation; 2) to develop long range policies, laying out at least tentative paths in the direction of the goals we should like to achieve. This second point is important. One of the chief difficulties the United States has faced in attempting to develop long range policies is the overabundance of departmental concern for the day-to-day business and the consequent subjugation of long range planning. Yet without such planning our policies would have a tendency to be dictated by what other states do—we could not take the diplomatic offensive. One criticism of the policy of containment rests in its essential negativeness in this respect. It implies that we "hold the line" around the borders of the East and necessarily wait for some action from Peiping or Moscow before making a retaliatory move. Such a policy means relinquishing to the opposition all the initiative—letting him choose the time and place for action. Such considerations underlie the oft-expressed proposal that the United States seize this initiative. We must have positive and not merely negative policies. But we cannot have a positive policy without

---

[7] White House Announcement of New Procedures for Overseas Interdepartmental Matters, March 4, 1966. Quoted in *The Secretary of State and the Problem of Coordination,* Committee on Government Operations, United States Senate (Washington, D.C.: U.S. Government Printing Office, 1966), p. 1.

[8] See Schlesinger, *A Thousand Days,* p. 276, where President Kennedy is quoted as saying, following the Bay of Pigs fiasco, "I must have someone there [CIA] with whom I can be in complete and intimate contact—someone from whom I know I will be getting the exact pitch . . . Bobby [Kennedy] should be in CIA."

[9] At present, with the resignation of McGeorge Bundy, this office is vacant. The work of the staff, however, continues.

having some idea of our long range goals. Thus the need for some agency that, in addition to concerning itself with the major issues of the day, attempts to outline more far-reaching goals and ways to achieve those goals.

In the attempt to meet this challenge through the use of the NSC, two distinct techniques have been developed. During the Eisenhower years, consistent with the general philosophy of running the executive as a staff system, the Council's twin functions of initiative and execution were institutionally divided between a Planning Board and an Operations Control Board (OCB). The former, in cooperation with the Council's Staff, would refine policy proposals emanating from a Department for consideration by the Council. After Council consideration and presidential approval, the OCB was responsible for ensuring that the various aspects of the policy were implemented by the Departments or agencies concerned.

Fundamentally, at both the Planning Board level and in the NSC itself, the system was essentially a committee system. This meant among other things, that although differences might have been aired, there was a tendency for them to be glossed over so that "consensus" might be reached. Alternatively, a proposal, if violently objected to, would be sufficiently altered to secure the acquiescence of all concerned. But what emerged from the alteration was the lowest common denominator of policy; that is, one with which nobody disagreed, one which again promoted blandness rather than definiteness in policy directives.

From this flowed another significant difficulty. Given the tendency toward bland consensus rather than precise policy, the wording of NSC policies was often vague, generalized, and ambiguous. As a result, each agency of execution, whether State, Defense, or one of the services, could interpret the policy as it chose. Thus the Operations Coordinating Board— a good idea on paper—was not always effective in overseeing execution of NSC policy since it was difficult for anyone to state authoritatively just what the policy was. Moreover, the Board itself continued the committee system with consequences similar to those just mentioned.

As a result of these considerations, Presidents Kennedy and Johnson eliminated the distinction between planning and execution—both the Planning Board and the OCB have been abolished—and placed responsibility for long range policy development in the Departments, with the State Department given clear pre-eminence in the area. As a result the National Security Council has met less often since 1961, and has been used primarily as an action agency for policies arrived at before submission to the Council, and as an instrument for dealing with problems of immediate concern.

An excellent example of the latter, and one which illustrates a number of other points concerning NSC operations, was the missile crisis of 1962.

The Missile Crisis[10]

On Sunday, October 14, 1962, an American U-2 conducted aerial recon-
naisance over the western end of the island of Cuba. The primary purpose
of the mission was to check on the installation of Soviet surface-to-air
missiles (SAMs), as well as the increasing amounts of other Soviet military
aid being channeled into the Cuban armed forces. Further, there was just
the possibility that something new and different in the way of Soviet aid
might be detected.

To the Kennedy administration, "new and different" meant surface-to-
surface missiles, capable of inflicting nuclear damage on the United States.
President Kennedy had more than once indicated that there would be no
serious objection on the part of the United States to the Soviets supplying
defensive weaponry (such as the anti-aircraft SAMs) to Castro, but that
we would not countenance the introduction of offensive missiles (for
example, medium and intermediate range missiles) in Cuba.

When the photographs taken by the U-2 pilot had been developed and
analyzed, however, they indicated clearly that the Soviets were indeed in
the process of constructing "offensive" missile sites. By the evening of
October 15 the CIA had reported this to McGeorge Bundy, the President's
Special Assistant for National Security Affairs, and the following morning
Bundy informed the President. The missile crisis was on.

Actually there were two distinct aspects of the crisis: 1) what should be
the American reaction to the Soviet move? 2) how best to implement the
policy agreed upon? In addition, of course, the crisis could not be considered in the abstract: was it a feint to lure us into action so that the
Soviets could counter attack in a much more critical area, Berlin? How
would American policy be interpreted in the rest of Latin America, and
among our NATO allies? Above all, on the dimly perceived horizon there
loomed the terrible spectre of nuclear war as the only alternative to
acquiescence. Finally, it should be noted that whatever was decided had to
be arrived at quickly—before the Soviets succeeded in getting their missiles
in Cuba operational and announcing the *fait accompli* with suitable
Khrushchevian dramatics.

The first act of the President provides an excellent example of the fact
that institutional forms are not necessarily indicative of the policy-forming
process. He asked his Special Assistant McGeorge Bundy to call a meeting
of some fifteen people upon whose advice Kennedy was to base his deci-

---

[10] This case study is based primarily on Schlesinger, *A Thousand Days*, Chapters
XXX and XXXI and Theodore Sorensen, *Kennedy* (New York: Harper and Row, Publishers, 1965), Chapter XXIV. Where discrepancies occur Sorensen has been taken as
authoritative. There is obviously much more to the episode than can be related here.
For example, this account leaves out our efforts in the U.N. and OAS. The major
purpose here is to give a description of the processes of government in crisis.

sions. This group, referred to eventually as the Executive Committee of the National Security Council, was composed of people "who had little in common except the President's desire for their judgment."[11]

The task of the Committee in the first instance was to produce an adequate response. Though the specifics of who took what positions are, for the most part, not a matter of public record, there is evidence that the group met more as individuals than as representatives of their respective Departments or agencies. An interesting characteristic of the process was that the President did not attend every meeting of the Committee, feeling that his presence might inhibit a discussion that had to produce results rapidly as well as intelligently.

Essentially, the alternative responses ranged from doing nothing to invading Cuba. For a variety of reasons it was felt that *something* ought to be done (especially with regard to the Soviet Union as opposed to Castro)—though few if any members of the Committee advocated invasion, at least as the initial response.

The issue came down to a naval blockade *versus* an air strike against the missile sites. On this the Committee was seriously divided. The technique used to resolve the division was to appoint subcommittees, each to develop a "scenario" of what would eventuate if the particular alternative were selected. The critical objections to the air strike were 1) it could not feasibly be confined to the missile sites, and 2) the questions of warning. If we did not warn of the strike in advance, Soviet citizens might be killed. Further, as Robert Kennedy is reported to have argued persuasively, it would put us in the position of Japan at Pearl Harbor. Yet, if warning were

---

[11] Sorensen, *Kennedy*, p. 674. The "regular" members of the committee included:

State Department: Dean Rusk
                     George Ball (Under Secretary)
                     Edwin Martin (Assistant Secretary for Latin American Affairs)
                     Alexis Johnson (Deputy Under Secretary)
                     Llewellyn Thompson (Soviet expert; former Ambassador to Moscow)
Defense Department: Robert McNamara
                     Roswell Gilpatric (Deputy Secretary)
                     Paul Nitze (Assistant Secretary)
                     General Maxwell Taylor (Chairman, Joint Chiefs of Staff)
CIA: John McCone (Director)
                     Robert Kennedy
                     Douglas Dillon
                     McGeorge Bundy
                     Theodore Sorensen
Occasional Members: Adlai Stevenson (Ambassador to the United Nations)
                     Vice President Johnson
                     Dean Acheson (former Secretary of State)
                     Robert Lovett (former Secretary of Defense)
                     Donald Wilson (Deputy Director of USIA)

given, it could only be in the nature of an ultimatum in which any head of state would find it impossible to acquiesce.

By October 18, the President had opted for a blockade, but he did not receive full support from the Committee for this position until the next day, when it became clear that a blockade would be an *initial*, not necessarily the only response. That is, the blockade had the great merit of dealing directly with the lesser half of the problem: keeping more missiles from coming into Cuba. At the same time it would enable further consideration—and allow the Russians to back down more gracefully—concerning what to do about the missiles already in Cuba.

It was on Monday night, October 22, less than a week after the initial meeting of the Executive Committee, that President Kennedy announced the fact of Soviet missiles in Cuba and our response to that fact. The blockade, or quarantine as the President preferred to call it, was to go into effect the next day.

From one point of view the story ends here—the policy having been set, the next move was up to the Soviets. But it was necessary to keep the Committee in daily session, pending Soviet reaction. Nor was this all. Having established a blockade, there were still several unanswered questions: 1) Suppose a Russian ship ignored the American demand to stop and be searched? 2) How near should the United States Navy permit Soviet ships to approach Cuba? Should the island be ringed, or should American ships search out Cuba-bound Soviet ships on the high seas, as the Navy wanted to do? 3) What should be done in case of an attempt to interrupt our continuing surveillance of the island? These questions illustrate that it is one thing to arrive at a policy decision and quite another to carry out that policy effectively.

While the six tense days between the President's speech and the Premier's ultimate response ground on, the President ordered the Navy not to intercept Soviet ships in the high seas far from Cuba and to disable (by destroying its rudder), but not to sink any ship refusing a request to stop. He refused to put into effect the prepared plan of action—bombing a SAM site—when a Soviet missile shot down a U-2 plane (killing the pilot who had flown the October 14 mission).

In each case the underlying reason was simply to do everything possible to let the Soviets back out as gracefully as the situation permitted. And in fact missile-laden Soviet freighters eventually turned around and steamed home. Yet at the same time preparations had to be continued for the eventuality that the Soviet Union would refuse to remove the existing missiles within Cuba—preparations that included an air strike and, potentially, the invasion of the island.

After a succession of notes between Kennedy and Khrushchev—some of the latter's being sufficiently contradictory as to indicate less cohesion in Moscow than in Washington—the Soviet leader announced on Sunday,

October 28, that in return for an American commitment not to invade Cuba all missiles of an offensive character would be removed. The two-week crisis was over.

If nothing else, this episode illustrates the dreadful loneliness with which a President must make decisions on matters of national security. Regardless of advice, intelligence, and indications of support, it was the President alone who had to make the crucial decisions—decisions that could have eventuated in literally total disaster. Nor, it is well to keep in mind, were these decisions confined to those elaborated by the Executive Committee. For example, if the original decision to destroy a SAM missile site in the event that an American U-2 aircraft was shot down had not been reversed by the President, the whole crisis might have escalated into war.

Largely because of this, it is understandable that no President will feel constrained to consult a governmental table of organization in order to discover from whom he should seek advice in time of crisis. The fact that the Executive Committee was composed in large part of men whose official positions would lead one to expect their inclusion was due primarily to the President wanting men he could trust in those positions. It is significant, on the other hand, that the CIA and Joint Chiefs of Staff were represented by two different persons than had advised the President at the time of the Bay of Pigs.

Finally, it should be noticed that Congress played virtually no role in the crisis. *After* a policy had been decided upon, congressional leaders were called to Washington for a briefing by the President; but in no sense was there any consultation with Congress while the policy was being developed. This was not due so much to any presidential desire to exclude congressional participation as it was to the necessity for secrecy and speed.

The Pentagon

The accompanying chart shows the general organization of the Defense Department. Two or three points call for special comment. Atomic energy, so important to our total military effort, is under the control of a separate civilian agency, the *Atomic Energy Commission.* Liaison between that Commission and the Defense Department is maintained through a Military Liaison Committee. Information on all matters relating to the military uses of atomic energy is provided by the Commission through the Committee to the Defense Department. Of course, basic questions such as whether or not to produce the hydrogen bomb remain decisions of the President.

Research and development with respect to space exploration are in the province of a separate agency, the National Aeronautics and Space Administration.[12] Since, however, the line between the peaceful and military

---

[12] See *United States Government Organization Manual,* 1966–67, pp. 470–74.

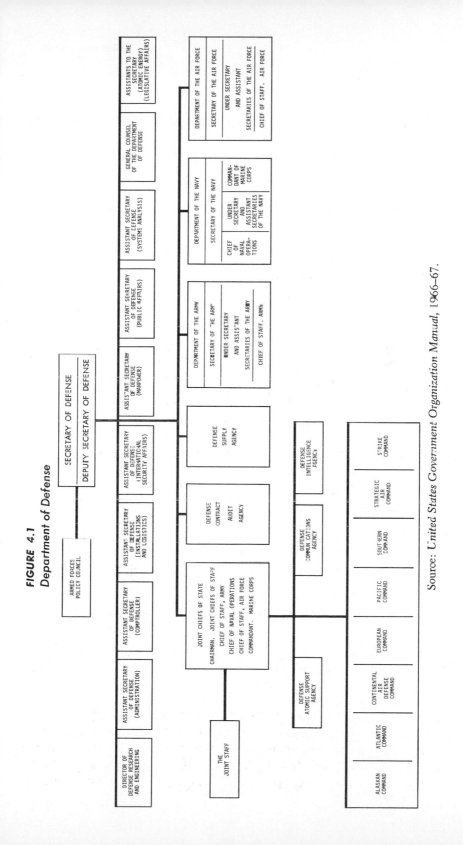

FIGURE 4.1
Department of Defense

Source: *United States Government Organization Manual*, 1966–67.

aspects of mastering outer space is thin, if not invisible, the efforts of this agency are most important to Defense.

At the top level there is the *Armed Forces Policy Council*, composed of the Secretary and Deputy Secretary of Defense, the Secretaries of the three services, the Chairman of the Joint Chiefs of Staff, the military heads of the three services, and the Director of Defense Research and Engineering. This Council advises the Secretary of Defense on broad policy relating to the Armed Forces. The *Joint Secretaries* is the formal manifestation of the responsibility of each service secretary to the Secretary of Defense.

The *Joint Chiefs of Staff*, composed of a chairman and the military leaders of the three services, is in a somewhat unique position. As the chart indicates it is subordinate to the Secretary of Defense, charged with advising him on basic military strategy, and also the President's chief adviser on military matters. Since the chairman ordinarily attends the NSC meetings, lines of authority between the President and JCS do not always pass through the Secretary of Defense. In a sense, then, members of the JCS wear two hats: 1) individually they are the military head of their respective services; 2) collectively they are the advisers on grand military strategy to both the Secretary of Defense and the President. The exact relationship between JCS and the Secretary of Defense will thus depend to a great degree on the desires of the President. Moreover, there is nothing to prevent a President from appointing a personal assistant on military policy, who then might well stand between the Joint Chiefs and the President. A primary reason for doing so is that since the Chiefs wear two hats, their natural tendency is to see grand military strategy in the perspectives of their own service. It can be argued that a military man in the White House office, removed from the Defense Department, can advise the President on over-all strategy from a more objective vantage point. Presidents Roosevelt and Truman had such an assistant in Admiral Leahy, and although President Eisenhower dispensed with the office, President Kennedy re-established it in the person of General Maxwell Taylor. General Taylor, now retired, holds the office of Special Consultant to the President under President Johnson.

In terms of supervision, the fundamental problem faced by the Secretary of Defense has been that of making certain that the military remain the servants, not the masters, of policy. His position with respect to the three service secretaries and their military counterparts has been strengthened from time to time, but he must still rely on Congress and the President for support.

This situation brings up an interesting and difficult question: granted that *within* the executive branch there should be an opportunity for all qualified voices to be heard in the determination of policy—once that policy is formed, should there be the right of dissent in public or before Congress? Suppose, for example, that the Secretary of Defense, with the

President's approval, decided that research and development of long range (over 1500 miles) missiles should be carried out by the Air Force alone, and that the Army should cease further work on such missiles. Suppose that the budget requests to Congress reflected this—that is, cuts in the Army request, increases in Air Force requests, for missile development. Should Army generals who disagree with the Secretary's decision have the opportunity to state their position before Congress, in the hope that the latter may in effect "overrule" the Secretary? If so, is the Secretary's position as *chief* of the Defense Department meaningful? If not, is not Congress being deprived of expert advice on which to base opinions concerning the feasibility of the Defense Department's proposals?[13]

As we shall see below, this type of problem is a very real one and has arisen more than once in the post-World War II era. By and large, though not without some bitter infighting, military leaders have been allowed to speak their pieces in such situations. The line between insubordination and the exposure of differences for the public welfare, however, has not as yet been clearly defined—perhaps it never could be.

Basic to this ambiguous position of the Secretary of Defense as head of his department is what might be called the functional inertia of the services. Even though Unification implied coordination of military effort among the three services, it did not end bitter disputes concerning the proper role of each in any grand strategy. Primary reliance on air power, for example, might well make naval leaders feel not only that the Navy was being slighted but also that our national security was being jeopardized by insufficient recognition of other factors. Indicative of this was an episode that produced just such feelings and was known popularly in its time as the "Revolt of the Admirals."

The Revolt of the Admirals[14]

In the spring and summer of 1949 the problems involved in unification of the three services, and in the related, more basic, question of grand military strategy, were given public airing in a congressional investigation of unification and strategy. What prompted the investigation was the growing feeling on the part of many admirals that "unification" was becoming "domination," specifically by the Air Force over the Navy. One of the inducements to Navy acquiescence in unification had been the appointment of a known supporter of naval power, James Forrestal, as first Secretary of Defense. When Louis Johnson succeeded Forrestal, however, he gave indications of placing increasing reliance on strategic bombing as the kingpin of our defense efforts. Illustrative of this was his order to stop

---

[13] On this point see Maxwell Taylor, *The Uncertain Trumpet*, pp. 112–14.

[14] The description of this episode is based on an unpublished manuscript by J. Dale Chastain of Chatham College.

all work on a 65,000-ton super aircraft carrier, which was interpreted as a complete victory of the Air Force over the Navy.

Bitterness within the Navy reached a point where one of the Navy's most noted airmen, Captain Crommelin, made public a confidential letter from Vice Admiral Bogan, commander of the First Task Fleet in the Pacific, to Secretary of the Navy Matthews. Bogan asserted that it would be "sheer balderdash to assume that there has been anything approaching unity . . . Bickering is still the rule." And referring to the doctrine of strategic air power, with its consequent diminution of the role of the Navy in the total defense effort, he asserted "we are fearful that the country is being, if it has not already been, sold a false bill of goods."[15]

Shortly thereafter, Crommelin admitted he had "leaked" the letter to the press, hoping it would "blow the whole thing open and bring on another congressional investigation. . . ."[16] The Captain was suspended and the House Armed Service Committee began public hearings into the dispute.

The Navy's position was not confined to the fact that it was getting a "raw deal" in unification. Rather the admirals argued that the basic assumptions underlying the "raw deal" were really at issue. They argued that reliance on strategic bombing as a major deterrent to war, and as a weapon for victory if war should come, was dangerous. Regarding its use as a deterrent, Admiral King asserted that its effectiveness "depends on the amount of fear it will instill in the would-be aggressor. This is a matter of speculation."[17] As a weapon for victory, the Navy had still greater doubts. Naval arguments in this connection were essentially that: 1) Strategic bombing of the Soviet's basic war-making plant could not prevent its initial success in overrunning Western Europe. 2) Should the latter occur, the Soviets would control vast reservoirs of war capabilities that we would be most reluctant to bomb, since it would involve atomic destruction of our traditional allies in Western Europe. 3) Although air power, and within it, strategic bombing, are important, it is equally important to be able to strike effectively at the enemy's

> armed forces and the transport system which moves him and his supplies. The targets must have a direct connection to the fighting which our troops and our allies are conducting. Bombing of cities and industrial areas will not have an immediate and direct effect in delaying or stopping the advance of enemy armies.[18]

It is important to note in this "revolt" the fact that not only is unification on paper sometimes quite different from unification in reality, but also

---

15 *The New York Times*, October 4, 1949.

16 *Ibid.*, September 11, 1949.

17 *Unification and Strategy*, Hearings, U.S. House Armed Services Committee, 81st Congress, 1st Sess. (Washington, D.C.: U.S. Government Printing Office, 1949), p. 253.

18 *Ibid.*, p. 238. The remarks are those of Admiral Halsey.

that underlying the organizational question of the Navy's role in unification was the doctrinal question of the validity of strategic air power as the
basis of our military strategy. This problem in turn raises the question of
whether, in an age of nuclear warheads and ballistic missiles, a "unified"
military organization makes sense so long as it is based on the traditional
tripartite functions of land, sea, and air forces.

At the same time, interservice competition may well serve to produce
innovation, as is often remarked about the development of the polaris
missile capable of being fired from a submerged submarine, thus providing
the Navy with an important role in our nuclear defense program. Further,
in an age of mutual nuclear deterrence, "traditional wars" involving
conventional army, navy, and air force units may prove to be the real
military challenge—as in Korea and Viet Nam.

PROBLEMS OF CONTROL

The description of the organization for security is partial thus far.
Besides the agencies and departments mentioned, there are countless
interagency committees and liaison offices, not to mention those extra-
organizational devices for coordination: the telephone and the luncheon
date. How is this maze of organizational activity controlled? How, that is
to say, is security policy generally—and within that framework, military
policy specifically—made responsive to the "will of the people." Broadly,
this problem of control has two aspects: 1) control over the executive by
the Congress and the people and 2) control within the executive by the
President and his civilian assistants over the military.

An Over-View of the Problem

Generally speaking, what has already been said about the roles of the
President, the Congress, and the people in foreign policy holds true for
military policy as well. If anything, the problems are more acute.

In the case of the public, the lack of information—not to mention
expertise—on military matters, which results from the necessary secrecy
such matters involve, means that even the attentive publics have comparatively very little impact. Although it is true that veterans' organizations
such as the American Legion concern themselves with military policy, it is
usually in terms of supporting the position taken by military leaders in the
government rather than on the basis of independent positions that may or
may not be in harmony with the professional military.

In at least one instance however, a combination of what we have called
mood and vigorous assertion of a position by a number of interest groups
apparently did have an important effect on a military proposal. This was

the idea of universal military training, proposed by the executive but forcefully opposed by a number of organizations, especially church groups, which argued that it was inconsistent with our traditions and would open the door to futher encroachments of the military on the civilian control of our society. Yet even in this case, public action was in fact reaction to policy emanating from the executive. And it is difficult to think of many instances of a similar nature, or any instances in which attentive publics have taken an active role in the development, as opposed to approval, of military policy.

As we have already noted, Congress also faces great handicaps as an organ of control. Its military affairs committees are faced with the same problems of information and expertness as are its foreign relations committees. Further, there is as yet no single committee that could be called the legislative counterpart of NSC. The organization of Congress is essentially based on the traditional distinction between military and foreign policy. Any sort of security policy developed in Congress will necessarily be a haphazard conglomeration of compromises among the appropriations, foreign relations, and military affairs committees, as well as all the other committees whose domain will be affected by security matters.

As in foreign policy formation, probably the most effective device for congressional control of the military is the power of the purse. But again, the constitutional provisions are vitiated by the circumstances of contemporary military affairs. In the first place, a decision on military policy today often commits expenditures over a period considerably longer than two years. Once Congress has agreed to such a decision, in the form of the first appropriations, it can change its mind only at the cost of the great sacrifice of the already expended funds. And second, since we live in an age of fantastic technological change, research on and development of new weapons must proceed constantly, even though the cost is enormous. Yet Congress, for lack of both information and expertness, is for all practical purposes coerced into making the necessary appropriations, lest the "Russians beat us to the punch." Added to this is the fact that in five or ten years three-fourths of these weapons may be obsolete. Congressmen have expressed concern with this situation. As the chairman of the Joint Committee on Atomic Energy once declared, the choice seemed to be "financial ruination" or "atomic devastation."[19] But with our security apparently at stake, and in the absence of any real evidence other than that provided by the military, it is not surprising that Congressmen feel constrained to vote the requested funds.

Within the executive branch, the problem of control of the military concerns the relationship of the civilian and military authorities. This

---

[19] Quoted in Richard C. Snyder and Edgar S. Furniss, Jr., *American Foreign Policy: Formulation, Principles, and Programs* (New York: Holt, Rinehart & Winston, Inc., 1954), p. 375.

means that military policy, as developed by the military, must undergo the constant scrutiny of civilian chiefs, and likewise that in any combined councils of decision-making, the civilian viewpoint must be sufficiently represented to prevent the military members from overwhelming control. One good example of an attempt to promote the latter goal was the reorganization of the NSC in 1949, at which time the three service secretaries—who had originally been members along with the Secretary of Defense—were removed and the Vice President was added as a formal member. To achieve the first goal, an executive order of 1953 transferred such functions as integrating research and development, coordinating procurement, and translating strategic plans into industrial requirements, from boards within the Department to the Secretary of Defense. Further reorganization in 1958 was aimed in part at placing over-all control of research and development in the hands of the Secretary of Defense, as well as assuring his complete control over the internal organization of the department.[20] Congress, however, retained the right of veto over any order of the Secretary to "abolish, merge or transfer functions" in the department.[21]

Regardless of what institutional changes are introduced, civilian control in the development of military policy faces a number of obstacles resulting from the crisis we face, the developments of science, and the new status of the military. The general nature of the problems will be indicated, followed by a case study illustrative of many of them.

The New Technology

On August 5, 1945, the word "mushroom" to most people was a noun connotative of steaks and gravy. On August 6, it became an adjective, descriptive of a cloud, connotative of unparalleled, almost inconceivable, destruction. Since that time a considerable portion of our national resources, material and human, have been expended in the development of nuclear military weapons large and small. Nor has technological research and development been confined to the explosive power of nuclear weapons; of necessity considerable attention has been paid to the means of delivery of nuclear and conventional warheads, as well as to the use of nuclear power to propel war craft.

The basic problem raised by this new technology is whether our policies, military and/or foreign, have in fact become the consequences of, rather than the controlling factor in, technology. More specifically, the new technology raises questions concerning military strategy, the strain on our internal economy, the foreign policies we pursue, and the logic of our

---

[20] See Frederich C. Mosher, "Old Concepts and New Problems," *Public Administration Review*, XVIII (Summer, 1958), 169–71.

[21] *The New York Times*, August 7, 1958.

military organization. Questions that are new, terrifying, and complex—but questions we cannot escape.

Secrecy

Closely connected with the problems of the new technology is the attendant question of the great secrecy that is needed in developing weapons. This has at least two important consequences. 1) It precludes effective debate on policy alternatives even by Congress, much less by the public—at least to the extent that policies themselves are determined by our military capabilities. 2) It entails an extensive elaboration of governmental controls to preserve secrecy, which consequently limits individual liberties. The second point is perhaps best discussed as an aspect of the contemporary dangers to civil liberties generally. An illustration of the first point is the fact that the decision to produce the hydrogen bomb was made solely within the executive branch; there was no public or even congressional consideration of this basic policy decision. If the decision were, in effect, merely one concerning the best way to carry out an already agreed upon policy, this fact would not be of crucial importance. But if this decision had important consequences for security policy generally and foreign policy specifically—as it did—then the necessity for secrecy meant another increment in the wall separating policy-formation from popularly elected representatives of the people.

The Growth of the Military

It is perhaps difficult for a person who has grown to maturity since the end of World War II to imagine a time when important military leaders were not intimately concerned with fundamental policy decisions. Yet, traditionally, and until recently, there were few admirals and generals, and they were outside the main stream of American social, economic, and especially political life. Partly because of our new position in the world and partly because of the training involved in the development of a professional military officer, the military today has become very much a part of the warp and woof of our society.

The current esteem for military leaders also has its roots in our traditions. Even in the days when the military played no significant role in the development of major public policies, it was accepted as a kind of political axiom that the Army won wars in the field while the diplomats lost them at the conference table. Despite the fact that men not only control but are controlled by events, the resort to war carries with it implications of failure by the civilian statesman and of need to use the military to "solve the problem." As General MacArthur put it:

"When all other political means fail, you then go to force; and when you do that, the balance of control, . . . the main interest involved, the minute you reach the killing stage, is the control of the military. . . . You have got to trust [the military] . . . at that stage of the game when politics fails, and the military takes over."[22]

As long as a situation in which "the military takes over" is considered the abnormal case, the implications of prestige are not very important. But when the military becomes a vital factor in the formation of the crucially important public policies, this prestige has profound repercussions. Our fundamental policy of containment, for example, was influenced in large measure by the then Joint Chiefs of Staff. When this policy became the subject of sharp criticism on the part of opponents of the Truman administration, what action would have been more natural than to call on the Chairman of JCS—General Omar Bradley—to explain (that is, defend) that policy? But there were military men of equivalent prestige who disagreed with containment and favored the Gibraltar approach to security policy. It is just as understandable that the political opponents of President Truman used these military leaders to support their position. Thus the spectacle of Senator Taft, supported by men like Generals MacArthur and Wedemeyer, debating with the Truman administration, which was supported by General Bradley. Exactly the same kind of situation arose under the Eisenhower administration when Generals (notably Maxwell Taylor and Matthew Ridgway) began to criticize "massive retaliation."[23] These actions mean that the military is now no longer confined to the rule of supplying expert advice about possible alternative policies ultimately made by civilians; rather, they themselves have become politicized. By the growth of the military, then, we mean not only that military considerations have come to occupy a pre-eminent position in the councils of policy-making. We mean also that the military leaders have come to take an active role in the political debate concerning fundamental policy decisions. At least three dangers are inherent in this situation.

The Military Mind

First, we must recognize the potential dangers arising from the infusion of military thought processes into democratic decision-making. The implications of this danger have been forcefully detailed by a former member of the State Department; a gentleman whose perspective as a civilian policy-maker, working with the military, makes his remarks especially relevant:

The military are always disposed to make their estimates in terms of theoretical military capacity. If Guatemala is under a hostile regime (like the Arbenz regime of a decade ago), they may express alarm at the fact

---

[22] Quoted in Hoopes, "Civilian-Military Balance," pp. 225–26.
[23] See p. 123.

that the oil fields of Texas are within bombing range of it, even though there is no possibility that Guatemala will bomb Texas. In 1950 they were alarmed because, by sending our occupation forces out of Japan into Korea, we were leaving the way open for China to invade and conquer Japan. In practical terms this was nonsense, since it was not realistically conceivable that, under the circumstances of the day, China would actually undertake the reduction of Japan and the military pacification of the Japanese people. It was, however, in response to the insistence of the military, based on this fantastic fear, that we were moved in to intervene in the Chinese Civil War, sending our fleet into the Formosa Channel to create a diversionary threat to the Chinese flank. Our present entrapment on Formosa and the Chinese off-shore island is the direct consequence of a move that had no other purpose than that of preventing an invasion of Japan which was quite out of the question. . . .

It is simply not true that the military know best when it comes to matters which can be denominated military-strategic. The vision to which they are trained is too narrow, too technical, too crude. The fact that they are human, moreover, repeatedly makes it proper to discount their recommendations in terms of a political bias that may be unconscious—just as it might be proper to discount the military recommendations of some French Generals with respect to Algeria. Here, too, the President and his civilian advisers, including the Secretary of State, may *agree* with the judgments of the men in uniform, but should never feel themselves obliged to *accept* them.[24]

While there is no precise definition of "the military mind" the phrase itself indicates certain predispositions, inculcated by rigid training, that are inappropriate for forming public policy. Professor Richard Snyder and Edgar Furniss list five attributes that seemed to represent a consensus on just what the military mind involves:

1) rigidity in thought and problem analysis—the rejection of new ideas and reliance on tradition rather than on lessons learned from recent experience; 2) inadequate weighing of nonmilitary factors in military problems and inability to understand complex politico-military relationships; 3) an authoritarian approach to most social issues and situations accompanied by a disrespect and disregard for civilian authority; 4) insulation from nonmilitary knowledge or anything beyond what is narrowly defined as militarily relevant; 5) judgment of policy goals and techniques primarily in terms of military force and total victory from total war. Clearly these qualities would rarely be found completely dominant in any one military leader. Rather they typify collective attributes which are shared in at least a minimum degree by all military personnel.

As those authors put it:

The problem which arises from inappropriate habits of military thought is twofold: first, to minimize and counterbalance such habits in the training and organization of the military; and second, to minimize the impact of such habits on the policy-making process.[25]

---

[24] Louis J. Halle, "Lessons of the Cuban Blunder," *New Republic*, CXLIV (June 5, 1961), 13–17.

[25] Snyder and Furniss, *American Foreign Policy*, p. 369.

The military, in attempting to meet the first problem, has developed a number of schools where officers are trained in the political-economic aspects of international problems. Further, the State and Defense Departments have at least experimented with exchanging personnel to develop mutual expertise in each other's problems.[26] These efforts in themselves, however, are no guarantee that military considerations will be tempered by appreciation of other factors involved in any situation. Officers may just as well be produced who, because they understand the point of view of their civilian counterparts, are just that much more effective in persuading them to their viewpoint. The second problem is usually approached by strengthening civilian representation on important bodies—for example, the removal of the three service secretaries from NSC—or by buttressing civilian control over military leaders, as was done by executive order in 1953 and legislation in 1958. The efficacy of such attempts brings up the second danger resulting from the growth of the military.

Who Defines Reality?

It must be remembered in discussions of the "military mind" that not all military men reveal the attitudes encompassed in the term. Furthermore, those attitudes are not confined to people who wear Army or Navy uniforms. It can hardly be overemphasized that policy formation is as much influenced by the policy-makers' conception of the problem as by anything else. Given certain assumptions about the world, conclusions as to how to meet problems may follow automatically. The important thing is whether or not those assumptions are correct. In other words, if public debate on policy issues occurs within the context of an essentially military analysis of the world situation, alternative policies based on alternative assumptions are effectively precluded from consideration. The debate over containment is a good example, as the arguments rested on the views of military leaders regarding the proper security policy for the United States. But if military considerations are all that underlie security policy, the two are then equated; and the equation is not necessarily valid, especially in time of peace. Containment essentially concerns the most effective military way to deal with the Soviet threat. Such an argument tends to ignore the fact that other, nonmilitary, considerations may be involved.

To take a recent example, when the government of the Dominican Republic was overthrown in the Spring of 1965, the Johnson administration was faced with at least two competing versions of reality:

1. The policy goal of the highest priority in the Western Hemisphere is to keep Communism out. The Castro regime in Cuba represents Communism in this part of the world, and is bent on exporting it. The Dominican revolutionists—admittedly leftists—meant, or might have meant, the ad-

[26] *Department of State Bulletin*, Vol. XLIV (June 30, 1961).

vent of Castroism in another Caribbean country. It was therefore absolutely necessary to intervene with troops to prevent the forceful acquisition of another territory by Communist imperialism. Even if there were some doubt as to the true nature of the revolutionists—as there had been about Castro—the risks of further Communist penetration of the Western Hemisphere were too great not to take decisive, that is military, action.

2. Whether or not Communism represents a real threat in the Western Hemisphere is secondary to the challenge of social and economic development. That is, even if Communism is a threat, the best way to combat it is through combating the conditions which lead to upheaval. Therefore, the primary emphasis of United States policy ought to lie in the direction of attempting to help Latin American countries to meet the revolutionary aspirations of their people. From this point of view the Dominican revolution should have been supported rather than resisted— indeed, military intervention put the United States on the side of resistance to change and fundamentally worked against the best interests of the people of not only the Dominican Republic but also the United States.

Notice that in neither case does one set of considerations monopolize the basis of policy. No proponent of the military intervention would discount the importance of social change in Latin America; no opponent of such an analysis would say that Communists do not represent a real threat. The question is one of emphasis. For although military and political considerations are inextricably bound up with one another, there is a difference between the military implications of a foreign policy, and the political implications of military policy. The point here is not that either of these alternative ways of picturing the world we live in is "right" and the other "wrong." Rather, as long as essentially military assumptions underlie our security policy, nonmilitary approaches may not even be discussed. Herein lies the greatest danger resulting from the growth of the military in authority and prestige. If the civilian leaders of government, executive and congressional, accept the essentially military assumptions about the problems of security policy, civilian "control" is no longer control in any meaningful sense. It was, after all, civilians as well as soldiers who urged President Johnson to intervene in the Dominican Republic.

Even though an alternative view of reality has been—at least apparently—developed in this instance, there are at least two reasons for the tendency in our society to accept the military picture of reality. The first, mentioned in another connection, is the matter of prestige. No other group of experts, with the possible exception of the physical scientists, can approach the prestige of the military. If, for example, a group of distinguished economists and political scientists should argue for increased economic aid, even at the expense of military build-up, and this should be opposed by military leaders on the grounds that such a shift in emphasis might jeopardize our "security," there is little doubt which group of experts would be listened to. The military has, in contemporary parlance, "paid off"; economists and political scientists have yet to demonstrate their utility to the same degree.

Second, there is a natural enough tendency for any public official, military or civilian, to "play it safe." In our example of the Dominican Republic, the military analysis was strictly in terms of the here and now. A Communist regime existed in Cuba; a revolution looking very similar to Castro's was underway: therefore, a misguided sense of delicacy about military intervention could have been fatal. On the other hand, the potential decisiveness of the revolutionary movements in Latin America is just that: *potential*. We have no way of knowing what the next ten or even five years will bring in the form of political, economic, or social change in those areas. Support of Latin American revolutions can be justified only in vague terms of what the world will be like in the future; crushing the Dominican revolution is an immediate military necessity. Can we afford to gamble military security for long run political gain? Such considerations may be understandable, but they should not becloud the fact that the vague, long range, nonmilitary factors are those which may be crucial.

Finally, there is a third danger—in a sense the converse of the first. This concerns the possibility of an admiral or general using the prestige gained as a military expert to influence nonmilitary policy. This question arose a few years ago in connection with the support some leading military men have given to anti-Communist movements of the radical right such as the John Birch society. It is a highly debatable point to assert that Communist infiltration is the number one danger to American society; in any case the competence of a general to make this assertion is no greater than that of anyone else. Yet, his influence may be out of all proportion to his competence, because of his prestige as an "expert on security." Although this has not been a common occurrence, it was sufficiently prevalent to cause the Kennedy administration to issue orders restraining such activity.[27]

NATIONAL SECURITY: POLICIES AND ALTERNATIVES

It is always dangerous to generalize about vast and complex policy questions; however, the postwar national security policies of the United States may be grouped into three distinct phases, each corresponding to a particular administration—Truman, Eisenhower, Kennedy-Johnson.

Following an initial period of rapid disarmament, the Truman administration was forced to rearm for the Korean conflict, commit itself to a peacetime alliance in the form of NATO, and pursue what looked like an endless nuclear race with the Soviet Union, once the latter had succeeded

---

[27] *The New York Times*, June 18, 1961, contains a survey of incidents along this line. See also, the *Des Moines Register*, August 11, 1961.

in exploding an atomic weapon. Yet, under President Truman little thought was given to developing a strategic doctrine commensurate with the revolutionary transformation science and technology had wrought in military capability. Rather, military policy was viewed as a matter of remaining "more powerful than the Russians," especially in the nuclear field, but if necessary, as in Korea, in conventional forces as well.

When the Eisenhower administration took office in January, 1953, one of its first concerns was a re-examination of our total national security program as it had evolved under President Truman. The resulting proposals, dubbed almost immediately the "New Look," provide excellent illustrations of the kinds of problems involved in developing security policy, as well as a graphic example of the interconnection between foreign and military policies and domestic capabilities. The New Look was announced by the Secretary of State, defended in terms of military strategy, and based largely on domestic economic considerations.

Much of the debate surrounding the New Look tended to obfuscate some of the main issues involved. This was true for at least three reasons: 1) Because it implied certain criticism of the Truman administration's policies, it brought forth arguments from those associated with that administration, not excluding the former President himself; the issue thus became involved in the general Republican versus Democratic political hassle; 2) Beginning in January, 1955, the Eisenhower administration was faced with a Democratically controlled Congress, which meant that the budgetary underpinnings of the New Look faced congressional examination that, by natural party inclination, would be unsympathetic; 3) The New Look became involved in the campaigns of 1956 and 1960, and neither congressional nor presidential campaigns are notable for the calmness of debate and the measured consideration of proposals. But this obfuscation itself is important; for, to the extent that policy proposals are debated before Congress and the electorate, one must expect the lack of precise issues, logical arguments, and positions defended with no thought to party considerations. Partisan politics is democratic politics, and to expect major policy issues to be formulated in a "nonpolitical" atmosphere is either to demand the impossible or to remove the issues from democratic processes.

"More Bang for a Buck"

Table 4-1 provides ample evidence of the significant expansion of defense expenditures over the last fifteen years (figures rounded off to nearest billion):

It should be noticed that although the Korean fighting accounted for a tremendous increase in spending, armistice did not produce a rapid decrease in the defense budget. Rather, it was felt by the Truman

TABLE 4-1

Fiscal Year (Billions of Dollars)

	Total budget expenditures	Major national security expenditures
1949	40	13
1950	40	13
1951	44	22
1952	65	44
1953	74	50
1954	68	47
1955	65	41
1956	67	41
1957	69	43
1958	72	46
1959	81	46
1960	78	46
1961	80	46
1962	88	51
1963	93	53
1964	98	54*
1965	97	52*

*Not including special appropriation for Viet Nam.
Source: *Statistical Abstract of the United States, 1960.*

administration that Korea should teach us a lesson: we cannot rely on our atomic superiority alone to prevent aggression. In the words of former Secretary of State Acheson:

> There [Korea] the attack had to be met—and was met—on the ground where it occurred. And this, in turn, required the raising, equipping, supplying and training of forces, our own and others, which could do this.
> So a sound military program . . . requires [in addition to a great atomic striking force] forces that can deal on the spot with lesser aggressions which, if unchecked would go far to undermine the integrity, and certainly the power, of the free world. . . .
> Now the military program we have been discussing cannot be acquired on the cheap. It is very expensive indeed.[28]

But do we need, or are we *able*, to stand that expense? Essentially the New Look, recommended by the Joint Chiefs of Staff and approved by the

[28] From "Instant Retaliation: the Debate Continued," *New York Times Magazine* (March 28, 1954), p. 13 ff. Reprinted, in part, in Herbert L. Marx, Jr., ed., *Defense and National Security* (The Reference Shelf, XXVI, No. 6), 98–103.

National Security Council, was a military program designed to ensure national security at a bearable cost. Three things were involved: 1) reshaping our military power around our air-atomic advantage; 2) gradually disengaging American forces from exposed positions; 3) arriving at a stabilized budget that our economy could be reasonably expected to bear over the long haul. As Secretary of Defense Wilson put it, "The increasing capabilities of new weapons and new techniques are sweeping into discard the practice of gauging military strength solely by count of men, and a census of ships, tanks, guns and planes."[29] By gearing our defense program to the technological revolution, the ever-mounting burden of armaments could be diminished. In terms of the relationship of military policy and our economy, then, the New Look meant that it was unnecessary, if not impossible, to attempt to create and maintain large conventional armies and navies of the World War II variety as well as a nuclear striking force. Rather, by the judicious use of the weapons our technological superiority was producing, we could develop both strategic and tactical striking forces at greatly reduced cost. Table 4-2 indicates the budgetary manifestations of this, as the New Look was proposed for fiscal 1955.

Simply stated, the underlying question concerning the budget of the New Look was, is it enough? When Congressmen held hearings on these budget proposals, they did not confine themselves to listening to the civilian members of the administration; they also called in military leaders. It would border on insubordination for an admiral or general to disagree publicly with the budget proposals; however, on several occasions Congressmen have almost urged the military leaders to ask for more. In the 1956 hearings, for example, after the Air Force Chief of Staff, General Nathan Twining, admitted that the budget "meets only our essential needs on a minimum basis," one Congressman asked if there was anything the matter. "Can it be corrected by dollars? If it can be, why have you not got them? If there is anything the matter with you this Congress will give you the dollars. You know it. You are literally and figuratively the white-haired boy here." General Twining replied, "We can always use more dollars,"[30] and in fact, the Congress eventually appropriated around $900 million for the Air Force over the original budget request."

This clearly illustrates a basic dilemma faced by Congress: how can it be sure that economies in defense are not risking national security? They have the word of the Joint Chiefs of Staff, but this word is given in the context of two important considerations. As Admiral Radford, former Chairman of

────────────

[29] From "Wilson Explains Program to Gain Maximum Defense Without Waste," *New York Herald Tribune*, October 12, 1954. Reprinted, in part, in Marx, *Defense and National Security*, pp. 39–44.

[30] *Department of Defense Appropriations for 1957*, Hearings, U.S. House Subcommittee on Appropriations, 84th Congress, 1st Sess. (Washington, D.C.: U.S. Government Printing Office, 1956), pp. 764, 769.

TABLE 4-2

Fiscal Years (Approximate Billions of Dollars)

	1949	1950	1951	1952	1953	1954	1955	1956	1957	1958	1959
Army	5.2	4.0	7.5	15.6	16.2	12.9	8.9	8.7	8.6	9.1	9.4
Navy	4.4	4.1	5.6	10.1	11.9	11.3	9.7	9.7	9.7	10.3	11.6
Air Force	1.8	3.6	6.4	12.7	15.1	15.6	16.4	16.5	16.9	17.5	19.0

Based on a chart in *The New York Times*, January 17, 1957, and the *Statistical Abstract of the United States*, 1960.

JCS, has said, it is not the business of JCS to concern itself with fiscal policy. Also, it was fundamental to the Eisenhower program that defense effort should be on a "pay-as-you-go basis." With this in mind it is not difficult to see how Congressmen (especially Democratic Congressmen in the case of the New Look) could argue that fiscal policies—a desire to balance the budget—had determined military strategy rather than vice-versa. And how can any Congressman, in the absence of expertise and military information, be blamed for wanting to "play it safe"? As the above episode illustrates, congressional controls on the military through control of the budget may well have the opposite effect from that intended. It may mean that Congress will act as a friendly court of last resort for military men whose initial budget estimates have been cut substantially by their civilian chiefs.

One other difficulty in attempting to arrive at maximum security at a price we can afford is that of rapid technological change. Assuming air-atomic weapons as the nucleus around which our defense effort revolves, what happens when scientific research demonstrates the possibilities of intermediate and long range missiles replacing aircraft? Inevitably, development of missiles must be pushed, but this can be very costly, especially when each service has its own missile program. The substantial increases in the budget proposals for all three services for fiscal 1958 resulted in part from the current emphasis on missile development, which costs in the billions of dollars. If the New Look offered the advantage of flexibility in military policy, the cost of that flexibility was necessarily high.

Balanced Forces Versus Air-Atomic Power

Although critics of the New Look argued that it was a program designed to make big wars out of small ones because it necessarily relied on nuclear air attacks as the deterrent of aggression, administration leaders at all times took pains to point out that this was not necessarily the case. Rather, as Admiral Radford asserted, it was ". . . a matter of emphasis. We are putting emphasis on our advantages—our long suits—in other words, on modern air and naval power, on new weapons, on a highly mobile and offensively equipped strategic reserve."[31] But if that was true in principle, there were important people who argued that in practice too much reliance was being placed on our "long suits," which would not be used if they were effective. These important people were represented in the military by Army leaders, for both the Air Force and Navy were involved in air-atomic strategy. The Army argued that with Russian development of air-atomic power roughly equivalent to our own, a state of "mutual deterrence" would be reached. Neither side could afford an all-out atomic assault on

---

[31] From a statement made before the Senate Foreign Relations Committee on April 14, 1954. Reprinted in Marx, *Defense and National Security*, pp. 58–59.

the other, for fear of retaliation. In such a situation, the military threat was one of potential conflict between ground forces. This meant that a wise military policy would include emphasis on manpower, armed with tactical nuclear weapons as well as the conventional type.

Typical of such opinions were those expressed by former General Matthew Ridgway, upon his retirement, after having served as Army Chief of Staff on the JCS during the first two years of the Eisenhower administration. In a letter to the Secretary of Defense he wrote:

> . . . with [the] improvement of Soviet air defense capability, the United States nuclear-air superiority will have lost most of its present significance.
> . . . military power . . . must be real and apparent to all concerned, and it must be capable of being applied promptly, selectively, and with the degree of violence appropriate to the occasion.
> It is my view that the commitments which the United States has pledged create a positive requirement for an immediately available mobile joint military force of hard hitting character in which the versatility of the whole is emphasized and the preponderance of any one part is de-emphasized.
> While a "mobile ready force" element is provided for an published policy statements, the actual development of a mobile ready force must [at present] compete with increasingly emphasized continental defense, and with, in my opinion, overemphasized nuclear-air requirements. . . .[32]

The question of emphasis on air-atomic power was not the only important military implication of the New Look. A little discussed, but equally important, question concerns the implications of centering a military effort around atomic weapons of any variety. The problem here is whether it will ever be possible to fight a *local* atomic war. Although it is possible, in theory, to distinguish between tactical and strategic nuclear weapons, it can be argued that once such weapons have been used, the side that begins to lose in any conflict will naturally resort to larger and larger warheads. The resultant reciprocation will necessitate the ultimate weapon, the thermo-nuclear bomb. The logic of this argument is historically buttressed by the concept of fighting until unconditional surrender by the opposition has been obtained, a concept thoroughly ingrained in twentieth-century thinking by both of the world wars.

The New Look and Security Policy

There is probably no better contemporary illustration of the relationship between military doctrine and total security policy than the questions raised about the New Look. On January 12, 1954, Secretary of State John Foster Dulles explained how that program related to American security policy in a now famous address to the Council on Foreign Relations. After

---

[32] The letter is reprinted in Edgar S. Furniss, Jr. (ed.), *American Military Policy* (New York: Holt, Rinehart & Winston, Inc., 1957), pp. 141–48.

pointing out that attempting to meet local Communist aggression on its own terms, as in Korea, meant that we were accepting the enemy's superiority in manpower and not bringing our superior technology to bear, the Secretary went on to say:

> . . . Local defense will always be important. But there is no local defense which alone will contain the mighty landpower of the Communist world. Local defense must be reinforced by the further deterrent of massive retaliatory power. A potential aggressor must know that he cannot always prescribe battle conditions that suit him. . . .
>
> The way to deter aggression is for the free community to be willing and able to respond vigorously at places and with means of its own choosing.
>
> So long as our basic policy concepts were unclear, our military leaders could not be selective in building our military power. If any enemy could pick his time and place and method of warfare—and if our policy was to remain the traditional one of meeting aggression by direct and local opposition—then we needed to be ready to fight in the Arctic and in the Tropics; and in Asia, the Near East, and in Europe, by sea, by land, and by air; with old weapons and with new weapons.
>
> . . . This could not be continued for long without grave budgetary, economic, and social consequences.
>
> . . . The New Look means that henceforth we shall depend primarily upon a great capacity to retaliate, instantly, by means and at places of our own choosing. That permits a selection of military means instead of a multiplication of means.[33]

The initial question raised by the speech was its real meaning. Was the United States pinning its defense against any and all forms of aggression on massive retaliation by our Strategic Air Command, or was massive retaliation, as the Secretary stated in a subsequent interview, a means of supplementing local defense? There was a good deal of speculation on this point, but the continued emphasis on air-nuclear weapons, coupled with the explanatory remarks of the Secretary of State himself, seemed to mean that the chief instruments of deterrence would be the Strategic Air Command and its naval counterpart.[34]

To the extent that "massive retaliation" implied the possibility of strategic nuclear bombing as the chief deterrent to aggression, a number of important questions were raised. The first of these concerns credibility. If

---

[33] The transcript of the entire speech may be found in *United States Department of State Bulletin*, XXX (January 25, 1954), 107–10.

[34] In a press conference following his "massive retaliation" speech Secretary Dulles is reported to have said, "What I meant . . . was that if you have the capacity to strike an aggressor at the points which will hurt him, the deterrent power of that is sufficient so that you do not need to have local defense all around the twenty-thousand-mile perimeter of the orbit of the Soviet world because your deterrent power, to a large extent, reinforces your local power so that you do not have to depend upon having forces-in-being to stop an attack in its tracks anywhere it could occur because you rely primarily upon deterring that attack, not necessarily upon being able to stop

strategic bombing is going to deter an aggressor, he must be convinced that in fact strategic bombing will follow aggression. And if aggression has so far not resulted in the use of nuclear weapons, as it did not, for example, in Korea, will it in the future? Relevant to this question is the fact that the Soviet Union is increasing *its* capacity for massive retaliation, and if nuclear weapons were not used when the United States had a clear superiority will they be used now that Russia is capable of a nuclear bombardment of the United States?

This notion of mutual nuclear capability has led a number of people to argue that strategic bombing, while remaining a mutual deterrent to all-out war, will become less and less effective as a deterrent to local aggressions of the Korean variety. Suppose that tomorrow, they say, the Soviets were to invade Pakistan. The basic question facing the United States would be: is the defense of Pakistan sufficiently important to retaliate massively (that is with nuclear warheads) against the Soviet Union, when we know that the Soviet Union can retaliate massively against us? As one student of military policy put it, the corollary to massive retaliation is simply that there is no alternative to peace.[35] This means that we would either have to choose some policy other than massive retaliation or let Pakistan fall to the Soviet Union.

In terms of security policy, then, massive retaliation—the doctrinal manifestation of the New Look—raised questions as to our capacity for flexibility in dealing with the Soviet Union. If our policy is one of resistance to Communist encroachments on the non-Communist world, but our chief weapon of resistance is massive retaliation (which the Russians are able to reciprocate), any encroachment must result in success for the aggressor, or all-out nuclear war, or abandonment of massive retaliation. Critics of the policy have pointed to Korea, Indo-China, Hungary, and Laos as precisely the kind of situation that presents problems of foreign policy for which we cannot find suitable answers, in view of our reliance on massive retaliation. As it affects the specifics of foreign policy, the argument against massive retaliation was: 1) Foreign policy to be effective must be backed by military power, and 2) Reliance on thermo-nuclear power, in the face of Soviet possession of it, means that in any negotiations with the Soviet Union we deal either from weakness or must be prepared to risk total nuclear war; 3) Total nuclear war will not be resorted to in any but the gravest emergencies; 4) As a result we have little or no basis of power for negotiating issues of less than the gravest emergencies—for example, Korea, Indo-China, Hungary, Laos, and West Berlin.

---

it." Text of the press conference on March 16, 1954, reprinted in part, Marx, *Defense and National Security*, pp. 64–71.

[35] See the article by Henry Kissinger, "Force and Diplomacy in the Nuclear Age," *Foreign Affairs*, XXXIV (April, 1956), 349–66.

Graduated Deterrence

What the critics of massive retaliation emphasized primarily was flexibility of response. If, in other words, mutual nuclear deterrence will allow the Communists to nibble the West to death with local actions on the perimeter of our containment line, how can we deal with the nibbles?

One suggested line of thought in this connection has been the development of the concept of graduated deterrence.[36] This involves the notion, essentially, of making the punishment fit the crime. It accepts two premises underlying the New Look: 1) capability for massive retaliation is fundamentally necessary, and 2) we should use our technological superiority to offset the manpower advantages of the Communists. It seems obvious that massive retaliation must be retained as the ultimate deterrent to an all-out nuclear attack; the point is that, of necessity, it is limited to that function. For local situations the doctrine of graduated deterrence requires that the West employ sufficient military power to deter or defeat any aggression, short of precipitating an all-out conflict. This means creating a distinction between *strategic* and *tactical* nuclear weapons and applying, or threatening to apply, nuclear weapons only to the point of successfully meeting the local challenge.

Implicit in this doctrine is the concept of limited war. If all wars must be fought to "victory"—that is, unconditional surrender—then tactical nuclear conflict will ultimately result in all-out nuclear war as the enemy is pushed further and further into defeat. Admittedly, the notion that "in war there is no substitute for victory" would be difficult to remove from the American mind—witness the tremendous dissatisfaction with the ultimate turn of events in Korea. But if local aggression is to be met on American terms, with weapons based on our technological advancement, if we are not to try to meet manpower solely with manpower, and if we are to prevent little wars from becoming big wars, the proponents of graduated deterrence would say that limited wars, fought for specific and limited purposes, must become part and parcel of American thinking.

Proponents of this line of thought had been urging it from the middle 1950s, and with the advent of the Kennedy administration the doctrine took on an official aura as many of its adherents were given important positions in Washington. Yet the notion is not without problems of its own. The chief of these concerns the feasibility of realistically distinguish-

---

[36] For discussion of this concept see Rear Admiral Sir Anthony Buzzard, "Massive Retaliation and Graduated Deterrence," *World Politics*, VIII (January, 1956), 228–37; Henry Kissinger, "Military Policy and the Defense of the Grey Areas," *Foreign Affairs*, XXXIII (April, 1955), 416–28, as well as his article cited above; Paul Nitze, "Atoms, Strategy and Policy," *Foreign Affairs*, XXXIV (January, 1956), 187–98; and William Kaufmann ed., *Military Policy and National Security* (Princeton, N.J.: Princeton University Press, 1956), pp. 12–38.

ing between tactical and strategic nuclear weapons. Especially as our commitment to South Viet Nam has become larger, there still seemed to be no way in which tactical nuclear weapons could be employed without risking escalation to a major nuclear exchange.

The problem of escalation has caused the doctrine of graduated deterrence to be regarded, with increasing frequency, as inadequate. We might note, in passing, that graduated deterrence (insofar as it was confined to nuclear weapons) would seem to be the doctrinal analogue of many of our missiles: outmoded before being used. What military analysts both in and out of uniform have increasingly stressed—and what the Kennedy administration appeared to be moving toward—is the need for as much flexibility as possible. This, in light of the criticisms of graduated deterrence as originally conceived, means building up our conventional forces to the point where, conceivably, nuclear war—providing such an attack was not made on us—would not have to be fought. This idea sounds logical and certainly desirable, but its feasibility is questionable.[37]

Expense is a basic consideration. None of the proponents of a program for the build-up of our conventional forces have suggested the diminution of our nuclear capability, although there has been some difference of opinion as to how great our stockpile needs to be. Such a build-up means increasing our over-all defense expenditures by as much as $two to $three billion annually. As long as such crises as Berlin can excite Congress and the public, such budget increases may be forthcoming; but will they be sustained over the long haul? Clearly, the Eisenhower administration thought this would unbalance the budget disastrously; economy was one of the chief rationales of the New Look. To disagree with the New Look is not automatically to dispense with its justification. Thus, if we are to continue (to paraphrase the President) to build our forces to the point where we are not faced with the horrible choice of surrender or nuclear war, the American people and their representative in Congress are going to have to make real financial sacrifices, to an extent never before demanded of them in peace time. This became increasingly apparent as the financial commitment to a domestic Great Society had to give way to the necessities of the tremendous build-up of conventional forces in Viet Nam (requiring something like $12 billion over and above the regular defense budget in fiscal 1966).

A second question arising out of the policy of flexible response is: will our nuclear arms never be used first? This has several aspects. One concerns strategic attack on our country; if we deny ourselves the right to strike pre-emptively, it is clear that our nuclear deterrent, if it is to be meaningful, must be able to withstand a first blow. This necessitates

---

[37] The literature on current military doctrine is nicely summarized in Urs Schwarz, *American Strategy: A New Perspective* (New York: Doubleday and Company, Inc., 1966), especially Chaps. VII and VIII.

expensive programming for "hardening" our permanent launching sites (by going underground) and/or developing movable, or moving, launching sites (as from nuclear powered submarines). Thus, to reemphasize, a build-up of conventional military power does not by any means lessen our nuclear efforts. Another aspect concerns Europe. If the Soviets launched a conventional attack in central Europe, would we be committed under any and all circumstances not to use nuclear weapons? If so, are we not sacrificing our superior technology, which was supposed to have substituted for Soviet manpower superiority? If we do use them, might not escalation ensue? Here, one can only say that doctrine is at best ambiguous, though at least one official of the Kennedy administration is reported to have said that in Europe it is conceivable that we would use nuclear weapons before they were used against us, given the alternate possibility of defeat.[38]

Finally, the question arises: will conventional arms be enough in situations involving a mixture of Communist military expansion with local revolutionary movements, as in Viet Nam. It is not too farfetched a conclusion to assert that if the Viet Nam experience teaches anything, it is that military doctrine—no matter how sophisticated—cannot be divorced from political, social, and economic conditions in an area where domestic revolution is present. To state the issue baldly: will all the green–bereted counter–insurgency forces in the world suffice, if the Viet Namese peasants identify with the National Liberation Front and see the Americans as little more than substitutes for the imperial Frenchmen who preceded them?

These questions are raised to illustrate the tremendous complexity of developing military doctrine, rather than as criticism. But one thing is clear. Regardless of whether massive retaliation alone, graduated deterrence, or some alternative doctrine is developed in the future, military and foreign policies are mutually interdependent. This means that the development of military doctrine incorporating the great and continuing technological advances of our time and the meshing of that doctrine with the goals of our foreign policy is one of the great, if not the greatest, challenges facing our country today. Finally, whether or not this challenge can be met depends ultimately on the capacity and the willingness of the nation as a whole to underwrite a rational national security policy.

THE ROLE OF THE MILITARY IN A DEMOCRATIC SOCIETY

Implicit in this challenge is the integration of the military into our policy-making processes. This involves the recognition of some basic points that deserve re-emphasis.

---

[38] See interview with Deputy Secretary of Defense Roswell L. Gilpatric in *U.S. News,* June 19, 1961.

The New Role of the Military

However regrettable it may be from the point of view of the traditional place of military men and military thinking in American society, it seems an inescapable corollary of the revolutionary transformation of America's position in the world that the military has played and will continue to play a central role in public affairs.

It is certainly clear that our national security constitutes one of the crucial problems with which our government is faced. And it is just as clear that Americans can no longer afford to await the coming of an international holocaust before preparing for it, as we have been so prone to do in the past. What the atomic age means, if it means anything, is that the preservation of our security is an everyday, continuing task of *preventing* all-out war, while at the same time deterring local aggression. Such a job calls for preparedness above all; preparedness in terms of military strategy and power. This in turn means that military men and military considerations must play an important part in the development of policy.

Military Security and Democratic Values

To say that the military is important, however, is not to say it should be predominant. In the broadest sense the preservation of our national security does not mean only the military defense of the United States; security means also the preservation of values held by Americans, preeminent among which is liberty. In these terms, the risk implicit in the new role of the military is that in our excessive concern with physical security we will permit the militarizing of our society to the point of undermining the liberties that lie at the basis of that society. This danger has been expressed in terms of the trend toward the garrison state, a state in which all other values are subordinate to the requirements of military security. As Professor Harold Lasswell has written:

> . . . To militarize is to governmentalize. It is also to centralize. To centralize is to enhance the effective control of the executive over decisions, and thereby to reduce the control exercised by courts and legislatures. To centralize is to enhance the role of the military in the allocation of national resources. Continuing fear of external attack sustains an atmosphere of distrust that finds expression in spy hunts directed against fellow officials and fellow citizens. Outspoken criticism of official measures launched for national defense is more and more resented as unpatriotic and subversive of the common good. The community at large, therefore, acquiesces in denials of freedom that go beyond the technical requirements of military security.[39]

[39] Harold Lasswell, "Does the Garrison State Threaten Civil Rights?" *The Annals*, 275 (May, 1951), 111.

Further, this trend toward the garrison state is induced as much by the tendency to view the world through military lenses as it is by having military men in high places.

Recently this concern with the increasing militarization of our society has evoked criticism. If over-concern with security may result in the garrison state, it is argued, over-concern with the preservation of liberal democratic values jeopardizes our very survival. "Previously the primary question was: what pattern of civil-military relations is most compatible with American liberal democratic values? Now this has been supplanted by the more important issue: what pattern of civil-military relations will best maintain the security of the American nation."[40]

Striking the Balance

Preoccupation with democratic controls may blind us to the very real need for considering strategic-military factors in our foreign policy. But to say this is not to say that such factors are the *only* relevant ones, or in many cases even the predominant ones—the preservation of our national security includes values as well as territory. If we can no longer afford to ignore military considerations, we cannot ignore everything else. If there is potential conflict between democratic values and military requirements, surely we can afford neither to destroy the values nor ignore the requirements. Rather it is incumbent upon us to develop the capacity for weaving the military fiber into the cloth of our total security policy, remembering always that the military is properly the servant and not the master of our society.

BIBLIOGRAPHICAL NOTE

The new role of the military in American public affairs is considered in Samuel P. Huntington, *The Soldier and the State: The Theory and Politics of Civil-Military Relations*, 1957, and Arthur A. Ekirch, Jr., *The Civilian and the Military*, 1956.

As the title indicates, Alfred Vagts, *Defense and Diplomacy: The Soldier and the Conduct of Foreign Relations*, 1956, devotes considerable attention to the role of the military in the development of foreign policy in the form of a historical analysis.

The chapter, "The Role of Military Institutions and Agencies in American Foreign Policy," in Richard C. Snyder and Edgar S. Furniss, Jr.,

---

[40] Samuel P. Huntington, *The Soldier and the State: The Theory and Politics of Civil-Military Relations* (Cambridge: The Belknap Press of Harvard University Press, 1957), p. 3.

American Foreign Policy: Formulation, Principles, and Programs, 1954, is an excellent short analysis of contemporary problems concerning the role of the military.

William W. Kaufmann, ed., *Military Policy and National Security*, 1956, and Henry Kissinger, *Nuclear Weapons and Foreign Policy*, 1957, deal with the concept of deterrence. A later book by Kissinger, *The Necessity for Choice*, 1961, contains modifications in the writer's thinking on deterrence. An excellent overview of American security policy may be found in Urs Schwarz, *American Strategy: A New Perspective*, 1966. A later book by Kaufmann, *The McNamara Strategy*, 1964, is definitive for the Kennedy years.

Walter Millis, *Arms and Men: A Study in American Military History*, 1956, after relating American military history, discusses the impact of atomic weapons on war, as does Bernard Brodie, *Strategy in the Missile Age*, 1959.

Paul Hammond, *Organizing for Defense*, 1961, is an excellent analysis of the American military establishment. Senator Henry M. Jackson ed., *The National Security Council* (Jackson Sub-Committee Papers on Policy-Making at the Presidential Level), 1965, is valuable for the understanding of that body.

The threat posed to individual freedom by the new role of the military, and what can be done about that threat, is the subject of Harold D. Lasswell, *National Security and Individual Freedom*, 1950.

transportation

ROBERT H. SALISBURY

People who talk about transportation often talk of "the trans-portation industry," "the transportation problem," and propose "the transportation policy" for the future. This attitude, in which all persons and groups engaged in transportation are thought of as performing the same economic function and therefore as a single monolithic group, has typified much of the debate on policy in the field. But even a cursory examination of the industry reveals that there is not one transportation industry but several. The interests of the railroad, truck, airline, and bus companies are not identical. On the contrary, they behave according to different economic imperatives, they compete with varying degrees of vigor both across industry lines (for example, trucks versus railroads) and within given industries (for example, TWA versus Eastern Airlines), and they seek very different policy goals through government. The conflicts are numerous and shifting and involve not only various interests within transportation but also other segments of the society.

Thus in order to understand transportation *policies* we must look at transportation *politics*—the conflicts of interests that give rise to policy demands. And to understand the interests involved in transportation politics, we must understand the economic forces that shape the interests at stake. If the emphasis in this discussion is on economic matters, it is because these are the factors of which transportation politics is made.

TRANSPORTATION ECONOMICS AND POLITICS

The size of the transportation industries in comparison with the rest of the economy is deceptive. Only the railroads loom large in the American economy in terms of assets or employees. But size does not determine the political significance of economic activity so much as the relationships between particular economic and social groups. In this respect the significance of the transportation industries can hardly be overstated. Perhaps no other single economic function is more central to the entire economic life of a people so mobile and technically interdependent as Americans. The size and character of the political and social community is much dependent upon the degree to which means of transportation and communication break down physical isolation and promote mobility of people and goods. The location and development of centers of trade and industry are closely related to the available transport facilities. Rivers and harbors, mountain passes and, in modern times, rail lines and highways have had incalculable consequences for every aspect of the social system.

Further, as an economic system reaches the stage of industrialization of the United States—marked by extreme mobility of persons and goods and incredibly complex interdependence of millions of people and billions of dollars worth of products—the system of transportation is of first importance to all members of the society. Thus public concern with transportation is bound to increase as the society grows more complex, and the result of increasing concern is seen in the growth of governmental policy.

"Consumers" of Transportation

Since transportation costs are also an important factor in the costs (and thus the profits) of virtually all businesses, the size of these costs will be a matter of direct and deeply felt concern to many people. If a user of steel should find the price of steel too high, he may sometimes be able to substitute aluminum or wood. But the user of transportation services is often unable to find alternatives. Either he ships his products to market or he does not sell them. In the past there was typically only one seller of transportation service available. The railroad was so far superior to the horse that a shipper had no real choice. And if there was only one railroad available, then the shipper was at its mercy in a very real sense. For many decades in the United States there was a strong tendency toward railroad monopoly of transportation, particularly in areas outside the larger cities. Although the situation has been substantially changed by the rise of motor and air transportation, the earlier tendency toward monopoly has been a major factor explaining why shippers used *political* power to control transportation costs while relying more upon *economic* power to secure lower costs on raw materials and labor.

Farmers have been particularly vulnerable to railroad power. Many agricultural crops are perishable if they cannot be taken to market quickly, and transportation is a principal item of cost to a farmer who may provide his own labor but who cannot carry his own cattle to market. The transportation industries loomed as industrial giants against the solitary farmer, and the latter often felt at the mercy of the railroad so far as economic bargaining power was concerned. But inequality in the economy might be redressed in the political arena. There, greater numbers and general rural overrepresentation could give farmers the opportunity to control transportation costs that they could not control through economic bargaining. This resulted in the early farmer organizations, such as the Granger movement, having as a central goal the control of transportation rates. The establishment of regulatory commissions at state and national levels came about largely as the result of efforts by the agricultural protest groups. The attempt to solve farm problems by regulating rates gave way in later years to the more fundamental goal of gaining governmental support for farm prices. Also, the rise of competition in transportation has made rate regulation less important to farmers and indeed to most shippers. It is important to recognize, however, that the earlier conflicts over transportation—roughly, those prior to the first World War—were between the railroads and their allies on the one hand, and the shipper groups, particularly farm groups, on the other. Since that time, and more relevant for our concerns, the conflicts have been largely among various groups *within* the transportation industries.

In explaining the extensive political action concerning transportation, one other general factor should be mentioned. If transportation is basic to the economy in peacetime, it is doubly so in war. Since military affairs are pre-eminently a governmental responsibility, in time of military stress governmental action is almost inevitably directed toward the transportation industries. The first World War, particularly, brought significant government action in transportation in the form of government seizure and operation of the railroad system which had broken down in the attempt to meet wartime demands.

The Interest Groups

Transportation politics involves the interests of a wide range of groups that, either because of direct concern or because of alliances with transport groups, devote much effort toward influencing public-transport policy. These groups cannot all be dealt with at length, but it is well to understand the nature and functions of the more significant ones.

Carrier Organizations. The organized mechanisms through which the various industries speak are trade associations. The railroads have formed the most comprehensive of these: the Association of American Railroads, which includes railroad firms doing 97 per cent of the business in North America (including Canada and Mexico). The present AAR was established in 1934 through a merger of several other more specialized organizations. It provides many services to the industry through research into common problems, through technical assistance of many kinds, by enhancing cooperation among various companies in handling such joint problems as the use of freight cars, and by mobilizing the resources of the industry to meet emergencies. The AAR also appears to provide the machinery through which disputes between rail companies can be resolved and competition moderated. On the political front, the AAR *is* the railroad industry. The Association is regularly among the leaders in reported expenditures for lobbying, and it carries on broad-gauge propaganda campaigns on behalf of the railroad point of view. The AAR is the chief spokesman for the railroad interests on matters of public policy.

The motor carriers too have established an association linking the major firms in their industry, the American Trucking Associations. This federation of state associations was formed in 1933 to perform for the motor carriers the same sort of task that the AAR does for the railroads. Although a wide variety of motor carriers are eligible to join the ATA, a much smaller proportion of those eligible has actually done so, compared to the AAR. Motor transport is engaged in by firms ranging from very small—one truck and one owner-driver— to very large, and by many types of carriers: for example, common and contract, taxicabs and interstate trucks. Many smaller carriers do not feel the need to carry on a broad campaign on the political front. Their chief competition comes not so much from railroads as from the large truckers who dominate the ATA; in turn, the large truckers have found that one of their most persistent problems is the control of rate-slashing by small truckers. As a result the ATA represents only a segment of the motor carrier industry—the larger interstate truckers—although on questions of national policy it is clearly the most active segment.

Air carriers have established an even more exclusive organization, the Air Transport Association. Only scheduled airlines are eligible to belong. Since one of the most vigorous disputes in air carrier policy-making has been whether the "nonskeds" were to be allowed to operate, the Air Transport Association has been far more involved in intra-industry disputes than have other carrier organizations.[1]

The American Waterways Operators speaks for the water carriers plying the lake, river, and intercoastal water routes of the United States. Water transportation accounts for about one-sixth of the total ton-miles of shipping in the United States, but the political significance of water carriers is quite different from that of the other forms of transportation. Although water transportation is low in cost, it is slow and limited in the markets that it can serve. Much of the cargo transported by water is handled by private carriers, such as subsidiaries of steel or aluminum firms carrying raw materials to processing plants. Despite substantial federal aid to improve river and harbor facilities and local government help on port facilities, the business of water carriage has not been very profitable. The

---

[1] See Robert Bendiner, "The Rise and Fall of the Nonskeds," *The Reporter*, XVI (May 30, 1957), 29–34.

carriers themselves are not very strong, either economically or politically. The major political force supporting the interests of the water carriers has been the various local groups seeking federal money for rivers and harbors construction.

"Satellite" groups. Many other organizations are active in one phase or another of transportation policy. Any major policy battle will find impressive lists of organizations established along regional or state lines or on the basis of some specialized function supporting—or appearing to support—one or another of the major carrier groups. The labor organizations of each industry are also significant. Railroad brotherhoods may make wage demands on management and Teamsters may go on strike against trucking firms, but on questions of national transportation policy the labor group of each industry is generally found on the same side as management. Organizations such as the American Automobile Association and the Transportation Association of America frequently take positions on controversial transportation questions and the latter, at least, has been referred to as a railroad "front" group.[2]

Shippers and suppliers. Industries in which transportation is a big part of total cost of products are often active in transportation politics. Indeed, as we have noted, it was these groups that provided much of the early impetus for regulation of railroads. These industries are typically those whose products are high in bulk and low in value, such as most farm products, coal, cement, and the like. Shipper interests have also been organized along sectional lines. For example, in the 1930s southern shippers mobilized their political resources in an attempt to eliminate what they regarded as discrimination in rate structures. Industries that supply products to the transportation industries also have a considerable interest in the economic success of their customers.

Financial control groups. Of very considerable importance in the group struggles over transport policy, especially when the railroads are involved, are what may be called financial control groups.[3] These groups include: 1) persons in positions to make vital decisions, who 2) are associated primarily with financial institutions such as banks or investment houses rather than with transportation firms as such. In the railroad industry the need for large capital investment has always been great, and when the foreign capital that had provided much of the early railroad investment was replaced by American capital around the end of the nineteenth century, J. P. Morgan, Andrew Mellon, E. H. Harriman, and other financiers entered the scene to reorganize and consolidate many of the railroad systems and to take over many of the key centers of decision in the industry. Trucking firms have not needed as much capital and consequently have remained largely outside the orbit of finance capital.

---

[2] See Senate *Report* Number 26, pt. 2, 77th Congress, 1st Session (1941).

[3] See Merle Fainsod, Lincoln Gordon, and Joseph C. Palamountain, *Government and the American Economy*, 3rd ed., (New York: W. W. Norton & Company, Inc., 1959), pp. 254–57.

The importance of the finance groups cannot be estimated with any confidence, since little real documentation is available for recent years. Certainly the potential power of these interests is great, and it is fairly clear that in the past financiers played a major role in shaping railroad policy. The fact that the same groups are also allied with much of the rest of basic American industry gives a powerful potential to the railroads in their conflicts with other carriers. It would appear, however, that the financial control groups are not completely united in behalf of the railroads. Such conflicting interests as lower rates for the transportation of steel may prevent the railroads from mobilizing the finance groups to vigorous support of the railroad position.

TABLE 5-1

Chronology of Transport Regulation

1871 and following	Granger laws—state regulation of railroads.
1887	Interstate Commerce Act—created the Interstate Commerce Commission, prohibited rate discrimination, etc.
1890s	Supreme Court cases weakening 1887 Act.
1906	Hepburn Act—Enlarged authority of ICC to set maximum rates, extended its jurisdiction, and otherwise increased its power.
1910	Mann-Elkins Act—ICC control over long-and-short hauls and general rate schedules further increased.
1914	Shreveport Rate Cases—Supreme Court decision extending ICC rate control over much intrastate commerce.
1918–20	Government seizure and operation of railroads.
1920	Transportation Act of 1920—Further strengthening of ICC; effort to assist weaker railroads through "recapture clause" and by encouraging combination of roads.
1933	Emergency Transportation Act of 1933—Abandonment of "fair return on fair valuation" rule.
1935	Motor Carrier Act—Bringing interstate motor carriers under jurisdiction of ICC.
1938	Civil Aeronautics Act—Establishment of Civil Aeronautics Board with authority to regulate rates and service of air carriers.
1940	Transportation Act of 1940—Extension of ICC authority to water carriers; statement that transport regulation should henceforth utilize each type of carrier to its best advantage.
1958	Transportation Act of 1958—Made it easier for railroads to reduce particular rates and to curtail intrastate service.

THE DEVELOPMENT OF REGULATION

The Interstate Commerce Commission was established in 1887 as a basic part of the first great national attempt to regulate railroads.[4] The Granger movement had brought about regulatory commissions in some of the states, but railroad lines commonly extended beyond the boundaries of a single state, and state commissions lacked both constitutional authority and political power for adequate control. The ICC was to attack the problem on a national scale. The Commission was to be "independent" and expert. Its independence was to consist of freedom from direct pressure or influence of political party interests, and this independence was to be achieved by appointing members for fixed, overlapping terms, longer than those of the President, and by requiring that the Commission be bipartisan in composition. It was expected that long terms and the absence of political pressure would permit the Commission to develop the experience and expertise necessary to deal with the complex field of railroad regulation. It had been felt that one of the chief difficulties confronting the courts when they were called upon to restrain predatory railroad practices was their lack of really intimate acquaintance with the problems. A full-time group dealing with the problems could remedy inequities more swiftly and effectively than was possible in the courts.[5]

"Independence" was not a guarantee of the effectiveness of the Commission, however, nor was the Commission removed from the political scene. The courts could and did review its decisions with the early effect of sharply reducing ICC authority to control railroad practices. The agrarian protest groups that had provided the political impetus to establish the Commission lacked sufficient strength to give it continuing power. Indeed its very "independence" meant that the ICC was cut off from important political support, since no President or party could make much use of the Commission in building a majority. As a result the ICC achieved comprehensive control of rates, service, and financial structure of railroads only gradually.

By the second decade of the twentieth century the Commission had broad legislative grants of authority, the specific exercise of which was generally sustained by the courts. By this time, however, the political power and the economic interests of the railroads themselves had changed

---

[4] On the history of the ICC, see I. L. Sharfman, *The Interstate Commerce Commission*, 5 vols. (New York: Twentieth Century Fund, 1931–1935); R. E. Cushman, *The Independent Regulatory Commissions* (New York: Oxford University Press, 1941).

[5] On the theoretical virtues of independent commissions, see Marver H. Bernstein, *Regulating Business by Independent Commission* (Princeton, N.J.: Princeton University Press, 1955).

considerably. Railroad expansion had ended by 1916, and by that time more and more railroads found that their hopes of earlier years were not fulfilled. Although some fairly strong systems had been put together, many roads were in grave financial difficulty. For this reason, government control did not have the unpleasant taste that it might otherwise have had for the railroads. These changes in attitudes were speeded by the virtual collapse of the United States railroad system in the face of the demands of World War I. Seizure and operation by the national government was unavoidable in 1918, and when Congress revised basic public policy toward the railroads in 1920, it confirmed the view that the array of interests had changed drastically since 1887.

The Transportation Act of 1920 was designed to revive the railroads as a strong and healthy system, though still regulated against any predatory actions. Under the new policy, the railroads were conceived of as a *system* rather than as many firms with few formal connections. The new conception conformed more closely to the realities of railroad cooperation and control; they provided, in addition, the basis for one extension of ICC authority. The Commission was directed to draw up a plan under which the railroads would be consolidated into fewer and stronger companies; enough to provide some competition for each other, but few enough to avoid waste and duplication. After several years the Commission completed a plan calling for nineteen systems in various parts of the country. The Commission could not force combination in accord with its plan, however, and the railroads that did seek to combine did so along different lines. Until 1933, railroad holding companies were outside ICC jurisdiction, and combination through the holding company device could not be prevented. In 1940 the consolidation plan, having achieved little real reorganization, was dropped from the legislative mandate of the ICC.

The Act of 1920 transformed the relationship between the ICC and the railroads in still another way. The principal reason for establishing the Commission had been to provide for the regulation of railroad rates so as to prevent those rates from being discriminatory and too high. Prior to World War I the main business of the ICC was to hear and act upon complaints from shippers. If the complaint was found to be justified, the ICC was empowered under the Hepburn Act of 1906 to prescribe the maximum rate that could be charged. But the change in the philosophy of regulation which was embodied in the 1920 Act made protection of shippers only a part of the story. The railroads themselves had to be protected against too severe competition and against unwise management. Consequently, the 1920 Act authorized the ICC to set minimum as well as maximum rates. Rates were to be such that the railroad industry as a whole would earn a satisfactory return (5.5 per cent of their investment), and provisions were made to allow the weaker roads to "recapture" part of the earnings of the stronger roads when the latter exceeded the "fair return."

The recapture clause actually produced little but litigation, but the positive authority that the 1920 Act gave the ICC to regulate the whole rate structure of the railroad industry, in exact detail, was indeed significant. The ICC would still protect shippers, of course, but it would also provide a floor under railroad earnings to protect railroads against themselves and against the competing transport industries. The ICC was to become a confidant and friend of the railroads rather than an implacable adversary.

During the 1920s the rapid expansion of motor transportation made it clearly impracticable to assure railroad earnings simply by setting high rates. High rates would merely shift traffic to truckers without necessarily producing increased revenue for railroads. And when rising motor competition was followed by the railroads' severe financial distress during the Depression, it became clear that a more complex approach to the problems of transportation regulation would have to be developed. The Emergency Transportation Act of 1933 marked the beginning of a new era in transportation policy. The ICC was no longer to attempt to guarantee the railroads a fixed percentage return on their investment nor even to base rates on the value of investment. Instead the Commission was to "give due consideration, among other factors, to the effect of rates on the movement of traffic; to the need, in the public interest, of adequate and efficient railway transportation service at the lowest cost consistent with the furnishing of such service; and to the need of revenues sufficient to enable the carriers, under honest, economical, and efficient management, to provide such service." Thus the ICC was to view the problems of the railroads as part of a broader transportation industry, and the criteria the Commission was to apply were made a great deal more flexible than before.

Another side of the railroads' difficulties was dealt with in 1935 when commercial motor carriers were brought under ICC control. Many states had enacted regulatory statutes aimed at trucks, but these had not provided adequate protection for the two major groups concerned: the railroads and the larger truckers. The railroads, of course, resented the general lack of rate, safety, and service controls that contributed to the competitive advantage motor carriers often enjoyed over railroads. They sought to bring the motor carriers under ICC supervision to equalize some of these conditions. Larger truckers were not averse to federal regulations, even though it might entail some loss of advantage vis-à-vis the railroads, for the large truckers were troubled by competition, often of a "fly-by-night" sort, from small one-truck carriers. The latter were quite numerous during depression days, since money for a down payment on a truck and a tankful of gas set a man up in business. Such businesses usually did not survive long, but with a great many of them continually appearing, the confidence of shippers in the trucking industry was faltering. The large truckers were willing to trade ICC control of themselves for protection against too easy entry into the trucking business by small truckers. The

Motor Carrier Act of 1935 provided that "certificates of public convenience and necessity" must be obtained to engage in business as common motor carriers, protecting the continued right to operate of all existing carriers through a "grandfather clause."

The authority of the ICC had long (since 1906) been extended to cover oil pipelines, express companies, sleeping-car companies, and refrigeration and storage services, and in 1940 all common carriers operating on domestic waters were brought under Commission jurisdiction. In 1942, freight forwarders—middlemen who collect and consolidate small shipments of goods, ship them in carloads, and unload and deliver them—were added, as were rate-making bureaus of the several industries in 1948. Thus all the major carrier groups except the airlines were made subject to ICC control.

In 1940 the basic statement of transportation policy was revised to take fuller account of the new competition in the transportation industries. The ICC was directed to:

> . . . provide for fair and impartial regulation of all modes of transportation subject to the provisions of the Act, so administered as to recognize and preserve the inherent advantages of each; to promote safe, adequate, economical, and efficient service and foster sound economic conditions in transportation and among the several carriers; to encourage the establishment of reasonable charges for transportation services, without unjust discrimination, undue preferences or advantages, or unfair or destructive competitive practices . . . to the end of developing, coordinating, and preserving a national transportation system by water, highway, and rail, as well as other means, adequate to meet the needs of the commerce of the United States. . . .

In effect, the Transportation Act of 1940 placed the many transportation industries under ICC control and specified that that control was to be exercised in such manner as to produce "sound policy," with the criteria for determining "soundness" largely left undefined. In turn, this meant that the contending groups in the transportation industries would all conduct continuous campaigns within the framework of ICC authority to secure the maximum advantage.

In one sense, of course, the Commission has broad discretion and authority to shape the whole transportation system of the United States, airlines excepted. Not only are questions of rates, service, and competition among carriers within the authority of the ICC, but the less dramatic, yet important functions of prescribing safety devices, investigating accidents, controlling the issue of securities, and supervising accounting methods give the Commission extensive authority over the management of the carriers. Given the sweeping powers of the ICC, much is at stake for the carriers. Consequently, they devote much of their resources to the struggle for advantage, far more than any group not directly and primarily engaged in transportation. The ICC has thus been transformed from a symbol of antirailroad sentiment and an agency to protect shippers against railroad monopoly to an arena within which rival carriers contend for competitive advantage.

THE ISSUES

The political issues in the transportation field have varied, of course, over different periods of time and according to changing political and economic circumstances. Each type of carrier, as it developed, faced certain problems unique to it and found a particular environment with which to deal. But there have also been basic similarities in the issues that have faced each carrier, and as the field of transportation has become an arena of competition among several competing types of carriers, these similarities have become more relevant to an understanding of the field than the historical differences. We shall examine three broad categories of issues that have particular significances: 1) right of way and roadbed provision, 2) rates and service, and 3) combination, and cooperation.

Right of Way and Roadbeds

Each of the major railroads operate on roadbeds provided as the result of some form of government subsidy. In the earliest days of the Republic, highways were built with the help of the federal government. Canal boats operated on ways built with substantial assistance from public funds. In the early days of railroad development, state and local governments often tried to outbid each other in financial inducements to persuade the railroads to extend their lines through particular communities. And between 1850 and 1871, assistance amounting to nearly $500 million was extended to railroads in the form of federal land grants.[6] Probably only about 10 per cent of the total mileage built in the United States received land grant aid and most of this was located west of the Mississippi where the immediate prospects for profitable railroads were not good, due to the lack of settlers. Nevertheless, it is fair to say that the building of the railroad system in the United States received substantial help from government in the early stages of development. Without such help it is questionable if enough

---

[6] Federal Coordinator of Transportation, *Public Aids to Transportation* (Washington, D.C.: U.S. Government Printing Office, 1940), II, 3–103; Board of Investigation and Research, *Public Aids to Domestic Transportation*, 79th Congress, 1st Session, House Document 159 (1944), 105–88. Robert S. Henry argues that the value of the federal land grants was substantially less, perhaps 130 million. Also the federal government received considerable financial return since land-grant railroads were required until 1940 to carry mail for 80 per cent of the rates applying to other roads and until 1946 government military and naval personnel moved at much less than normal rates. "The Railroad Land Grant Legend in American History Texts," *Mississippi Valley Historical Review*, XXXII (Sept. 1945), 171–95.

capital could have been attracted to construct the western roads at such an early date, and this in turn would have meant much slower settling of the west.

All the transportation industries have received governmental help in getting established, however. All modern highways have been built by government. Airways have been developed by federal authority, and the charts, weather reports, radio-navigational aids, and airport facilities—the airlines' equivalent to railroad trackage, roadbed, and terminal—also were financed by public agencies. The vast majority of water transport facilities have been developed or improved through governmental action. Thus, all have been assisted in varying degree. The critical contemporary issues revolve around how much of the costs of these facilities should be borne by the particular transport group. Thus railroads have tried to force truckers to pay a larger share of the expenses of building highways, and both groups have urged that water carriers share more of the burden of improving river navigation.

Rates

Although public assistance to carriers for their roadbeds has usually been the first issue to arise, once the carrier is in full operation, the central issue soon becomes the rates charged. Particularly with respect to the railroads, the problems of rate regulation have monopolized attention since the latter part of the nineteenth century. A number of aspects of the general issue of rate regulation must be understood in order to talk sensibly about the problems. Three major issues—maximum rate control, valuation and rates, and discrimination among different shippers regarding rates will be considered here.

By spreading the network of their service throughout most of the United States, the railroads achieved a substantial position of monopoly in transportation. Most shippers had no real choice about which company would transport their products. Some areas, of course, were served by more than one railroad, and shippers in those areas could bargain between competing roads. In other areas, like much of the sparsely settled west, there was not sufficient traffic to permit the railroads to abuse their monopoly position, since this would merely keep away further settlement. But in many parts of the country the railroads did enjoy monopoly conditions, and as a result could set their rates as high as the shippers could pay without going bankrupt.

Since shippers, particularly farmers, had no way to combat railroad rates in the market place, they turned to the political arena. The passage of state and later national legislation providing for regulatory commissions empowered to fix maximum rates was the result of this effort. When the commissions were first established, it was widely anticipated that they would be able to curb the monopoly power of the railroads and reduce rates to levels bearing reasonable relation to the costs of the service. However, the complex forces at work were more involved than they had appeared to be, and many unforeseen problems developed.

The Interstate Commerce Act of 1887 provided, among other things, that the Interstate Commerce Commission could review rail rates and, if the Commission found the rates to be too high, it could order them to be changed. Only "just and reasonable " rates were to be permitted. The Supreme Court held quickly, however, that the ICC had no power to specify the rates to be charged,[7] and so a railroad could change a rate found to be unjust by a fraction of a cent and make it legitimate. The support of the railroads by the courts effectively emasculated the ICC's authority, and it was not until the passage of the Hepburn Act of 1906 that the Commission was given specific power to set maximum rates. The Mann-Elkins Act of 1910 extended the Commission's authority over rates by empowering the ICC to suspend proposed rate increases while examining their reasonableness, and to consider the rate schedules as a whole rather than confining attention to specific rates. As a result of these changes, the authority of the ICC to control the maximum rates charged was fully established.

Nevertheless, this authority was not sufficient to control the profits that railroads might earn. The definition of what rates were "just and reasonable" depended not solely upon what the shippers thought was fair, but what brought the railroads a "reasonable" return on their investment. The Supreme Court held in *Smyth v. Ames*[8] that "just and reasonable" rates were those that assured the railroads of a "fair return on a fair valuation" of the railroads' investment. This formula was designed to protect the railroads from overly zealous Commission action that might result in a rate reduction below the amount necessary to keep the railroads in business. The railroads were able, for a number of years, to argue that the rates set by the ICC were not fair, and it was difficult to demonstrate that they were.[9]

"Fair return" was generally agreed to mean a return of between 5 and 8 per cent on the investment. The really difficult problem was how to determine the "fair value" of the investment. The early days of railroad promotion had seen a considerable amount of financial manipulation that severely inflated the paper value of the railroad investment without actually adding any productive facilities. Were these paper assets to be included as part of the base upon which the percentage return the railroad

---

[7] *Cincinnati, New Orleans and Texas Railway Co. v. Interstate Commerce Commission*, 162 U.S. 184 (1896).

[8] 169 U.S. 466 (1898).

[9] For a convenient summary of the development of these doctrines see D. Philip Locklin, *Economics of Transportation*, 4th ed. (Homewood, Ill.: Richard D. Irwin, Inc., 1954), chap. 17.

was entitled to earn would be figured? Even if this problem were solved, how was the value of the railroad plant to be calculated? If the *original cost* of building the railroad, minus depreciation, were used as the basis for rate-making, this would reward the wasteful construction that often characterized railroad building. If the *cost of reproduction* of the facilities were used, this would give the railroads the benefit of increases in the general price level that had occurred since the railroad was built. Or if a compromise—the *prudent investment* of a reasonable man—were used, who was to determine what was prudent and what was not? The issues raised by the "fair return on a fair valuation" formula were immensely difficult and so long as the courts insisted that control of railroad rates must also guarantee the railroads a fair return, the railroads were given an important weapon to stave off the rigors of control. By taking ICC rate decisions to the courts and protesting that the rates were unfair, the railroads were able to protect some of the fruits of their monopoly position in transportation. When this monopoly position gave way before motor and air competition, the question of maximum rate control lost much of its original significance, since monopolistic rates might merely force shippers to use the other means of transport.

Rate discrimination. Rate discrimination was another type of controversy that grew during this period of 1870 to 1917. This issue was one of discrimination by carriers in the rates charged competing shippers for the same service.[10] Rate discrimination took two different forms; discrimination against specific shippers producing the same product, and discrimination between different localities. In the early days of agitation for rate regulation, one of the main charges against the railroads was that lower rates were being extended to a few favored shippers as part of a concerted effort to eliminate competition and build the trusts. A particularly flagrant example of this practice was the granting by the Marietta and Cincinnati of a rate of $.10 a barrel to Standard Oil for a particular haul of crude oil, charging smaller oil companies $.35 a barrel for the same haul, and giving Standard the additional quarter. Rebates of rates and special rates were sometimes induced by competition between railroads for a large shipper's business, but more often they appeared to be part of the movement toward monopoly that marked so much of American business in the late nineteenth century.

The Interstate Commerce Act of 1887 contained prohibitions against rebates to favored shippers and generally outlawed discrimination among persons. These prohibitions were strengthened by later legislation, and this aspect of discrimination in rates was substantially eliminated, so far as it was possible for governmental action to do so. It remains true, however,

---

[10] For more extended discussion of these problems see Dudley F. Pegrum, *Transportation: Economics and Public Policy* (Homewood, Ill.: Richard D. Irwin, Inc., 1954).

that since rival shippers do not ordinarily ship in exactly the same quantities or over equal distances, charges of favoritism through different rates not accurately based upon cost differences continue to be made.

It has proved far more difficult to eliminate discrimination in rates between *places*. The situation in which the railroad charged the same product more for a short haul than a long haul was a fairly common type of such discrimination in pre-regulation days. Usually this type of discrimination resulted from the fact that competition over the longer haul forced the railroad to reduce its rate, whereas for the shorter haul the railroad enjoyed a monopoly. Obviously this sort of discrimination had serious disadvantages for the city or manufacturer located on the short haul. Higher transportation rates mean a weaker competitive position vis-à-vis the manufacturer in a city served by more than one railroad. The 1887 Act prohibited charging more for a shorter haul than for a longer haul, when the former was contained within the latter, over the same line in the same direction. Railroads could receive specific exemption from the prohibition, and the prohibition applied only when the two hauls were under "substantially similar circumstances." However, the Supreme Court held that competition between railroads over the longer haul made the circumstances dissimilar,[11] and it was not until the Mann-Elkins Act of 1910 that the "similar circumstances" clause was dropped and the blanket prohibition enforced. Railroads can still apply for and obtain specific exemptions for specific rates when the ICC finds that lower rates for a longer haul are necessary to meet (but not to undercut) competition from other carriers.

Another aspect of rate discrimination which had profound consequences for the economic development of the nation was the discrimination between different *regions* of the country. The railroads of the United States were built in three fairly distinct groups, each serving a different type of economy, each separately controlled, and each cut off from the others by river barriers.[12] The eastern roads served an area that already was emphasizing manufacturing, and the rate structure of this region was designed to encourage the shipment of manufactured goods to other parts of the country. In the South, the rail rates were fixed to encourage the flow of agricultural products northward, and the southern roads recouped by charging high rates on the shipment of manufactured products. The railroads west of the Mississippi followed the same pattern as the southern roads. The result was that, although the cost of transporting manufactured goods by rail was actually lower in the South than in the Northeast, the rates were higher in the South, and rates were higher in the West than in the South. The rate structures developed by the three groups of railroads

---

[11] *Interstate Commerce Commission* v. *Alabama Midland Ry. Co.*, 168 U.S. 144 (1897).

[12] On the development of basic rate structures, see Marvin L. Fair and Ernest W. Williams, *Economics of Transportation*, rev. ed. (New York: Harper & Row, Publishers, 1959), chap. 22.

were designed to maximize their profits, and when rates were brought under the control of the ICC, it was very difficult to discard the main outlines of transportation rates for the whole nation.

In the years around 1900, effective control of many southern and western railroads came into the same hands that controlled the eastern roads—those in centers of financial power—thus assuring united opposition among the railroads to any proposals for scrapping the sectional classification. The effects of this system were mainly to make it difficult for manufacturing, particularly of basic industry products, to develop in either the South or West where transportation costs for manufactured goods were so high. Not until the TVA was established and sought to promote industrialization in the South were there politically effective protests against the discriminatory rates.[13]

The Transportation Act of 1940 specified that no unreasonable preferences be given in the rate structure to any region or territory and, after revising the rate structures to make them more equitable as between sections, the ICC finally put a uniform classification into effect for all territory east of the Rocky Mountains. Transportation costs are not the only factor, of course, affecting the economic development of an area; other factors also have worked in the past to keep manufacturing concentrated east of the Mississippi and north of the Ohio. Nevertheless, more equitable transportation rates appear to be one of the factors contributing to the expanded industrialization of the South and West during recent years.

The discussion of discrimination in transportation rates has focused on the railroads. Discrimination in rates charged by the newer types of carriers has been a much less significant policy problem. Rates of water carriers, motor carriers, and airlines all tend to be set with reference to railroad rates. If particular rail rates are low, other carriers will charge low rates in order to compete. The temptation to discriminate in rates in order to attract more business generally has been strongest for railroads.[14] Railroads must bear heavy fixed costs of investment in plant and rolling stock, roadbed, administrative overhead, and so on, which must be paid whether or not there is any business. It is therefore to its advantage for a railroad to get additional business even at rates which do not fully cover its total costs—that is, fixed plus out-of-pocket costs—so long as the rates cover out-of-pocket costs and contribute something to fixed costs. Thus a railroad may try to cut its rates in order to secure extra traffic in competitive markets. The truckers' cost structure is not so likely to induce them to set rates that discriminate between one customer and another. The major part

---

[13] The Southern Governors' Conference also became active on this issue. See H. C. Nixon, "The Southern Governors' Conference as a Pressure Group," *Journal of Politics*, VI (1944), 338–45.

[14] See Locklin, *Economics of Transportation*, pp. 138–41 and 685–86.

of their cost are out-of-pocket costs—those extra expenses incurred for each additional piece of business done—such as wages and gasoline.

Service

The problems of the adequacy of transport service cannot be entirely separated from those of rates discussed previously, since service at rates that are too high is not adequate service from the point of view of the shipper. But the provision of service that is satisfactory in quantity and quality to both the shippers and the carriers has engendered considerable conflict among several interested groups, and this conflict has resulted in governmental action. The problems of service have two main aspects— the *addition* of service at the behest of would-be shippers or of new transport firms anxious to tap a promising market, and the *abandonment* of service in unprofitable markets by carriers seeking to cut their losses at the expense of the few remaining customers in the area to be abandoned.

In the early days of railroad building, many communities, as well as states and finally the federal government, offered substantial assistance in order to persuade the railroads to go through a particular locality or area and provide their invaluable service. Many of the communities in the Midwest and West expected that massive growth and commercial success would follow the railroad, and many railroads were built in hopes that turned out to be only dreams. The railroad system expanded beyond the needs of the economy, and despite the reorganization and concentration of control that took place in the early twentieth century, many railroads found themselves in awkward financial condition and were unable to continue operating many of their lines at a profit. However, by this time many communities had come to depend upon these lines. To abandon the service, local interests feared, would make virtual ghost towns of these communities. Clearly, all the available political resources of the communities where abandonment was threatened would be mobilized to resist. This resulted in the Transportation Act of 1920 providing that no interstate lines could be built or abandoned without permission of the ICC. State commissions exercised similar authority over intrastate lines. Thus the problem was frankly made political rather than simply a question of business judgment of the profit and loss situation.

As motor and air travel have increased, however, the railroads have steadily sought, and eventually received, permission to abandon unprofitable service, particularly passenger lines. Since 1920 more than 40,000 miles of railroad line have been abandoned while only about 10,000 miles of new line have been built, a shrinkage of the railroad network in the United States of about 12 per cent. Under the Transportation Act of 1958 the ICC was authorized to permit railroads to abandon intrastate runs even when abandonment was opposed by state regulatory authorities. The abandonment of rail service is often necessary to the financial health of the railroads, but the social health of communities may depend upon retaining railroad service. The problems are difficult to solve, but they are unavoidable in a dynamic society where people and industry are continually shifting locations.

The older carriers serving older markets may have sought retrenchment of service, but the newer forms of transportation and the newer markets have tried to obtain expanded service. Common motor carriers and airlines must receive certificates of convenience and necessity from the ICC and CAB respectively before being allowed to add new routes and before new firms can compete over established routes. The rationale of regulation here is based upon the memory of railroad overexpansion and the resulting financial troubles, plus the fact that the airlines have, until very recently, required government subsidy to make them profitable. To these considerations must be added the concern of existing carriers to resist the expansion of service; for example, railroads seeking to limit truck service, or one airline trying to maintain a monopoly over a particular route against the threatened competition of another airline. The communities to be served are on the side of the new carriers, and in this situation the long-term victory generally has gone to those who desire increased transportation service.

Competition, Cooperation, and Combination

One of the most difficult subjects to discuss accurately and dispassionately in the whole field of public policy is the degree of competition existing among the firms of an industry. Even when all the necessary data are available, which they seldom are, reasonable men continue to disagree about what the data mean. These problems are as hard to handle in the field of transportation as they are elsewhere. But an attempt to grasp the extent of competition or cooperation within the many transportation industries is fundamental to an understanding of public policy in the field and of the political activities of many groups interested in transportation questions.

Competition among several firms to assure reasonable prices and service has never been regarded as being as desirable in transportation as it is in most of the economy. Since the latter part of the nineteenth century, transportation (meaning until recently railroads) has been regarded as a public utility for which competition could not function as an adequate regulator. Government regulation had to be substituted to hold prices and service at levels acceptable to the public. This image of transportation was never entirely accurate, since even in the days of railroad domination of transportation, several railroad companies competed for traffic in many of the markets of the country, particularly the major cities, such as Chicago,

New York, and Philadelphia. It was primarily the rural areas and agricultural shippers who faced one-railroad monopoly.

In the late nineteenth and early twentieth centuries, public policy toward transportation was directed largely toward the restoration of competition in transportation, through preventing the pooling of revenues, by breaking up railroad combinations under the Sherman Act and so on.[15] Following the near disastrous failure of the railroads to provide adequate service during World War I, public policy underwent a shift as the desire of the railroads themselves to decrease competition and a widespread public desire to shore up a financially weak railroad system coincided. The Transportation Act of 1920 aimed to assist the overexpanded industry by encouraging consolidation and merger, while guaranteeing to the industry as a whole a stable financial return. Consolidation of railroads into fewer and stronger units is still often considered as a way of improving their competitive position. Several large eastern lines have joined forces in recent years. Initiative continues to rest with the railroads, and federal authorities, mainly the ICC and the Justice Department, serve as referees, approving some consolidations and opposing others on anti-trust grounds.

Governmental limits on competition. In addition to encouraging certain consolidations of railroads, governmental authority has been used in other ways by the carriers to reduce the competitive pressure within each transportation industry. The rationale in each case is that by preventing extreme competition the firms of the industry are made financially stronger and are thus able to operate more efficiently over the long run. Two major techniques to moderate intra-industry competition are *control of entry* and *minimum rate control.*

Control of entry is a useful device for reducing competition only if the industry is sufficiently attractive that entry by new firms is sought. For many years the railroad industry has not been attractive enough, and few firms have sought to obtain permission from the ICC to offer rail service— almost none in recent decades. Interstate trucking, on the other hand, has offered financially promising opportunities, and thousands of applications for permission to enter the industry have been filed with the ICC. A basic part of the original legislation providing for federal control over interstate trucking—a provision that helped secure support from the larger existing trucking firms for the whole Motor Carrier Act of 1935—guaranteed the right of continued operation to all existing firms, but provided that new firms thereafter would have to obtain certificates from the ICC that the service they proposed to offer was "in the public interest." Existing trucking firms thus secured a measure of protection against an ever-growing

---

[15] An early but thorough treatment of this general problem can be found in W. Z. Ripley, *Railroads: Rates and Regulations* (New York: Longmans, Green and Co., Inc., 1912).

number of companies engaged in motor transport, and competition was correspondingly moderated.

Airlines likewise must secure permission from the Civil Aeronautics Board before inaugurating service or expanding routes.[16] The basic regulatory legislation affecting airlines was passed in 1938 and provided "grandfather rights" to protect existing firms in their right to continue to operate. Since the regular airlines often have not operated at a profit, the control of entry was concerned not so much with regulating competition among airlines as with protecting the meager earnings of the existing companies.[17] Even in recent years, when some of the major trunk airlines have made substantial profits, and repeated demands by new firms to be allowed entry to the industry have arisen, the CAB, supported by the existing airlines, has resisted these pleas and by refusing entry to new firms has moderated the competitive pressures upon the airlines.

Governmental action to prevent carriers from setting excessively low rates has quite a different purpose than the control of maximum rates. Maximum rate control is designed to limit the profits of the carrier who is in a relatively monopolistic position; this sort of control is asked for by shippers. *Minimum rate control* is designed to prevent "cut-throat competition" among the carriers and is desired by the carriers themselves. Particularly among the railroads, but also among small truckers, there is often the temptation in the face of competition to reduce rates below the actual cost of providing the service, to attract more business. If the carrier can stand the temporary loss, the hope is that the competitors will be forced out of business and that the losses will be regained later by raising the rates again. If the carrier can thereby put to work idle equipment, he may not lose very much money even though his rates are not equal to his total costs. However, unless the lower rates bring a larger volume of business to the whole transportation industry, frequently all that happens is that some of the firms go bankrupt. Except for air passenger traffic, the volume of transportation traffic does not change much with rate changes, and, as a result, price-cutting competition, which is particularly common in time of depression, tends to throw the whole industry into chaos. Even shippers do not necessarily welcome these rate wars, since the rates will not stay low, and the violent fluctuations in rates and service are difficult to deal with in planning business operations. The result of these considerations is that the ICC and the CAB are empowered to establish minimum rates for the carriers under their control.

The ICC requires that rates be at least equal to the added cost to the

---

16 See Richard E. Caves, *Air Transport and Its Regulators* (Cambridge, Mass.: Harvard University Press, 1962).

17 See Civil Aeronautics Board, *Role of Competition in Commercial Air Transportation* (Washington, D.C.: U.S. Government Printing Office, 1952); G. E. Hale and Rosemary D. Hale, "Competition or Control IV: Air Carriers," *University of Pennsylvania Law Review*, CIX (1961), 311–360.

carrier of providing service and that the rates be no lower than necessary to meet competition. Prior to 1958 a railroad often had difficulty in setting rates below those of a competing water carrier or trucker in order to win back business. However, the Transportation Act of 1958, in response to the pleas of the railroads, provided, "Rates of a carrier shall not be held up to a particular level to protect the traffic of any other mode of transportation." Thus minimum rate control is to be used to moderate intra-industry competition by preventing destructive rate wars but not to prevent rate competition between one transportation industry and another.

THE NEW COMPETITION

The rise of competing forms of transportation has substantially altered the problems of public policy in the field. No longer do railroads constitute monopolistic giants able to dominate whole sections of the country with their financial power. Instead they are, in the words of a recent Commerce Department report, the " 'sick man' of transportation." We have noted that interindustry competition—trucks versus rails versus airlines versus water carriers versus pipelines—is the dominant form of competition in transportation. Hence our subsequent discussion will concentrate on this, ignoring the considerable but less politically exciting intra-industry competition that exists.

Table 5-2 shows how dramatic the shift in traffic from railroads to other carriers has been in recent decades. The corollary has been that railroad earnings since World War I have been lower than a financially healthy industry should enjoy. The financial excesses and overbuilding of the early days of railroad monopoly came home to roost when motor carriers began to take away business and earnings fell. The Great Depression exacerbated the trouble and drove many roads into bankruptcy; however, this did permit them to reorganize their capital structures along sounder lines. Not until World War II did railroad earnings begin to recover. But even the heavy traffic and relatively good income of the war period were not an unmixed blessing, for enormous strain was placed on already obsolete equipment. At the end of the war railroads were faced with hardening competition, which could be met only with new and modern equipment, since a major drawing card of motor and air carriers was speed and comfort of service. Wartime earnings might have given the railroads an outside chance to renovate their plants and hold more of the traffic, if it had not been that war was followed by seven years of substantially uninterrupted inflation. Rising costs were not so serious for motor carriers, since they did not have such a huge investment in obsolete and worn-out equipment.

The result of this situation was that railroads had to seek large rate

TABLE 5-2

Percentage of Domestic Intercity Traffic Carried by Major Types of Transportation

	1916	1939	1949	1959	1964
Railroads					
Passenger-miles	98.00	8.7	9.3	3.04	2.05
Freight ton-miles	77.2	62.2	60.6	45.4	43.51
Motor Carriers					
Passenger (including private automobiles)	—	90.5	88.5	91.3	92.11
Freight	—	8.0	10.6	21.9	22.69
Inland Waterways					
Passenger	2.0	.5	.4	.28	.32
Freight	18.4	17.8	15.8	15.2	16.34
Petroleum Pipelines					
Freight	4.4	12.0	13.0	17.3	17.36
Airways					
Passenger	—	.25	1.8	4.4	5.53
Freight	—	.002	.025	.05	.098

Sources: Data for 1916 from Marvin Fair and Ernest Williams, *Economics of Transportation* (New York: Harper & Row, Publishers, 1950), p. 132. Data for other years from *Annual Reports* of Interstate Commerce Commission of 1941, p. 9; 1951, p. 20; 1960, p. 10; 1966, p. 59.

increases in order to make any progress in modernization. Between 1946 and 1952, rates were increased an average of 78.9 per cent. This did not help to win back business from the trucks, and during the same period the motor carrier share of traffic rose from 7.28 per cent to 16.21 per cent of the volume and considerably more of the value.

Since 1952, prices have risen more slowly, and the railroads have tried in various ways to improve their competitive position. Part of their effort has been to modernize their operations. Such innovations as "piggy-back" service have begun to win back some business. The elimination of costly passenger runs has proceeded slowly but steadily. Some large railroad consolidations have permitted more efficient operation, but most observers agree that the railroad system is still not organized or operated along optimum lines, and that further consolidation and more imaginative innovation are needed.

The fact that detailed governmental regulation of transportation exists has made the new competition an intensely political matter. In seeking more flexibility in dealing with labor matters, the railroads must meet pension levels established by Congress and work through the special machinery established under the Railway Labor Act to mediate railway labor disputes. The railroad brotherhoods are allies of the companies in their battles with the truckers, but in the face of declining railroad employment the brotherhoods fight hard to protect as many jobs and rights as possible against, for example, automation. On several occasions the President has had to intervene in labor disputes.

More significant in the railroads' political drive to compete successfully has been their quest for greater flexibility in rate-making. As explained earlier, because of their heavy fixed costs, railroads often find it advantageous to reduce particular rates even below their full costs in order to increase their business. However, the ICC has and uses the power to set rates exactly, and any changes must be approved by the Commission if there is any protest made. Naturally, rival carriers are likely to object to lower railroad rates so that even when they are ultimately approved they may not take effect for many months after they are proposed. The Transportation Act of 1958 granted somewhat greater freedom regarding rate-making by providing that rates of one carrier should not be held up simply in order to protect another; but the ICC still controls the specific rates.

The railroads contend that without greater flexibility, and perhaps other types of assistance too, they will not be able to remain solvent, and our basic transportation system will deteriorate. The rival carriers argue, on the other hand, that the railroads' dire predictions are exaggerated and that, given the power to shift rates at will, the railroads will cut rates long enough to drive the motor and water carriers out of business, then raise rates again to monopolistic levels.

On several occasions proposals have been made by executive agencies to increase the ability of the railroads to compete. President Eisenhower appointed an Advisory Committee which reported in 1955, advocating that the ICC authority to suspend rate changes and to set specific rates be substantially reduced. Again in 1960 the Department of Commerce issued a report making some seventy-eight specific recommendations dealing with transportation problems. Many of these dealt with enlarging the rate-making freedom of carriers. These proposals have been widely discussed as "railroad proposals," and the AAR and ATA have purchased considerable national advertising to defend and attack them.

Other suggestions for helping the railroads in recent years have included providing government loans to enable railroads to modernize their equipment more easily. The Transportation Act of 1958 included a provision of loan guarantees for this purpose. A number of railroads have sought to curtail drastically their passenger service, on which the ICC estimated a deficit of more than $500 million incurred in 1959 alone. Other roads have sought to attract more passengers by providing more attractive accommodations. However, the number of passenger runs has greatly declined, and many roads seem willing to confine themselves to "expense account" luxury service only.

If transportation policy is to move toward permitting intercarrier competition to serve as the mechanism for keeping rates and service at adequate levels rather than relying upon detailed regulation, however, any proposal will be a "railroad proposal." Flexibility in rate-making is a goal sought primarily by railroads because it is the cost structures of the railroads which make rate flexibility important. Truckers rely more on their advantages in service, while water carriers depend on the cheapness of their rates to attract business. Railroads, competing with both, seek flexibility.

ARENAS OF CONFLICT

The ICC

Whatever adaptation of the regulatory framework is to be done must be done by governmental action, and the competition among the carriers must take them constantly into the arenas of decision. A major arena, of course, is the ICC. The policy declaration contained in the Transportation Act of 1940 stated that decisions of the ICC were to insure that each type of carrier preserved its inherent advantages, and that no carrier was to be given any preferred position. But when rival carriers are in conflict over the whole range of policy decisions, any decision the ICC makes is bound to benefit some interests and hurt others. It has been argued that the Commission has tended over the years to favor the railroads by granting rate changes when requested and by encouraging the extension of regulation to other carriers.[18] On the other hand, the administrative delays associated with the regulatory process are serious handicaps for railroads, for which rapid improvement is most essential.

Congress, President, and Courts

Although many of the basic decisions concerning transportation interests are made by specialized agencies like the ICC, the major institutions of the national government are, of course, intimately involved in this policy struggle. Congress writes the basic legislation setting forth the policies the ICC is to follow, and, as we have seen, important transportation legislation has been produced every few years of this century. Legislative questions of indirect effect on transportation interest, such as many tax issues, frequently induce the affected groups to mobilize any influence they have on Capitol Hill. Annual congressional decisions determining how much money the ICC is to be allowed to spend to enforce its rules and to

---

[18] See Samuel P. Huntington, "The Marasmus of the ICC," *Yale Law Journal*, Vol. 61 (1952), pp. 467–510; Charles S. Morgan, "A Critique of 'The Marasmus of the ICC,' " *Yale Law Journal*, LXII (1953), 171–226.

investigate rate cases may also be of great consequence. In the early days of the Commission the lack of funds was a major factor forcing the Commission to retreat to a relatively passive approach toward rail regulation. Appropriation control as well as general legislative authority are important weapons, potential or actual, that make Congress an important arena for conflicts among transport interests. The significance of the legislative arena to transportation interests can best be seen, perhaps, by the fact that in the eighteen years between 1946 and 1964 the Association of American Railroads reported more than $50,000 lobbying expenditures in twelve years, the American Trucking Associations spent that amount eight times, the Transportation Association of America five times, and several other transportation-related groups spent sums of that magnitude in one or two specific years.

The President, indeed much of the executive branch, is frequently involved in transportation politics. Of course, members of the ICC must be appointed by the President with the consent of the Senate, and this could give the Chief Executive considerable opportunity to shape Commission policy. Appointments run for seven years, however, and the chance that a single President could remake a Commission is not good. At any rate, Presidents have not appeared to try to direct transportation policy in this manner. More important examples of executive influence can be seen in the recommendations of several presidential commissions that have studied both the administration and policies in the field. Several other proposals have been made to transfer some or all of the control of transportation industries to an executive department directly under presidential authority. In 1966 President Johnson proposed and Congress approved the establishment of a Department of Transportation. Although regulatory functions would remain with the several independent commissions, the new department would encompass the transportation safety and service functions now scattered among several agencies, and more important, would focus the attention and resources of the nation on solving both technological and economic problems that have so long plagued the transport industries. Such transfer would vitally affect the ability of particular groups in the transportation field to secure their interests. Railroads, for example, have generally opposed shifting authority away from the ICC to an executive department,[19] and all the transportation interests approached President Johnson's proposal with great caution. Maritime shipping interests were able to avoid being included in the new department, preferring their existing arrangements with the U.S. Maritime Commission.

The courts have played an important role from time to time, as noted before, in shaping transportation policy as they followed particular formu-

---

[19] See David B. Truman, *The Governmental Process* (New York: Alfred A. Knopf, Inc., 1951), p. 421.

las for determining the fair value of railroad investment, or as they interpreted in narrow and restrictive ways the authority of the ICC. In recent years the courts have not had a major part in resolving conflicts in this field, but the judiciary remains a potential battleground for the interests at stake.

State and Local Government

Many agencies of state and local governments make decisions of interest to transportation groups. Federal regulatory authority is based on the constitutional power to regulate interstate commerce. Today this is a broad enough grant to embrace almost all rail and air traffic and much motor transport too. For example, since 1914 the courts have sustained federal control of rates for entirely intrastate traffic when such control is necessary to control interstate transportation effectively.[20] Nevertheless, states continue to be involved, usually through some type of commission, regulating rates on intrastate traffic such as interurban passenger lines. Motor carriers are subject to very extensive regulation respecting licensing, height, weight, length, and service. Many of these issues are the subject of bitter struggle between rival transportation groups as railroads and truckers bid for support from the state legislatures.[21] Indeed, restrictive state legislation seems to present one of the primary weapons by which railroads can reduce the competitive advantages of the trucks. State regulations of this kind are not unlimited, however, since the Supreme Court has from time to time struck them down for placing an "undue burden" on the free flow of interstate commerce.

All transportation interests must also be closely concerned with state and local taxation. Property taxes are particularly important to railroads. The huge investment in rolling stock, the trackage and right of way, and any terminal facilities are subject to taxes that place a burden on railroad income. Both the rate of taxation and the level of assessment are therefore of great concern. Gasoline and other state and local highway uses taxes represent an important cost of doing business to the truckers and thus draw much attention. In some states in the past, the stakes for transportation interests were so great that particular rail firms dominated virtually the entire political life of the state. Interest group conflicts have grown more complex and no firm today occupies the position that the Louisville and Nashville or the Southern Pacific once did in Tennessee and California

---

[20] *The Shreveport Case*, 234 U.S. 342 (1914).

[21] The struggle in Pennsylvania over truck weight restrictions was so intense that trucking and railroad associations *plus their respective public relations firms* became embroiled in a colorful lawsuit. See Andrew Hacker, "Pressure Politics in Pennsylvania: *The Truckers vs. The Railroads*," in Alan F. Westin, ed., *The Uses of Power* (New York: Harcourt, Brace and World, Inc., 1962), pp. 323–76.

respectively. Nevertheless, the decisions of state and local governments continue to attract the political attentions of transportation groups.

AVIATION POLICY AND POLITICS

The commercial aviation industry, although a transportation industry and competitive with motor carriers and railroads, carriers on its major political activities on a different front. It is regulated by separate administrative agencies, and while aviation interests do engage in such general transportation controversies as those related to highway construction, by and large, the air carriers resolve their conflicts separately. The Civil Aeronautics Board and the Federal Aviation Agency are the principal governmental agencies dealing with aviation problems. The CAB was established in 1938 when the basic policies of control were enacted. Prior to that time safety regulations and air mail rates were prescribed by various agencies, but little over-all control of the industry was exercised.

The FAA

The Federal Aviation Agency was established in 1958, superseding the Civil Aeronautics Administration.[22] The latter had been the agency in charge of administering the airways since 1938. It controlled flight patterns, provided navigational assistance, examined planes and tested pilots, administered the federal program aiding airport construction, and with the CAB, investigated air accidents. As the nation's airways became increasingly crowded, and especially as uncontrolled military planes presented a growing hazard to civilian craft, it appeared necessary to establish a stronger agency, and so the FAA was created. The FAA has enlarged responsibilities for air safety and airway development and is given an administrative position directly under the President to enhance its prestige. Its most important additional authority is to control the flight patterns of military as well as civilian aircraft. The Agency is in charge of the expanding program for constructing airport facilities adequate to handle the volume and type of airspace use found in the jet age. The FAA is also directing the program for increased ground control of air traffic.

The CAB and Competition

The major arena for airline disputes, however, is the Civil Aeronautics Board. The CAB is primarily concerned with economic regulation: controlling entry, fixing routes and approving expansion or abandonment of

---

[22] For an interesting discussion of the political activity related to this legislation see Emmette S. Redford, "A Case Analysis of Congressional Activity: Civil Aviation, 1957–58," *Journal of Politics*, XXII (1960), 228–59.

service, setting maximum rates, and determining air mail payments and subsidies. The industry now regulated by the CAB developed along lines quite different from other transportation industries. In the early years of aviation, the paramount concern of governmental policy was to develop aviation technology in time of peace which would be adequate in time of war. In the period following World War I, commercial aviation showed little likelihood of achieving commercial success without substantial assistance, so the air carriers were granted subsidy payments in the form of overpayments for carrying airmail. As commercial aviation developed and business expanded, various local communities sought service, and when airmail subsidies were expanded in 1934, the industry became somewhat more attractive.

After several shifts in the governmental control machinery, Congress established the CAB in 1938 as a semi-independent, regulatory agency. The CAB has been confronted with the task of encouraging what is still an infant and somewhat risky industry. This encouragement has taken the form of subsidies for financially weak firms, and limitation of the entry of new firms into the field. All firms operating at the time the 1938 legislation was passed were allowed under "grandfather rights" to continue operation. These firms are called "trunk" lines, and they handle more than two-thirds of the airline business. New firms seeking to enter the field of commercial aviation must secure certificates of convenience and necessity from the CAB. No new certificates for trunk-line operation have ever been issued.

By no means, however, has competition been entirely absent within the airline industry. The domestic trunk airlines compete with each other over many routes—often quite vigorously. When a new route promises to provide adequate traffic, several lines may seek CAB permission to serve it. The CAB is faced with difficult and intensely political problems as air traffic expands. In the first place, air traffic is almost all passenger traffic, and passenger traffic is greatest on a rather limited number of routes. The airlines naturally seek to serve these profitable routes. Since no route has enough traffic to make it profitable for all lines to serve it, the CAB limits the number of firms that can gain entry. Those lines denied access to choice routes and communities may thus come into severe conflict with CAB policy. Any policy limiting expansion of service would assist those firms already serving the major routes. The CAB for its part has had the obligation to protect the financial position of certificated lines. Hence, it has followed a conservative path in resisting proposals to enlarge service unless it was clear that the traffic justified the expansion. The CAB has also sought to strengthen the weaker companies whenever possible.

The task of the CAB has been made much easier by the extraordinary expansion in air travel. Passenger air-miles more than doubled between 1955 and 1963, and each year since has seen enormous growth. Airline earnings have been very strong in most cases. Only one trunk line has received any subsidy in recent years, and the majority of the feeder lines now operate without government help. Air travel rates have been reduced and the industry as a whole seems to be on a sound footing. Policy questions tend to center on such issues as expanding air service to smaller cities and enlarging airport facilities. To meet the latter problem federal assistance for airport construction has amounted to some $800 million in matching grants to state and local authorities since 1946, and air terminals are still almost as crowded as railroad stations are empty.

THE AMERICAN HIGHWAY SYSTEM

Although airplanes may be the most exciting aspect of the modern transportation revolution, the most significant development from the point of view of commercial transportation and nonmilitary governmental programs is the phenomenal rise of motor vehicle transport.

TABLE 5-3

Surfaced Road Mileage and Motor Vehicle Registration in the United States

	Surfaced road mileage	Motor vehicle registrations
1900	128,500	8,000
1920	369,122	9,239,161
1930	694,000	26,531,999
1940	1,367,000	32,035,424
1950	1,678,619	48,567,000
1958	2,083,108	71,502,000 (1959)
1963	2,252,647	86,297,000 (1964)

Sources: U.S. Department of Commerce, Bureau of the Census, *Historical Statistics of the United States, 1789–1945,* pp. 220–23; *Statistical Abstract of the United States: 1960,* pp. 550, 561; *Statistical Abstract of the United States, 1965,* p. 561.

The growth of the automotive industry and of the industries related to automobiles and trucks has wrought far-reaching changes throughout the economy and in the political and social system as well. The manifold effects of this development cannot all be considered here, but one area—highways—does deserve our concern. The direct clash of many of the transportation interests over proposed highway programs in recent years affords an opportunity to examine these forces in case-study fashion as they relate to an issue of the broadest social significance. The highway programs are important in their own right too, for they are of enormous size financially, involve all levels of government, and call into play values and interests ranging from reservation Indians (states containing reservations want the federal government to provide the whole cost of highways through the reservations) to national defense.

Development of American Highways

When the first automobiles appeared in the United States in the 1890s, the opportunities to drive them were severely limited. Although bicyclists had been trying to secure better roads, most of the roads outside the major cities were dirt tracks and even urban streets were often little more than mud. Long-distance transportation was almost inconceivable on these primitive roads; if motor vehicles were to have any future, highways had to be constructed for them. By 1900 many interest groups had begun to promote the cause of better highways.[23] The American Automobile Association, the American Road Builders Association, promoters of "named highway" projects like the Lincoln highway, and others built political support to "get the traffic out of the mud." Although from time to time ever since 1806 the federal government had provided funds for road construction, the principal responsibility had remained with the county or township. The roads were normally built either by citizens who thus worked off their road taxes or by convicts. State officials had begun to establish state highway programs with state administrative control by 1916, when the first major federal highway legislation was passed. The Federal Aid Act of 1916 authorized the expenditure of $75 million in those states possessing responsible highway departments. World War I temporarily checked the program but also dramatized the possibilities of motor transport.

The Federal Highway Act of 1921 set the basic pattern followed by federal programs until 1956. The Act provided that grants were to be distributed to states—one-third on the basis of population, one-third on the basis of area, and one-third on the basis of rural postal routes in the state. Each state was required to match the federal grant with its own funds and to submit to certain federally prescribed standards of operation. The Act also provided that a system of interstate and intercounty roads should be designated up to 7 per cent of the total road mileage which would serve as the focus for federal aid. In 1925 this focal system of arterial highways was narrowed to a total of 70,000 miles.

In 1944 a separate system was authorized to be referred to as the National System of Interstate Highways and not to exceed 40,000 miles (increased in 1956 to 41,000 miles). The routes of this latter system were to connect the principal metropolitan areas of the country and were to

[23] See F. L. Paxson, "The Highway Movement, 1916–1935," *American Historical Review*, LI (1946), 236–53.

receive a larger portion of their costs from the federal government. Also in 1944 federal aid was extended to urban extensions of routes receiving federal support in the rural areas. There are today four classifications of highways receiving federal aid; Interstate System, primary roads; secondary roads, and urban extensions. In addition, of course, states construct roads for which they receive no federal aid, as do counties and townships in some states. Cities are on their own so far as most of their street construction is concerned.

Highway finance. Throughout the first third of the twentieth century highway construction was expanded rapidly, and counties became utterly unable to finance the programs. Even at the state level, money from the property tax, the principal source of state and local income at that time, soon became scarce in the face of large capital expenditures for highways. At the national level the income tax was providing an ever greater share of the federal revenue and came predominantly from the eastern part of the country. Revenue for highway construction, however, was granted in larger proportion to the western states. Thus at both state and federal levels demands for new techniques to finance highways were heard, and the result was the gasoline tax, in most cases to be earmarked for highway construction purposes only. Through this tax the users of highways would provide the revenue to meet the costs of construction and maintenance, and the gasoline taxes imposed by federal and state governments have continued to be the principal source of revenue for highway purposes to this day.

Use of the gasoline tax and of other taxes imposed specifically on users of highways has not solved all the problems of highway finance, however. Most of the controversies that have developed in relation to highway problems in recent years have revolved around questions of finance. No one has successfully challenged the ever-increasing demand for highway construction and modernization as the traffic has grown; but how these highways are to be paid for has remained an area of disagreement. Truckers urgently want more and better highways but hope to avoid taxes that would bear especially upon them. Private motoring groups like the AAA also want an expanded highway program but hope to shift more of the financial burden onto the commercial vehicles which, because of their greater weight, account for a larger proportion of wear on the roads and necessitate heavier construction. Railroads and other competing groups seek to equalize what they consider to be an unfair advantage possessed by motor vehicles in not paying the full costs of their roads, and therefore ask higher taxes on trucks and buses. Farmers want to avoid paying taxes on gasoline used on the farm, and taxi drivers likewise oppose being taxed for the purpose of building highways they seldom see. Although some groups have argued that highway programs are so vital to national defense that part of their costs should be attributed to defense programs and paid for out of general revenue, this view has not so far been persuasive and financing highways from taxes on highway users has remained the basic principle. The only large-scale exception occurred during the Great Depression when highway projects were often built as relief measures to provide employment.

Although finance is central, many groups are interested in other aspects of the highway programs. Many farmers are disturbed, for example, by the shift in the emphasis of federal programs to construction of intercity routes and away from secondary and "farm-to-market" roads. There have been disputes between construction firms and labor groups over whether the prevailing wages of the area would have to be paid on highway projects. In the past, firms have sometimes imported workers to a high wage area to cut their costs, and labor groups tried successfully in 1956 to make sure that did not happen in the highway program. Proposals to increase taxes on the sale of trucks and buses and to tax rubber tires and retread rubber stimulated the affected groups to action. Problems of administrative organization—for example, whether to have state or federal officials determine the prevailing wage rates in each state—were matters of concern not only to the economic groups with stakes in the issue, but also to the affected bureaucracies. All these groups actively tried to shape the course of legislation respecting highways with varying degrees of success, and their activities provided a broad panorama of politics at work.

The Interstate System. During World War II, highway construction in the United States came to a virtual standstill while, at the same time, there was substantial wear and tear on highways, especially from military vehicles. When the war ended, the automobile population expanded rapidly, and the new cars moved at speeds that often made the old roads altogether inadequate. The financial problems of railroads, of which we have spoken, helped stimulate the shift to trucks as means of commercial transportation. The net result was a substantial demand for repair and modernization of old roads and construction of new high-speed arterial highways to handle the new traffic. Congress responded to these demands by authorizing $2.4 billion in total federal aid between 1948 and 1954. The biennial authorizations increased each two years of this period from $450 million to $875 million with an ever greater proportion being devoted to the interstate, metropolis-to-metropolis network. Despite these efforts the needs grew more rapidly than the appropriations, and from various sources proposals were made for long-range and massive efforts to overtake and get ahead of the highway demands.

Many states sought to meet the new demands by building toll roads. Following the prewar example of Pennsylvania, states issued bonds to be paid by the tolls received for use of the high speed, limited access superhighways over major long-distance routes. Through bond financing, these roads could be built in addition to those financed through gasoline taxes.

Motorists, especially long-distance truckers, received substantial savings in time and gasoline consumption. Some states found, however, that traffic on the new roads did not always provide toll revenue adequate to pay for the bonds, and problems of connecting toll routes for interstate travel were not always solved. As late as 1957, for example, the Kansas turnpike still ended in an Oklahoma farmer's field.

In 1954, both Congress and the President began to study the possibilities of a long-term multi-billion dollar highway program to be financed primarily by the federal government to meet the needs of arterial highways. In early 1955, President Eisenhower released the report of his Advisory Committee, which called for a program by all levels of government to cost $101 billion over ten years. Of this total, $27 billion was to be spent on the National System of Interstate Highways, $25 billion to come from the federal government and be financed through bonds issued outside the regular debt structure of the federal government. These bonds would be retired out of general revenue of future years. The Committee estimated that, with traffic continuing to increase and tax revenues from highway users also increasing, revenue would be adequate to pay off the bonds without raising taxes. The bond approach, however, would cost some $12 billion in interest charges during the life of the bonds. Many groups vigorously opposed the bond issue proposal, among them the American Automobile Association and the Association of American Railroads, although the American Trucking Association supported the proposal. Many congressional leaders argued that highways should be financed by increased user taxes and began to push in that direction.

One element of conflict in the situation involved competition between the political party groups in Congress as each tried to secure whatever advantages there might be in the highway programs. Senate Democrats sponsored a bill which finally passed the Senate providing for a five-year $12.25 billion program and preserving more of the traditional emphasis on primary and secondary roads than did the Administration plan. In the House, alternatives to the bond issue approach to financing were developed, and higher taxes were proposed bearing particularly heavily on the things used by trucks, such as diesel fuel and truck tires, rather than on things used by automobiles. The AAA and AAR supported these proposals, but the truckers and rubber manufacturers (and the American Farm Bureau Federation, which opposed any extension of the federal program) opposed the tax increases.

In 1956 the Administration agreed to accept the "pay-as-you-go" principle insisted upon by most Democrats. The proposed tax increases were scaled down somewhat as they affected trucks and buses, and the American Trucking Association supported the new bill. The AAA and the AAR continued to try to place a greater share of the costs of the program on the truckers, but the disagreements had been moderated sufficiently so that while many groups remained only partially satisfied, the bill finally passed without significant opposition.

The Federal-Aid Highway Act of 1956 authorized the largest roadbuilding program in American history. $31.5 billion were to be spent over a thirteen-year period of which nearly $27 billion were to come from the federal treasury. Primary and secondary roads and urban extensions of these roads received increased assistance matched in each case by the states affected. Roads through national parks, public lands, and Indian reservations, for which the federal government traditionally has taken responsibility, were allotted increased sums. The bulk of the funds, however—eventually close to $40 billion—was to be devoted to the Interstate System. The federal government pays approximately 90 per cent of the costs of this part of the program, and states are given credit for toll roads that fit into the system. The money for the Interstate System is apportioned among the states more in accordance with population than the other programs have been, which means that urban industrial areas receive greater benefits and farm groups fewer benefits than they have from past highway programs.

To provide revenue for the program, increased taxes were levied on gasoline and tires, and some special taxes were imposed on trucks and buses. These were increased still further in subsequent years, partly to boost the share to be paid by the truckers and partly to provide more cash for the program. The completion date for the Interstate System is 1972, but even as the new roads take shape other transportation problems demand attention.

Highway beautification. Beginning in 1958 Congress provided additional highway money to those states that prohibited the erection of billboards along the right-of-way of interstate system roads. The action added an additional dimension of conflict to highway politics, since many motels, restaurants and outdoor advertising firms strongly opposed the restriction. Most states eventually have accepted the restraint in order to receive the extra funds.

In 1965 the campaign against commercial defacement of the landscape was broadened with the passage of the Highway Beautification Act. Under its terms federal funds were made available for scenic improvement of highways, and in addition, the states were required to keep such eyesores as junkyards from offending the motorist's eye or suffer the loss of 10 per cent of their federal highway money.

Mass transportation. In a more and more urban society the most severe transportation problems have come to be those of moving about within the city. A substantial part of the Interstate System budget has gone to provide the urban portions of the new arterial highways. At the same time, however, local traffic and transit difficulties have continued to grow. Private automobiles choke the city streets, and mass transit systems— buses, streetcars, subways, and commuter trains—have lost riders and money at increasing rates. In 1964 Congress approved an Urban Mass Transportation Act to assist local communities in finding solutions. City governments, transit companies and suppliers, and commuter lines supported the effort; fiscal conservatives opposed it; highway interests remained neutral. The program authorized $375 million in grants and loans, but with San Francisco's new transit system alone costing almost three times this amount, the sum will not go very far. In any case, although there have been interesting experiments in new transit systems, few observers are confident that any final solutions yet exist for the transportation needs of the metropolis.

BIBLIOGRAPHICAL NOTE

Nearly all major areas of public policy that have received national legislative attention since World War II are treated with careful attention and full detail in Congressional Quarterly Service, *Congress and the Nation, 1945–1964*. Transportation policy is reviewed on pp. 517–61.

Full-scale treatments of transportation development and current problems may be found in Philip D. Locklin, *Economics of Transportation*, 5th ed., 1960; Russell E. Westmeyer, *Economics of Transportation*, 1952; Marvin Fair and Ernest Williams, *Economics of Transportation*, rev. ed., 1959; and Charles L. Dearing and Wilfred Owen, *National Transportation Policy*, 1949. Each of these volumes deals with the economic aspects of transportation and includes discussion of the historical development of public policy in this field. James C. Nelson, *Railroad Transportation and Public Policy*, 1959, and Ernest Williams, *The Regulation of Rail-Motor Rate Competition*, 1958, are very useful. Walter Adams, "The Role of Competition in the Regulated Industries," *American Economic Review*, XLVIII (1958), 527–43, stresses the desirability of greater competition in transportation. See also the symposium, "Transportation: Part I," in *Law and Contemporary Problems*, XXIV (1959), 529–732.

Few systematic studies of the organized interest groups active in transportation politics are available, but John G. Schott, *The Transportation Monopoly*, 1944; Arne C. Wiprud, *Justice in Transportation*, 1945; and Senate Report No. 26, pt. 2, 77th Congress, 1st Session (1941) contain valuable information about railroad groups. A number of recent congressional investigations have been revealing with regard to transportation interests.

Most general studies of transportation concentrate attention on the railroad industry. Students desiring more data about other transport industries may consult Charles A. Taff, *Commercial Motor Transportation*, 1952; G. E. Hale and Rosemary D. Hale, "Competition or Control IV: Air Carriers," *University of Pennsylvania Law Review*, CIX (1961), 311–360; and Richard E. Caves, *Air Transport and Its Regulators*, 1962.

The Interstate Commission is the subject of I. L. Scharfman's authoritative *The Interstate Commerce Commission* in four volumes, 1931–1935. A more recent analysis that emphasizes the ICC's relationship with the carriers it controls is Samuel Huntington, "The Marasmus of the ICC," *Yale Law Journal*, LXI (1952), 467–509. See also the discussion of Huntington's findings in *Yale Law Journal*, LXII (1953), 171–226, 561–74 and LXIII (1953), 44–63.

A brief but valuable history of the early years of highway development in the United States may be found in F. L. Paxson, "The Highway Movement, 1916–1935," *American Historical Review*, LI (1946), 236–53.

A thorough discussion of highway policy and politics is Philip H. Burch, *Highway Revenue and Expenditure Policy in the United States*, 1962. See also the valuable essay by Robert S. Friedman, "State Politics and Highways," in Herbert Jacob and Kenneth Vines, ed., *Politics in the American States*, pp. 411–46, 1965. Wilfred Owen examines mass transit in *The Metropolitan Transportation Problem*, 1965.

agriculture and natural resources

ROBERT H. SALISBURY

To understand the political climate within which American agricultural policy has been made, we must understand first the *ideology* surrounding farming in this country. At least since the days of Thomas Jefferson, when small farmers were beginning to look on manufacturers and merchants as economic and political enemies, farming has been vested by writers, newspapers, political orators, and farmers themselves with special qualities— qualities that made it right and desirable for government to protect farmers against those who would take advantage of them. Three broad themes run through this type of argument.

First, agriculture is regarded as logically prior to any other economic activity. All of us must eat before we do anything else. Farming is thus indispensable to the welfare of all, and if farmers are not given a "fair share" of material rewards then governmental action should correct the situation and place agriculture—the "first industry"—on a par with other occupational groups. Then too, farming is harder work and often less rewarding in a material way than work in most other fields. No eight-hour day, no minimum wage, no plush offices are available to the farmer. He rises before dawn, works fiercely all day, is isolated from his fellows, enjoys fewer of the comforts of urban life, faces myriad perils from nature, and gets relatively small cash rewards for his efforts. Moreover, his income is uncertain. Not only do the fluctuations in market prices and farming costs plague him, but a hailstorm at a critical time may destroy a year's crop and with it a year's income. Third, there is a strong strain in the talking and writing about American agriculture to the effect that farmers are better, more virtuous people than city dwellers. The city is the center of high crime rates and generally sinful activities—or, at the least, is filled with smoke and traffic. In the country, on the other hand, the air is pure, the grass is green, and man is part of nature's life-giving processes. For this reason too, then, farmers and farming deserve a preferred place at the hands of governmental authority.

The situation with natural resources is somewhat different. For most of our history the problem of resources was largely ignored; we had more resources than we needed, and in any event there was nothing that government need do, except see that the resources were handed out in a more or less equitable fashion. During this century, however, especially as a result of President Theodore Roosevelt's keen interest in the West, conservation of natural resources has become a major public responsibility at all levels of government. In addition, however, resources are to be *used* and a variety of interests compete for control of resource use. Both agricultural and resource policy are thus objects of intense political activity, and it is this dimension of the questions with which we shall be chiefly concerned.

FARM POLICY: ECONOMIC AND POLITICAL BACKGROUND

Farming is not only a way of life, it is a business. And admirable as the *way of life* may be, the *business* of farming has presented serious problems for decades. In the days when the pioneers settled the frontier and until after the Civil War, many farmers engaged in what was basically subsistence agriculture. They raised the food and fibers necessary to feed, clothe, and house their families, selling or bartering only enough to secure commodities, such as salt or calico cloth, that they could not supply themselves. Particularly in the Midwest of this period, where few people lived in cities, very little commercial agriculture took place.

The Agricultural Revolution

The coming of mechanization to farming, however, changed this pattern drastically. With a reaper and later with a combine, one man could harvest a wheat crop that formerly had required many men. Gang plows, improved seed, and other technological improvements made it possible for a farmer to raise enough crops not only to feed himself and his family but to sell in substantial quantities as well. To buy the new machinery the farmer needed cash, and by selling in the market a farmer could get cash. Farming on a cash basis meant that farmers would specialize, raising those crops that gave them the greatest returns in their climate and soil, rather than trying to raise all the needs of the family. By specializing and using machinery the productivity of the farmer increased, and with the cash received from selling his increased output a farmer could begin to buy not only machinery and the necessities he formerly had raised himself but also some of the comforts previously enjoyed by his city cousins. Thus today electric freezers, automobiles, and television sets are bought by farmers from the proceeds of commercial cash agriculture—radically different from subsistence agriculture.

Cash farming brought many advantages to farmers, but it also posed many problems—problems that have provided the basis for most issues of modern agricultural politics. First and foremost, cash farming made farmers dependent on markets: markets in which their products were sold and where the object was to secure the highest possible price, and markets where farmers bought at the lowest possible price the machinery and other products they now needed. In order for cash farming to be profitable, farmers had to secure more for the things they sold than they paid out for the things they bought; in the late nineteenth century, when cash farming really took hold, this did not always happen. For one thing, the markets in which farmers sold their products were distant. To reach them, transportation, usually by rail, was necessary, and thus farmers became dependent on railroads. Moreover, some markets were "rigged" by grain speculators or meat packers who on occasion conspired to hold down prices paid to the unorganized farmers. Even in an honest market, no individual farmer's product would be required to provide the needed supply of a commodity. The small number of flour mills or meat packers who bought from the farmers could often quite easily and legitimately play off one solitary small farmer against another. Nor could the farmer afford to wait until the price went up next year. His crop might spoil if it was not quickly sold or stored. The packer or miller, on the other hand, could wait. The tendency was strong, therefore, for farmers to operate at a disadvantage in selling their products.

At the same time, in the markets where farmers bought the things they needed, the manufacturers of farm machinery comprised one of the early trusts, and many other industries supplying farmers with indispensable commodities were few in number and highly organized. Again the solitary farmer was at a disadvantage. No manufacturer needed the custom of any specific farmer, yet no specific farmer could do without the manufacturer's product. Thus in selling and buying alike the farmer had less bargaining power than those with whom he had to deal.

A further problem was presented by the very fact of the farmer's increasing productivity. As machinery and technique improved, farmers could produce more and more. But an increasing output of a product will not bring the producer more income unless the demand for the product also increases. An expanding population in the United States meant more mouths to feed, of course, but farm productivity increased more rapidly than the population. Up to a point, as people earn more income they buy more food, so that as per capita income rose so did consumption of farm products. But as income rises a smaller and smaller proportion of income goes for food, and more money is spent instead on services, appliances, and luxuries. Farm costs have risen faster than income, so that during the 1950s alone the net income from farming fell from 42 per cent of the *gross* income to 31 per cent. The result of these tendencies has been that as the economy has expanded the farm sector has occupied a less important place and has secured a smaller proportion of the national income.

In the face of the higher incomes available from industrial work, a steady stream of farmers has left agriculture and moved to the city. In recent years the farm population has not only suffered a relative loss of numbers but actually is smaller than formerly. Those who remain work much larger farms (doubled in size since 1940), employ a huge investment in land and equipment (seven times larger than 1940), stress ever more scientific agriculture and steadily improve their productivity. Fewer farmers grow more food on less land than ever before. Nevertheless, they have been confronted over and over with the specter of falling prices and incomes.

T A B L E 6 - 1

The Decline of American Agriculture

Percentage of total national income going to farmers		Percentage of U.S. population living on farms	
1869–1879	20.5	1910	34.9
1899–1908	16.7	1920	30.1
1919–1928	12.2	1930	24.9
1933	8.9	1940	23.2
1940	7.4	1950	15.3
1950	6.9	1959	9.4
1959	2.9	1964	6.8
1964	2.3		

Sources: *Historical Statistics of the United States* and *Statistical Abstract of the United States: 1965.*

Difficulties in planning farm production also affect prices. A farmer plants a crop or breeds his livestock long in advance of the actual sale and must guess at the probable future price. If he guesses wrong and the price is below his expectation, he must salvage what he can by selling a larger volume of goods. The tendency is for each farmer to produce as much as possible. But if all farmers produce to the maximum, the supply will be so great that the bottom will fall out of the market price. Education and information on the nature and probable future state of the market can alleviate somewhat his tendency to overproduce, and the U.S. Department of Agriculture and state agriculture colleges carry out work of this kind.

But even so, without some sort of disciplined control, whether private or governmental, American farmers today tend to produce more than can be sold at prices that are satisfactory to them. The main exception to this rule has occurred during the three war periods of the twentieth century. During each period, foreign production declined and American demand increased, with the result that farm prices improved substantially.

The facts of farming as a business differ greatly from the values often expressed by those who extoll farming as a way of life. As a group in society, farmers are declining in numbers both relative to the rest of the population and absolutely. The economic strength of the farm sector of the economy likewise has been steadily reduced; virtually every other major industry has grown more rapidly than agriculture. The very productivity achieved through use of machinery and scientific techniques of farming often compounds the problems of securing adequate income. This situation did not develop all at once, of course. It has, however, been the dominant tendency since the permanent full scale shift to cash farming during and after the Civil War.

The Political Representation of Farmers

The economic and numerical decline of agriculture in American society has occurred in the context of the American political system, which has generally given to rural people political strength greater than their numbers alone would justify. In the United States Senate, a predominantly rural state with a small population like North Dakota has the same voting strength as a heavily populated, mainly urban state like New York. In the House of Representatives, seats are allotted to each state primarily on the basis of population, but House districts are drawn by state legislatures, and state legislatures in almost every state have over-represented rural interests. Thus even in the House, farmers have had a louder voice than mere numbers or economic strength would give them. Trying to recoup in the governmental arena the ground lost in the economy, farmers since the Civil War have often made political responses to economic adversity. The growth of large metropolitan centers in so many states, however, has made most Senators increasingly responsive to urban interests. The Supreme Court decisions requiring every state legislature to be apportioned on the basis of population are further reducing the political advantage of farm groups, and these changes will have profound effect on the processes and purposes of farmers in politics.

Early Governmental Programs for Agriculture

The early attempts to organize discontented farmers for purposes of recovering their power were quite differently focused than those of the more contemporary era. The Granger movement of the late 1860s and early '70s, the Farmers' Alliance, and the Populist Party were three important organizations drawing most of their strength from agricultural interests. The Populists, of course, organized as a party rather than a specifically agricultural interest group, but the main themes of all three organizations and of others during the latter nineteenth century were similar. The political program was twofold: 1) break up the trusts and combines of the business world through antitrust proceedings, and 2) regulate the rates charged by public-utility type enterprises. The image of the business firms with which farmers had to deal was one of conspiracy and monopoly, and the public policy goal was to control these monopolies through governmental authority. The image of business conspiracy was mingled with the image of agrarian independent and individualist virtue. These appeals continue to be heard in the rhetoric of agricultural debate. The policy objectives of farm organizations, however, have changed substantially. Antitrust action still receives support from farm groups, and the most consistent opponents of railroad rate increases have been the several agricultural organizations. But the main theme of farmer demands since World War I has been for direct governmental support of farm prices and income.

Although it took several decades to become fully operative, the idea early gained currency that the answer to the problem of declining farm prices was to increase those prices rather than try to decrease the prices of other commodities through antitrust and regulation. The first major step in this direction was the establishment of agricultural education and service agencies designed to teach farmers how to improve their methods, get bigger yields, and earn larger profits. Three major types of activity were undertaken in this direction and all three continue to provide important services today. In 1862 the federal government established an agency which later became the Department of Agriculture "to acquire and diffuse useful information on agricultural subjects." The Department confined itself to distributing free seeds and other similarly marginal functions for many years after its establishment. But beginning about 1900 the research and service functions of the Department were expanded until today over 70,000 employees supervise the expenditure of sums in the neighborhood of $2 billion.

In 1862 a second approach to raising farm standards of living was taken with the passage of the Morrill Act, which provided grants of public lands to endow colleges "for the benefit of agriculture and the mechanic arts." These colleges, in most instances, became far more than simply centers of agricultural research and training, but the latter have remained central functions. The agricultural colleges have continued as an important element in the structure of agricultural politics, and as such will be further treated below. Suffice to say, for the moment, that they represent the attempt to educate farmers to higher income.

The service and education efforts were supplemented shortly after 1900 by the development of the extension program. Extension was in one sense simply bringing education and research directly to farmers through face-to-face demonstration and training. This field education came to have more profound significance, however, with the organization and expansion of the extension program, which was financed after 1914 partly by federal funds, partly by state governments, and partly by private groups of farmers and businessmen. Extension became a focal point for organizing the more prosperous farmers who tended to be more receptive to demonstrations of new techniques. To some degree the emphasis on education, research, and extension programs as means of increasing rural prosperity has meant less support for direct programs of price support and production control. Accordingly, those commercial farmers not so clearly benefited by price support programs have emphasized education and research programs.

Direct Support for Farmers

All the major farm organizations have sought more direct governmental assistance, however. The "golden years" for farm prices, 1909–1914, were followed by the heavy demands and high prices of World War I, but, following the war, demand collapsed and so did prices. Throughout the 1920s, farm prices remained relatively low despite the prosperity of other sectors of the economy. During this period the American Farm Bureau Federation rose to prominence and power in farm politics and along with the older Grange began to seek various programs that would raise domestic prices. A number of proposals were made, through the "Farm Bloc" in Congress, and two versions of the McNary-Haugen bill were passed by Congress, only to be vetoed by President Coolidge.

The McNary-Haugen bills and several other proposals of the period were based on a generally accepted control device, the tariff. The idea was to "make the tariff work" through a "two-price" plan. Farm products were to be purchased by the federal government in quantities sufficient to raise the domestic United States price to acceptable levels. The stocks so purchased would be sold abroad at the presumably lower world price and the losses recouped by some type of equalization fee subtracted from the supported United States price.

McNary-Haugenism never was put to the test of operation, but the establishment of the Federal Farm Board in 1929 attempted a similar program without the foreign trade features. The Federal Farm Board was endowed with a revolving fund of $500 million, which was to support cooperative marketing associations. The associations were to stabilize farm prices by buying when prices were low and selling when prices were high.

The Board stepped in to buy large quantities of cotton and wheat as well as several other commodities. By 1931 the combination of general depression and a bumper crop resulted in huge surpluses, and the Board ceased operation after losing nearly $400 million.

The lessons of the Federal Farm Board failure were clear by the time the Roosevelt Administration took office in 1933. Price support programs could not succeed in raising price levels for farm products unless one of two other situations obtained; either demand increased or production declined. General depression and a relatively inelastic demand for farm products meant that in many cases production would have to be reduced in order to achieve price increases. Since farmers normally tended to increase production in the face of falling prices, and especially did so when the Farm Board would purchase the increase at artificially high levels, the inescapable conclusion was that governmental policy would have to include provisions to curtail production. The first Agricultural Adjustment Act of 1933, therefore, provided that the Secretary of Agriculture could contract to make payments to farmers in return for reducing acreage or for raising less livestock. Money for the payments was to come from a tax levied upon processors of basic farm commodities such as cotton ginners, meat packers, and flour millers. Cotton, tobacco, and potato production control was soon made mandatory for all growers if controls were accepted by two-thirds of the growers in referendum vote.

In 1936 this legislative program was declared unconstitutional by the Supreme Court on the grounds that the tax on processors benefited special interests rather than the general welfare and that the control of agricultural production was a state concern beyond the legitimate authority of Congress.[1] Congress quickly restored federal assistance to farmers by offering payments in return for taking land out of production of soil-depleting crops and for following other conservation practices. The object was to provide additional farm income under the guise of conservation, and crops designated soil-depleting were in fact those in excess supply.

In 1938 Congress passed new basic farm legislation restoring the policy of supporting agricultural prices and of providing for production controls when necessary. The processor tax was eliminated and the post-1937 Supreme Court—now a "liberalized court"—sustained the legislation as a legitimate regulation of interstate commerce.[2] The 1938 law established the basic elements of agriculture policy which continue in present-day legislation, and these will be discussed primarily as they are currently in operation.

---

[1] *U.S. v. Butler*, 297 U.S. 1 (1936).

[2] *Mulford v. Smith*, 307 U.S. 38 (1939); *Wickard v. Fiburn*, 317 U.S. 111 (1942).

The primary objective of the farm programs of the last several decades has been to increase farmer income. Without some means of controlling production, however, no price support program could operate except by incurring astronomical cost and collecting mountainous surpluses. We have seen that the 1933 AAA offered farmers payments designed to raise their income in return for taking land out of production, and that under the conservation label the 1936 legislation did likewise. Since 1938 there have been three principal ways by which the problem of production control has been approached: flexible price supports, acreage allotments, and marketing quotas. When the price support levels are permitted by law to vary, the Secretary of Agriculture may lower supports whenever it appears that there will be an oversupply of a commodity. It is hoped that the lower support price will encourage farmers to plant other crops instead. However, many farmers may be unable to grow other crops and may instead increase production so as to receive equivalent income at the lower per bushel price. Consequently, in the short run, although high support levels usually will encourage increased production of a commodity (and were used for this purpose during the war periods), low support levels may not result in decreased production.

In the light of this situation Congress has authorized the Secretary of Agriculture to call for referendum votes by growers of a commodity that promises to be in oversupply. If the growers approve by a two-thirds majority, they will be limited in the number of acres they may plant or in the amount they may market. The alternative to this production control is to accept a substantial reduction in the price support level. Farmers have usually voted to accept the controls, and when they do, a farmer who exceeds his acreage allotment is subject to fines and is ineligible for CCC loans. Acreage allotments are allocated by the Secretary of Agriculture and broken down by states, counties, and finally, by individual farms. At the local level they are administered by Agricultural Stabilization and Conservation committees elected by the farmers.

The acreage allotment system does not always achieve the desired reduction in output, however. A farmer may use fertilizer and other means to increase his per acre yield, or in some cases, he may take land out of production of one surplus crop but devote it to another. For some crops there are exemptions from controls for small producers. Moreover, Congress has provided minimum levels below which total acreage cannot be cut. As a result, for several of the basic crops the existing production controls have often been ineffective in achieving the twin objectives of eliminating surpluses and supporting farm income.

Other techniques have been tried to cut production with minimum damage to farmers. One particularly controversial one was the Soil Bank program passed in 1956. Leaders of both parties disputed this program bitterly at the time of its adoption, as each party sought to secure whatever electoral advantage might accrue to the sponsor. Under this program farmers would retire part of their acreage allotments in return for payments giving them a substantial portion of what they would have received had the acres been cultivated. In some cases, farmers were directed to engage in soil conservation practices on the retired acres. Sometimes whole farms were taken out of production. The program soon acquired a bad reputation, however, even among farm programs. Farmers often put their worst acres in the "bank," and some money was allegedly used in areas where the maximum vote yield was anticipated. Several hundred million dollars were spent without much apparent effect on surpluses, and the program was allowed to lapse in 1960. Variations on the same theme are still extensively used, however. Additional payments, called *diversion payments*, are given to growers of several of the basic crops who agree to cut their allotted acreage by an additional 20–50 per cent. Indeed, under present programs many farmers cannot qualify for the full value of the price support programs without divesting some of their acreage. Still more stringent controls are imposed on the production of certain commodities in the form of *marketing orders*. A wide variety of commodities—specialty crops such as fruits, fluid milk, and other items not readily stored for any length of time—are brought to market only under strict quantity control. Unless the farmer has a quota, for example, he cannot market milk in most parts of the country. Marketing quotas very effectively lead the farmer to curtail his production, and they have been more widely used in recent years. The great field crops—the so-called "basics"—rely on less stringent methods, however.

Parity and Price Supports

The standard against which farm prices, incomes, and policy arguments are measured is that of *parity*. Parity is a relationship—a relationship between the prices farmers pay for the things they buy and the prices farmers receive for the things they sell. Parity is not, of course, just any relationship between prices received and prices paid. It is rather an ideal relationship based on some period in the past. Until 1948 the base period—the ideal relationship—was 1909–1914, when farmers had enjoyed their greatest peacetime prosperity in this century. Thus a program guaranteeing full, or 100 per cent parity would mean that farmers would be assured prices for their products sufficient to give them buying power equivalent to the buying power of 1909–1914. If the prices of things farmers buy have doubled, then farm products should also bring twice the return.

Beginning in 1948, a "modernized" parity formula was introduced, though it did not become the mandatory formula until 1957. "Modernized" parity is figured by calculating the average price received by farmers for each commodity over the previous ten years, making certain adjustments to take account of changes in demand for various agricultural products, and then relating this figure to prices farmers pay for some 350 items. The resultant "adjusted base price" is then related to the 1909–1914 base to get the parity price. "Modernized" parity results in lower parity prices for many commodities, especially wheat and feed grains, while giving higher returns on such products as livestock.

Many Republicans have joined the American Farm Bureau Federation in proposing that the historic base period be eliminated entirely in calculating parity. Instead, support levels would be set at 90 per cent of the average price of the commodity for the most recent three years. Each year the base period would be moved up one year, and in this way, farmers would be protected against sudden fluctuations in their prices, but the level of supports would more closely approximate the free market price.

Full parity would mean full equality of purchasing power per bushel of corn or per bale of cotton with that of the base period. Actual legislative protection has not normally provided 100 per cent of parity. The 1938 legislation authorized price supports at from 52 to 75 per cent of parity; supports being pegged higher when supplies fell and lower when production increased. During the war period farm prices rose well above 100 per cent of parity, and the OPA was forbidden to put ceilings on farm prices until they reached 110 per cent of parity. When price controls were removed in 1946, farm prices rose still further to 115 per cent in 1947. From 1942 to 1955 Congress required prices to be supported at no lower than 90 per cent. During the war years farm prices were considerably higher than that, but price supports were used to encourage farmers to plant crops that were especially needed for the war effort. The Acts of 1948 and 1949 provided that price supports should range between 60 per cent (1948) or 75 per cent (1949) and 90 per cent of parity, depending on whether supplies were large or small. However, the application of this flexible principle was postponed several times and did not go into operation until 1955 and then only after a considerable struggle. Minimum support levels for such crops as wheat, corn, cotton and rice are now set at 65 per cent of parity, though, in fact, support prices have generally been somewhat higher.

Farm policy discussion has centered mainly around the so-called *basic* commodities. This group of major crops includes wheat, corn, cotton, tobacco, rice, and peanuts. Many other commodities are supported, however, when it appears likely that prices will be too low. Livestock, butter, and a long list of other products may be supported within the broad limits prescribed by Congress. The price at which each commodity will be supported is determined separately by the Secretary of Agriculture on the basis of the anticipated production and expected demand. Generally, the greater the expected supply in relation to demand, the lower the support price.

The principal mechanism by which prices are supported centers around the Commodity Credit Corporation. When the Secretary of Agriculture announces the support level for a crop, usually prior to planting time, this means that the Commodity Credit Corporation stands ready to grant what are called nonrecourse loans at the announced level. If the support level for corn is $1 per bushel, then, if the market price at the time of harvest is below $1, farmers may place their crop in storage and get a loan from the CCC of $1 per bushel. If at any time during the next year the market price exceeds $1, the farmer may redeem his loan and sell his crop. If, however, market prices remain below support prices, at the end of the year the CCC takes full possession, and the farmer keeps the loan money. It is in this latter case that surpluses are accumulated.

Under recent Democratic administrations a number of different approaches have been combined in various ways in an effort to give farmers income protection without accumulating surpluses. Such crops as wheat and cotton are sold, in part, on the world market. In order to make American wheat more competitive, growers now are governed by a kind of two-price plan, selling their "domestic" wheat at one price and their export wheat at another, lower, level. The over-all wheat price is satisfactory and, since the export crop is larger, surpluses are smaller. In cotton the same result is obtained by paying the grower in cash in order that he may sell to American cotton mills at the world price and still come out on top. In other crops, too, a bewildering variety of mixtures now exists with marketing orders, acreage allotments, diversion payments, income support payments, price support loans, and still other elements employed to meet the particular problems of each crop and each special group of farmers.

Surplus Disposal

Many commentators on the farm problem argue that the heart of the difficulty is the depressing effect of the existing stockpile of surpluses, and if these could be liquidated without damaging the present price structure, a free market for agriculture would again be feasible. In any case, the cost of storing the surpluses is a massive drain on the economy. The commodities in storage bins and warehouses cost nearly $1 billion a year just for storage.

A number of programs have been developed to attempt to use the surpluses in ways that will not hurt the farmers' market price. Among these are such welfare-oriented programs as the distribution of food for school lunches, unemployed persons, disaster-stricken areas, and welfare agencies. The most dramatic surplus disposal program, and practically the only farm-related program which all farm groups support enthusiastically, is Public

Law 480, the Agricultural Trade Development and Assistance Act of 1954. The main feature of this program is that the federal government sells surplus farm products overseas for foreign currencies which, in turn, are used in various foreign aid programs. The cost of this program was over $1 billion in 1960, but the international benefits are significant enough to draw the support of all interested groups. The only major problem arises when the sale of U.S. surpluses interferes with regular commercial sales from other countries, as occasionally happens. But however extensive the surplus disposal programs may seem, they have not gone very far toward eliminating the surplus problem.

The future for American farmers may be brighter than the recent past, however. Both at home and especially abroad the population explosion is an imposing fact. There are signs that American agriculture has shrunk enough to reach a tolerable balance with domestic demand for food and fiber, and the developing areas of the world look to the U.S. for help in developing more productive systems of agriculture. Thus the "farm problem" may again turn into a national asset.

Special Services

Although most political attention is devoted to issues involved in protecting farm prices, it should be noted that many other governmental programs provide services to farmers. The Federal Crop Insurance Corporation, the Rural Electrification Administration, The Extension Service, the Soil Conservation Service, the Farm Credit Administration, and the Farmers Home Administration provide credit, advice, information, and other benefits to enable farmers to operate more successfully. Some of the programs are, or have been, the subjects of considerable political struggle, but generally today they are only on the fringes of the main controversies.

THE POLITICS OF AGRICULTURE

Traditionally, farmers have been looked upon as a single homogeneous group, united in its interests and demands. The "Farm Bloc" has often been cited as the classic example of an interest group pursuing self-oriented policy objectives and appealing to whatever legislators or party leaders would help them. The "Farm Bloc" of the early 1920s secured the passage of a number of bills through the support of a bipartisan group of midwestern Republicans and southern Democrats. This coalition embraced the major commodity groups in agriculture and was led by the American Farm Bureau Federation. Much the same grouping continued to dominate farm policy-making throughout the New Deal period also. Whatever validity this conception may once have had, however, it bears little resemblance to the realities of farm politics as they have existed for more than a decade. Contemporary farm policy issues can only be understood in the light of conflicting interests and competing groups of farmers and their nonfarming allies.

The Commodity Bases

Farmers vary widely in the size of their farms, their investment, their education and background, and their income, but the most significant basis for political division is the fact that farmers grow many different crops. The conditions under which one crop is grown and marketed are often much different from another, and in many cases farmers growing different crops, or the same crop in different parts of the country, have directly conflicting interests. The dairy farmer producing butter competes to some extent with the cotton or soybean grower since the oils of the latter crops are used in margarine. The cotton grower in Georgia competes with cotton growers on irrigated land in California, and the two seek different farm policies. A fruit grower may care nothing at all about price support programs while a grain processor may care a great deal and participate actively in the policy struggle.

The diversity and range of specialized agricultural interests, some compatible and some conflicting, are immense and increasing all the time as farmers become more and more mechanized and scientific. Traditionally, the three largest commodity groups have been the growers of wheat, corn, and cotton. Two main types of wheat are grown in the United States: spring wheat is raised mainly in the upper Great Plains states, winter wheat grows mainly in the lower Great Plains. Other regions, such as the Pacific Northwest, also produce wheat, and many farmers elsewhere grow some wheat. Politically, though the "wheat states" are mainly the plains states, especially Kansas and the Dakotas. The geography of wheat growing is important, for the plains states are located in a marginal rainfall belt. That is, the adequacy of rainfall is always uncertain, and drought is an ever present possibility. This, in turn, means that while some years may produce bumper crops, others may produce little at all. Moreover, technological development has had enormous impact on wheat farmers. The broad flat fields of wheat are ideally suited to mechanical harvesting, resulting in greater productivity of wheat farmers, who by increasing the supply of wheat create a downward pressure on price, unless increased demand for wheat makes up the difference. But demand for wheat, especially American wheat, has not increased with production. When income levels rise generally, as they have in recent years in the United States, people eat less bread and cereal and more meat, vegetables, fruit, and dairy products. Prosperity for the economy as a whole does not, therefore, mean prosperity for wheat farmers. Finally, the United States has long exported wheat, but in the years since the Korean War, its export market has declined drastically. All these factors combine to make wheat farming a more risky type of farming than many other kinds, and wheat farmers tend to seek more governmental protection against those risks than do some other types of farmers.

By contrast, corn growers are relatively well-off and less enthusiastic about governmental aid for agriculture. Part of this difference relates to the different uses that farmers make of their crops. Much of the corn is fed to hogs and reaches the market as pork, and most of what is not consumed on the farm is sold for livestock feed. Generally in recent years, feed deficit areas, where grain is imported to feed to livestock, have opposed restrictive programs, while feed surplus areas have sought more governmental help. The corn-hog area is concentrated east of the wheat belt—in Iowa, Illinois, and Indiana. Here the weather is much more reliable. Prosperity has increased the demand for meat as it has for the milk and eggs that many farmers in this same area produce commercially, and corn-hog farmers are not dependent upon the export market. Technology has had some effect in corn growing, especially through the use of hybrid seeds, but the impact of machinery on the corn-hog producers has not been as great as it has on wheat growers. Corn-hog farmers are not necessarily pleased with market conditions and have sought some degree of governmental protection, but generally they have applied less political pressure than wheat growers.

The position of cotton growers in recent years has usually been somewhere between corn-hog and wheat farmers. Mechanization has increased cotton yields and irrigated cotton in Arizona and California has come along to compete with the old cotton South. Vast cotton-growing undertakings in Egypt and other former colonial areas have taken away much of our previous export market, but except when disease strikes, cotton production is fairly steady. Cotton farmers, especially from the "old" cotton areas, have sought more governmental assistance than corn growers but somewhat less than wheat growers.

Again, although these three crops, plus dairying, engage a substantial proportion of the American farmers, there are many other crop interests involved in farm policy struggles. However, the main lines of group activity and party conflict in recent years can be traced to these major commodity bases.

Farm Organizations

There are nearly as many farm organizations as there are commodities, but only a few of these are of major political importance. The largest by far is the American Farm Bureau Federation. Organized in 1919, the AFBF grew in close association with the Extension Service. County agents organized committees of leading farmers in the county to arouse enthusiasm and provide some of the funds for extension work. When these county bureaus were organized into state and national organizations the result was a powerful spokesman for the more prosperous and politically more active farmers. The AFBF has always had very close—at times semi-official—relations with the U.S. Department of Agriculture and with most of the land grant colleges. The main link has been the extension program, and although the use of county agents as recruiting agents for the Bureau has declined under pressure from other farm groups, the policy views of these three organizations remain in harmony. The Farm Bureau played an enormously influential role throughout the 1920s and 1930s, and took much credit for writing the New Deal farm legislation. The Bureau fought the Soil Conservation Service and other elements of the governmental bureaucracy for agriculture as potential rivals for power in farm politics. Not, however, until the Farmers' Union emerged in the postwar period as a cohesive organization, ready to work through the major parties for a full legislative program, was the AFBF presented with a real threat to its general position as principal spokesman for farmers on matters of public policy.

The Farm Bureau has been mainly a sectional alliance of midwestern corn-hog and southern cotton interests though in recent years the corn-hog interests have generally been dominant. It has moved more and more firmly to a position of opposing broad-gauge government assistance to agriculture; at most it advocates lower and more flexible price supports and fewer production restrictions. The AFBF seeks restrictions of many other programs, not including extension or land grant college work. The Bureau has tried to decentralize the administration of many farm programs in order to give more authority to state governments, with which the Bureau's relations are more dependable than they are with a sometimes Democratic national administration. The AFBF has been closely aligned, increasingly in recent years, with Republican leaders and warmly supported Republican Secretary of Agriculture Ezra T. Benson. The Bureau has always worked more closely with business leaders, especially the Chamber of Commerce, than other farm groups, as local businessmen have always been active in support of county agent work. As the Bureau has moved toward advocating greater reliance upon a free market in agriculture, its business ties have been strengthened, and Bureau spokesmen can be relied upon to assert a "conservative" position on a host of economic and social questions in addition to farm problems.

A second major farm organization is the Farmers' Educational and Cooperative Union, usually referred to as the National Farmers Union. The NFU is considerably smaller than the AFBF (ca. 300,000 *versus* 1,600,000), but in the past decade it has become the chief rival of the Farm Bureau. It advocates expanded governmental help for farmers: high price supports or production payments, more and cheaper federal credit for farmers, more stringent production controls, rural relief programs, and the like. The NFU emphasizes the "family farm" theme and attacks corporate farming and "big business." These policy demands reflect the interests of the NFU constituency, which is mainly located in the Great Plains wheat belt. In recent years the organization has gained members in other parts of the Midwest, especially among younger farmers with heavy investments yet to be amortized and in areas hit by drought.

The NFU has become increasingly identified with the leadership of the Democratic party and is partly responsible for the Democratic successes in the Plains states in recent years. It has also achieved a close alliance with organized labor groups and has won support from the bulk of the urban Democrats in Congress for high price support programs. The NFU vigorously opposed the Eisenhower administration generally and Secretary Benson in particular and has supported the Kennedy and Johnson administrations with an enthusiasm equal to the Farm Bureau's opposition. Since the late 1940s the Farmers Union and the Farm Bureau have been diametrically opposed on virtually every issue of farm policy and, indeed, on most other issues as well.

A third general organization of farmers is perhaps of more historical interest than contemporary political importance despite its considerable size. The National Grange was, in the latter nineteenth century, a powerful force in farm politics, but in recent years has had relatively little influence. The Grange today occupies a middle position between the Farm Bureau and the NFU and has been moving closer to the latter end of the spectrum.

Groups such as the National Council of Farmer Cooperatives and the National Milk Producers Federation may also play an important role on those farm questions of specific importance to their members, but they are not ordinarily in the forefront of the major farm policy struggles.

In addition, a number of specialized commodity groups have been organized in recent years, ranging from wheat growers and corn growers to cranberry growers and turkey raisers. This proliferation of groups, reflecting the growth of more diverse and specialized farm interests, is a close counterpart of the growing complexity of farm policy. One other general farm organization is worth mentioning, however, because of its unique approach to farm problems. The National Farmers Organization has attracted a considerable following, especially from disaffected Farm Bureau members in the Midwest, for its program of direct economic action. The NFO urges that all farmers join together to withhold their products from the market until the price is satisfactory. The NFO is perhaps significant mainly in reflecting considerable frustration and disenchantment among farmers with legislative programs of the past and a desire for something new to end their troubles.

CONTEMPORARY CONFLICTS

Efforts to get support for any major agriculture policy change must come to terms with two major trends among farm interests.

Partisanship in agriculture. To a very large extent, farm politics of the past decade has been bipolarized, with the Democratic–NFU–wheat farmers seeking expanded governmental assistance aligned against the Republican–AFBF–corn-hog farmers advocating less governmental involvement. These two general groupings were almost mutually exclusive throughout the 1950s; the Farm Bureau leaders had no success with a Democratic Congress, and the NFU hardly even tried to influence Republicans whether in Congress or the executive branch. The partisan character of the split has been revealed over and over again in congressional votes on farm policy and in the electoral efforts of the two rival organizations. The NFU almost invariably finds that Democratic legislators are the only ones who "vote right," while the AFBF finds similarly for the Republicans, and in election campaigns the two rival organizations have at times seemed to be virtually attached to the respective party headquarters. When Republicans occupied the executive branch, Farm Bureau sympathizers were prominent in the Agriculture Department. Since 1961, on the other hand, Farmers Union people have filled key executive positions. Presidential recommendations concerning farm policy have differed widely, depending on which party was in power. And in Congress the votes on farm issues have resulted in highly cohesive party alignments—nearly all Republicans opposing the large majority of the Democrats.

Partisanship is not complete, of course. A few plains state Republicans favor higher supports, and a considerable number of southern Democrats oppose them. The latter have become a kind of swing group. In most cases the majority of the defecting Democrats are southerners. If enough of them support the NFU-backed position, it will pass; if not, it will fail. Southern Congressmen, on these issues as on so many, are in a powerful position. They dominate the agriculture committees of Congress, and as a swing group on the floor, they can bargain very effectively. They have used this power to promote the interests of southern crops—cotton, rice, peanuts, and tobacco, especially—while preventing either the AFBF or the NFU from achieving their full objectives. Sometimes the big-city Democrats also oppose higher farm supports, but the NFU and the AFL – CIO have worked closely together to try to cement a working alliance whereby farm Democrats would support labor legislation in return for urban votes on farm bills.

Throughout the 1950s the partisan struggle centered around the issue of the desired price support level. The NFU–Democratic alliance sought to maintain price supports at 90 per cent of parity and to resist efforts to achieve greater flexibility, while the AFBF–Republican grouping tried to lower the support level. The former group won several temporary victories in Congress, but gradually price supports have been reduced anyway and the issues have begun to change.

Fragmentation of the farm bloc. A second direction in which farm politics has moved is toward a general fragmentation of interests with each commodity group seeking separate treatment and making what alliances it can. Until very recently, farm policy, although extremely complex, generally presented a facade of comprehensiveness. A single bill would apply to, and represent the interests of, a variety of major crops. But the trends of specialization in agriculture and the increasing intercrop conflicts of interest have made it virtually impossible to write general farm legislation any longer. After an unsuccessful attempt to get a general freeze on price support levels in 1958, the major bills considered were virtual grab bags of many separate and largely unrelated programs. The bill that finally passed consisted of programs for cotton, rice, corn and feed grains, wool, and tung nuts. In 1959 separate programs for wheat and tobacco passed Congress but were vetoed by President Eisenhower. In 1960 a dairy support bill was approved but another wheat bill failed to pass.

Since 1961 the Kennedy and Johnson administrations have proposed and Congress has passed several bills referred to as "general" or "omnibus" farm legislation. Yet in fact these acts have been more like compendia of separate commodity programs, many of which have little in common. The 1965 legislation, for instance, dealt in diverse ways with wheat, wool, feed grains, dairy products, cotton, and rice. More significant, in a way, was the fact that these programs will run for four years, longer than Congress has ever authorized before. Perhaps farm policy conflicts are at last beginning to recede. As a final note it may be observed that during the 1964 presidential campaign the traditional "farm issue" was hardly mentioned by anyone.

NATURAL RESOURCES

The United States is blessed with a wide variety of valuable resources that underlie the economic strength of the nation. But despite substantial abundance, few of these resources are available in unlimited quantities. Some vital materials like natural rubber are not found in this country. Others such as tin and tungsten must be imported to provide an adequate supply. And many resources including oil, water, and soil may be dangerously depleted in the future. In short, despite a great natural endowment, the United States faces problems of scarcity; problems that may not be as severe as those of some other countries but still give rise to political action and governmental response.

The definition of resources is not fixed. Coal was once the pre-eminent source of power. The development of large amounts of power from oil, gas, falling water, and atomic energy has greatly reduced the significance of coal. The technology of the industrial system and the state of economic development in the United States affect our conception of what constitutes a valuable resource.

Resource policy in the United States has been further conditioned by two other "givens." For one thing, much of the land—and the minerals, soil, forests, and water that go with it—was owned originally by the federal government. Some of this public domain was acquired by purchase, some by treaty, some by exploration. But since it was not private property, the government could not avoid responsibility for it. Secondly, the economic character of much resource development has made governmental action inevitable. If a firm wishes to plan in terms of 100 years and has sufficient capital to do so, sustained yield forestry may seem attractive, but probably it will not otherwise. Private development of atomic power has lagged in the United States because of the huge risks involved, and the original atomic bomb, of course, would not have been developed by private enterprise. In short, the cost and/or risks of some types of resource development are very large. Moreover, from projects like parks, flood control, and navigation assistance the benefits are diffused among perhaps millions of people. It becomes impossible to operate these projects privately, since neither the customers nor the size of the purchase are known. For all these reasons there exists a broad range of governmental programs and policy controversies concerning the development and use of the nation's resources.

Ideology in Resource Politics

That governmental authority should be invoked to deal with conflicts over the use of resources was inevitable, but the scale of operation and to some extent the direction could be disputed. The public domain might be handed over to homesteaders or reserved for parks and forests. Multiple-purpose dams might be built often or seldom, power might be sold at the dam or from transmission lines. The states or the federal government might control offshore oil. These and many more conflicts over policy may make enormous financial differences to groups concerned. In the process of seeking to secure their goals, the principal groups have developed sets of ideas and arguments to support their positions. Three general ideas have been especially prominent in this field: exploitation of resources by or for the benefit of private producers, conservation of resources by public authority, and exploitation of resources by public authority.

Historically, the first of these three positions was by far the most significant. The public domain was to be sold cheaply and sometimes given to private parties to encourage the growth and settlement of the nation. For the most part, private exploitation was uncontrolled. Charters were issued by public authority, and the courts were sometimes called upon to interpret the limits of private property rights. But there was little doubt in the minds of most people that American resources were unlimited and little suggestion that these gifts of a bountiful nature would have to be husbanded.

In the latter nineteenth and early twentieth centuries several factors combined to produce a different set of ideas about natural resources. As the population expanded, land values rose, and, especially in the latter half of the nineteenth century when farm prices declined, it became very attractive to settle low-priced homestead land, farm it as extensively as possible for the required five years, and then sell it at the increased value. This process resulted in bringing millions of acres into the most depleting kind of cultivation. The disappearance of great forests of the Great Lakes area was an inescapable fact by this time, and a number of people began to show concern over the fact that at this rate of cutting there would soon be no trees at all. Moreover, there developed during this same period a considerable body of scientific data about natural resources, especially forests, and the scientists were prominent in promoting new concepts of resource use. These concepts stressed orderly, efficient utilization of resources to secure the maximum yield at a rate that would maintain the supply into the indefinite future. This was the beginning of the conservation movement.

The scientists and their supporters began an extensive campaign of public education for governmental action to enforce conservation. Despite their zeal, however, it may be doubted whether conservation would have been written into public policy without other developments of the period. The technology of industry produced electric power, petroleum, and chemical giants whose dependence on long term supplies of natural resources placed these matters in a different light than had been held by the small-scale homesteader. Scientific management concepts in industry made planning and efficiency more acceptable politically. Finally, the general shift in political and social ideology away from *laissez faire* to acceptance of some regulation of business allowed the conservationists to become part of the Progressive Era.

The first great surge of conservationist policy by the federal government occurred during the administration of Theodore Roosevelt. The factors that led to conservation thinking all came into conjunction in the first decade of the twentieth century. In time, although conflicts developed within the original groups, the conservation movement gained new adherents from two other types of interests. With the general increase in prosperity and leisure time, recreation attracted more and more interest, and many wished to preserve areas for hunting, fishing, and other outdoor recreation. National parks, forests, and fish and game preserves thus became important political goals to these people. Also, what might be called an antiquarian aesthetic interest, a concern to preserve some of the natural beauties of the country unmarred by urban "civilization," animated more and more people, particularly writers.

Conservationists have sometimes been allied with and sometimes opposed to a third approach to resource use, that of public exploitation. This view is a part of the broader demand for governmental development and protection of human and natural resources. Sometimes the goal grows out of the inability of private enterprise to raise the capital necessary to undertake the project or from the fact that the benefits of the project are so diffused as to make profits impossible to secure. Both of these conditions, for example, make it very unlikely that private enterprise will construct large *multipurpose* dams. In many cases, however, the demands for public exploitation reflect a basic change in attitude toward resources. The feeling is that these resources belong to all the people of the country, not just a few, and that private exploitation, especially of the "strike it rich" or "cut and get out" type, is immoral and improper. There is not necessarily any thought of not using these resources, but only of using them to benefit as many people as possible. The assumption is that public dam construction, federal control of tidelands oil, or governmental development of atomic power will benefit more people than will private utilization of the resources involved.

All three of these general attitudes toward resources are prominent in the conflicts of today over natural resource policy.

LAND RESOURCES

The federal government at one time has owned nearly one and-a-half billion acres of land in continental United States, over three-fourths of the total land area. Over 400 million acres still are in the public domain, most of them in the western states. The story of the transfer of so much land from public to private ownership embraces much of American history. For the first years after the Constitution was adopted, the sale of public land was designed to bring revenue to the government. As the West gained greater political power, the emphasis was changed to using the public domain to encourage settlement, and successive Acts of Congress, culminating in the Homestead Act of 1862, made it easier and cheaper to secure private ownership of land. The Homestead Act provided that anyone over twenty-one, who was or intended to become a citizen, could acquire up to 160 acres of surveyed public land by living on the land for five years and making certain improvements. Grants of land were made to the states as early as 1787 to support common schools, and later to support universities and other institutions of the states. Land grants were made also to the railroads in the West and South.

The land policy throughout most of the nineteenth and early twentieth centuries was to encourage settlement of as much land as quickly as possible. In this process there was a good deal of fraud. The rapid increase of land values in some areas placed a premium on speculation. Much grassland was plowed only to blow away before the winds. Tacit encouragement was given to the illegal practice of entering the public domain and cutting the trees without pretending to settle. Cutting the forests permitted cultivation, which in turn often resulted in dust storms and erosion, since the forest cover no longer held the soil in place.

A change in direction regarding land policy came as a consequence of several factors. By the latter nineteenth century most of the choice land was gone. What was left was arid and distant from markets. The universal dream of owning a farm had lost some of its attraction as commercial agriculture suffered a prolonged slump. The erosion and waste of unrestricted settlement and cultivation had become a subject of more and more concern to the growing group of conservationists. In recent times, although homesteading is still possible, the principal actions of the federal government in this century have been to withdraw, reserve, and sometimes even purchase land to conserve and regulate the use of land resources.

Reservation of Public Land

The earliest actions setting aside public land for public use established Indian reservations. Usually these reservations consisted of land unwanted by anyone else. It is illustrative of the nature of resources, however, that as new mineral deposits were discovered and new uses were found for old materials, pressure developed to take back the reserved lands for private exploitation. Today Indian reservations contain much less than half the peak of 166 million acres reached in 1875.

National parks have survived in strikingly better fashion. As recreation and tourism have become major industries in many parts of the United States, the National Parks have had vocal defenders. Beginning with Yellowstone Park in 1872, more than 200 parks, monuments, and historic sites have been reserved from public land, or in some instances purchased from private owners. The National Park Service administers these lands. Political conflict is not absent from this activity. Recreation and conservation groups often seek to expand the park system or at least to increase the appropriations for its maintenance. Others may seek to exploit mineral or timber in, and build dams in or highways through, the parks. Moreover, as more and more people turn to outdoor recreation and the parks and campsites become increasingly crowded, these interests seek larger appropriations and thus come into conflict with a host of competing groups.

The enormous recent increase in demand for outdoor recreational facilities, coupled with the continued growth of urban population centers, has led to great expansion in programs, particularly in the direction of preserving the remaining scenic and wilderness areas in relatively pristine natural condition. The Park Service has spent nearly $1 billion to enlarge and improve its facilities since 1956. In 1963 the Bureau of Outdoor Recreation was created in the Interior Department to take the lead in planning and development of future facilities. The Wilderness Act of 1964 has led to the setting aside of nine million acres of undeveloped national forest land to be kept in a wild state. Federal policy now assists cities and counties in acquiring open spaces and preserving them against urban development. Thus the conservation movement has been strongly reinforced by the recreation demands of an affluent urban society.

Throughout much of the nineteenth century, lumbering was a major industry in the United States and timber one of the most vital resources. The great forests of the Great Lakes area were thoroughly cut over in this period, and the forests of the west were attacked recklessly. Taking their cue and their training from state-owned forests in Germany, scientific foresters began to campaign for public action to conserve the fast-dwindling tree supply. For some twenty years this campaign of scientists achieved little, but in 1891 a law was passed, almost unnoticed, that permitted the President to reserve portions of the public domain as *national forests*. Successive Presidents withdrew land from the public domain and slowly funds and administrative machinery were secured to manage the forests. Gifford Pinchot, Chief Forester under Theodore Roosevelt, was perhaps the outstanding leader in this movement.

Western states were the only ones really affected by this policy, since only in the West was there much public land remaining. In 1907 western interests finally secured legislation prohibiting further reservation in the western states. In 1911, however, the Weeks Act authorized the purchase of land for forest conservation, and, mainly in the 1930s, nearly twenty million acres were added to the national forests in this fashion. Most of the land purchased has been either in the South or in the Lake States of Minnesota, Michigan, and Wisconsin.

Most of the national forests are managed by the Forest Service of the Department of Agriculture. The forests are run on a sustained-yield basis, with private firms securing the right to cut timber by competitive bidding. Land included within national forests may also be leased in order to extract mineral resources. The Forest Service has been involved in some heated controversies concerning the administration of conservation programs. Rivalry has persisted between the Forest Service and the agencies now located in the Bureau of Land Management in Interior. Each agency administers much public land, and from time to time each has sought to unify public land management under its guidance. The agencies often diverge on policies respecting functions, such as control over grazing on public land, which they both perform. Each group tends to regard itself as the leading exponent of conservation and prudent resource use.

Water Resources

As the arable land in the public domain was occupied, pressure mounted to make some of the remaining land arable by irrigation. Some irrigation projects had been privately constructed since the Indian days, but not until 1902 did the federal government embark on a program to reclaim arid lands. The Newlands Act of that year provided that irrigation projects could be constructed, and the costs, without interest, were to be repaid over ten years by the homesteaders claiming the irrigated land or by the owners of private land benefiting from the irrigation. Homestead claims of irrigated public land were limited to 160 acres and private owners were likewise limited to the amount of water necessary to irrigate 160 acres. Most of the land suitable for irrigation actually turned out to be private land. The terms of repayment of construction costs have been extended to fifty years, thus allowing the land to become fully productive before payments are required. The 160 acre limitation has survived, although many groups seeking to irrigate larger areas under single ownership or hoping to speculate in land values have sought to abolish it. Today more than thirty million acres are cultivated under irrigation, and well over 200 dams have been constructed.

Until the Hoover Dam was authorized in 1928, the irrigation projects were aimed at a single purpose, reclaiming arid land through irrigation. Yet a dam built to store water for irrigation can also be useful for flood control and power production and possibly also for helping navigation. The Bureau of Reclamation of the Interior Department finally began to try to fulfill these several purposes with each project, and the costs of the project were allocated among the purposes served. The prospect of developing hydroelectric power through governmental action greatly enlarged the political scope of the Bureau's program. The demands for power in the West were potentially great, but so were the stakes of the private utilities and their allies in opposing public power. Moreover, this expanded multi-purpose operation of the Bureau of Reclamation conflicted with a rival bureaucracy, the Army Corps of Engineers. The Army Engineers had navigation and flood control as their main peacetime job. They operated with strong alliances throughout the country, whereas the Bureau of Reclamation was confined to arid regions. Thus one cannot today speak of irrigation programs apart from the broader conflicts of interests in water resources. Bureaucratic rivalry, public versus private power interests, and rivers and harbors "pork barrel" legislation are all involved.

More recently the controversies surrounding the use of water resources have been broadened as new problems arise and old ones fade. Thus the demand for irrigated farm land is less active in conditions of agricultural decline. The demand for water facilities for recreation has grown with dramatic intensity. Beyond these changes in emphasis, however, has been the rapid growth of concern for just plain water—to drink, to wash with, and otherwise to use. Water for human and industrial use \must be pure and plentiful. Population growth has combined with drought to create severe shortages, especially in the great urban centers of the northeast. Federal policy is aimed at ways to increase the potential water supply, by desalinization of sea water, for example, or reuse of water. This calls for research and demonstration, presently done with federal money. In addition, stringent federal controls have been enacted to require both local governments and private firms to take the necessary steps to stop pollution of both water and air. Federal funds are made available to assist in purifying local water supplies and in the process, of course, one cause of the shortage—pollution—will be diminished.

POWER AND ENERGY RESOURCES

The most important political issues surrounding the use of water resources in the United States have been those concerning the production and sale of hydroelectric power. Hydroelectric plants provide just under one-fourth of all electric utility power in the country. Many of these are privately owned, but government-owned utilities have increased until, federal and municipal together, public power accounts for more than one-fifth of the nation's capacity. Whether or not the production of hydro electric power by the federal government should be continued has become one of the central political conflicts of the day.

We have already noted that federal irrigation projects eventually were broadened into multipurpose projects producing power as well. In other parts of the country federal funds had been spent since the beginning of the Republic to improve navigable streams, to develop harbor facilities, and later, to control floods. Most of this work has been directed by the Army Corps of Engineers. The Corps has planned projects, usually in close association with the local interests involved, secured appropriations from a friendly Congress, and executed the plans for a wide variety of river and harbor improvements. Their warm relationship with the National Rivers and Harbors Congress, to which many influential congressmen belong, and the Associated General Contractors who actually build the projects, has helped make the Corps a very powerful agency in the federal government. Until recent years the Engineers did not build projects producing hydroelectric power. Their prime concern was, and still is, navigation and flood control. However, a dam built to store flood waters can be used also to produce power, and since 1936 many of the Corps' multipurpose projects have included power as one objective.

Electric Utility Regulation

The gradual emergence of the federal government as a major producer of electric power occurred during the same period that another evolutionary process was underway, that of increasing regulation of private electric power companies. When electric power first became commercially feasible in the 1880s, local governments regarded the electric companies as community benefactors and sought to advance their success. Utility franchises were often awarded without regard to possible abuses of power on the part of the companies. By the early twentieth century, however, electric power had become a monopoly in most areas, and in addition, many electric companies had been joined together in colossal utility empires. Protests against excessive rates brought about the establishment of state regulatory commissions in most states, but these commissions were long hampered by inadequate funds and limited authority. Under these limitations and extensive publicity campaigns by the utilities, the commissions suffered the same fate that other regulatory agencies, including federal commissions, have so often suffered—"capture" by the industry they are to regulate.

During the 1920s the names of men like Samuel Insull came to be associated with massive and intricately organized utility combines, so large and so complex as to defy even the most vigorous state commission efforts to exert regulatory authority. With the coming of the Depression many of these empires collapsed, but even before that public protests against these "interests" gave rise to a lengthy federal investigation. The result, after a bitter legislative struggle, was the passage of the Public Utility Holding Company Act of 1935. This Act gave the Securities and Exchange Commission broad regulatory authority to regulate the financial structure and operation of utilities. Particularly controversial was the so-called "death sentence" clause preventing holding companies beyond the second degree; that is, no more than two holding companies might be pyramided on top of an operating gas or electric utility. Through the enforcement of this statute, utilities were to be kept relatively small and simple enterprises, at least by comparison with the fantastic complexities of the earlier empires. Thereby, the investor in utility stocks would be protected, and the political power of utilities would be contained, enabling state regulation to be more effective in holding down rates.

Another line of increasing regulation began with the establishment of the Federal Power Commission in 1920. Originally, this body was responsible simply for licensing hydroelectric development on public lands and navigable waterways. As rate regulation of electric utilities became a matter of increasing public controversy, the FPC authority was enlarged, notably in 1935, and it became a full-fledged regulatory commission. Today, in addition to licensing, the FPC supervises accounting and financial practices of licensees and has authority over wholesale rates of those electric utilities engaged in interstate commerce. The Commission approves rate schedules on power produced by the Interior Department or under the supervision of the Army Engineers.

Public Power

The low cost power from national government projects is, in most cases, sold at wholesale by agencies of the Interior Department. The Bonneville Power Administration, the Southwest Power Administration, and the Southeastern Power Administration handle power from groups of projects while others are marketed through the Bureau of Reclamation. This power is usually sought by a number of competing customers, including municipalities, rural electrification cooperatives, and private utilities. Under the law, preference must be given "to public bodies and cooperatives," and private utilities may obtain for resale only what power is left. Private power advocates do not always oppose dam construction projects which have many purposes. They do oppose the preference clause, however. Indeed, they oppose federal marketing of power altogether and would prefer that federally produced power be sold only at the dam, or "busbar." Unless the government builds transmission lines to bring the power to the communities and cooperatives, these agencies are often unable to take advantage of the preference clause, and the private utilities are able to dominate the field. The Army Engineers usually support the utilities in their preference for sale at the busbar, and, accordingly, the Engineers do not market power as does the Interior Department. Interior builds transmission lines whenever it can secure the necessary appropriations, but this is one of the several issues over which public power advocates do battle with private power groups.

The TVA. Probably the most dramatic phase of American natural resource policy at any time of our history has been the establishment and growth of the Tennessee Valley Authority. TVA has been much studied by observers from other nations who hope to apply the lessons learned to their own resource development problems. At the same time, it has been a continuing focus of controversy in American politics. The establishment of TVA in 1933 was the culmination of a long and lonely struggle of a few Congressmen, notably Senator George Norris of Nebraska. They had campaigned for more than a decade for a comprehensive, multipurpose, valley-wide program to develop all of the potentialities of the Tennessee River. The logic of valley-wide development was compelling. Rather than have many separate and only vaguely coordinated projects, the idea was to integrate into a single system the flood-control, navigation, and power projects and to plan consciously the rehabilitation of the whole valley region.

Logic, of course, was not all that was involved. TVA was intended to produce electric power and to buy out existing private utilities. It was to raise the economic level of the whole region and in so doing to work enormous changes. Many interests would benefit from these changes, but many others would lose—notably, the utilities. More important was the fact that TVA became a symbol of broad-gauge governmental action to promote welfare. Those opposing TVA regard this as an interference with private enterprise, upsetting to existing relationships and interests, and in the long run producing less welfare. The supporters of TVA, and of other public power projects, argue that its larger resources enable government to undertake projects, like valley development, that private enterprise could not and would not afford. Moreover, a central theme of New Deal endorsement rested in the ability of TVA to provide a "yardstick" by which the performance of private utilities could be measured against that of public enterprise—in an effort to keep rates at the lowest level compatible with prudent management. Each side produces statistics and rationalizations to support its position; symbols such as "creeping socialism," "monopoly," and "public interest" are invoked; but neither group convinces its opponents.

The Tennessee Valley Authority is a semi-autonomous corporation, governed by a three-man board of directors appointed by the President. Regular operating expenses are paid from TVA's own revenue, and the Authority is much less subject to control and supervision than are most government agencies. TVA has engaged in a broad program. Floods have been substantially curbed and an even river flow is maintained all year, permitting navigation for over 600 miles. The income level in the valley area was raised from 40 per cent of the national average in 1933 to 60 per cent of that average in 1950. Huge amounts of power have been supplied to the Atomic Energy Commission projects at Paducah, Kentucky, and Oak Ridge, Tennessee. Much private industry has been attracted to the Valley by the low cost power. TVA has priced its power in a manner calculated to stimulate its widest possible use. As a consequence, from one of the lowest per capita consumption rates in the nation, the region has changed to one of the highest, and in turn, all kinds of economic activity have expanded on this base of low cost power.

The low cost of public power, in TVA and elsewhere, is an issue about which reasonable men do not agree. It is clear that the *price* of TVA power is less than half the nation's average. It is not so clear whether this price accurately reflects the cost to the government of producing the power, or whether, on the other hand, it amounts to a subsidy to the Tennessee region. A number of arguments are made pro and con, but two seem to be central: taxes and cost allocation. Private utilities, of course, pay taxes to federal, state, and local authorities on both their physical assets and their income. These taxes are costs that the utilities must cover in their rates. TVA pays no taxes, though it does make payments to state and local governments in lieu of taxes. These payments admittedly are lower than the utility tax burden, however. The utilities claim that if taxes were subtracted TVA income would have failed to cover its costs. TVA supporters deny this, and the nature of TVA costs makes it difficult to reach an objective conclusion. The costs of construction facilities used only to produce power may accurately be calculated and compared with income. But many TVA facilities are multipurpose. What proportion of the joint costs should be allocated to power as against flood control and navigation? Almost any decision on this question is arguable, and the contending interests do not accept each other's conclusions.

TVA is the largest producer of electricity in the nation with assets worth some $2.5 billion. The system serves an 80,000 square mile area including most of Tennessee and parts of six other states. However, neither congressional appropriations nor TVA's own power revenues were adequate to maintain the Authority's growth rate, estimated at about 12 per cent a year. For several years TVA sought the power to sell revenue bonds on the open market in order to finance expansion. President Eisenhower recommended such legislation on several occasions, but the opposition of private power companies, the National Association of Manufacturers and kindred conservative groups, and those who feared the loss of congressional control over TVA's construction budget blocked passage until 1959. When the bill finally passed, it permitted TVA to issue up to $750 million in bonds, but in a gesture to private power interests, the bill also limited TVA's service area to substantially that served at the present time. Almost all recent TVA activity has been in constructing steam plants which now supply over 50 per cent of TVA's power. The larger symbolic issue of "public power" remains in force, however, and TVA still brings ideological and partisan fire to the eyes of many in and near Congress.

TVA seems firmly established and successful. Yet its example of comprehensive, multipurpose river basin development under a single authority has not been followed in other parts of the country. Proposals to establish authorities of other major river basins have received little support in recent years. Even the recent Democratic Administrations have substituted the more limited goals of comprehensive planning and coordination of the many agencies, national and state, which are involved in river basin activities for the single authority modeled after TVA.

Dixon-Yates and Hell's Canyon. A dramatic example of the political conflict over public power was the Dixon-Yates contract controversy of 1954–1955. The Atomic Energy Commission's demand for TVA power was becoming so great that the supply for other users, notably the City of Memphis, Tennessee, was threatened. TVA proposed to build additional facilities, but the Eisenhower Administration chose instead to have the Atomic Energy Commission contract with a utility group headed by Dixon and Yates to supply power to Memphis. Involving very little risk to the private utility, the contract was hailed as an advance for private enterprise. Public power and TVA supporters fought the contract vigorously, both in Congress and during the 1954 elections, and "Dixon-Yates" became a major slogan in the party battle. The Eisenhower policy withstood these attacks, however, until 1955. First, it was discovered that a man had helped the government draw up the contract while also employed by the investment firm that would handle the Dixon-Yates securities. This "conflict of interest" added considerable fuel to the fire. Then the City of Memphis decided to build its own power plant, thereby making the Dixon-Yates facilities unnecessary, and the contract was cancelled.

The political struggle over public power is further illustrated by the dispute over Hell's Canyon. This magnificent gorge on the Snake River offers one of the largest remaining potential sources of hydroelectric power in the nation. The Truman Administration wanted to build one high dam there as part of a comprehensive plan for federal development of the whole Columbia River basin. The Idaho Power Company wanted to build three smaller dams in the same gorge with private funds, but their proposal would have prevented future multipurpose development of the area. The Democratic Interior Department objected to the Idaho Power plan and so long as they did so, the FPC would not grant the necessary license to the company. With the inauguration of a Republican administration in 1953, however, the Idaho Power proposal was accepted as providing an opportunity to put "partnership" to work, letting private enterprise show what it could do. Interior withdrew its objections and in 1955 the FPC granted the license. A broad public power alliance continued to fight for public development of the site as they had fought against the Dixon-Yates contract. Labor groups, the Farmers Union, the American Public Power Association, and assorted other liberal organizations joined to support some Democratic Congressmen who were making an issue of Hell's Canyon. They argued that this was a "giveaway" of irreplaceable resources to interests who could not develop the full potential of the gorge and who would charge high prices for whatever power was produced, thus retarding the growth of the Northwest area. Efforts were made to reverse the FPC license in the courts but to no avail. In 1956 and after, Senate Democrats endeavored to pass legislation preventing further private development in Hell's Canyon, but this also failed, and the private facilities were finally built.

Hell's Canyon and Dixon-Yates were major campaign issues in 1956 and 1958, and, in the Northwest, where public power is of great importance, they undoubtedly helped elect a number of Democrats to Congress. The partisan character of the question was reflected in the debates and votes on power issues in Congress during these years, and the rival slogans of "partnership" and "giveaway" were widely used in extensive public relations campaigns to mobilize the political energies of the electorate pro and con public power development. Yet outside the areas immediately affected by the proposed projects, not much excitement was kindled over these questions.

There is little doubt that the question of power development has greatly receded as a political or economic issue. Its symbolic appeal is insignificant in comparison with civil rights or the war on poverty. Its economic relevance is moderated with the growth of enormous productive and power capacity. Accordingly, it gets scant attention from President or Congress. Even a proposal such as Barry Goldwater was alleged to have made in 1964—to sell TVA to private interests—is hardly taken as a central theme, pro or con, of most political campaigns. "Public power" is one of the "old" ideological and economic issues.

Petroleum

From the modest beginning of petroleum production in Titusville, Pennsylvania, in 1859, oil has grown to become one of the most significant resources in the United States, and indeed in the world. The early use of petroleum to light kerosene lamps was significant in the latter nineteenth century, but the gasoline and diesel engines of the twentieth century have made petroleum crucial to the transportation and defense systems of every nation. The result has been a mighty economic complex of interests throughout the world with substantial power. At the same time, oil as an irreplaceable natural resource raises severe problems of conservation.

In the United States, more than twenty states produce petroleum, but Texas, California, Louisiana, Oklahoma, and Kansas account for over three-fourths of the production. Oil is normally found in pools that may vary substantially in size, the larger extending over a considerable area. If a well is drilled and taps a pool, the normal property rights entitle the owner to pump as much oil as he can. But a pool usually lies under many properties and one well may pull the oil out from under another owner's land. To avoid this, other wells will be drilled, as many as possible, by each owner in order to pump the maximum amount of oil from his property before others siphon it away. Thus, in the absence of controls, discovery of a large field will be followed by a rush to drill and pump. This sort of exploitation is both wasteful and uneconomic. When so many wells are drilled much of the natural pressure in the pool is lost and consequently much of the oil cannot be recovered. Also, much of the oil may run off at the surface in the scramble to drill and pump. Furthermore, a large unregulated field will produce huge quantities of oil that will hit the market hard and drive down the price.

Consequently, when some of the big strikes were made in Oklahoma and Texas, oil companies demanded some regulatory mechanism to save themselves from their own destructive competition. Oklahoma enacted legislation in 1915 authorizing the state Corporation Commission to estimate "reasonable market demands" and to limit production to that amount. The Commission was to prorate production among well owners. During and following World War I, however, demand for petroleum increased substantially and the Oklahoma plan was not put into effect. But in 1931 the huge East Texas field was brought into production, and the price of oil collapsed. The governors of Texas, Oklahoma, and Kansas acted swiftly to control production. An interstate compact was formed, originally without waiting for Congress to consent, to assure that all three states would limit production. Each state proceeded to prorate production among the mines of the Oklahoma system. The Texas Railroad Commission lacked authority to do this, but for a time its orders were enforced by martial law, and eventually the required legal authority was secured. The states called their regulation "conservation measures" but specified that both economic and physical waste were to be prevented.

Twenty states joined the interstate compact, but state action alone did not sufficiently guarantee effective production control. If one state refused to cooperate, there were no sanctions available to force its adherence to the program. Hence it was necessary for federal authority to back up the control machinery. Today the Bureau of Mines in the Interior Department makes monthly forecasts of consumer demand for petroleum products, divides these into estimates for each state, and sends these forecasts to the producing states. The states legally need not follow these estimates, but they all do. Each state prorates its quota among its wells and the federal government forbids shipments in interstate commerce that are in violation of state quotas.

Regulation of production is not the only major governmental action affecting oil. Since oil is such a vital resource and is irreplaceable, exploration must be encouraged to discover new pools. Just how much encouragement is necessary is a matter of dispute, but the political power of oil interests is great and one result is the "depletion allowance." 27.5 per cent of the gross sales of oil and gas producers (but not to exceed 50 per cent of net revenue) is exempt from federal income tax. Other mineral producers also receive depletion allowances, though none as high as 27.5 per cent. The depletion allowance unquestionably expands greatly the net return from oil and gas production. The "Texas oilionaire" has been made possible, in part, by this allowance which permits him to keep more of his income. Oil producing interests have used this capital to move into other industrial areas; for example, securing control of the New York Central

Railroad, and into active politics. To a considerable extent, the oil depletion allowance provides the money that, in turn, secures the influence and power needed to preserve the depletion allowance against those who would reduce it.

Natural Gas

Among natural resources none has come into more striking prominence recently than natural gas. The use of natural gas for heating, power, and in manufacturing has been multiplied more than a dozen times in the past twenty years and spread geographically from the Southwest, the major producing area, to most of the nation. Gas is usually associated in nature with oil and often provides the pressure forcing the oil out of the ground. For years natural gas was burned off as waste, but the development of seamless steel pipe made it possible to transport gas by pipeline over long distances and thus made it as commercially significant as fuel.

The natural gas industry is divided into three phases; production, transportation, and distribution. There are several thousand producers, located mostly in the Southwest. About twenty of the producers, however, are corporate giants who also control pipelines that carry the gas to market. Some of the distributors also control pipelines, but most companies engaged in this phase of the business are local gas companies. Local gas companies are public utilities with a monopoly of the business in a given area. As such their rates and service are regulated by state commissions.

Under the Natural Gas Act of 1938, interstate transmission of natural gas and its sale for resale have been subject to rate and service regulation by the Federal Power Commission. However, neither state nor federal regulation began until after the gas had been produced and entered interstate commerce. Thus the rates paid by the consumer, though regulated, actually "floated" on top of the unregulated producer's price. Moreover, for the integrated producer-pipeline owner this meant that by charging himself high rates for the gas he produced he could escape much of the impact of regulation of the transportation rates. Some members of the FPC, notably Leland Olds, held that effective regulation of interstate transportation required also regulation of production. In 1949, when Olds was nominated by President Truman for another term on the FPC, the oil and gas interests successfully prevented his confirmation by the Senate. A bill specifically exempting the production price of gas from FPC control was passed by Congress in 1950 and vetoed by the President. The FPC, however, then decided that it lacked the authority under the 1938 legislation to control the production price. The Supreme Court reversed the Commission in 1954 and directed it to set "just and reasonable" prices for gas entering the pipelines.

President Eisenhower announced that he favored legislation to withdraw this authority from the FPC, and when, in 1955 and 1956, a bill designed for this purpose was considered by Congress, it had Administration support. The argument of the proponents of the bill was mainly that the rapidly increasing demand for gas made it necessary to encourage maximum expansion of production. Many gas utility companies opposed the bill, however, on the grounds that it would raise the prices they paid for their gas. A large number of northern and eastern cities, labor groups, and other consumers of gas joined in this opposition. The bill nevertheless passed the Congress, but not before one Senator announced that a lawyer lobbying for passage had given $2500 to the Senator's campaign manager. President Eisenhower thereupon vetoed the bill, approving its purpose but condemning the "arrogant tactics" of its supporters. In 1957 supporters of the bill engaged in still more blatant efforts to win support, despite the fact that they had had clear majorities in Congress plus the support of the President, and again the tactics "snatched defeat from the jaws of victory." Supporters shied away and little effort has been made for the bill since. Natural gas conflicts, like so many other resource issues, drew sectional lines of division between representatives of producing areas, especially the Southwest, and representatives of consumer areas. Some Democrats tried to make a party issue out of what they termed "another giveaway," but in contrast to the public power issues, some Democratic leaders in Congress supported the bill while a number of Republicans opposed it. It appeared further that voters were substantially indifferent, at least outside the producing areas. Meanwhile, the FPC has been struggling to regulate gas production rates and has been having a very difficult time with an unwanted task. Unlike a public utility, gas production is highly competitive, and the traditional regulatory formulas are not readily applicable.

Atomic Energy

The amazing technological developments of the twentieth century have transformed much of the economic, social, and political life of the world, and the changes already experienced may be merely a prelude to the future. Surely one of the most fundamental changes has been in the field of energy resources where atomic and thermonuclear energy have drastically altered the nature of international relations. The impact of atomic energy may be almost as great on the economic development of the United States, when the power needed to run machines and heat buildings can be drawn economically from atomic reactors. Atomic energy is potentially unlimited in quantity, and as the power needs of the nation continue to increase and other sources of energy are depleted, the public policies affecting atomic development will eventually be of vital significance.

Unlike any other resource in the United States, atomic energy was purposely developed as substantially a total federal monopoly. The enormous capital outlay of $2 billion was required to perfect the atomic bombs of World War II, and it seems clear that no other source than government and no other purpose than world war could have combined to produce successful controlled atomic reaction so quickly. But there was a war, and Hiroshima and Nagasaki were bombed, and atomic energy had arrived. The military importance of atomic energy was so great, however, that civilian uses could be explored only under the strictest control. Since the American position in the world following World War II depended for several years on its atomic weapons monopoly, the strictest sort of secrecy was thought necessary concerning these matters. Some argued that this meant that control of atomic development should continue to be vested in the military as it had been during the War. This proposal was rejected in favor of civilian control, to be exercised by an Atomic Energy Commission of five members appointed for five years by the President, with the consent of the Senate.

The AEC was established by the McMahon Act of 1946. Its original authority over atomic development was great, and only a limited role was provided for private enterprise. This was an unprecedented act, but it dealt with a subject of unprecedented importance. The discretion granted the AEC was great, and the departure from standard images of American economic organization was also extreme. Many criticisms were leveled at the AEC, culminating in substantial revisions of the law in 1954. The secrecy and security provisions were attacked as inadequate, and when it appeared that atomic secrets had been given to the Soviet Union, the program was pulled into the whole loyalty-security conflict. The decision of the AEC to sever its relationship with physicist J. Robert Oppenheimer on security grounds was followed by a considerable debate over the desirability of some of the security restrictions. Many argued that fewer restrictions would enable freer communication among scientists which would lead, in turn, to more rapid advances.

Another area of controversy developed as rapid strides in technology made it apparent that economically feasible, peacetime atomic power was just over the horizon. This brought forth the whole range of public and private power interests. As a result of this dispute the 1954 legislation opened the atomic power field to private development subject to licensing by the AEC. As of 1964 some thirteen nuclear power plants were in operation. Although these plants are still largely experimental, there is little doubt that nuclear power will be economically feasible within a very few years. When that time comes there need be little public concern about running out of power and energy resources, of course, since nuclear power is almost literally infinite in potential supply. What will become of great public concern will be the fate and possible redevelopment of those areas of the country whose prosperity has depended on their production of the older energy resources. Coal producers will demand renewed attention and assistance and perhaps even oil and gas interests will face economic decline. In any event, the politics of resource conservation and development will continue as a lively field of conflicting interests.

BIBLIOGRAPHICAL NOTE

There is much literature concerning the complex field of agricultural politics and policy. Leading works treating its historical development are Richard Hofstadter, *The Age of Reform*, 1955; Murray R. Benedict, *Farm Policies of the United States, 1790–1950*, 1953; Fred A. Shannon, *American Farmers' Movements*, 1957; and the United States Department of Agriculture *Yearbook, Farmers in a Changing World*, 1940. Contemporary issues are discussed in Lauren Soth, *Farm Trouble*, 1957, and Edward Higbee, *Farms and Farming in an Urban Age*, 1963. The political side of agricultural policy is examined in Charles M. Hardin, *The Politics of Agriculture*, 1952; Grant McConnell, *The Decline of Agrarian Democracy*, 1953; Wesley McCune, *The Farm Bloc*, 1943, and *Who's Behind Our Farm Policy?*, 1956; Reo Christianson, *The Brannan Plan*, 1959; and William Block, *The Separation of the Farm Bureau and the Extension Service*, 1960.

Natural resources policies and politics are considered in some detail by Clair Wilcox, *Public Policies Toward Business*, 3rd ed., 1960; Barrow Lyons, *Tomorrow's Birthright*, 1955; Norman Wengert, *Natural Resources and the Political Struggle*, 1955. A recent review of natural resources in the United States is Hans H. Landsberg, *Natural Resources for U.S. Growth*, 1964.

A good discussion of land resource policies can be found in Marion Clawson and Burnell Held, *The Federal Lands: Their Use and Management*, 1957. A series of articles on water resources may be found in *Law and Contemporary Problems*, XXII (1957), nos. 2 and 3, entitled "River Basin Development and Water Resources." A fine general treatment is John V. Krutilla and Otto Eckstein, *Multiple Purpose River Development*, 1958. John Ise reviews park development in *Our National Park Policy*, 1961. The political struggles over grazing are well discussed in Phillip O. Foss, *Politics and Grass*, 1960.

Arthur Maass' study of the Army Engineers, *Muddy Waters*, 1951, is valuable. Among the numerous works on TVA, Roscoe Martin, ed., *TVA: The First Twenty Years*, 1956, is particularly useful. Aaron Wildavsky's study of *Dixon-Yates*, 1962, is excellent.

Policies concerning a number of other river basins have been examined by social scientists including Charles McKinley, *Uncle Sam in the Pacific Northwest*, 1952, Marian Ridgeway, *The Missouri Basin's Pick Sloan Plan*, 1955; Wm. Leuchtenberg, *Flood Control Politics: The Connecticut River Valley Problem*, 1953; Roscoe Martin, *River Basin Administration and the Delaware*, 1960.

Case studies of resource control including oil and gas can be found in Emmett Redford, ed., *Public Administration and Policy Formation,* 1956.

The politics of atomic energy programs are treated in Morgan Thomas and R. M. Northrup, *Atomic Energy and Congress,* 1956. Prospects for the future are examined in Philip Mullenbach, *Civilian Nuclear Power,* 1963.

All of these policy areas are reviewed in detail in Congressional Quarterly Service, *Congress and the Nation,* 1945–1964.

government
and
business

RICHARD W. TAYLOR

Government regulation of business is one of the most controversial and complex issues of domestic politics. Not only do
students of government offer a variety of judgments on the relation between business and government, but businessmen themselves give divided counsel on whether, when, and how the
government should intervene in the economy. The advice offered, moreover, usually turns on ideological assumptions that
are more likely to confuse than to enlighten.

Political platforms illustrate the murky air of charge and
counter-charge. The Republican Party entered the 1964 presidential campaign with a platform charging that the Democratic
administration had "violently thrust federal power into the free
markèt in such areas as steel prices, thus establishing precedents
which in future years could critically wound free enterprise in
the United States . . ." Republicans discounted the Democratic Party's position in advance: "Dominant in their council
are leaders whose words extol human liberty, but whose deeds
have persistently delimited the scope of liberty and sapped its
vitality. . . . Such leaders are Federal extremists." But the
Democrats would not debate on such terms. They too wanted
to reach the business mind. "The American free enterprise system is one of the great achievements of the human mind and
spirit," the Democratic platform stated. "It has developed by a
combination of the energetic efforts of working men and women,
bold private initiative, the profit motive, and wise public policy,
until now it is the productive marvel of mankind." The difference in tone can be accounted for as the difference between the

"outs" and the "ins." Although it is clear from these statements that Republicans feel that they differ from Democrats, it may well be doubted that the 1964 election contest was over which set of phrases would win.

The purpose of this chapter is to clarify the obscurity in which conflicts of interest express themselves and to examine the differences within the business community and between business and government. To understand the process of governmental involvement in the economic order will require 1) an examination of the nature and organization of property, 2) a description of contesting groups in the economic struggle, and 3) an inquiry into the manner in which group pressures manifest themselves in the public efforts to maintain competition. The difficulties in application of the competitive model will be especially exemplified. Problems of direct regulation of an industry will be exemplified in the operations of the Federal Communications Commission; and the alternative of public ownership will be briefly examined.

PEOPLE, POLITICS, AND PROPERTY

Wealth when protected by law is called property and when used in business is called assets. When government intervenes in economic affairs it usually alters property rights and affects the assets of individual enterprises. For example, a real estate code defines the rights of holders of deeds, but these rights may be altered by a zoning ordinance. A merchant may purchase goods for sale at his price, but his right to determine the selling price may be altered by a price control statute. Both employer and worker may have the feeling that they have a natural right to bargain regarding terms of employment, but minimum wage laws and legislation legitimizing collective bargaining may interfere; both minimum wage and labor legislation interfere with the owner's freedom to employ at will and serve to control his use of property. Many different laws affect property relations. Insofar as businessmen wish to protect their assets through governmental action, laws will define the character of their property rights, and the process of securing and repealing these laws involves politics. Viewed in this way, the law of property may be regarded as the foundation of economic activity and a principal means of public regulation of business activities. Conceptions of property and the law are constantly changing under the impact of technological and organizational revolutions, which have produced the modern capitalist economy in the United States. One of the central questions is whether or not the ideology of free enterprise, which is usually advanced to justify this system, has kept up with these revolutionary times.

The Legal Foundations of Capitalism

A fascinating chapter in the legal history of property in the United States is its common law origin. John R. Commons has demonstrated that in early common law, property was identified with a "thing" or "skill" possessed by an individual.[1] According to this early conception, land and buildings erected thereon provide good examples of the "thingness" of property; whereas the right to the fruits of one's labor from the field or shop provide examples of the occasionally inconsistent "skill" or labor theory of property. In the common law, the "thing" conception of property was generally considered a most important right, a right prior to the creation of society and superior to the worker's "skill property." Commons calls property in things *corporeal* property.

An example of how the courts applied this *corporeal* theory of property is provided by the history of Granger legislation and the attempts of agricultural America to protect itself against what farmers thought to be exorbitant rates by railways and grain elevators. To prevent such abuses the Illinois legislature enacted legislation prescribing maximum charges for the storage of grain. This legislation was regarded by the owners of grain elevators as an interference with their natural right to do as they pleased with their property. Some members of the court sympathized strongly with this group of owners, but the majority of the court felt that this regulation by the State of Illinois was justified. The majority in the case of *Munn v. Illinois*[2] used the *corporeal* theory of property when they reasoned that whereas the fixing of prices might interfere with the profit-making capacity of grain elevators, it did not deprive the owners of any property. The grain elevators were not taken from the owners; rather, some of the conditions limiting the owners' power to use the property were legislatively redefined. However, even the majority did not follow this theory completely because they did not wish to sanction all similar price regulation statutes. To justify this particular limitation on this property the majority had recourse to the words of an English common law justice, Lord Chief Justice Hale, who two-and-a-half centuries previously had explained that when private property was "affected with a public interest, it ceases to be *juris privati* only." Although the majority provided this qualification, they maintained primarily the *corporeal* view of property. This view of property is occasionally expressed today when we describe a man owning much real estate as "a man of property."

Soon the *corporeal* concept of property, however, was found to be inadequate as a legal device to deal with the complex problems of modern

---

[1] The following is from Commons, *Legal Foundations of Capitalism* (New York: The Macmillan Company, 1924), pp. 225–82.

[2] 94 U.S. 183 (1877).

business and technology. Modern business largely involves the exchange of pieces of paper such as contracts, promissory notes, stocks and bonds, and bank checks and paper money, and these pieces of paper under the *corporeal* view (if consistently applied) are worthless *per se*. Under the pressure of business, a new view of property as a bundle of rights has developed, according to which these pieces of paper become claims against others and evidence value; that is, they describe relationships between people. It is these *relations* that are significant since governmental institutions interpret them and require performance of the duties stated therein. This is the domain of *incorporeal* property, a bundle of rights that courts will enforce against the persons who have made commitments through some form of contract. As these bundles of rights were defined by law-makers, the older common law concept of property as a physical thing was changed in business law to make prices the crucial feature of the business relationship.

Business found it necessary, moreover, to secure additional protections for *incorporeal* property by expanding the significance of this concept. Businessmen have been anxious to protect their market by trade-marks and tariffs, their inventions by patents, their going concern value in good will, and their profits through price-fixing devices. These efforts have been directed toward the creation of what Commons calls *intangible* property. He says:

> . . . it was not until the new idea of "intangible" property arose out of the customs and actual terminology of business magnates of the last quarter of the nineteenth century that it was possible . . . to make the new distinctions which clearly separate from each other not only ownership of debts, but also the ownership of expected opportunities to make a profit by withholding supply until price is persuasively or coercively agreed upon. This ownership of expected opportunities is "intangible" property.[3]

Of one aspect of *intangible* property—good will—he says, it "can be seen and felt—not in commodities, but in the transactions of business; and felt, not in consumption and production, but in the confidence of patrons, investors, and employees."[4] Manifestly, *intangible* property refers to no definite thing, nor does it refer to a contract or promise made by two parties. It is *intangible* in the sense that it refers to anticipated profits on the basis of present market conditions that are protected by law or it refers to expectations for profit stemming from changed market conditions, which have resulted from changes in the law. Hence when a private utility extracts a promise from the government that it will always receive a profit in return for submitting to public regulation, the private utility has extracted from the government *intangible* property in terms of a *promised*

---

[3] Commons, *Institutional Economics* (New York: The Macmillan Company, 1934), p. 5. Quoted with the permission of Mrs. Anne Commons Polisar.

[4] Commons, *Legal Foundations of Capitalism*, p. 273.

income on investment, no matter what may happen. Furthermore, when some group proposes to change this guaranty in such a way as to reduce the future profit expectations of the company, the private utility is likely to struggle to maintain its *intangible* property rights. It will argue that it would be deprived of its property (meaning anticipated profit) without due process of law.

The *intangible* property concept provides a useful tool for examining the aspirations of various groups as they seek help from the government to protect their present markets or to secure new ones. A monopolistic business will defend itself against a government antitrust suit in such a way as best to protect its market; a would-be competitor may well endeavor to support a government antitrust suit by supplying information, or it may go to Congress to get legislation that might break up the market control by the monopoly. The Lanham Trade Mark Act (1946), passed by Congress at the behest of business interests wanting to protect their markets, vested an almost absolute property right in peculiar marks that distinguish particular lines. The object was not to promote competition, but to protect future profit expectations by controlling markets. Such market protections that individualize the products of different corporations also facilitate their advertising programs. Coca Cola can be sure that no other manufacturer of thirst quenchers can legally duplicate either their name or their container; they have legal control over both because they own them as *property*.

Property receives its meaning in the context of the conflict of economic interests. Most changes in the significance of this concept have come about under the pressure of business interests. When business activity was hindered by the *corporeal* conception of property, courts and legislatures were persuaded by businessmen to add *incorporeal* property. Finally, under the demand for protection of markets and profits the concept of *intangible* property was also added. This last concept helps to explain the strivings of various interests as they seek government aid to protect their assets or to deprive others of their *intangible* assets. The property system becomes a means of understanding the relations between government and business.

When we speak of "property rights," we are merely using a shorthand expression describing the rights of persons to ownership and control over things and expectations. This may be illustrated from the field of patents; when an invention is patented, the patent is the right of the owner to exclusive control over the invention for the prescribed seventeen years. In practical terms the exclusive control means the right to exclude others *or* to charge a price for the invention; it may also mean that the owner may decide whether or not his patent is to be used by anyone. It is not the invention that has the right but the man, and this man may not even be the person who made the invention. Nonpropertied persons often seek governmental aid in modifying or destroying existing property rights.

Property, in short, is a bundle of rights defined and protected by government as well as subject to change through governmental processes. It is the means whereby economic possessions are legally identified. In our country the states have primary responsibility for defining corporeal and incorporeal property. As state lines provide no useful boundaries for the large national markets, intangible property has become largely determined by national laws and regulations.

The Organization of Property

The changes in legal rules that resulted in the dissociation of the thing owned from the right to own correspond to some fairly fundamental changes in the manner of business organization and the marketing process. The technological revolution has had its counterpart in an organizational revolution. First the steam engine and then electric and internal-combustion motors have helped transform our economy from an agricultural to an industrial one, and from one of many local markets to one with a huge national market. The large-scale factories required by modern technology have involved to a considerable degree the replacement of the individual businessman by the corporate device. The corporate form of organization is a legal construction that makes possible the collection of a large amount of capital from a large number of different persons through the device of stock ownership. The corporation itself is only partially controlled by the owners, the job of running the corporation being largely delegated to management. This divided and mulitiple ownership through stock owner-ship is encouraged through the device of limited liability as well as limited responsibility. The separation of ownership from management has simpli fied and unified the administration of corporate assets and has made possible the perpetuity of the legal personality independent of the life of stock or bond holders.

Along with this commercial revolution the forms of ownership of the earlier period have continued to survive. The data summarized in Table 7-1

TABLE 7-1

Number of Sole Proprietorships, Partnerships, Corporations, and Total Receipts

Forms of Business Organizations	Number of businesses in thousands			Total Receipts in millions		
	1947	1954	1962	1947	1954	1962
Sole Proprietorships	6,624	7,715	9,183	$101,124	$144,000	$178,420
Partnerships	889	959	932	60,687	79,000	73,673
Corporations	552	698	1,268	528,632	758,000	895,121

suggests that there is still a considerable economic role for the private entrepreneur. There are still young men who invest in land to build a farm; the retail business continues to embrace a large number of small establishments. The partnership continues to be a popular form of organization for retailing and for a number of professions, especially law and investment brokerage. However, statistics suggest also that these forms of ownership are of rapidly declining importance. According to the Federal Trade Commission (FTC), the 100 largest corporations in 1962 accounted for 47 per cent of the total manufacturing assets and 58 per cent of manufacturing profits after taxes.[5] (Incidentally, this is almost one-fourth of the entire manufacturing assets of the world.) Even these figures underemphasize the concentration of control that accompanies this ownership. The economic power reflected by these statistics of business concentration controls other businesses. For example, in the automobile industry the relationship between the marketers of automobiles and the producers is determined by contracts controlled by the producers. Approximately $3 billion are invested in garages and facilities owned by these agents, and although called "independent businessmen," they can hardly be considered as such. As Berle says, "their policies, operations, and in large measure, their prices are determined by the motor company whose cars they sell."[6] Other devices for concentrating power in the economy include the interlocking directorates (directors of one company holding similar responsibilities in other, occasionally competing, companies), control of patents and licenses, as well as trade associations and mergers. Some of these we shall have occasion to discuss later, but a most important reason for this large-scale concentration of control is the activity of government itself.

The device of incorporation has not been exploited as a means of governmental regulation. The responsibility for incorporation has remained dispersed in each of the fifty states, although there is no constitutional barrier against the national government taking on this job. This responsibility for incorporation has rested lightly on the states, their activities being more permissive than regulatory and frequently motivated by the desire for tax revenues. For example, one state advertised for potential incorporators as follows:

> Incorporate in Arizona: Complete in one day. Any capitalization, least cost, greatest advantages. Transact business anywhere. Laws, bylaws, and forms free. Stoddard Incorporating Co., Phoenix, Arizona.[7]

In the corporation, the states have provided a device to facilitate the large accumulations of assets necessary to carry on modern business while the

---

[5] *Annual Report of Federal Trade Commission, 1964*, p. 37.

[6] Adolph A. Berle, *The Twentieth Century Capitalist Revolution* (New York: Harcourt, Brace and World, Inc., 1954), pp. 27–28.

[7] W. Z. Ripley, *Main Street and Wall Street* (Boston: Little, Brown & Co., 1927), p. 29.

potential capacity of this device for regulation has been largely ignored. New Jersey laws in 1888, permitting corporations to own and vote shares of stock of other and occasionally competing companies, provided a legal formula that encouraged additional concentration of industry under the holding company device. Especially in the utility field this device was exploited to create holding companies of the second ("grandfather holding companies"), third ("great-grandfather"), and even higher degrees, a method of organization that permitted a few people with relatively small investment to control large economic empires. Under the pressure of business interests, the national as well as state governments have often framed other policies that have encouraged the development of large concentrations of business.

These two facets of modern industrial organization—the corporation and its large size—have resulted in other changes in the conception of property. Under the older forms of ownership two attributes of property were combined—the creative and productive aspect, and the consumption and enjoyment aspect—and this combination reflected the genuine possibilities of a handicraft barter civilization where the producer put his skill to the work of creation, the product of his efforts becoming his to use and enjoy. Under the newer forms of ownership, the corporate device has separated ownership from control. A person can still invest money, but he grants the corporate management all power to use that capital to create, produce, and develop. The investor retains virtually no control over the product, although he may retain a right to share in the earnings, and in return he has an investment that has the advantage of being quite liquid— it can be sold for money—without interfering with the ongoing productive process. What is true for capital investment is also true for labor. Labor is impersonalized; the employee of large factories rarely knows which of the products he has helped to create, and he has no control over what he is to help to produce, or over the finished product. The worker receives instead liquid wages, which he can use to purchase many of his family's requirements in a vast market.

From this brief survey of changes in property and industry, one may conclude that government has constantly been involved with the fortunes of commerce. Not only does the law of property lie at the base of the economic system, but public revenues, the maintenance of internal order, and foreign policy are affected by conditions of economic growth and development. It is not surprising, therefore, that government protects property, and that these protections (as well as the notions of what property is) change as economic conditions change. The legal alterations of property are largely the product of political conflict, because the direction of change as well as its instruments become political issues. To be sure, many important business decisions—automation, for example—are made with little reference to the public decision-making process.

Groups Representing Business and Their Language

The verbal frame of reference—ideology—of most citizens is that private ownership and control of property is the rule, and government regulation or ownership of property is the exception. This belief is heralded in the political party platforms and exemplified in the discussions of businessmen. Even though the government creates property rights and protects them, the fundamental assumption is that governmental regulation of property requires justification. This ideological opposition to public interference is expressed in the Constitution, our literature, the editorials of newspapers, the statements of organized business, and even in the constitutions of a good number of trade unions. Accordingly, the American economy is generally called a free enterprise economy, meaning freedom from governmental control along with governmental action against invasion of property rights. As one searches for the specific content of this ideology, he finds, as our political history evidences, that a host of different and conflicting points of view can happily coexist within this frame of reference.

The National Association of Manufacturers (N.A.M.), an organization of about 16,000 manufacturing firms and corporations, has provided a fairly representative exposition of this ideology. In 1946, one of its committees published a report, which states that the individual enterprise system ". . . is interwoven inseparably into the whole fabric of American life," and that observance "of the principles of [this system] . . . has brought more benefits to the-people than were ever obtained under any other economic system in history."[8] Among the principles that the NAM regards as fundamental are 1) the competitive character of the economy, 2) the freedom to enter and leave various occupations, 3) the freedom and sanctity of contract, 4) "the right to accumulate property, as an incentive to the full use of productive activity," and 5) the freedom to invest money in profitable enterprises. These economic principles are supported, according to the NAM, by "a distinctive philosophy,"—one that "regards the individual as of supreme importance, fundamentally responsible for his own welfare and entitled to the benefits he earns." In this system, the government's responsibility is restricted to the protection of private property, the enforcement of contracts, and the maintenance of "certain conditions essential to the operation of an individual enterprise economy."[9]

Other representatives of business interests, such as the more influential and less conservative United States Chamber of Commerce, express funda-

---

[8] *The American Individual Enterprise System: Its Nature, Evolution, and Future* (New York: McGraw-Hill Book Company, 1946), I, 5. A provocative, logical and economic criticism of this document appears in Richard Schlatter, *Private Property* (New Brunswick: Rutgers University Press, 1951).

[9] Quotations are from *The American Individual Enterprise System.*

mentally the same economic point of view. This organization, endeavoring to represent business in general, has a particular need to express positions in general abstractions, because it represents to some extent competing and opposing practical business interests. These generalities cover these conflicts of interest to protect organizational size and unity. A very carefully devised policy-making procedure insures the moderation of potential conflicts of interest, and at the same time seeks to make a forceful public posture before Congress and the Executive with the Chamber's annual *Policy Directions.*

The policies incorporated in this document constitute the positions of the U.S. Chamber of Commerce. These policies have been either adopted by a majority of the delegates at the annual Congress of American Industry, or they have, in exceptional situations, been the result of a compl cated referendum process; interim policies may also be made in extraor dinary circumstances by action of two-thirds of the Board of Directors. The formal procedure obscures much educational and committee work through which extensive consultation between the Washington office and constituent organizations is achieved. These constituent organizations include 3600 local, state, regional, trade, and professional associations and over 25,000 business members—firms, corporations and individuals. Over 800 individuals serving about thirty committees reflecting different segments of the economy are active in the development of policy. Meeting regularly, these committees study, with the assistance of staff reports, various industrial issues in order to prepare for the Board of Directors reports with recommended policy declarations. The Board's function is to determine whether a proposal meets the requirement of the Chamber's by-laws—namely that it is an issue "national in character, timely in importance, and general in application to business and industry." By definition much controversial material may be excluded from general policy consideration by the application of this principle. Should a proposal meet these tests it is submitted for clarification and review to the Committee on Policy, which may modify it and incorporate it in a "Preliminary Report." This "Preliminary Report" is submitted to member organizations more than six weeks prior to the annual meeting so that delegates may inform themselves in advance regarding the issues that the Congress of American Industry is to decide.

The annual May meeting of the U.S. Chamber is an impressive event in Washington. Delegates representing constituent Chambers of Commerce in every state of the union flock to Washington to visit the sights, to visit with their Congressmen, and to carry through the legislative business of the Chamber. Prior to the meeting, opportunity is given to get the Policy Committee to submit additional resolutions; however, these efforts are generally unsuccessful for the immediate annual meeting. The annual meeting may approve, reject, or amend proposed policies, order a referendum, or refer the proposal to the Board of Directors for additional committee consideration. The annual meeting elects its president and listens to reports of many Chamber activities including the Chamber-sponsored efforts to get more businessmen in politics, which has led to the *Action Course in Practical Politics*. Although the action course is officially nonpartisan, it is intended to increase the interest of businessmen in securing election to public office. The Chamber has found that it is easier to persuade fellow businessmen who have secured election of the merits of their proposals, than it is to persuade other individuals. The Chamber is also able to mobilize businessmen by the information it provides through its periodical, *Congressional Action*, which is distributed to encourage letter writing and other types of political action.

Another organization representing still less conservative business viewpoints is the Committee for Economic Development. This organization, composed of 200 leading businessmen and educators, depends almost entirely on its research reports and educational campaigns. The statement of action of the CED exemplifies its appeal to reason:

> Through this business-academic partnership, CED endeavors to develop policy statements and other research products that commend themselves as guides to public and business policy; for use as texts in college economic and political science courses and management training courses; for consideration and discussion by newspaper and magazine editors, columnists and commentators, and for distribution abroad to promote better understanding of the American economic system.[10]

Organizations that oppose some of the positions of business groups are likely to use some of the same generalities that businessmen use to convince public officials of the virtues of their proposals. Although these generalities are not likely to clarify issues, the language of political conflict and ideological justification often does signal the nature of the concern. Since groups seek as broad support as possible to achieve a specific goal, it is tactically effective to secure such support by appealing to those abstractions that unite rather than the specifics that divide; hence the frequent obscurity of political discussion. One of the best examples of this tendency is the use of the word "competition," one of the basic concepts of the free enterprise theory.

Competition and Monopoly in Technical Language

What types of facts are designated by "competition" and what kinds of economic controls constitute a competitive market? At the outset it should be noted that lawyers and economists attach different meanings to the terminology. Economists have distinguished three characteristic types of

---

[10] Taken from the back cover of Walter H. Wheeler, Jr., *Distressed Areas in a Growing Economy* (New York: CED, 1961), this statement appears with the description of organization and purposes on all published materials of this pressure group.

market, the *competitive*, the *oligopolistic*, and the *monopolistic* market. The competitive market is one embracing many buyers and sellers—where buyers are economically free to buy from a multitude of sellers after evaluating the relative quality of goods and services as well as prices. Similarly, vendors are free to sell to those vendees who are willing to pay the highest prices. Theoretically, quality as well as price is subject to negotiation and bargaining, but market price will be determined by the relation between supply and demand. For the lawyer, as will be explained later, competition refers to all those market conditions that have not been legally defined as monopolistic and illegal.

The direct opposite of a competitive market is the *monopolistic* market in which either one buyer or one seller controls the complete market. The Aluminum Company of America exercised such a control of the aluminum market in the United States until after World War II; this company was in an economic position to sell aluminum at any price it wished or to withhold sales if it chose. For this reason, Alcoa was subject to periodic suits brought by the government. Periodically, the U.S. Government has also instituted proceedings under the Sherman Act against the partial monopoly of the Atlantic and Pacific Tea Company because its extensive retail market gave it economic power to control the price of goods sold to it and to its competitors. Court decisions supported the government's contention that the A&P was in effect a monopoly because as a buyer it controlled prices of a number of items on the market in spite of the fact that it was not the sole buyer.[11] The Aluminum and the A&P examples illustrate the two sides of the market on which *monopoly* may operate.

In fact the word "monopoly" has other connotations. When it was originally introduced into the English language by the utopian Thomas More in 1516, it described the destruction of competition brought on by the English enclosure legislation. Its early legal use, and occasionally its encyclopedia use today, was to describe the patents granted by the Crown giving exclusive right to manufacture and/or to sell specified products. This British use explains why the struggle against monopoly in that country has been generally a struggle against one prerogative of the Crown. On the other hand, in the United States "monopoly" has often been the product of economic combination by private individuals, and consequently, the struggle in this country against monopoly has generally taken the form of opposition to large-scale concentrations of privately controlled wealth. It is

---

11 See, for example, *U.S. v. A & P*, 173 F. 2d 79 (1949). In this case, to which reference will be made later in the text, the Circuit Judge Sherman Minton explained that "The buying power of A&P was to so use its power as to get a lower price on its merchandise than that obtained by its competitors. This policy, as implemented by 'direct buying,' was referred to by top officers of A&P as a two-price level, the lower for A&P and the higher for its competitors. It used its large buying power to coerce suppliers to sell to it at a lower price than to its competitors on the threat that it would place such suppliers on its private blacklist if they did not conform, or that A&P would go into the manufacturing business in competition with the recalcitrant suppliers."

partially for this reason that not until the last part of the nineteenth century did courts begin to expand the common law to make illegal those restraints on the market caused by private economic actions as well as by public grants. Today, "monopoly" is generally used to designate a wide variety of devices for eliminating competition.

Rarely do single firms obtain a complete monopoly. More likely is the reduction of competition by some kind of combination or cooperation among competing firms. In some areas a few concerns dominate the market, a condition economists refer to as *oligopoly*. Oligopoly arises when these powerful concerns are not subject to market influences but rather influence the market themselves. Some oligopolies have been the result of government antitrust suits against monopolies, for example in tobacco, aluminum, and steel. Oligopoly in flour milling and automobile industries has arisen from market conditions. On the market, oligopoly may be facilitated through intercorporation agreements or informal devices independent of trade association or explicit agreement.

Recent experience has shown that a competitive market is hard to maintain. Both buyers and sellers often have a direct interest in controlling the market, so that they will not have to depend on the whims of competition to insure a supply of products or to be able to sell them at a satisfactory price. Whether control of the market is secured through economic or political action, this control may impede the freedom of either buyers or sellers or both, as the case may be, to bargain freely with respect to price and quality of the monopolized product.

There are a variety of methods whereby reductions of competition may be achieved. Loose combinations—that is, the collaboration by separate firms in one industry—may result from formal agreement or merely from tacit understandings. Close combinations—complete integration under one management—may be accomplished through a voluntary merger, or through some type of predatory activity that results in the union of two or more previously competing corporations. Combinations may be either *horizontal* or *vertical*. A horizontal combination is the joining together of separate businesses engaged in the production or sale of the same or similar economic goods. A vertical combination is the integration of various stages in the productive process from raw materials to marketing of finished products. Each of these different types of combination involves a lessening of competition on the market with respect to entry, price, or quality or some combination of these.

An additional method by which competition is controlled and often monopoly created is by public grant. According to some authorities, government is itself the chief creator of monopoly. A franchise to an urban transit system, a license to a radio or television station, a certificate of public convenience and necessity to a private electric company, or a professional license to practice medicine all usually have the effect of reducing competition or eliminating it, no matter what the stated purpose of the grant is. Indeed, a multitude of transit or electric power companies serving the same district is uneconomic because of the high investment cost and the lack of public convenience. The purpose of medical licensing is to prevent the untrained or quacks from competing with the medical profession.

The existence of technological forces that tend toward large-scale enterprise and the fact of state and national encouragement of a number of monopolistic conditions raise the question of what should be done in those markets where competition does not serve as a regulator. There are, broadly speaking, three possible alternatives, each with its important advocates. One alternative is that technological forces should be allowed to control the market since large-scale enterprise is efficient; according to this view, there should be no restraint by government except in those situations where the economic power is used in a way opposed to public policy.

A second alternative favors "bust the trusts," meaning that the government should use its legal weapons simply to break up monopolies except where a specific monopoly is clearly in the public interest. The third alternative is a compromise position between the other two: government should foster competition where this will encourage production and distribution, but it should take steps to control directly either through *ownership* or by *positive regulation* those industries that can only be carried on monopolistically; in other industries, where competition is restricted by economic forces to a few large corporations, the government should also protect the public by such regulations as are necessary. In this latter case, public authorities should intervene only when private economic power is used to frustrate public policy. These three positions, each of which has many advocates, reflect competing claims that can be resolved only in the political and the economic market places.

Another controversy surrounds the question of how competitive the United States economy really is. Many economists argue that the competition is declining. They use the facts of economic concentration, the concentration of investment in large banking and insurance institutions, and the increasing role of government in the economy to buttress their case. While some welcome these facts, others complain. Those who welcome the decline of competition argue that the increase in technological efficiency and economic security produced by these facts more than justifies the decrease in competition and the values that such competition theoretically might achieve. Those deploring the assumed decline of competition argue along two lines. One group holds that the decline of competition has been brought on by governmental interference, such as the granting and protection of monopolistic rights as in patents or in franchises to private utilities. The second group complains that the decline of economic competition has been the result of predatory large-scale business activities that the government has not attacked vigorously enough.

Many businessmen and economists argue, on the other hand, that competition is increasing. They use different sets of facts to justify their position. Some of these authorities point out that only large-scale enterprise has the capacity to deal with other large businesses. In the event that a business cannot purchase the raw materials or finished products at prices they consider reasonable, they put their hired scientists to work in the laboratories to discover substitutes. In any event, according to this view, there are few things for which no reasonable substitutes are available. When prices, services, or quality are unsatisfactory, there is always some other business eager and able to invade the market by providing an alternative product or method.

The question of whether competition is increasing or declining is indeed controversial. This is a political fact with which we must deal just as we deal with the political fact that most citizens believe in the virtue of competition. Students of business organization and economics may well be permitted to continue to study this question and, perhaps, come to some scientific conclusion. However, this study is an academic process; and until there is general agreement on these economic facts, we must continue to concern ourselves with the political facts relating to competition.[12]

PROTECTION OF COMPETITION

Republicans and Democrats in the 1964 election campaign were united, as we have seen, in supporting competition and in favoring the full enforcement of the antitrust laws. "Trustbusting" has been a sacred cow of U.S. politics during this century, as almost uniformly reflected in the ritual of the political party platform. However, there have been wide variations of governmental behavior. Some of these have been reflected in the changes of the law by congressional enactment or court decision. Perhaps as significant have been the changing styles of administrations as they mixed the variety of techniques of governmental action explored in Chapter 1. Public ownership, criminal and civil sanctions, taxation, expenditures, publicity and investigations, licenses and franchises have all been used to promote desirable market conditions. Significantly, these devices have frequently been employed by independent regulatory commissions such as

---

[12] Regarding such controversies one of the most sophisticated students of scientific method writes, "The wisdom of absolutes, verities, facts, will be regarded as present before us in society, but not as potentially the master of knowledge or of life. Yes, even 'facts' must lose their sophisticated claim to dominance. My naiveté will regard everything as fact, even a wrong theory: and will admit no claim to independent actuality for any fact whatever as opposed to any non-fact whatever. But how indeed can a sociologist do other, when the world and life and mind are all his jumbled field?" Arthur F. Bentley, "New Ways and Old to Talk about Men," *The Sociological Review*, Vol. XXI (1929), 38, as quoted in *Life, Language, Law* (Yellow Springs, Ohio: Antioch Press, 1957), p. 23.

the Federal Trade Commission, and these agencies have quasi-legislative and quasi-judicial powers as part of their responsibility to enforce the law. To answer the question whether the United States really has an established antimonopoly policy requires an examination both of the standards set by the statutes and of the behavior of the public officials, who apply these standards to practical circumstances.

Competition and Monopoly in Nineteenth Century America

The problem of monopoly became a serious issue during the late nineteenth century when radical changes in the economy took place, largely as a consequence of technological innovations in transportation and steel. These changes laid the foundation for the large business unit and the transformation of the market. The small firm gave way to the large firm with its greater technological efficiency, while the local market gave way to the national market. This process was facilitated by various financial manipulations involved in industrial combinations and by aggressive behavior such as price wars, espionage, preferential rebates, and even violence. Insofar as these activities were designed to prevent competition, to increase the size of business, and to establish economic empires, the problem of monopoly was evident. The growth of bigger business units posed a threat to many smaller vested interests and resulted in agitation from injured groups and reformist elements for government regulation and a policy of "bust the trusts." Neither the common law nor state legislation was able to prevent these "abuses," and the injured groups turned their attention to Congress and the national political parties. Under the threat of possible third party competition, reluctant Democrats and Republicans in Congress finally passed the Sherman Act of 1890, which was to become the cornerstone of governmental efforts to protect the competitive system.

The Sherman Act

An appeasement measure to combat the Populist Revolt, the Sherman Act did not result from either careful congressional committee investigation or from extended congressional deliberation. It was a simple, rather general piece of legislation, containing but eight brief sections. Section I made illegal "every contract, combination in the form of trust or otherwise, or conspiracy in restraint of trade or commerce among the several States, or with foreign nations." Section II was more inclusive in that it declared that "every person who shall monopolize or attempt to monopolize or combine or conspire with any other person or persons to monopolize or attempt to monopolize any part of the trade or commerce among the several States or with foreign nations shall be deemed guilty of a misdemeanor." The first section was directed only against the practices of two or more parties in their efforts to restrain commerce, whereas the second section is much broader in that it is not limited to two or more concerns nor is it limited by method of contract, conspiracy, or combination. The second section declared any monopoly illegal regardless of whether trade was restrained or not and whether or not it was the product of conjoint activities. However, the act provided no definition of the terms "monopoly," "restraint of trade," or "to monopolize."

The object of the Sherman Act was to maintain competition in interstate and foreign commerce. By neglecting to define what was meant by certain key words, however, the statute was left quite vague. In the event of a conflict between the common law (where not every monopoly or restraint of trade is illegal and where judges are guided by the principle of "reason") and the Sherman Act, which declares every monopoly and restraint of trade illegal, a broad avenue for judicial discretion was left open. Nor is the Constitution explicit on what is, and is not, interstate and foreign commerce. In the face of congressional reluctance to support the Justice Department with funds to carry through antitrust litigation, and in the face of similar executive lethargy, judicial discretion in favor of "monopoly" interests in the community has often been left unchallenged, while judicial opinions unfavorable to some large industrial combinations have often been reversed by acts of Congress. The vagueness of the Sherman Act itself makes possible conflicting interpretations of such phrases as "restraint of trade" and "monopolize or attempt to monopolize." These conflicting interpretations have been used by a variety of interests to persuade succeeding Supreme Courts that particular monopolistic activities were either monopolistic or not. Depending always on the type of controversy and on a judicial sense of fitness, and occasionally on the particular political-economic situation, the courts have interpreted, reinterpreted, muted, and occasionally strengthened efforts to preserve competition.

Lack of clarity of purpose only partially accounts for the shifting antitrust policy. The sanctions that have been used to enforce antitrust policy have been both inappropriate and weak in relation to the economic purposes of the Act and to the power of the interests that have practiced monopoly. These sanctions are criminal and civil. Penalties for criminal violation of the Sherman Act are limited to a maximum of a $50,000 fine (before 1955 legislation it was $5000) and a year's imprisonment. Penal sentences have been only sparingly used, and until 1961 almost always only against labor unionists and racketeers, not businessmen. However in *U.S.* v. *Westinghouse et al.* (1961)[13] seven executives of electrical companies received unprecedented jail terms and fines were levied against the thirty-

---

[13] *U.S.* v. *Westinghouse et al.* (1961); for Judge Ganey's statement see *The New York Times* (Feb. 7, 1961), p. 26. There is no reported opinion in this case; the defendants all pleaded guilty or *nolo contendere*.

two corporate defendants and forty-one other officers. In the past, fines have been imposed in a good number of cases and have varied from $200 to $638,000 for individual defendants. However, to achieve the purpose of protecting competition, these criminal sanctions seem quite unrealistic. If the Sherman Act is supposed to promote an economic situation of competition, its concern is not primarily with such questions as criminal intent and reform of misdemeanants.

Furthermore, monopolistic results may be easily achieved without any collusion or criminal intent to monopolize. Businessmen are often very much like players at cards or baseball; they too wish to score all the tricks or runs. If this hazardous analogy may be carried a bit further, a comparison from the card game of bridge may show how the competitive game may be rigged without intent. We need only hypothesize that all four players are using the same strategy, for example Culbertson's; in this case the results of the game are merely determined by the lay of the cards and by no intent to predetermine the result. Manifestly, each side is attempting monopoly by securing all the tricks; however, both sides agree (without even thinking about it) to divide the market by making rules of fair play and by using common strategy. There is, consequently, team effort to monopolize the results; there is collusion to divide up the market; and the results are almost entirely determined by the way the cards are dealt.

Similarly, we may describe the industry where the managers of the apparently competing corporations have received a similar training, can secure bank loans at the same rate of interest, read the same trade papers, and study figures presented to them by cost accountants who follow the common practices of their trade. In place of the deal of cards, we substitute the variety of resources and markets, and we should not be surprised if the market was divided up not through the competitive situation but through the realistic appraisal of apparently competing businessmen as to which market they might most profitably serve. Another possibility in which criminal intent is inappropriate is the situation in which a business merely through efficiency might become large and achieve a monopoly status because it serves the public better than former competitors. Finally, the financial penalties are inappropriately small to act as deterrents to multimillion dollar monopolies; to be sure, few businessmen look forward to having the criminal tag placed on them, but this tag, as we have noted, is rarely levied against them.

Other remedies provided by the Sherman Act have proved of varying degrees of usefulness. One rarely used section authorizes courts to entertain suits by private persons who have been injured by monopolistic activity. If the suits are successful, courts are required to assess triple damages on the offending party. One reason for the infrequent use of this section is that private parties generally do not have the resources to provide the investigative groundwork for securing proof. Another reason is that the defendants are frequently permitted to plead *nolo contendere* to public indictments, a plea that prevents the government from presenting its case. This means that injured parties do not have this potential government assistance.

The strongest civil remedy the government may use is the court injunction, which may take the form of dissolution, divestiture, and divorcement proceedings. The injunction is designed to prevent named parties from continuing alleged illegal acts. However, dissolution, divestiture, and divorcement proceedings are drastic and rarely applied, for this type of action requires the complete destruction of the illegal combination, which would injure the property interests of stockholders and other investors who are certainly not culpable. A much favored device of much more moderate character is the *consent decree* whereby the government and offending persons or corporations come to an agreement regarding the particular activities that the guilty party will cease.

Neither the simple prohibitions of the Sherman Act nor its inappropriate sanctions, however, provide the main cue to the economic significance of this legislation. To find this significance, one must inquire into the economic practices of various lines of business and the ensuing economic and political pressures on competitors, consumers, campaigners, elected officials, and administrators of the law. As Dean Acheson has explained:

> Now it is characteristic of those who have had the good fortune to escape the study and practice of law that to them the law is—or seems to be—both simple and clear. It would not occur to them, for instance, that the plain and simple words of the Sherman Anti-Trust law do not apply to professional baseball because it is a sport and not a business, but do apply to professional football and boxing because they are both sports and businesses. A lawyer knows only too well what Longfellow meant when he wrote, "And things are not what they seem."[14]

The anomalous situation wherein contracts of baseball players are given a property status while contracts for boxers and footballers are not can be explained in terms of a special situation arising out of the history of these sports in their relation to the law. (Litigation following the removal of the Milwaukee baseball franchise to Atlanta may reopen this question.) Other paradoxical decisions can also be successfully explained in terms of special circumstances.

Sherman Act Cases

To illustrate the way in which economic circumstances and conflicts of interest give varying contents to the words of the law, a brief survey of the treatment of a variety of different situations is in order. Since a full survey

---

[14] Dean Acheson, "Foreign Policy and Presidential Moralism," *The Reporter* (May 2, 1957), p. 13. Printed with the permission of the publisher.

of the different types of cases is impossible, what follows is merely illustrative. Three questions will be considered.

First, what is the "interstate commerce" covered by the Sherman Act? One of the earliest cases arising under the Act was against a New Jersey holding company, the American Sugar Refining Company. The object of this action was to prevent this holding company from monopolizing interstate commerce in sugar. The government's case was directed by Attorney General Olney who had spent much of his time in his official position trying to persuade Congress to repeal the Sherman Act on the grounds that it would prevent the natural development of the economy. The Attorney General's feelings were reflected in the majority opinion of the Supreme Court, which reasoned that the American Sugar Refining Company, in spite of the fact that it controlled 98 per cent of the refined sugar capacity in the United States, was not subject to the Sherman Act. This was because manufacturing was not commerce, but *prior to commerce.* Professor Edward Corwin has asserted that the "effect of this holding was to put the Antitrust Act to sleep for a decade, during which period most of the great industrial trusts of today got their start."[15] Since according to the opinion of the court *manufacturing* was not *commerce*, sugar refining was only subject to state regulation; and because the states were incapable of controlling giant interstate operations such as the sugar monopoly, this decision was the signal for the first great period of corporate mergers (1897–1903).

The Supreme Court has considerably broadened its conception of commerce since the sugar trust case. In 1899 following the change of one judge on the High Bench the ruling was modified to include *manufacturing* as part of *commerce.*[16] The broad sweep of national power with respect to commerce was more recently indicated in another sugar case,[17] in which the Supreme Court held that the Sherman Act applied to a loose combination of beet sugar refiners who had agreed among themselves on the buying price for sugar beets grown in their state, California. The sugar combination argued that the purchase of sugar beets by California firms in California was purely a local matter and beyond the reach of the Sherman Act. The Court held, nevertheless, that "the artificial and mechanical separation of 'production' and 'manufacturing' from 'commerce,' without regard to their economic continuity, the effects of the former two upon the latter, and the varying methods by which the several processes are organized, related, and carried on in different industries or indeed within a

---

[15] Cf. Edward S. Corwin, *The Constitution and What It Means Today* (Princeton: Princeton University Press, 1947), p. 37. The sugar trust case is *U.S. v. E. C. Knight,* 156 U.S. 1 (1895).

[16] *Addyston Pipe and Steel Co.* v. *U.S.,* 175 U.S. 211 (1899).

[17] *Mandevelle Island Farms* v. *American Crystal Sugar Company,* 334 U.S. 219 (1948).

single industry, no longer suffices to put either production or manufacturing and refining processes beyond the reach of Congress' authority."

Insofar as the commerce clause of the Constitution is concerned, the tendency of court decisions in recent years has probably been to broaden the scope of the Sherman Act beyond the intentions of its legislative authors. In the *Mandevelle* case the Court provided this test for the exercise of national power, "a showing of actual or threatened effect upon interstate commerce" that would be "substantial." However, earlier courts held to a more restrictive interpretation. For example, it was not until 1944 that interstate contracts for insurance were held subject to regulation by the national government. Under an old rule of the Supreme Court, the insurance business was regarded as intrastate commerce. According to this rule, combinations of insurance underwriters could operate free of the restrictions of the Sherman Act. Through a suit against a combination of nearly 200 stock companies operating in eight states, the Antitrust Division sought to bring insurance under control of the Sherman Act. In *U.S. v. South Eastern Underwriters Association* this combination was held to be a monopoly, and Justice Black explained a new inclusive view of the extent of the commerce power:

> Our basic responsibility in interpreting the Commerce Clause is to make certain that the power to govern intercourse among the states remains where the Constitution placed it. That power, as held by this Court from the beginning, is vested in the Congress, available to be exercised for the national welfare as Congress shall deem necessary. No commercial enterprise of any kind which conducts its activities across state lines has been held to be wholly beyond the regulatory power of Congress under the Commerce Clause. We cannot make an exception to the business of insurance.[18]

Second, what contracts or combinations does the Sherman Act prohibit? Although the tendency of the court has been to expand the meaning of interstate commerce, the Court has generally followed a narrow interpretation of the terms "monopoly," "to monopolize," and "restraint of trade." One of the first cases concerning the question of whether or not the Act prohibits all monopolistic activities is *U.S. v. Trans-Missouri Freight Association.*[19] In this case the government sought to enjoin a loosely knit association of railroad companies that fixed rates so that there would be no competition in rates. The opinion of the Supreme Court, written by

---

[18] 322 U.S. 533 (1944). The rule that insurance was intrastate commerce preceded the Sherman Act, *Paul v. Virginia,* 8 Wall. 168 (1869). After the S.E.U.A. decision the status of insurance became more complex when Congress legislated in 1945 that the continued regulation and taxation of insurance by the states is in the public interest. A three-year moratorium on the application of the Sherman Act to cooperative rate fixing was established so that states could implement new rate fixing mechanisms. See Martin Lindahl and William A. Carter, *Corporate Concentration and Public Policy,* 3rd ed. (Englewood Cliffs, N.J.: Prentice-Hall, Inc., 1959), pp. 442–445.

[19] 166 U.S. 290 (1897).

Justice Peckham, stated that the "language of the act includes every contract, combination in the form of trust or otherwise, or conspiracy, in restraint of trade or commerce among the several States. . . ." The majority of the Court felt that the Sherman Act prohibited *all* monopolistic activities in interstate commerce. From this position the Supreme Court has retreated. Indeed, Justice White, for the minority, argued in this case that the Sherman Act outlawed only "unreasonable" restraints of trade, and Justice White's view became the settled opinion of the Court in the *Standard Oil Company* case in 1911.[20]

Although the court in this case declared the Standard Oil monopoly illegal, the prevailing opinion (written by Justice White) incorporated the distinction between "reasonable" and "unreasonable" restraints of trade. Thereafter followed a period of considerable uncertainty on the part of businessmen as to what actions violated the Sherman Act and what did not. Consequently, many businessmen asked Congress to clarify this matter. The consumers and small enterprisers, anxious to have a strict construction of the Act, urged Congress to pass legislation to catalogue the various economic practices that would restrain trade. Mindful of these pressures, political parties promised strengthening of the law on these and other grounds, and this activity provides the background for the Clayton and Federal Trade Commission acts.

Besides introducing some general confusion into the interpretation of the Sherman Act, the "rule of reason" assisted the development of a remarkable double standard under which the courts became more lenient toward close combinations than toward loose combinations. Part of the reason for this leniency toward close combinations derives from their unitary character. Although it is fairly easy to dissolve a trade association like the Trans-Missouri Freight Association or the South-Eastern Underwriters because they include separate corporations with separate managements who are cooperating in a manner that can be easily prohibited, the remedy for close combinations is not as simple, because separate ownerships and managements are not involved but the property interests of generally innocent investors are. Hence the courts have been reluctant to order dissolutions of close-knit combinations.

Third, does bigness itself constitute restraint? In general, large size has shared the same advantages under the "rule of reason" as have close combinations. The arguments of courts at least until after World War II generally followed the doctrine that mere size was no sign of monopoly. Thus a series of opinions following *U.S.* v. *United States Steel Corporation*[21] held that the law should not handicap the economic efficiency that the courts have assumed to be a concomitant to large size. This view was most cautiously expressed by Justice Cardozo who explained:

---

[20] *Standard Oil Co.* v. *U.S.*, 211 U.S. 1 (1911).

[21] 251 U.S. 417 (1920).

> Mere size, according to the holding of this court, is not an offense against the Sherman Act unless magnified to the point at which it amounts to monopoly . . . but size carries with it an opportunity for abuse that is not to be ignored when the opportunity is proved to have been utilized in the past . . .[22]

This tolerant position toward large businesses was maintained until 1945, when District Judge Hand ruled that the size of the Aluminum Company of America amounted to a restraint on the entry of potential competition.[23] At present the Supreme Court's position is to condemn size unless dissolution would mean a substantial loss in technological efficiency.[24] Hence, large size no longer has the same advantages as close combinations under the "rule of reason" and judges are more likely today to regard economic size as an aspect of economic power that may itself prove restraining on potential and actual competition.

Businesses under indictment frequently defend themselves by pointing out that size is merely a relative matter. One small grocer in a small town with no competitors for many miles may have an effective monopoly, whereas a large industrial combination such as Du Pont or the United States Steel Corporation may be subjected to considerable market control either because of competing large scale enterprises or because of the countervailing power of raw material suppliers and purchasers. One should point out that this argument does not conform to the competitive model with which this section was introduced. It is essentially an argument that oligopoly in this specific business will achieve better results. Opponents of large-scale enterprise do not view this argument favorably, and the courts have increasingly held that the Sherman Act barred this type of monopolistic activity.

Summary of Sherman Act Cases

The account of the Sherman Act and its enforcement suggests conflict between a variety of different groups to give it different meanings, as owners and corporate managers feel their property in things or expectations is affected. As a consequence, the Act itself has had special and different meanings in the field of transportation, professional athletics, insurance, and the production and marketing of sugar. Although the Act declares all monopolies to be illegal, under the "rule of reason" integrated close combinations have generally been carefully protected, large size has only recently become suspect, and only loose combinations have been easily broken up. What types of activities the government may reach with the

---

[22] *United States* v. *Swift & Co.*, 286 U.S. 106 (1932).
[23] *U.S.* v. *Aluminum Co. of America*, 148 F. 2d 416 (1945).
[24] Examine, for example, *U.S.* v. *Columbia Steel Co.*, 334 U.S. 495 (1948).

Sherman Act under the "interstate and foreign commerce" clause of the Constitution has also been controversial. We have noted that the status of insurance changed after the *South Eastern Underwriters* decision. Congress has shared responsibility for modifying the antitrust policy. After courts held that regional bureaus setting rail rates were illegal, Congress passed the Reed-Bulwinkle Act legitimizing this type of rail industry cooperation subject to ICC control.

Considering the character of the Sherman Act, and the diverse interests seeking to make it mean different things, there should be no wonder at the variety of attitudes that may be expressed toward a particular type of monopolistic activity such as price fixing. This variety has been put on the record by the Kefauver subcommittee of the Senate Judiciary Committee which investigated administered prices in the electrical industry following the decision in *U.S.* v. *Westinghouse et al.* (1961).

> *Mr. John K. Hodnette,* Executive Vice President, Westinghouse: I would hate to see the [Sherman] law changed in any great respect because, as I have indicated, I think it is a good law.
>
> *Senator Kefauver:* Your companies have gotten together, gotten the same price, and it may not be violations of law, but it is evidence that there is no competition, no price competition. The anti-trust laws are supposed to bring about competition.
>
> *Mr. Hodnette:* This is the most competitive industry I have ever seen. If there is one any more competitive than this, I don't want to get into it. And the prices that are charged to these standard products are determined by competition. They are determined by competition over many years of improvement in design and innovation. . . .
>
> *Senator Kefauver:* I know, but I mean I am just wondering where the competition is when you offer to sell 3,000 at $15.60 and General Electric offers to sell 3,000 at $15.60. Where is the competition?
>
> *Mr. Hodnette:* The free competition has driven the price down to that point, Senator.
>
> *Mr. Peter Chumbris,* Minority Counsel for the Committee: "Mr. Hodnette, I believe you testified earlier in 1956 . . . the Department of Justice was investigating because you were cutting the prices too low, I mean the industry, not just you, Westinghouse.
>
> *Mr. Hodnette:* This is what I understood the investigation was for.
>
> *Mr. Chumbris:* In other words, sometimes you are being charged with price-fixing, as you were in 1949 and 1959, and other times you may be charged with predatory pricing practices, if you go too low?
>
> *Mr. Hodnette:* This is the complexity of the law. We are in between. This is right.

Senator Kefauver: Well, where you are really competing on prices, I do
not know of anybody in the Federal Government that is going to fuss at
you, as long as you do not do it on a predatory basis, having in mind
driving the little fellow out of business by selling below cost.[25]

The Clayton Act

Part of the surge of public opinion behind the election of Woodrow
Wilson to the Presidency in 1912 stemmed from a popular reaction against
executive and judicial enforcement of the antimonopoly policy. Businessmen were not altogether sure what the "rule of reason" applied to and they
naturally wanted the greater security that comes from knowing what is
legal and what is not. Small enterprisers were opposed to large competitors
who had the economic power to force them out of business. Labor unions
were very much handicapped by virtue of the very rigid enforcement of the
Act against them, even though its author, Senator Sherman, had specifically explained that this Act was not to apply to trade union activity.
These pressures resulted in a number of different types of legislative
proposals that were to some extent finally included within the Clayton and
Federal Trade Commission acts.

The legislative history of the Clayton Act shows that one of the directions of this pressure was toward an explicit enumeration of monopolistic
practices that Congress should outlaw. The purpose of this specific listing
of illegal acts was to take discretion away from the courts under the "rule
of reason." However, Congress found the task of enumeration overwhelming, although the Clayton Act is primarily a remnant of this effort. In
sections 6 and 20 of the Act, Congress sought to exempt legitimate trade
union activity from the Sherman Act, while in sections 2, 3, 7, and 8
various specific activities that interfered with competition were proscribed.
Three specific evils are prohibited: 1) price discrimination, 2) exclusive
agreements, and 3) interlocking directorates or the purchase of stock in
competing concerns. These prohibitions are limited to circumstances where

---

[25] *Hearings* held before the Subcommittee on Antitrust and Monopoly of the
Committee on the Judiciary, May 10, 1961, Ward and Paul, Washington, D.C., pp.
2081, and 2104–7. Another company, General Electric, had an explicit directive 20.5
which stated that "No employee shall enter into any understanding, agreement, plan
or scheme, expressed or implied, formal or informal, with any competitor, in regard
to prices, terms or conditions of sale, production, distribution, territories or customers;
. . . nor engage in any other conduct which in the opinion of the Company's counsel
violates any of the anti-trust laws." Yet one old GE executive justified price fixing by
saying, "Sure, collusion was illegal . . . but it wasn't unethical. It wasn't any more
unethical than if the companies had a summit conference the way Russia and the West
meet. These competitor meetings were just attended by a group of distressed individuals who wanted to know where they were going." Richard A. Smith, "The Incredible
Electrical Conspiracy," *Fortune* (April, 1961), reprinted with other relevant documents
in *Administered Prices*, Hearings before the Subcommittee on Antitrust and Monopoly
of the Committee on the Judiciary, U.S. Senate, 87th Cong., 1st Sess., Part 27, p.
17097.

these activities substantially interfere with competition in interstate commerce. Furthermore, the Clayton Act made corporate officers personally liable for violations, and it facilitated the bringing of suits by injured parties under both this Act and the Sherman Act. Responsibility for enforcement was lodged jointly in the Department of Justice and the Federal Trade Commission.

Other aspects will be considered, but here we may examine the specific provisions of the Clayton Act with regard to close combinations. This Act seemed to establish a more rigorous standard for holding companies than the existing interpretations of the Sherman Act. Section 7 provided "That no corporation engaged in commerce shall acquire, directly or indirectly, that whole or any part of the stock or other share of capital of another corporation engaged in commerce, where the effect of such acquisition may be to substantially lessen competition. . . ." This provision was generally regarded as meaningless and ineffective because the Supreme Court ruled that:

> The statute does not forbid the acquirement of property, or the merger of corporations pursuant to state laws, nor does it provide any machinery for compelling a divestiture of assets acquired by purchase or otherwise or the distribution of physical property brought into a single ownership by merger.[26]

Since there was an easy way for a holding company to avoid the operation of Section 7, this provision did not prevent a practice that Congress presumably tried to forbid.

The Federal Trade Commission (FTC), representing the spokesmen for small business and the consumer, repeatedly sought amendment of the law, efforts that were finally crowned with success in the adoption of the Celler-Kefauver Anti-Merger Act of 1950. Section 7 of the Clayton Act was amended to prohibit both asset and stock acquisitions. This gave the government added power to deal with these mergers.

Curiously, Antitrust Division action starting in 1949 also may have invigorated the Clayton Act on these mergers, for the Supreme Court in 1957 reversed a dismissal of a government suit against du Pont de Nemours & Co.[27] involving intercompany stock holdings of the General Motors Co., activities which it declared came under the ban of Section 7 of the Clayton Act. In 1961 the Supreme Court finally ordered the du Pont Co.[28] to divest itself of the 23 per cent of General Motors stock which it held. Du Pont had been convicted of using its position to ensure that GM purchase a considerable proportion of the du Pont production of automotive finishes and fabrics. This was a vertical combination through stock acquisition, a

---

[26] *Arrow-Hart & Hegeman Electric Co.* v. *FTC*, 291 U.S. 587 (1934).

[27] *U.S.* v. *E. I. du Pont de Nemours & Co.*, 353 U.S. 586 (1957).

[28] *U.S.* v. *E. I. du Pont de Nemours & Co.*, 81 S Ct 1243 (1961).

FIGURE 7.1

Number of Corporate Mergers by Presidential Administrations, 1921–1961

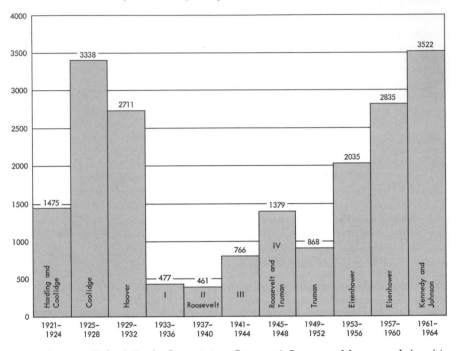

Sources: Federal Trade Commission, *Report of Corporate Mergers and Acquisitions* (House Doc. 169, 84th Cong. 1st Sess., 1955); and *Statistical Abstracts of the U.S.*, 1965, p. 503.

type of combination that the government had never attacked before under Section 7. Furthermore, the acts of acquisition took place between 1917 and 1919, and they were finally brought to trial in 1954. This case appears to suggest a significant change, for the Supreme Court has given a much more forceful interpretation to the original Clayton Act than it had previously; seemingly, it has revitalized the old Section 7, and a less permissive view of combinations may be in the making.

The first proceeding to interpret the Celler-Kefauver Act amending Section 7 of the Clayton Act illustrates some of the difficulties inherent in court enforcement of the antitrust laws. The case of *Brown Shoe Co.* v. *U.S.*[29] got under way in 1955 and took seven years before litigation was completed in 1962, twelve years after the law passed. Substantial staff time is required to carry a case like this through the courts. This case was exceedingly complicated in that it concerned both vertical and horizontal

---

[29] 370 U.S. 294 (1962).

combinations. Brown Shoe Company, which was the third largest seller of shoes with both manufacturing and retail operations, acquired the G. R. Kinney Co., which was the eighth largest seller and also had both manufacturing plants and retail stores. The government charged that the merger would lessen competition because Brown would force the Kinney outlets to sell Brown shoes and because competition would be eliminated between Brown and Kinney. The court accepted this argument, and the divestiture decree provided Brown with three alternatives: 1) a public offering of Kinney stock, 2) a sale of Kinney to another company, or 3) a transfer of Kinney shares to Brown stockholders. Brown complied by the sale of Kinney to F. W. Woolworth Company. This type of litigation of course takes a long time. Although courts in recent years have generally supported the more forceful interpretation of Section 7, mergers have increased greatly during the Eisenhower, Kennedy, and Johnson administrations as Figure 7.1 illustrates. This is, indeed, also true of corporate concentration.

The Federal Trade Commission Act

To assist in the enforcement of the Clayton Act, the Federal Trade Commission Act was also passed in 1914, creating an administrative commission of five members with rule-making, administrative, and judicial functions. The FTC was empowered to define and forbid unfair and dishonest methods of competition in interstate commerce, including deception in advertising. It is supposed to enforce the Robinson-Patman Act of 1936, which amended the Clayton Act to illegalize transactions through which chain stores and other large purchasers receive discounts, rebates, and other concessions that do not always correctly reflect all legitimate costs when these practices diminish competition or injure competitors.

In carrying out its many duties, the FTC:

1. Enforces laws against unfair competitive practices of businesses, unless this responsibility has been vested in some other agency by special legislation;
2. Works out lists of unfair practices (examine the appendix of any *Annual Report* of the FTC) by holding conferences in which industries are encouraged to avoid such practices;
3. Issues "cease and desist" orders when unfair practices continue;
4. Advises businesses so that they can be encouraged to avoid violating the law, and requires reports from them covering various aspects of their operations;
5. Scrutinizes acquisitions of stock and corporate structures in order to prevent interlocking directorates and ownership of stock in competing firms;
6. Investigates trade practices and economic conditions in foreign countries

where these practices may affect the foreign commerce of the United States; and

7. Institutes widespread investigations on the basis of which recommendations may be forwarded to Congress for new legislation to protect competition and business ethics.

Since the Department of Justice can compel testimony only through the grand jury, investigations of Clayton Act violations are often processed through the FTC, which may require persons to answer questions.

The Commission employs three different procedures: 1) the *stipulation* procedure by which defendants admit violations and agree to abandon objectionable practices (the admission may subsequently be used to support a cease-and-desist order); 2) the *industry conference* to secure industry-wide compliance with codes of fair competition; 3) legal enforcement action based on formal complaints that may result in a cease-and-desist order enforceable by the national courts. The types of practices with which the FTC deals fairly effectively can be illustrated from the record of stipulations achieved in a recent year.

> Among the deceptions were claims that: A throat lozenge containing an antibiotic cure prevents or shortens the duration of the common cold; an analgesic tablet is of aid in arresting the progress of arthritis, rheumatism, sciatica, or neuritis; a vaporizing device or chemical compound used in it reduces the incidence of infection or the spread of communicable disease. . . . In other stipulations, a manufacturer of home-freezers and two distributors of freezers in combination with food purchase plans agreed to discontinue claims that savings in food costs will pay for the freezer. . . .[30]

The concentration by the FTC on deceptive business practices has led to charges that this agency has been ineffective in dealing with patterns of corporate concentration. Following the 1960 election President-elect Kennedy appointed James M. Landis, an advisor to the late President Roosevelt on regulatory problems and a former member of three regulatory bodies, to make a study of these agencies. Following his report Congress accepted a 1961 reorganization plan that centralized some responsibility in the FTC chairman and speeded the procedures for handling complaints. Over a long period, however, the FTC has depended more on cooperative arrangements with industry, such as the Industry Guide Program established during the Eisenhower administration in 1955, because there have been inadequate funds to support extensive compulsory actions. In 1963 this Industry Guide Program was strengthened; the *1964 Annual Report* gave unprecedented "emphasis on the use of industry guidance methods as alternatives . . . to formal adversary actions," and it declared that whenever a law violation was identified, the Commission, instead of applying the simple . . . method of halting individual violators, undertook to find

---

[30] *Annual Report of the FTC*, 1955, pp. 68–69.

out if their competitors were doing likewise. If they were, the Commission then decided how best this competitively generated evil could be eliminated . . ." The new procedure gives the FTC wide discretion in deciding whether or not 1) to start formal proceedings, or 2) to accept mutually agreed upon assurances of discontinuance of unlawful activities.

Industry conferences, industry guides and the constant evaluation of business practices through the Business Advisory Service have provided alternative routes by which cooperation between the FTC and business has been achieved. Some of the guides, such as those issued on cigarette and tire advertising, remain controversial. Often these conflicts lead to legislative investigation and occasionally they lead to substantive legislation.

Exceptions to Anti-Monopoly Policy

Along with the handicaps placed by Congress on the enforcement of the antitrust laws through inadequate appropriations, a series of exceptions have been made to the general antimonopoly policy. Legislation to protect creative activity through the patent and copyright has always constituted an exception. These exceptions have been defended on the grounds that inventiveness and creativity should be encouraged by the government. Patents have often been protected even when they are owned by others than the inventor and when they have been used as means for creating an economic monopoly. Further exceptions exist under national and state agricultural policies, transportation, electric power, communication, gas, banking, meat packing, and insurance. Some of these exceptions are described elsewhere in this volume.

Among the most politically controversial efforts against price competition has been the movement to shackle the chain stores in order to preserve small independent businesses. This movement was most powerful during the depression and has been considerably moderated in recent more prosperous times. It has been characterized by a relatively disorganized attempt to tax the chains out of existence through state legislation, and by efforts at price fixing through "fair trade" and "unfair-practices" acts at the state level and the Robinson-Patman Act and the Miller-Tydings Act at the national level.

A number of different groups have been involved in various ways in these efforts by independent druggists and grocers to protect themselves against the more efficient services offered by the chains. Producers have frequently welcomed these efforts in order to improve their bargaining position with the chains. Many wholesalers, and competitors, have been similarly interested in moderating the power of the chains. Agriculture has been divided through astute politicking on the part of the chains, which have tried to prove to farmers that the chains' efficient marketing system could be more advantageous to them.

The first attack on the chains came largely through state legislative initiative by the passage of laws designed to cripple chains by *taxation*. During the depression this type of legislation had additional support from those desirous of finding new sources for state revenues; some of the additional taxes could even be justified on the grounds that the chains have a tax advantage over independent grocers because of their relatively higher turnover of stock. However, many of the twenty-seven state laws taxing chains were declared unconstitutional by state courts. Even though the U.S. Supreme Court upheld this type of legislation with respect to national constitutionality, the effort to tax the chains out of existence has not succeeded.

Subsequent efforts were directed toward *resale price maintenance* legislation. This type of legislation followed two forms. The "fair trade" laws, adopted in forty-five states, are designed to prevent price slashing of trademarked goods through private agreements between producers, wholesalers, and retailers. The "unfair-practices" legislation, adopted in thirty-one states, generally impose a prohibition on the sale of all commodities on either wholesale or retail markets at "below cost of production." These types of legislation are designed to restrain price competition within the states where legislation is effective.

Under considerable pressure from these same influences, Congress adopted the Robinson-Patman Act of 1936 and the Miller-Tydings Act of 1937. The latter act suggests the strategy of anti-chain store forces in that it amends the Sherman and Federal Trade Commission Acts to exempt resale price agreements in interstate commerce when products are shipped into "fair trade" states. The objective of this act was to expand the reach of this type of anti-chain legislation to products involved in interstate commerce.

The relative futility of this type of legislative approach is best illustrated by the legislative history of the Robinson-Patman Act. This act was the result of a conflict in interpretation of Section 2 of the Clayton Act, which prohibited price discrimination against small firms when such discrimination substantially interfered with competition, except when price differentials were based on "differences in grade, quality, or quantity," when they made "only due allowances" for differences in selling or transportation costs, or when they were made "in good faith to meet competition." The independents claimed that this section as interpreted permitted precisely the type of unreasonable quantity discounts that made possible the destructive predacity by the chains. The chains retorted that their activities were more efficient and consequently more economical. Statutory loopholes and judicial interpretation in effect prevented the use of this section to protect the independents.

The major organized force working for the Robinson-Patman Act was the U.S. Wholesale Grocers' Association; the original bill, indeed, was written by the general counsel of this organization. The USWGA secured the support of the retailers, and partial support from manufacturers and agricultural producers, with the chains in opposition. The proponents secured the support of Representative Patman, who had launched an extensive investigation of the whole issue, and Senator Robinson. Under the pull and push of a variety of pressures as well as general congressional confusion, this bill was wedded to another proposal, the Borah-VanNuys bill, which moderated the act in such a way that the chains were not substantially interfered with and agricultural and industrial producers were protected. As a consequence, the final law prohibits only excessive and unreasonable use of chains' mass buying power to discriminate against the independents. The chains have continued to grow and the independents have lost more of their market. On the other hand, wholesalers and producers have greater protections against the buying power of the chains.

The history of efforts to shackle the chains suggests a basic confusion in the idea of competition. Does competition mean a large number of sellers and buyers on the market actively seeking a share of the market? Or does competition mean the right of more efficient businessmen to drive the less efficient out of the market? Should established small independent businesses be given a continuing property right in the market in the face of more effective marketing techniques? Does the large size of the chains carry with it not only the power to abuse but actual abuse of their economic power against horizontal competition and vertical suppliers? The Federal Trade Commission, which had made an extensive investigation of this problem in the early 1930s, concluded that the commission should be given the power to proceed by the case-by-case method to expand the notion of unfair competition, but these recommendations were lost amid the pressure by retailers and wholesalers for their own pet bills.

POLITICS OF REGULATION

Although competition is the norm, in some fields public policy has been designed to prevent competition rather than foster it. Occasionally the government has created monopolies, in much the manner described by Thomas More, through the issuing of franchises; in these instances efforts have also been made to provide special regulation to insure adequate service and rates. The enterprises so regulated have generally been called "utilities" or as the Supreme Court described them in *Munn* v. *Illinois* "businesses affected with the public interest." Until the New Deal, business generally included under this concept was characterized by special economic circumstances, which were thought to make public regulation peculiarly appropriate. These included situations in which duplication of service was uneconomic or physically difficult, as for example, street railways, gas works, electric light and power, sewage, and water; businesses requiring heavy investment, with capital turnover occurring only over a long period and giving rise to decreasing costs with increased use of facilities, for example in rail transportation; and those in which publicly necessary services required the use of public rights of way, and where experience suggested that competition was undesirable, for example, electric power requiring parallel poles or street railways requiring parallel tracks. However, the concept of "business affected with the public interest" has expanded so that traditional notions of "public utility" as a closed concept have vanished even from the legal terminology.

Regulatory policy has tended to pass through roughly three stages. First, there has been a promotional stage, exemplified by large land grants to rails and subsidies for the location of electric power plants by local communities. Second, there has been a state regulatory stage, which usually broke down because interstate corporations could not be controlled by a state. The third stage, national regulation, has sometimes been encouraged by the regulated industry; more frequently the industry prefers state regulation. (National entrance into the field does not preclude state regulation. In many areas, electric power production, for example, federal and state regulatory authorities have established cooperative programs.)

The seven most important national regulatory commissions are the Interstate Commerce Commission, the Civil Aeronautics Board, the Securities and Exchange Commission, the Federal Trade Commission, the Federal Power Commission, and the National Labor Relations Board.

These commissions seem to have a life cycle. At first, there was widespread support for them and a vigorous program of regulation. This was followed by a middle-age slowdown, and then finally the incapacity of old age. Perhaps this life cycle reflects a "political fact of life," the more "independent" an agency is from normal executive and legislative controls the more dependent it is on support from regulated industries.

Periodically, regulatory agencies are attacked from all quarters. Regulated interests complain of bureacratic red tape. Consumers charge that the agencies fail to protect the general public. And there has been no lack of suggestions for improving the operations of the regulatory commissions. From the President's Committee on Administrative Management in 1937, from the Hoover Commission in 1949, from congressional committees in 1957, and most recently from a study by James M. Landis, there have come a series of recommendations. But the modest changes in administrative organization that have followed these recommendations have not had dramatic consequences in either policy changes or in the alteration of the political environment in which these agencies have functioned. This may be exemplified again in the regulation of television.

Regulation of Television

To understand the pattern of regulation of television, some understanding of the technical problems in designating portions of the radio spectrum is required. In the first place, radio paths differ; some types of transmission require wider portions of the spectrum than others. An FM broadcast requires a channel twenty times wider than an AM broadcast, while a TV broadcast of picture and sound requires a band 200 times the width of an AM program. Furthermore, low frequencies are capable of transmitting radio signals, but higher frequencies are required for FM and TV. Secondly, the distance that a signal may be transmitted depends not only on the power of the signal but the length of the wave. Powerful radio signals may interfere with less powerful ones on the same band at great distances, especially at night because after sunset "skywaves" are often forced back to earth by a ceiling of electrical particles known as the ionosphere.

Regulation by the FCC of radio and television deals principally with two issues, making policy for the allocation of broadcast channels and licensing of individual public and private broadcasters. At the present time AM broadcasts are confined to the lower end of the scale and FM and TV have the high ends of the spectrum. Briefly, the range for AM is between 1535 and 1606 kilocycles, FM occupies the range between 88 and 108 megacycles on the VHF (very high frequency) band, and TV occupies the remaining range between 54 and 216 megacycles on the VHF band as well as 470 to 890 megacycles on the UHF (ultra high frequency) band.

One way to appraise FCC performance is by examining the manner in which the regulated communications industry has dealt with the often conflicting pressures for commercial success and program variety. President Kennedy's first FCC chairman, Newton Minow, inaugurated his term of office with the charge that TV programming was a "wasteland," and this charge aroused a storm of protest from the broadcasting industry. Minow's successor, William Henry, carried on this theme in his first address before the National Association of Broadcasters. While complaining about the lack of industry support for an effective policy to deal with advertisers and TV advertising, he contended also that the industry was not anxious to support individual broadcasters who were engaged in original programming experiments. He said:

> Your contrasting reactions to these two struggles—overcommercialization and Pacifica Foundation—cast a disturbing light on the basic motivations of an industry licensed to do business in the public interest. And you might similarly gain insight into the reasons why, for all your magnificent

services to the public, your critics remain vocal. When you display more interest in defending your freedom to suffocate the public with commercials than in upholding your freedom to provide provocative variety—when you cry "Censorship!" and call for faith in the founding fathers' wisdom only to protect your balance sheet—when you remain silent in the face of a threat which could shake the first amendment's proud oak to its very roots—you tarnish the ideals enshrined in the Constitution and invite an attitude of suspicion."[31]

These opinions provide one context in which the interests of the industry and the administration of the law may be examined.

Interests and Television

There are seven distinguishable interests concerned with television: the broadcasters, the entertainers, the advertisers, the manufacturers, the distributors of television sets, the repairmen and the viewers. The broadcasters include not only the stations which own licenses, but the three networks and the American Telephone and Telegraph Company as well.

The television licensee typically has a small business with construction and annual operating costs amounting to about $250,000. His profits are generally high, averaging in 1952, 85 per cent on depreciated cost of physical property. Although physical construction costs for a station are relatively modest, TV properties have sold for as high as $12,500,000. The licensee is organized through the National Association of Broadcasters, which wields great power in government. During the Kennedy administration, the NAB was led by former Florida Governor LeRoy Collins who was the 1960 chairman of the Democratic National Convention.

The networks control a large proportion of the programs and advertising on most television stations. Curiously, the networks are not subject to regulation by the FCC. The American Telephone and Telegraph Company is involved in television through a patent agreement with the Radio Corporation of America. It leases to the networks the facilities by which programs are carried over coaxial cables for rebroadcast through the nation. The Radio Corporation of America, popularly known as RCA, also produces television sets and through its subsidiary, the National Broadcasting Company, owns one of the major networks.

Entertainers are variously organized. First, there are the producers of independent programs who provide live and filmed programs for sale to networks, advertisers, agencies, and stations. Second, there are unions of

---

[31] Address by E. William Henry, Chairman FCC before the NAB, April 7, 1964. The Pacifica Foundation runs a number of subscription radio stations on the West Coast. It was alleged by some groups to have carried obscene programs and to have a subversive management. The Foundation had carried live broadcasts of a variety of political expression including the Radical Right and Communists, and following the 1964 renewal of its license by the FCC it was challenged again for a live late evening broadcast by homosexuals who described their social problems. This and a number of other circumstances led to an FCC warning in 1965.

musicians, actors, technical personnel, as well as the American Society of Composers, Authors, and Publishers (ASCAP), which collects royalties for owners of music copyrights.

Advertisers should be distinguished from the advertising agencies and the station representatives. Advertisers purchase time either on local stations or on national networks for spot announcements or elaborate shows. The advertising agencies may be in competition with the networks and the independent program producers in developing programs, but their primary task is to develop national campaigns to sell this and that and persuade industries that they can be helpful in securing time to sell their product. They receive a 10 per cent discount in the purchase of TV time, and consequently can provide considerable services for a prospective advertiser without additional cost. Approximately thirty station representatives specialize in the sale of spot announcements for local stations. They compete with both networks and advertising agencies.

The manufacturers and distributors of TV sets have a definite interest in the expansion of broadcast services, but they also have large sums tied up in inventories of equipment already produced. Consequently, while the development of color TV undoubtedly produced a new demand for equipment, there was a violent controversy over which type of color system was to be developed. Although Columbia Broadcasting System received permission to develop their own color system, the courts and the Korean War intervened to the benefit of RCA and NBC whose system was finally elected by the FCC for development.[32]

Whether the consumer of television likes what he sees or is merely hypnotized is a matter of great debate. Chairman Minow of the FCC and Professor Claire Wilcox argue that the consumer is the forgotten man who does not even, as is claimed by the broadcasters, receive his entertainment free. What is needed, they insist, is more vigorous FCC action to force the broadcasters to improve the quality of their programs. On the other hand, broadcasters contend they provide the public with a wide range of entertainment and in developing programs they keep the wishes of the television audience constantly in mind. The viewer, they argue, gets what he wants. Underlying the debates is another issue of public policy. Should television serve the needs of the mass audience only or should programs be developed for specialized audiences of more limited size?

Current Issues of TV Regulation

The almost unlimited discretion given the FCC in the Federal Communications Act has not resulted in expeditious resolution of controversies in the broadcast industry. Aside from the issues of allocations and the

---

[32] Much of the preceding discussion depends on Claire Wilcox, *Public Policies Toward Business*, rev. ed. (Homewood, Ill.: Richard D. Irwin, Inc., 1960).

granting of licenses, which have already been discussed, there are serious problems relating to advertising, monopoly, and civil liberties.

The FCC has the power to relegate advertising to station breaks or otherwise limit its omnipresence. However, to a considerable extent, advertising controls the programming of TV and pays the production bill. Consequently, until now the FCC has largely accepted the broadcasting industry's view that advertising be unregulated, and negative actions that have been taken have been confined largely to deceptive advertising uncovered by the Food and Drug Administration and the FTC. The Landis report to President Kennedy recommended that there be more coordination between these latter two agencies and the FCC.

Mr. Landis also recommended that there be some coordination between the FCC and the Department of Justice regarding the issue of monopoly; licenses are not to be issued to those convicted of violating the antitrust laws. However, competition is difficult to define if it might theoretically exist between communications media as well as within one particular industry. The pattern of development of the communications industry has been in the direction of rapid concentration of power, not only by networks, but within regions among different media such as newspapers, radio, and television. As a consequence, a fourth of the AM stations and three-fifths of the TV stations are owned by newspapers. This has lead to competition between ownership interests; a competition which has not often been visible to the viewer. One way of expanding competition would have been to require all TV to move to the UHF band. But this was successfully opposed by the Association of Maximum Service Telecast which represented the TV industry and secured a compromise requiring all new television sets to be built to receive UHF signals. The spread of community antenna television (CATV) is an alternative means for providing competition to local television monopolies. In early 1966 the FCC assumed regulatory control over CATV, and asked Congress to determine how its regulatory authority should be used.

Regulation and use of the airwaves provide peculiar civil liberties difficulties. To prevent biased programming the FCC has favored prospective licensees who promise to serve the whole community, not those who propose to serve parts of it. Whatever test is applied relative to programming represents, however, a regulation of the communications. The FCC has had to face a variety of criticisms, as has the broadcasting industry, with respect to programming and denial of access to proponents of a variety of different views. Perhaps the problem of the radio editorial and the issue of political broadcasts will exemplify these difficulties.

The FCC in the Mayflower decision of 1941 denied radio stations the right to editorialize. This ruling required "balanced discussions" when controversial issues were raised. Under the pressure of broadcasters this decision was modified in 1949. Stations are now permitted to editorialize as long as they permit contrary opinions to be heard. However, there is no obligation to present controversial issues, and the only manner in which the Mayflower and subsequent rulings have been policed has been on the basis of private complaints from listeners. Under present rulings, for example, an atheist has no right to purchase time to answer the proponents of religion, who apparently have little difficulty purchasing time to present their views, because the FCC has not felt religion a matter of public controversy.

Civil liberties are also involved in the problem of political broadcasts. Section 315 of the Federal Communications Act requires stations to record all requests for political broadcast time. It also requires that if political broadcast time is granted to one candidate it must be granted to any opponent under equal conditions. Furthermore, a station may not censor a political broadcast, and charges for political broadcasts are not to exceed the charges for comparable use. The purpose of these provisions is to protect equal access to the air for political contestants. In spite of the law, there have been complaints that some stations do not apply these rules with equity. Moreover, small political parties do not have the financial resources to pay for equal time no matter what the merit of the ideas they expound.

In the 1960 election year Congress amended Section 315 of the Communications Act to eliminate the equal time requirement insofar as minor party candidates for President and Vice President were concerned. This legislation made possible the controversial Nixon-Kennedy debates. However, a serious value problem was presented to proponents of democracy who were asked if democracy requires only that those who are likely to be victorious have a right to express their views. However, it is practically impossible for the few communications outlets to provide means so that everyone can be heard. Even so, the practical question is serious when there are as many as seventeen candidates who say they are running for President as was the case in 1960. Consequently, in the eighty-seventh Congress, legislation was introduced to make this exemption from Section 315 permanent.[33] This issue dragged along in the eighty-eighth Congress where, following the assassination of President Kennedy, Democratic strategy dictated the defeat of this proposal in 1964; Republicans complained that President Lyndon Johnson did not wish to face their candidate, Senator Goldwater, in a repeat of the Nixon-Kennedy confrontation.

---

[33] *Review of Section 315 of the Communications Act* Hearings before the Communications Subcommittee on Interstate and Foreign Commerce, U.S. Senate, 87th Cong., 1st Sess., 1961. Incidentally, this preliminary study shows that in spite of the vast amount of free time granted the major parties, Presidential, and Vice Presidential candidates they spent as much in 1960 on TV as in 1956.

When public pressure is overt and well pronounced in one direction the FCC and Congress generally can be expected to act. However, on most issues public concern is not clearly manifested in the communications area unless some clear moral misdeed provides a spark. Movement for reform of the FCC had to await the discovery of scandal, and a scandal was uncovered by Professor Bernard Schwartz. Mr. Schwartz was employed by the House Commerce Committee to inquire into the regulatory commissions, and he was fired by the same committee when he found and proposed to expose violations of the law that were politically embarrassing to the powerful congressmen and the incumbent administration. Some of these violations implicated members of the FCC. Although his principal discovery was that the FCC issued broadcast licenses on the basis of political and economic preferment rather than on the basis of publicized criteria, what caught the public attention was the fact that Chairman Doerfer and other commissioners received free entertainment from the NAB while at the same time charging the government for expenses of attending professional meetings. One commissioner was found to have accepted substantial sums of money from an applicant for a TV license, who subsequently proved successful. These revelations stirred the public conscience in the direction of reform.

The Kennedy Administration's answer to these charges and the long series of unresolved controversies has proven to be the traditional American remedy, namely reorganization. Following the Landis study of December, 1960, Kennedy sent a message to Congress in which he recommended, for all regulatory agencies, the centralizing of responsibility under the chairman and the decentralizing of decision-making by permitting the chairman to delegate many responsibilities to individual commissioners or subordinates. These ideas were subsequently incorporated in Reorganization Plan 2 for the FCC. This proposal included the elimination of the controversial Review Staff, which had the duty of preparing justifications for FCC decisions.

President Kennedy's proposals for FCC reorganization came under a flood of criticism from the TV industry as well as congressmen.[34] Some critics of the President's proposals argued that to centralize responsibility for the administration of the Commission in the hands of its chairman would create a communications czar. These same critics, and others, complained that decentralization of decision-making would infringe on the

---

[34] *Broadcasting Magazine,* April 17, 1961, published a list of ten Senators and thirteen representatives with direct or family property interests in the TV industry. A nephew of Speaker Rayburn was FCC Commissioner Bartley.

rights to appeal. Newspapers joined the NAB and a majority of the sitting FCC commissioners in opposing the proposed reorganization.

The legislative strategy of the opponents of the President's reorganization plan was to insist that although the purposes of the plan were laudable, the method was inappropriate. (According to the Reorganization Act of 1961 the President may submit reorganization proposals to Congress. If either House does not *veto* within sixty days, they go into effect.) This position was taken by Governor Collins for the NAB, who pointed out that the President's plan eliminated the right of appeal; he felt this should be done only by ordinary legislation. After Chairman Oren Harris of the House Commerce Committee, which would have jurisdiction over such legislation, promised to bring in new legislation, even the Democratic leadership in the House joined all the Republicans to *veto* the FCC reorganization by an overwhelming 323–77.

Following defeat of the President's plan, Congress considered several bills[35] designed to improve the operations of the FCC. Neither the Kennedy Administration nor congressional leaders recommended support for the Landis proposal that a special office on telecommunications policy be established. A Harris bill reflecting largely the views of the TV industry emerged from the House. It provided that a minority of three commissioners of the seven-man FCC could veto any delegations of authority or refusals to hear appeals. A FCC-sponsored bill, which provided that the principle of majority rule would apply on delegations and appeals, was introduced into the Senate; finally a modified version of this proposal was adopted at the end of the 1961 session.

The strategies of the various contestants in this struggle should be examined. Initially, President Kennedy tried to reform policy by a quiet reorganization program. The TV industry resisted and enlisted the aid of congressmen sympathetic to its position. The House disapproved the President's reorganization proposals after congressional leaders promised that the goals the President was seeking would be better obtained through legislation. This strategy invited the Democratic administration to seek widespread public support. FCC chairman Newton Minow, a Kennedy appointee, entered the fray and became a regular participant in the public forum by appearing on TV; the FCC held its own hearings in June to publicize the alleged programming defects of the TV industry. Eventually,

---

[35] Discussion of the issues relative to Reorganization Plans 1–4 pertaining to the SEC, FCC, CAB, and FTC may be found in *Hearings*, Subcommittee on Government Operations, House of Representatives, 87th Cong., 1st Sess., May 18, 19, 1961. Senate Republicans took the leadership in killing the SEC reorganization. Discussion of the Harris Bill H.R. 7333 and the FCC alternative known as the Pastore Bill S. 2034 may be found in *Federal Communications Commission Reorganization*, Hearings before a subcommittee of the Committee on Interstate and Foreign Commerce, House of Representatives, 87th Cong., 1st Sess. on H.R. 7333, June 13–15, 1961.

the Administration obtained the support it needed for most of the goals it sought.

The 1961 Act denied to the FCC chairman authority to delegate minor responsibilities, but it did give a majority of the commissioners the right to make these delegations. Furthermore, appeals could be rejected without giving reasons, and the commission was given considerable discretion with respect to granting oral arguments on exceptions to agency decisions. And, finally, the Review Staff was abolished. The manner in which this legislation influences the TV industry, however, remains to be worked out in the working relationship which develops between the industry and the FCC.

This chapter has examined the experience of two regulatory agencies, the FTC and FCC. Neither agency has left a record of energetic leadership in the making of policy. Both stand accused of delaying justice. To some extent these difficulties arise from their own organizational form as quasi-legislative and quasi-administrative bodies; to some extent it is the consequence of the character of their political support. Their "independence" has been from both presidential control and his political responsibility. Moreover, Congress has not provided either legislative or financial support. In the face of this separation these agencies, particularly the FCC, have sought the friendly support of regulated industries. There should be little wonder that, on occasion, even courts have ordered reversal of commission decisions because of the impropriety of the influence exerted on commissioners. It may be doubted that either administrative reorganization or new personnel will alter the situation without a clearer and more effectively expressed public opinion.

PUBLIC OWNERSHIP

Direct public regulation of business follows four characteristic methods. 1) The states provide a basic statutory framework for the definition and exchange of property. 2) Regulatory schemes exist principally at the national level to promote competition. 3) Regulatory agencies have been given authority by both state and nation to regulate those industries in which competition has not insured satisfactory service. 4) Public ownership and operation of business is an alternative which is frequently ignored, perhaps because its presence constitutes a challenge to the prevailing ideology of free enterprise. The Socialist party has ceased as an electoral group, and discussions of "creeping socialism" have sometimes been replaced by discussions of "federal extremism." In spite of this declining interest there are some significant examples of public enterprise such as the Tennessee Valley Authority and the Atomic Energy Commission. The Post Office constitutes a large public monopoly. The nation's public school systems and state college and university systems are important public businesses, while the sale of public lands as well as rentals constitutes a major source of national revenue. In addition, more than two-thirds of the cities own their own water works; about 2000 run their electric systems, almost 100 own their gas works, a growing number of cities (over fifty) own their local transit systems. Public ownership is not as extensive at the state level, but North Dakota has experimented with a wide variety of state ownership projects such as banks and grain elevators. In other states one frequently finds state liquor stores, and occasionally some kinds of insurance and housing programs.

According to the Department of Commerce, in 1957 public businesses accounted for approximately $4.2 billion of national income or a little more than 1 per cent; however, these figures did not include the Post Office, educational systems, or public lands.[36]

Among the reasons for public ownership are necessity, accident, and choice. One municipality after another has been forced either to buy out or to subsidize bankrupt municipal transportation firms, and the national government may well be forced into the same choice with some railroads. Accidental development of public enterprise is illustrated by flood control development resulting in the construction of public dams, which may also be used to generate electric power; publicly owned liquor stores have been the incidental byproducts of state alcoholic beverage control. Experience with voluntary assumption of public ownership of national parks and forests, atomic energy patents, and many state and local enterprises has requently proven beneficial.

However, public control does not automatically resolve the issue of public accountability. Decisions still must be made regarding what the public wants and can afford. The nepotism which pervades private business has its counterpart in patronage and political preferment in public business. How to hold a public corporation politically accountable is a fundamental question, difficult to resolve. This last issue was faced in a particularly acute form in the recent controversy between Congress and the States of New Jersey and New York regarding the Port of New York Authority.

The Port of New York Authority

In 1921 the Port of New York Authority was established by New York and New Jersey with congressional sanction. Its general purpose is to facilitate transport to and from Manhattan Island; this public corporation is empowered to plan, lease, buy, or build all types of transport facilities, and it may finance construction by borrowing to be ultimately repaid through tolls which it sets. It owns all the tunnels under the rivers, many bridges, bus terminals, docks, and the major civilian airports in the New York area.

---

[36] *U.S. Income and Output, 1958* (Washington: Government Printing Office, 1959), p. 131.

The Authority is managed by a board of twelve commissioners, six appointed by each governor of the participating states. The commissioners appoint an executive director who administers the many programs. Although the Port Authority has managed to make substantial profits and has expanded its activities, in a democracy, efficiency of public agencies is only one standard to measure their success. For how are they to be held accountable to the electorate?

It is doubtful if the voters of New York and New Jersey have much control over the operation of the Port Authority. Congress has only a tenuous interest in its operations, and its legal capacity has occasionally been questioned. In 1959, when the Authority proposed to build a jet port in Morris County, N.J., complaints from residents of the area produced a House Judiciary Committee investigation of the Authority. Mr. Tobin, executive director, refused to produce for a subcommittee subpoened records, pleading he was accountable to the governors of New York and New Jersey. Subsequently Mr. Tobin was convicted of criminal contempt in the United States District Court for the District of Columbia, Judge Youngdahl in effect upholding the right of Congress to examine the operations under such interstate compacts. However, an appeal on behalf of the States of New York and New Jersey was won in the Court of Appeals on behalf of Mr. Tobin. The appeal was decided on the narrow ground that the Authority had produced all the documents that could be expected under the congressional resolution authorizing the investigation, but in the *dicta* the Court expressed the opinion that Congress did not have authority to alter the terms of its consent to an interstate compact under the Constitution. The Supreme Court declined to review the Court of Appeals' ruling. Consequently, it may be true that the twelve commissioners do operate this $800 million business affecting the lives of millions of people without being held directly politically accountable for their actions. However, they do need substantial support from the Governors of the compacting States.[37]

CONCLUSIONS

These various devices of public ownership, the regulation of private utilities, the protection of competition, the proper supervision of radio and television suggest that the economy of our country is much more complex than the few brief words quoted earlier from the statement of the National Association of Manufacturers could suggest. One sees combined a number of different patterns of ownership and control:

---

[37] Cf. Richard H. Leach, "War on the Port Authority," in R. J. Tresolini and R. T. Frost, *Cases in American National Government and Politics* (Englewood Cliffs: Prentice-Hall, 1966), pp. 10–18.

1. At the base there is private property, which is defined and protected by law.
2. Most of the extraction of raw materials and the manufacturing and distributive industries are operated by corporations where ownership is separated from the control of property.
3. Much of this property that is involved in production and exchange is under a variety of additional positive governmental controls.
4. Some property like the postal system is completely under government ownership and control.
5. In an earlier chapter we have observed that some property, such as the Federal Reserve Banks, is under private ownership but under government operation.
6. And some property is publicly owned but privately operated. Portions of the Merchant Marine, Atomic Energy patents, and the air waves for which government issues licenses remain in the public domain but are privately controlled.

It would be hard to imagine a single theoretical standard by which all these varieties of property could be measured for their ethical or public utility. The types of property as well as the types of control are fundamentally the product of group pressures, and any method of ownership and control is only as good as the presently predominating interests wish it to be, which is merely to say again that this lack of system seems to serve a lot of different people more or less effectively depending on their particular points of view.

BIBLIOGRAPHICAL NOTE

N. J. Ware, *Wealth and Welfare*, 1949, provides a short history of the development of the U.S. economy. A. G. Papandreou and J. T. Wheeler, *Competition and Its Regulation*, 1954, carefully compares the economist's concept of competition as distinguished from the lawyer's concept of competition. Public regulations to foster competition are described, court decisions are analyzed, and recommendations are made for the improvement of the present laws.

J. R. Commons, *Legal Foundations of Capitalism*, 1924, and *The Economics of Collective Action*, 1951. The "institutional" approach to economics is well illustrated in these two volumes. The late Professor Commons views economic behavior in a context as broad as society itself and is concerned with the close relation between the activities of public officials and private groups in the economic process. B. Gross, "The Coming Revolution in Economic Thought," in *Life, Language, Law: Essays in Honor of Arthur F. Bentley*, 1957, Ch. IV, is a brilliant essay that relates the "institutional" approach to modern developments in economic theory.

J. Bauer, *Transforming Public Utility Regulations*, 1950. As well as describing modern regulation of private utilities, this volume makes recommendations for improvements.

H. C. Simons, *Economic Policy for a Free Society*, 1947, one of the best defenses of the free enterprise economy, claims that government is the chief creator of monopoly. Professor Simons argues that monopolies of both labor and business should be destroyed in order to protect and improve our economic system. W. Adams and H. M. Gray, *Monopoly in America*, 1946, agrees with Professor Simons that government has been responsible, to a large extent, for the creation of monopoly power, but argues that the protection of competition is primarily a governmental responsibility which should be pursued through more vigorous and effective regulation.

J. M. Clark, *Alternative to Serfdom*, 1948, is a modest defense of governmental planning that provides one of the most careful discussions of the issues involved in public regulation.

J. A. Schumpeter, *Capitalism, Socialism, and Democracy*, 1950. A defender of the private entrepreneur, the late Professor Schumpeter is both pessimistic about the future of capitalism and the capacity of socialist planning to achieve better results. This is must reading for defenders of "free enterprise" as well as advocates of alternative economic systems. J. K. Galbraith, *American Capitalism*, 1952 tries to show that the size of a corporation is not necessarily an index of its capacity for interfering with the competitive economy. The "countervailing power" of suppliers and purchasers is frequently sufficient to place a large corporation under adequate social control. A. A. Berle, *The Twentieth Century Capitalist Revolution*, 1954, contends that the corporate managers are replacing the politicians as the modern statesmen and that corporation law is becoming modern constitutional law.

Emmette S. Redford, *American Government and the Economy* (New York: The Macmillan Company, 1965) is a useful recent text covering the range of subjects examined in this chapter. Students of the regulatory commissions will find James Landis, *Report on Regulatory Agencies to the President Elect*, 1960, and Bernard Schwartz, *The Professor and the Commissions* (1959) stimulating. James E. Anderson's *Emergence of the Modern Regulatory State* (1962) provides a brief history of regulatory policy in the U.S.

government
and
labor

JAMES M. BURNS

If we live in an era of Big Business and Big Government, surely we must talk in terms of Big Labor too. The total labor force in the United States—men and women over the age of fourteen employed or seeking work—is about seventy-five million. This number rises by about a million a year. Of the total labor force, about one of every four workers is a member of some union. Most of these trade union members are organized in the once separated American Federation of Labor and Congress of Industrial Organizations. "Labor" in the broadest sense dominates the American economy; and the part of labor that is organized wields tremendous economic and political power. The announcements of the AFL–CIO on a national problem reverberate in the White House and in Congress; the head of the AFL–CIO must be reckoned as one of the dozen or so most influential persons in America.

Individual unions also hold great power, especially when concentrated in particular areas. One of the largest unions, the United Auto Workers, heavily influences the politics of Michigan, and its policies and demands in bargaining with the great automobile companies influence the pattern of collective bargaining throughout the country. Pennsylvania politics would be much different without the Miners Union. Some of the craft unions, such as the Carpenters and Bricklayers, intimately affect politics in their localities. Labor as a whole is well represented in the lobbies of Washington and the state capitals.

Labor leaders like to proclaim that unions in America are "as American as America itself." To some extent this is true. The tremendous variety of labor unions reflects much of the variety of the whole economy and society. Thus we have not

8

only unions of auto workers and carpenters, but also of radio and television actors, of bank clerks, of government workers, of Pullman porters, of tug boat operators, and of hundreds of other types of occupations. On the other hand, organized labor is not a simple mirror of the whole body of Americans employed by others. Some employees are highly organized; others—for example, farm laborers, office secretaries, department store clerks, domestic servants, college professors—are under-organized or not organized at all. Some unions are strong and independent; others are small and weak, or perhaps dominated by an employer. These distinctions and qualifications are important ones to keep in mind in considering the labor policy of government and labor's influence on it.

HISTORICAL BACKGROUND

The efforts of American workers to organize and improve their situation are part and parcel of the history of America as a whole. Trade unions in the modern sense are about as old as our system of government. The great forces that have affected America—industrialization, urbanization, wars, depressions, prosperity, and above all economic growth—have shaped the American labor movement. But the impact has not been a one-way affair. Organized labor, especially in more recent years, has significantly affected government and public policy, just as the politics and government of Washington and state, county, and local capitals have influenced labor. This situation is also true of the relation between labor and employers. Labor organization has been, to a large extent, a reaction to the organization and practices of businessmen, just as the latter have continually modified their policies one way or another to cope with the demands of organized labor.

Hence we must visualize the development of government labor policy —including the *absence* of government policy—as in large part a response to the economic and political changes in the relation of labor and employers, this relation in turn being ceaselessly affected by basic economic, political, and social changes. For the sake of convenience we may divide the historical development of labor and labor policy into four broad periods.

The First Hundred Years

The first trade unions date from about the time that George Washington first took office as President. Prior to this time there had been, of course, guilds of skilled workers. But the typical organization of a small workshop was a master and a few apprentices, and such a relationship had made organization in the modern sense almost impossible. With the impact of the industrial revolution, however, important changes took place in the relations in the shop. Markets broadened, shops expanded in size, simple machinery was introduced, businessmen looked around for cheaper labor, the apprenticeship system declined, the relations between manager and worker became more impersonal, and a more distinct wage-earning class developed. The first unions were formed mainly by skilled craftsmen reacting against these new developments. By 1800 there were craft societies of carpenters, cabinetmakers, weavers, hatters, and a variety of other occupations.

It was only natural that employers would react strongly to the new organizations, and they often did so in a hostile manner. Employers formed associations of their own to deal with the workers, and they turned to the law and the courts for weapons against the workers' "illegal" organizations. The judges turned to the old English common-law doctrine of conspiracy to find journeymen shoemakers and other groups "guilty of a combination to raise wages." It was partly in protest against this alliance between the employers and the government that many workers turned to the Jeffersonian and Jacksonian political movements during the first half of the nineteenth century.

The first unions were often rather feeble and could be destroyed by depressions or by hostile employers or judges. As the nation expanded, however, the unions took more and more secure footholds, and by the mid-nineteenth century hitherto isolated labor groups in various cities had formed links with one another and were establishing national unions. Once established, the unions began to experiment, not always consciously, with various ways of operating. Some workers' groups used only economic weapons, such as the strike and the boycott. Others were more concerned with political action, forming workingmen's parties, even joining hands with farmers restless over economic conditions. Other unions turned to embryonic radical movements. Still others, like the notorious "Molly Maguires" resorted to terroristic tactics that led in turn to disorders, destruction, and bloodshed.

The climax of union labor's "first century" came in the form of the Knights of Labor. At first a secret organization, the Knights grew with amazing speed during the 1880s. Its importance lay in its attempt to become one great nationwide union of all types of workers and in its willingness to use political as well as economic weapons. For a time the Knights had spectacular success, increasing in size to 700,000 members and supporting some successful strikes. But its supremacy was short-lived. Disunity developed among the heterogeneous elements in the organization. Skilled workers felt that their interests were not sufficiently represented as against other workers. A number of strikes sponsored by the Knights failed badly. The leadership was often inept. By 1890 the experiment of one grand union using economic and political methods had failed.

What was government labor policy during the first hundred years? To a great extent it was nonexistent, as compared with the extensive labor legislation we have today. But the *absence* of policy was in itself important. It often meant that workers and employers were left to fight out their battles without interference from the government. Lack of concern over labor and working conditions by the government in turn reflected more basic factors: the prevailing ideology of *laissez faire* that, especially in the latter part of the period, emphasized the desirable operation of automatic and "natural" economic laws without intervention by the government; the emphasis in popular thinking on the Horatio Alger, Jr., "success story" of the able young man climbing the economic and social ladder; the fact that millions of workers were immigrants who could hardly speak English and who had little power to influence government; the organizational weaknesses of unions and their tendency to cave in when depressions struck.

One aspect of the negative or hostile government labor policies during this period was the role of the *courts*. In the *absence* of legislation—that is, action by the popularly elected lawmakers, who on occasion might be influenced by union pressure—judges used old, common-law doctrines against labor's "conspiracy" to combine. For example—to take a case shortly after this period—during a conflict between a union and a metal company in the metal trades, a court enjoined union leaders from boycotting the company; when the leaders persisted with the boycott, the court sentenced them to jail. In another case, a court prohibited the unionization of a coal mine without the consent of the owners.

The American Federation of Labor, 1890–1932

While the Knights of Labor were declining, a new organization of workers was gaining strength nationally. Under the leadership of a shrewd cigar maker named Samuel Gompers, the American Federation of Labor embraced not the ambitious program of the Knights but practical, "bread-and-butter" unionism. Gompers and his associates generally believed in capitalism and strove to improve labor's lot within that system. They favored local autonomy for the AFL's member unions, emphasis on economic tactics such as the strike and picketing, and avoidance of "class warfare" and other radical ideas. The AFL proved its durability when it survived the economic crises toward the end of the nineteenth century.[1]

The AFL's political tactics were the counterpart of its economic tactics. In general Gompers tended to fear government—to him it was less an agency that could help labor than a distant power to be feared. His main objective was to prevent employers from using the government—legisla-

---

[1] E. E. Cummins, *The Labor Problem in the United States* (New York: D. Van Nostrand Company, Inc., 1935), p. 135.

tures, governors, judges, and officials—to thwart labor's effort to improve economic conditions. Hence for some time the AFL had a limited and rather negative political program.

The government's relation to labor toward the end of the nineteenth century seemed to vindicate labor's suspicion of government. President Cleveland, as well as a number of state governors, used troops against strikers. Laws were passed limiting the effectiveness of strikes, picketing, the boycott, and other economic weapons. An important example of labor's difficulties with government was the Sherman Antitrust Act of 1890. Passed ostensibly to prevent illegal combinations by businessmen, the act was used against combinations of *workers*—that is, against labor unionism itself. Court injunctions, too, were often obtained by employers to thwart economic action by unions.

Disheartened by such developments, faced by the competition of more radical groups such as the "Wobblies" (Industrial Workers of the World), and impressed by the political successes of British unionists, the AFL decided in the early 1900s to enter politics a bit more actively. A program was formulated demanding such reforms as sanitary inspection of shops, liability of employers for injury or loss of life, the eight-hour day, child labor laws, free schools and textbooks, and even municipal ownership of private utilities. "We have long, patiently and in vain waited for redress . . ." labor proclaimed. If government did not respond, labor threatened to appeal to the voters.[2] During the following decade the AFL pursued a political tactic of trying to "help our friends and defeat our enemies."

Woodrow Wilson's election in 1912 with a Democratic Congress was hailed as a great victory for labor's heightened interest in political action. For labor, the "New Freedom" meant the Clayton Act, which seemed to exempt labor from the onerous provisions of the Sherman Act, more influence for the AFL in the administration of the Labor Department and the labor policies of other government agencies, greater access to the Administration and to Congress, and passage of a bill establishing the eight-hour day for most railroad employees.[3] During World War I the Federation achieved an important place in the war administration; and the war and employment boom helped it achieve its organizational high point, until then, of almost two million members.

The next fifteen years, however, brought American unionism to its lowest ebb in decades. Despite the prosperity of the 1920s, organized labor failed to augment either its economic or political power. Membership fell off, and little effort was made to organize millions of workers in the large mass-production industries such as automobiles and steel. Union strength

---

[2] "Labor's Bill of Grievances," *American Federationist* (May, 1906), pp. 293–96.

[3] Cf. A. S. Link, *Wilson: The New Freedom* (Princeton, N.J.: Princeton University Press, 1956).

fell off even more during the early 1930s under the impact of the Great Depression. There were few government programs to protect workers against the ravages of unemployment and wage cuts. "Men are afraid, working men are filled with fear," declared William Green, Gompers' successor as head of the AFL.

There were some bright spots for labor during these frustrating years. Union leaders scored an important legislative victory in 1932 with the passage of the Norris-La Guardia Act. Sponsored by two progressive Republicans, Senator George Norris of Nebraska and Representative Fiorello La Guardia of New York City, this act declared that, in order to protect the public interest, workers should be free to form unions without interference from employers. Recognizing that the "individual unorganized worker is commonly helpless to exercise actual liberty of contract and to protect his freedom of labor," it declared that workers may select representatives of their own choosing. It made yellow-dog contracts (contracts prohibiting workers from joining unions) unenforceable in federal courts and drastically limited the issuance of labor injunctions in other respects. But the act established no agency to enforce its provisions.

Some states also were still taking the lead in passing laws favored by labor. For example, more than half the states by 1932 had replaced the common law with statutes prohibiting blacklisting (listing of names of union leaders and organizers so that they could be denied jobs in other companies). Some industrial states and some states run by progressive politicians (such as LaFollette in Wisconsin) had passed extensive social welfare legislation, such as minimum wage laws for various types of employees, but unfavorable court decisions on the constitutionality of such laws under the Fourteenth Amendment discouraged the states from more decisive action; moreover, there was always the problem that the more drastic the labor laws, the more businesses might threaten to leave the state.

Aside from these bright spots for labor, the 1920s and early 1930s were a period of stagnation. Long committed to the essential features of a laissez-faire economic system, the Federation seemed to be as demoralized as most business. Some workers tried militant economic action, such as desperate strikes, or even turned to socialist or communist movements, but nothing seemed to help much as depression tightened its grip on the American economy.

The New Deal
and After

The inauguration of Franklin D. Roosevelt in 1933, like that of Woodrow Wilson twenty years before, brought a sharp change in the political climate for labor. Although the unions were not powerful enough politically to be decisive, leaders of the AFL and of other unions had given far more support to Roosevelt than to President Herbert Hoover in the presidential race of 1932, and once again labor had access to the Administration and to Congress. In the very first months of the New Deal, union leaders such as Green and John L. Lewis, head of the United Mine Workers, took an active part along with representatives of employers and other groups in framing the National Industrial Recovery Act, the most important domestic legislation of the early New Deal. Under the famous Section 7a of the NIRA, labor was "guaranteed" the right of collective bargaining. Benefiting from this provision and from increased employment, union membership and morale soared during 1934 and 1935. But so did divisions within labor. Restless at the continued conservative leadership of the AFL, eager to organize the great mass-production industries at a time that seemed ripe, and hopeful of building up a stronger labor alliance with the New Dealers, a group of unions under Lewis' leadership broke away from the AFL and established the CIO (then called the Committee for Industrial Organization, later changed to Congress of Industrial Organizations). Soon the rivalry between the AFL and CIO was dominating the world of labor organization.

In 1935 the Supreme Court declared the NIRA unconstitutional, and with it, of course, Section 7a. The court's decision, however, coincided with a leftward turn in the New Deal and helped bring the enactment of what was the most important labor legislation until that time, the National Labor Relations Act. Like Section 7a, the new act was designed to guarantee labor's right of collective bargaining, free from any employer domination or even influence, to all workers in concerns employing persons in interstate commerce or in industries substantially affecting interstate commerce. Unlike Section 7a, however, the act spelled out five types of unfair labor practices which employers were forbidden to engage in: 1) interfering with employees' rights of collective bargaining, 2) dominating or in any way influencing labor unions, 3) discriminating against union members in either hiring or firing, 4) discriminating against any employee because he took advantage of his rights under the law, and 5) refusing to bargain collectively with the properly designated representatives of the employees.[4]

Perhaps even more important than the terms of the Wagner Act was the vigor of its administration. The act provided for a National Labor Relations Board, and President Roosevelt appointed as members of the Board three men who were strongly "pro-labor" in the sense that they believed thoroughly in an act deliberately designed to improve labor's

---

[4] For an excellent brief treatment of the Wagner Act and its early administration, see Robert R. R. Brooks, *Unions of Their Own Choosing* (New Haven, Conn.: Yale University Press, 1939).

strength in collective bargaining. With the stimulus of the Wagner Act, unions gained further in membership and in economic and political power, although they were somewhat weakened by the deepening split between the AFL and CIO.

Four other enactments during Roosevelt's first two terms that extended the government's protection of labor were:

1. *The Fair Labor Standards* (Black-Connery) *Act.* This act was passed in 1938 under President Roosevelt's leadership after a sharp struggle within the Democratic Party between northern and southern members of Congress. The act excluded from interstate commerce any goods not produced in accordance with certain standards, established a forty-four hour week (to be changed to forty-two hours in the second year and forty hours thereafter), a minimum wage of $.25 an hour (after one year to be raised to $.30 an hour, and after seven years to $.40 an hour), and barred the use of oppressive child labor (defined as the employment of children under sixteen, or of children between sixteen and eighteen in dangerous or unhealthful occupations). Although many exemptions were written into the bill, especially for agricultural or food processing workers, the legislation served as a basis for further extension of its coverage.

2. *The Public Contracts* (Walsh-Healey) *Act.* Passed in 1936, this legislation provided that contractors with the federal government (which also meant, under the grants-in-aid system, many state agencies) must pay not less than the prevailing minimum wage for comparable work, observe the eight-hour day and forty-hour week, and meet various other requirements relating to working conditions.

3. *Settlement of labor disputes.* Amendments in 1934 strengthened the Railway Labor Act of 1926, which had established agencies for the mediation of labor disputes in the railway field. Under the terms of the original act a National Railroad Adjustment Board was created to bring representatives of railway management and labor into direct contact with each other, and the National Mediation Board, supposed to be impartial to either side, was set up to mediate differences between the two parties. The 1934 amendments forbade railway employers to "influence or coerce" their employees in regard to union organization.

4. *Social security.* Social security is treated separately in this volume, but it may be pointed out here that labor, as a group traditionally exposed to economic insecurity, was especially interested in the legislation passed in 1935 for unemployment insurance and old age compensation.

As labor's organizational, economic, and legislative strength increased during the 1930s, so did its political strength. Labor groups—especially the CIO—formed political action groups in support of Roosevelt in the 1936 and succeeding elections. So influential was organized labor after the 1940 election that it was given an unprecedented role in the administration of defense programs during World War II. It had an equal place with management in the National War Labor Board, which had the job of mediating, and in effect arbitrating, wartime labor disputes. The Conciliation Service, established in 1913 in the Labor Department to aid in the settlement of labor disputes, was also expanded to handle the flock of employer-employee conflicts that rose during the war.

Following the war there was a reaction to organized labor's newly won political and economic influence. While the unions were able to help elect Harry Truman in 1948 and retain their influence with the White House, Congress was often controlled by majorities reflecting popular feeling that labor power must be checked. By far the most important legislation responsive to these developments was the Taft-Hartley Act, described in the following section of this chapter. At the state level, too, laws were passed restricting union activity; many of these were modeled after the Taft-Hartley Act on the national level. The election of Dwight Eisenhower showed the limitations of union strength in presidential elections, for most of the union leadership supported his Democratic opponent, Adlai E. Stevenson. Although President Eisenhower seemed to follow a policy of "benevolent neutrality" toward labor issues, he gave generally broad support to the Taft-Hartley Act and appointed men to the National Labor Relations Board who took a far less pro-labor approach than had the earlier appointees.

The election of John F. Kennedy to the Presidency in 1960 with wide union backing aroused organized labor's hopes that the new President's policies and appointments would swing the balance of government intervention back to the friendly posture of the New Deal and Fair Deal years. So it did—to a degree. The activist young President worked closely with labor leaders on his legislative program, appointed some of them to major Administration posts, and often invited them to White House conferences and ceremonies. And he sympathized with their continuing effort to repeal or modify the Taft-Hartley Act. But Kennedy and labor had their differences. The President feared that if he asked Congress to modify the measure, the legislators might pass an even more anti-labor law. Kennedy pressed the unions for support of his wage-price guidelines. And in the face of a looming, costly railroad strike, he signed the first straight compulsory arbitration law in the nation's peacetime history.

President Lyndon Johnson maintained the generally friendly relations with labor that his predecessor had established. Although the new President, in line with pledges in both the 1960 and 1964 Democratic Party platforms, specifically requested repeal of Section 14(b) (the so-called "right to work" provision) of Taft-Hartley, he was too much concerned for his other legislative proposals to go all-out for repeal. The new President's successful efforts to pass Medicare and other social welfare legislation, however, gave the relations between the White House and organized labor a degree of rapport never achieved before. Still, in the turbulent politics of America, there was no certainty as to how long the alliance would last.

NATIONAL LABOR POLICY TODAY

The Taft-Hartley Act

The keystone of national labor policy today is the Taft-Hartley (Labor Management Relations) Act of 1947. As noted, this legislation was a response to a decade of dissatisfaction on the part of employer, farm, and middle-class elements to what they considered to be the excesses of labor. So strong was this feeling that even though President Truman vetoed the bill, two-thirds majorities were mustered in each chamber to overturn the veto and enact the Taft-Hartley bill into law. Republican control of Congress (for the first time in a decade and a half) was the main reason for the bill's passage, but it could not have been adopted without the support of a great many Democrats, especially from the South. Technically the act was simply a series of amendments to the Wagner Act; in effect, it represented a significant departure from the 1935 act in the direction of the idea that organized labor had become such a strong force in the economic and political life of the nation that it, like business, must be more closely supervised by the national government.

The Taft-Hartley Act is really a collection of rather diverse policies grouped together in one omnibus affair.

Unfair Labor Practices of Labor Unions

The most important provisions of the Taft-Hartley Act outlined unfair labor practices of *unions*, in contrast with the concern of the Wagner Act with unfair labor practices of *management*. The latter were retained, and supplemented with the following unfair labor practices:[5]

1. To restrain or coerce employees in the right to join or assist a union or to refrain from joining or assisting a union.
2. To restrain or coerce an employer in the choosing of his representatives for collective bargaining or adjusting of grievances.
3. To cause or try to cause an employer to discriminate against an employee in violation of the union-shop provisions of the Act.
4. To require, under a permitted union shop, an initiation fee for new members that the National Labor Relations Board finds "excessive or discriminatory under all circumstances."

---

[5] Adapted from Richard A. Lester, *Labor and Industrial Relations* (New York: The Macmillan Company, 1951), p. 324.

5. To refuse to bargain collectively with an employer where the union involved is the certified bargaining agent.
6. To cause or try to cause an employer to pay a sum "in the nature of an exaction," for services which are not performed or not to be performed.
7. To engage in, or encourage employees to engage in, a strike or concerted refusal, in the course of employment, to use or otherwise handle or work on any goods or to perform any services, where the object is to force or require:
   a. any employer or self-employed person to join any labor or employer organization.
   b. any employer or other person to cease using or dealing in the products of another person or to cease doing business with any other person.
   c. another employer to recognize an uncertified union.
   d. any employer to violate a Board certification.
   e. any employer to assign particular work to employees in a particular union or trade unless that employer is failing to conform to an order or certification of the Board.

Some of these provisions merit brief elaboration. Probably the most important of the unfair labor practices by a union (or by its agent) in the list above are the antiboycott and antistrike provisions under paragraph 7. After many years of almost complete immunity from the courts, secondary boycotts by unions (that is, a boycott by a union of products of a firm dealing with another firm that might be strikebound) were made subject to injunctions and damage suits. Moreover, the antiboycott and antistrike provisions of paragraph 7 are sharpened by further sections of the Taft-Hartley Act. Not only are items under paragraph 7 made illegal as well as unfair labor practices, but the National Labor Relations Board is required to give them priority of handling over all other cases.

It was obvious that such provisions as these, although somewhat more specific than the unfair practices by employers in the Wagner Act, would require considerable interpretation by the National Labor Relations Board as specific cases came before it. Much would depend, in short, on the make-up of and procedure of the Board. Believing that the Board under the Wagner Act had served unfairly as both judge and prosecutor, Congress made the NLRB's General Counsel independent of the Board and gave him supervision over all attorneys and employees in the regional offices, where cases would first be handled. Thus the General Counsel became the key figure in the agency. At the same time, the Board was enlarged from three members to five, holding overlapping terms of five years each.

Other Provisions of the Taft-Hartley Act

Union shop. One of the oldest and most acute issues between labor and management has been the question of whether a union can compel employees to become members of the union. Under the *closed* shop the would-be employee must join the union before being hired. Under the *union* shop a firm may hire union or nonunion workers, but after a specified period of time, usually a month, all employees must join the union. The Wagner Act had specifically authorized employers and unions to make closed shop agreements if they agreed to do so. The Taft-Hartley Act, on the other hand, made the closed shop an unfair labor practice. As for the *union* shop, the Taft-Hartley Act authorizes it only when the union is certified as the representative of the employees, when a majority of the employees eligible to vote have cast a secret ballot authorizing it, and when state laws do not prohibit it. All this "sounds complicated and is complicated. The aim is to prevent the union from using exclusion or expulsion from membership as a job penalty."[6] And under Section 14(b) of the Act (see pp. 282–283), *states* were permitted to enact laws banning the union shop.

Bargaining unit. A key problem under the Wagner Act has been deciding what bargaining unit an employer must (or must not) bargain with. NLRB decisions as to the bargaining unit—for example, whether office workers and skilled workers should be included in one unit along with the great number of unskilled and semiskilled workers—had often been very difficult and controversial ones, for they not only antagonized employers but also rival union groups, such as AFL craft workers. The Taft-Hartley Act made significant changes in this respect. Supervisors and foremen were removed from the definition of employee, and hence management could refuse to bargain with them if they should form unions. More important, the Board was restricted in its power to determine "appropriate bargaining units." It was prohibited from certifying as a bargaining unit any general union admitting to membership plant guards and watchmen (the latter could of course form separate unions of their own); from including professional employees in the same bargaining unit with nonprofessional workers unless a majority of the former voted for such inclusion; and from denying to skilled craft employees a separate bargaining unit simply because a previous NLRB decision had included such employees in a broader unit (the Board could continue to include them in the broader unit only if a majority of the craft employees so voted in a secret balloting).

Union publicity and loyalty. Unions could take advantage of the law for purposes of collective bargaining only after filing with the Secretary of Labor information on union affairs including the following: name and principal address of the union, names, titles, and salaries of the chief officers, amount of dues and initiation fees, regulations regarding membership qualifications, election of officers, calling of meetings, levying of special assessments, authorization of strikes, methods for raising union

---

[6] *Ibid.*, p. 323.

funds, participation in union benefits, and methods of and grounds for expelling members from the union. Unions were required to furnish the Secretary and their memberships a financial statement showing total assets and liabilities, amounts and sources of receipts, and information as to the purposes of the disbursements.

More controversial than the above provisions was a requirement that before a union could qualify for the benefits of the Act it must file affidavits to the effect that none of its officers was a member of the Communist party, or of any other organization that advocated the over-throw of government by force or by illegal or unconstitutional methods. It is to be noted that the law did not require such affidavits as such, but only if the union wishes whatever government support—such as certification as a bargaining unit—that the act might provide.

Labor-management disputes. On the grounds that the Secretary of Labor should not have control over an impartial mediation agency, the Taft-Hartley Act transferred the mediation and conciliation functions of the United States Conciliation Agency to a new, independent agency, the Federal Mediation and Conciliation Service. Important new procedures were set up for handling disputes. The parties must, as part of their duty to bargain in good faith, give sixty days notice in advance of a proposed termination or modification of an agreement and, within thirty days there-after, notify the Federal Mediation and Conciliation Service and any state service with jurisdiction. Under the law, the Federal Mediation and Conciliation Service may enter a case at the request of either of the parties or on its own initiative.

Whenever in the opinion of the President a threatened or actual strike or lockout will, by affecting all or a substantial part of an industry, imperil the national health or safety, he may appoint a board of inquiry. This board must report the facts of the dispute but without any recommenda-tions. The President may then direct the Attorney General to seek a court injunction to enjoin such a strike or lockout. If the federal court finds that the situation does threaten to jeopardize the national health or safety and issues an injunction, the board of inquiry is reconvened and, if the dispute continues, must report again to the President within sixty days with respect to the dispute, including a statement of each employer's last offer of settlement. Within the next twenty days, there must be a secret ballot on the *employer's last offer* and the results certified to the Attorney General. Thereupon the injunction of the court must be dissolved and a strike becomes legal. The President then submits a full report to the Congress along with such recommendations as he may wish to make.

The Act also made it unlawful for any labor organization (as well as any business corporation) to make certain political contributions or ex-penditures. The restriction applied to national elections (both presidential and congressional), to primary elections relating to the selection of presidential and congressional candidates, and to related political conventions and caucuses.

It was made illegal for any person employed by the federal government or by any of its agencies or corporations to take part in a strike. The penalty for striking was immediate discharge, forfeiture of civil service status, and ineligibility for re-employment for three years. Government employees were still allowed, however, to join unions and bargain with the government.

The "check-off" (an arrangement under which management assumes the job of deducting union dues and fees from the workers' pay and turning them over to the union) was restricted except upon individual written agreements with each worker.

Welfare funds were illegalized unless based upon written agreements.

The Act made unions specifically subject to suits for breach of contract, and both unions and employers were made liable for acts of their agents (although awards could not be enforced against individual union members).

Taft-Hartley's First Twenty Years

What has been the experience of labor and government during the first decade and a half of the Act's application? Organized labor of course greeted the Act with intense hostility, dubbing it, with considerable exaggeration, as the "slave-labor act." Many employers felt that the Act did not have enough teeth and would make little difference in curbing what they considered to be excessive labor power. Most Americans probably welcomed the Act as a desirable, if not perfect, experiment in redressing the balance between labor and management. A Gallup poll, a year after the Act went into effect, indicated that 16 per cent of those questioned favored outright repeal, while 13 per cent liked the Act as it was. Of the great middle group favoring modification rather than repeal of the Act, 14 per cent wanted liberalization of the law (in favor of labor) and 12 per cent favored a more restrictive measure.

Such reactions were somewhat ambiguous, however, because the Act included such a great diversity of separate policies. Experience with several of its specific policies has been somewhat more meaningful.

"Redressing the balance." Has the Act succeeded in achieving a "fairer" balance between management and labor? There is little agreement on this score because definition of a "fair balance" is itself a major issue. Certainly the Act has not destroyed or "enslaved" organized labor as a whole. The unions have continued to grow in size, although not at the rate of a decade or so ago. Some union leaders charge—and with considerable justification—that the Act, mainly through the famous Section 14(b), has made far more difficult the organization of workers in the South, although "little Taft-Hartley Acts" in the states are also a roadblock to organization.

The Act has had some effect in protecting individual union members and nonunion members against abuses of labor power. For example, the Board has given force in certain situations to the provision that a union cannot compel an employer to discipline members for any reason other than failure to pay union dues or fees.[7] The number of charged unfair labor practices, despite the fears of union leaders, continued to be preponderantly against the employer.

Effect on labor-management peace. Here again the verdict must be less than definite, because legislation is only one of many factors affecting industrial peace. The conciliation procedure of the Act has failed to avert several serious and lengthy strikes during the past decade; on the other hand, during much of the decade the number of man-days of labor lost through strikes and lockouts has been rather low compared with the decade before (comparing two such different periods, however, is quite difficult). After a year and a half of experience under the Act, one director of the Federal Mediation and Conciliation Service stated that the eighty-day injunction tended to postpone collective bargaining and actually to delay dispute settlements.

Effect on union status. The Act has not had a profound effect on the union shop or the closed shop. Of the many thousands of union shop polls conducted by the Board, the workers voted overwhelmingly for the union shop. As for the *closed* shop, its prohibition has not been very effective. The closed shop is found mainly in the craft industries, where the vast majority of employees and a great many employers have lived with the system for a long time and have little wish to change it. Few employees opposed to the closed shop have the inclination or resources to file a complaint against it with the Board. Hence thousands of workers continue as members of "bootleg" closed shops.

Union leaders also feared that the Taft-Hartley Act would make unionization more difficult and have a depressing effect on union membership. There is evidence that the Act, combined with the effect of "little Taft-Hartley laws" in the states, did frustrate unionization under some conditions, especially in the South. The rate of growth of union membership nationally did slow down during the 1950s; union membership even declined—by almost a million—during the 1950s. It has been argued, however, that more fundamental causes might lie behind the decline in union membership: for example, the growth of white-collar employment; the flow of labor from the North to anti-union areas of the South; and the higher ratio of women in the labor force.[8]

Loyalty tests. Although many union leaders attacked the loyalty provi-

[7] C. A. Daugherty and John B. Parrish, *The Labor Problems of American Society* (Boston: Houghton-Mifflin Co., 1952), p. 770; and Herbert R. Northrup and Gordon Bloom, *Government and Labor* (Homewood, Ill.: Richard D. Irwin, Inc., 1963), pp. 139 ff.

[8] James E. Anderson, *Politics and the Economy* (Boston: Little, Brown & Co., 1966), p. 250.

sions of the Act as unfair and discriminatory, most unions complied with them. Some of the noncomplying unions were led by men who were strong foes of communism but who opposed loyalty tests in principle and who considered their unions so entrenched that government support under the Act was unnecessary. For example, John L. Lewis, a strong anticommunist, refused to sign the required affidavit. Other noncomplying unions were influenced or dominated by left-wing leaders—in some cases Communist Party members or sympathizers—and such unions suffered considerable loss of strength because of their leaders' refusal to sign the required oaths. Union leaders challenged the constitutionality of the loyalty requirement, but a closely divided Supreme Court sustained the provision.[9] Congress later repealed this provision, however, and substituted another that disqualified members of the Communist Party from holding office in a labor union. The Supreme Court, again by a divided vote, held this latter provision to be an unconstitutional bill of attainder.[10] Though it did not specifically reverse its earlier decision, the thrust of the majority opinion and other more recent decisions suggests that the present Court might have held the original Taft-Hartley loyalty tests unconstitutional. At any rate, there are no longer any loyalty tests within the Taft-Hartley law or any other federal regulations that relate to labor unions.

Effect of limitation on political contributions. This provision of the Act has had mixed results. On the one hand, union heads, feeling that the provision was directed unfairly at labor's rightful political activity, took test cases to the courts. In 1948 the Supreme Court held that the provision could not extend to publication of editorials in union publications advising members on how to vote, but it did not pass on the constitutionality of the provision as a whole.[11] On the other hand, the provision has compelled unions to change their methods of financing political activity by setting up special funds for the purpose (rather than allotting political action funds from the general union treasury), and in this sense the provision has undoubtedly handicapped labor in its political activity.

In conclusion, it may be said that the Taft-Hartley Act has neither "destroyed free labor," as some union leaders charged it would, nor has it had as fully a "cleansing" or balancing effect as some of its proponents hoped. Some of the latter, indeed, have had second thoughts about the advisability of bringing government so much into the delicate area of labor-management relations as the Taft-Hartley Act has done. Many union members and some union leaders have come to accept—or at least to "live with"—the majority of the Act's provisions. Parts of the Act have had much of the effect expected, others have failed to have any important

---

9 *American Communication Association v. Douds*, 339 U.S. 382 (1950).

10 *United States v. Brown*, 381 U.S. 437 (1965).

11 *United States v. Congress of Industrial Organizations*, 335 U.S. 106 (1948).

influence on labor behavior, and still others have important side effects that have created new and unexpected problems.

Wages and Hours Regulation Since 1938

The standards established by the Fair Labor Standards Act on its passage in 1938 were so low that they did not have a major influence on wages except in certain industries, such as textiles. The constitutionality of the Act was upheld by the Supreme Court in 1941 after the high bench had become dominated by appointees of President Franklin D. Roosevelt. By the time the $.45 minimum wage went into effect in 1945 the post-World War II inflation was already getting under way and beginning to make the enforced wage limitations obsolete. After a long political struggle Congress in 1949 raised the minimum wage to $.75, and in 1956, after President Eisenhower had recommended an increase to $.90, and organized labor to $1.25, Congress set the minimum at a flat $1. In 1961 a Congress with Democratic majorities, under pressure from President Kennedy, raised the minimum (in two steps) to $1.25, and brought under the minimum wage and over-time provisions of the Act about three-and-a-half million more persons, making a total of twenty-seven million persons covered by the measure.

The huge Democratic, pro-labor majorities in both House and Senate after the 1964 election wished to honor the pledges of the Democratic party platform and of Democratic Presidents to boost the minimum wage floor higher. Many Congressmen also felt that a higher minimum wage would help in the war against poverty. In 1966 a new law increased the $1.25 non-farm minimum wage floor by stages to $1.48 by February 1967 and to $1.60 by 1968, and extended minimum wage coverage to an additional eight million employees. The most notable feature of the measure was its extension of minimum wage coverage to certain farm workers; for years Congressmen from rural districts had managed to exempt agricultural employees. Congress, however, would not go all the way; it established a "split-level" wage floor that provided only $1 to the farm workers, to be increased in steps to $1.30. Over thirty-seven million workers will be covered under the revised law.

Sometimes government seeks to keep wages *down* rather than up. Such was the case during World War II and the Korean war. During World War II the National War Labor Board, composed equally of representatives of industry, labor, and the public, was established to settle disputes between unions and management and to help stabilize wages in the battle against inflation. During the Korean war Congress authorized an Economic Stabilization Agency with subsidiary wage and salary boards, again with tripartite representation, with the power to keep salaries and wages from soaring under the stimulus of war spending. Presidents Kennedy and Johnson repeatedly urged labor to observe their wage guidelines.

The Landrum-Griffin Act of 1959

During the late 1950s the public became increasingly concerned about union malpractices that seemed far beyond the reach of the Taft-Hartley law or other federal legislation. A Senate Committee on Improper Activities in the Labor or Management Field found that small employers, union members, and the public at large were the victims of extortion, improper picketing, and secondary boycotts; that officials in certain unions had used coercion and violence against their own members; and that union officials conspired with employers through "sweetheart contracts" to deprive employees of their rights. The committee, closely covered by press and television, paved the way for the passage of the Labor-Management Reporting and Disclosure (Landrum-Griffin) Act of 1959.

The law is far more comprehensive than its name suggests. Its first title is a catch-all "Bill of Rights for Labor" that would insure all union members equal rights to choose candidates and vote in union elections; guarantee certain rights of free speech and assembly; restrict the manner in which dues and initiation fees can be increased; and require both employers and union officials to report on any money received by the latter from employers with whom the union is bargaining or whom the union is seeking to represent. Subsequent sections of the measure regulate the administration of trusteeships (local unions taken over and managed by the national union); police union election and removal-from-office procedures; require bonding of union officials; prohibit certain categories of persons with criminal records or communist affiliations from holding union office; and amend the Taft-Hartley Act to broaden restrictions against secondary boycotts and picketing. Following passage of the Act over 50,000 unions submitted reports on their internal government and operations. Thousands of complaints by union members and others have been made to the Department of Labor; many investigations have been conducted by the Department; but in only a very small minority of cases (mainly involving misuse of union funds) has legal action been necessary. But even these few cases stand as a warning to unions against corruption and abuses.[12]

State Labor Policy

The great mass of national labor policy is paralleled by extensive labor legislation in the states, although there are, of course, great differences between the states, especially between industrial and rural areas. Four main

[12] Major provisions of the Landrum-Griffin Act are treated in Northrup and Bloom, *Government and Labor*, Chap. 6.

objectives of state labor laws are: 1) protection of the safety and health of workers, 2) reasonable working conditions and wage scales, 3) settlement of industrial disputes, and 4) regulation of labor relations, including the power and activities of unions.

Safety and health. It was in this area that states pioneered, long ago, as the industrial revolution brought grave problems of health and safety affecting not only workers but whole urban populations. State laws prescribe minimum conditions of safety in industrial establishments; for example, active parts of machinery such as flywheels and saws must be protected, fire escapes installed, and adequate lighting provided. Every state prohibits children from occupation in hazardous industries. Women are excluded from occupations that might endanger their health. States also require technical qualifications for such jobs as elevator operators and railroad engineers for the benefit of both the employees and the people they serve. States have long been concerned also with occupational diseases involved in occupations where workers come into contact with poisonous or deleterious substances, such as lead.

Workmen's Compensation. This is another traditional state activity. Years ago, whenever an accident occurred, an injured employee had to institute a lawsuit in order to recover damages; but often he might lack the necessary funds, long delays were likely, and he might have trouble proving his case. As a remedy, laws were urged that would give all injured employees compensation without regard to fixing blame. Compensation laws, now found in all states, provide for payments to injured workers according to some established law; the amount usually varies with the seriousness of the injury and the amount of the employee's wages. Compensation varies widely from state to state and has tended to be low, especially in the light of inflation.

The fact that about 15,000 workers are killed at work each year, and perhaps two million seriously hurt, puts a heavy burden on the machinery of workmen's compensation. The machinery is not as modern as it might be. It was the aim of the original workmen's compensation to keep procedures swift and simple, through automatic benefits established by a predetermined schedule and quickly paid to the injured men. But questions as to how much compensation a worker is entitled to, whether or not the injury arose in the actual course of employment, and the extent of the disability, often takes months of litigation, with appeals up through administrative agencies and the courts. In some states the procedures have become so burdened by litigation that it is not much different from the common law system under which damage suits in the old days were usually heard.

Wages and working conditions. All states have enacted some laws concerning the length of the working day. Children especially have been protected against exploitation, and almost all the states have laws restricting the hours of labor of women in specified employments. Decades ago states also began to restrict the hours of men in occupations considered especially dangerous or unhealthful. *General* hours regulation came later, and only after encountering severe constitutional challenge. In a famous case, for example, the Supreme Court vetoed a New York law limiting the hours of bakery workers to ten a day.[13] The states continued to pass legislation, however, and later laws were upheld as changes took place in the make-up of federal and state courts. A number of states today have general hours regulation; the reason the number is not greater is less a matter of constitutional power than the fear of losing industry to other states.

As for minimum wages, Massachusetts was the first state to pass a minimum wage law, in 1912. The early state laws applied only to women and children. Minimum wage legislation in Oregon was challenged on constitutional grounds and was ultimately sustained in the Supreme Court by an even vote of four to four. Later, however, the high court voided minimum wage laws in several states, only to reverse itself during the New Deal period. In the case of minimum wage laws affecting men as well, only a handful of states have passed such general legislation, partly because of the competitive position of the states, and partly because a great deal of the most important industry comes under the terms of the federal statute.

Settlement of industrial disputes. Many states have agencies of mediation and conciliation, which usually work closely with labor and management (and with federal mediation officials) in trying to bring about settlements of strikes and lockouts. Especially interesting is the attempt of one state—Kansas—to "solve" industrial disputes through compulsory means. In 1920 Kansas abolished the right to strike, lockout, picket, and boycott in certain essential industries, established a court of industrial relations with power to fix wages and set working conditions, and made decisions of this court binding on all parties concerned. The plan met strong opposition from labor and from some employers, and it was later declared unconstitutional by the Supreme Court.

Regulation of unions and collective bargaining. As noted above, for many years unions had to face hostility from courts and legislatures, which considered them combinations to restrain trade, but the legality of unionism came to be securely protected. A far more controversial question has concerned the *practices* of unionism—the closed and union shops, sympathy strikes, boycotts, and the like. State legislation, like federal, has oscillated from antipathy toward many of these practices in the 1920s, to a more favorable posture in the 1930s, to the reaction against labor of the late 1940s. Thus many states passed "little Taft-Hartley Acts" that were modeled after, or in many cases went beyond, the federal law.

As in the case of the federal Taft-Hartley Act, the most important and

13 *Lochner v. New York*, 198 U.S. 45 (1905).

controversial aspect of the state legislation has involved the union shop and the closed shop. Eighteen states at the latest reckoning have passed so-called "right-to-work" laws prohibiting the union shop or any other form of compulsory union membership. The key provision in such laws is that no employer may compel a worker to join a union or remain a union member as a condition of holding a job. (Such union agreements are legal under the Taft-Hartley law, but this law gives a green light to the states to ban such agreements if they so wish.) Most of the states with such laws are southern or rural, but the passage of a "right-to-work" law in Indiana, along with recent revelations of corruption in some unions, makes it seem likely that other industrial states might pass such legislation.

Meantime, the controversy rages on. Backers of "right-to-work" laws contend that compulsory unionism destroys individual freedom by penalizing workers economically if they do not join unions, and that by joining unions, workers become subject to union dictatorships. Opponents of such laws argue that they are passed solely to weaken the power of workers to bargain effectively with employers, and that enactment of anti-union shop legislation provides a "free ride" for employees who want all the benefits of unionism without joining the union and contributing dues and other help. Union leaders hope that by taking a strong line in favor of ethical practices in corrupt unions they can prevent public opinion from being mobilized behind further "right to work" legislation.

LABOR'S ORGANIZATION AND POLITICAL ACTIVITY

Roughly speaking, of the approximately seventy-five million people in the total working population of the United States, about eighteen million are organized in some type of union. Hence, as noted previously, on the average less than one employed person out of every four is a union member. But averages, of course, are deceptive; in fact there is a great diversity in union organization from industry to industry. About two-thirds of the workers in manufacturing industries are organized, while other workers—such as farm hands and gas station attendants—are little organized, and still other types of employees are not organized at all. Union membership in the same occupation sometimes varies considerably from area to area. It is important to keep this great diversity of union membership in mind as we seek to assess the effect of labor on government and of government on labor.

The Shape of Union Labor

The great bulk of union membership is organized in the relatively new national organization called the American Federation of Labor and Congress of Industrial Organizations. With about twelve million members, the AFL-CIO is a federation of essentially (but not wholly) independent national unions. Dominating the AFL-CIO are some of the old, powerful craft unions that once made up the core of the original AFL, such as the United Brotherhood of Carpenters and Joiners of America and the International Association of Machinists, along with several "industrial" unions that came to power in the old CIO, such as the United Steelworkers of America and the Textile Workers Union of America. Of the 141 national unions in the AFL-CIO at the time of its beginning in 1955, 109 had been formerly affiliated with the AFL and thirty-two with the CIO.[14]

We hear so much of the big international unions in the AFL-CIO, such as those mentioned above, that we tend to overlook many of the lesser ones. But these are important too, both in themselves, and in their demonstration of the great variety of occupations organized under the AFL-CIO today. They include, for example:

Air Line Pilots Association
The Journeymen Barbers, Hairdressers and Cosmetologists' International
    Union of America
International Alliance of Bill Posters and Billers of America
International Broom and Whisk Makers Union
American Federation of Musicians
International Association of Siderographers

In size of membership the individual unions vary widely. The auto workers, machinists, and steel workers number about a million each, the carpenters about 800,000, and the electrical workers about 750,000, while at least a score of the small craft unions of skilled employees embrace fewer than 10,000 members each. In 1957 the AFL-CIO ousted its largest affiliate, the Teamsters, with about 1,400,000 members, because of its failure to clean house.

Besides the affiliated international unions and organizing committees, the membership of the AFL-CIO also includes: 1) directly affiliated local unions, 2) state and local central bodies, and 3) trade departments. In contrast with its relation with the international unions, the AFL-CIO has considerable direct control over these three types of organizations. The first of these are usually transitional bodies that sooner or later might be embraced in an existing international union. The state and local central

---

[14] Arthur J. Goldberg, *AFL-CIO: Labor United* (New York: McGraw-Hill Book Company, 1956), Appendix L.

bodies are simply combinations of unions at the state and local level, largely for political and civic purposes. The trade departments were established in the old AFL and served as a means of uniting similar types of craft unions in pursuit of common interests; for example, the Building and Construction Trades Department represented the joint interests of nineteen building and construction unions. These trade departments were continued in the merged organization, and a new one—the Council of Industrial Organizations—was added to give some identity and representation to the industrial unions that had comprised the old CIO.

Over three million unionized American workers in about fifty unions are not affiliated with the AFL-CIO. Many of these union people are in one of the three important national unions, the United Mine Workers of America, the Railroad Brotherhoods, or the Teamsters. The Mine Workers, numbering over half a million members, once received more publicity, under its fiery chief John L. Lewis, than any other union, largely because of the serious strikes it has precipitated in the coal industry. The Mine Workers, under Lewis, took the lead in breaking away from the AFL and forming the CIO, then abandoned the CIO to become independent, later joined the AFL, and has since been independent of the big national organization. The Teamsters, under James Hoffa, have been in poor repute in recent years.

Almost half a million railroad workers are organized into four railroad brotherhoods (trainmen, locomotive engineers, conductors, and firemen and enginemen), which never affiliated with the AFL or CIO. Half a century old, these unions have had a special position partly because of the close governmental regulation of the railroad industry. They are fairly stable organizationally and tend to be middle-of-the-road or conservative in union political action. The Brotherhoods' lobbyists in Washington are considered highly effective and often work with AFL-CIO representatives on matters of mutual concern.

Besides the national and international unions, such as the above, there are hundreds of local unions that have declined to affiliate nationally. Such local unions range all the way from truly autonomous and vigorous organizations to associations that are secretly or even openly dominated by the employer. Most local unions are at neither of these extremes; they exist mainly to afford the workers recreational and social activities, but are also able to bargain collectively and more or less effectively with management.

The Internal Government of Labor

The crucial feature of the government of the AFL-CIO is that, like that of the United States of America, it is *federal* in form. Power lies mainly in the various national and international unions that make up the AFL-CIO. But again, as in the case of the national government, important powers and functions have been delegated to the "parent" body. The Constitution of the AFL-CIO, which is somewhat longer than the Constitution of the United States, reflects both the unity and disunity of the many unions that make up the huge organization.

The AFL-CIO Constitution sets forth the principle that the integrity of each international union in the organization shall be maintained and preserved. The executive council (see below) has the authority to issue charters or certificates to new members of the organization but not in any case where there may be created a conflict with the jurisdiction of existing unions in the AFL-CIO; the rights of existing unions, in short, are fully protected. Aside from its important power to admit and expel from membership, the AFL-CIO has "no explicit controls, other than *persuasive* ones," with regard to the activities of its member unions. "Each conducts its own affairs, policies, and activities, negotiates its own contracts, collects its own dues, and expends its own money."[15] A member union may be expelled by a two-thirds vote at the national convention.

This convention is the ultimate authority of the AFL-CIO. Voting is based on the membership strength of the member unions (a "nominal" vote is granted to state and local federations). Regular conventions are to be held every two years, but special conventions may be called. Delegate strength is roughly proportional to the size of the member unions, with the smaller unions getting a little "bonus."

Between conventions the AFL-CIO is run by an Executive Council composed of the principal officers of the federation—president, secretary-treasurer, and many vice-presidents—elected by the convention. Members of the council are supposed to vote as individuals rather than as representatives of the member unions to which they belong. The council has power to carry out convention decisions and "to take such actions and render such decisions as are necessary and appropriate to safeguard the best interests of the federation and its affiliated unions." By far the most important position in the AFL-CIO—and one commanding prestige throughout the nation and even the world—is that of President, who serves as a full-time officer. He works with a small executive committee drawn from the Executive Council. Finally, there is a General Board, consisting of all the members of the Executive Council, the heads of all the member unions, and the heads of trade or industrial departments, which serves as a kind of "baby convention" to which the Council may refer policy questions.

Since the AFL-CIO is a federation of largely independent unions, it is at the level of its member unions that we must look for the decisions that shape the day-to-day policies and activities of American unionism. Historically, these unions are amalgamations of local organizations, and hence one might expect to find the same form of federalism here as exists in the organization of the AFL-CIO. In fact, the local units had to surrender

---

[15] Quotations from Goldberg, *AFL-CIO: Labor United*, p. 111.

much of their autonomy in order to build a strong enough national organization to meet severe economic and political challenges from outside. Hence the national organizations usually have strong direct controls over the affairs of the local units. The supreme authority and legislative body of the national union is the convention, composed of delegates from local organizations, which can make decisions about virtually all union matters. As in the AFL-CIO, executive boards or councils make decisions between conventions. There is a "General President" who usually has considerable power and in some cases, as with Lewis in the Miners, has dictatorial powers if he wishes to wield them. The larger unions have "bureaucracies" made up of paid assistants such as union organizers, lobbyists, publicity men, and clerical assistants.

At the great base of the AFL-CIO are the tens of thousands of local organizations. These organizations conduct the day-to-day business of unionism, such as holding meetings of workers, carrying on negotiations with employers, conducting strikes, and running a great variety of social, recreational, and political activities. Locals may be organized in many ways —on an occupational or craft basis or on a plant or multiplant basis. In addition to regularly elected officers who earn their main living as regular workers, most unions have business agents, who are full-time paid employees. Serving as "contact points" between the local union and the rank and file are shop stewards, who are usually elected by union members in each department of a plant, and who handle grievances that employees have against management.

Labor in Politics

With eighteen million unionists and with many millions more among its members' families, organized labor might be expected to have a paramount role in the nation's politics. But in fact, labor's aims have often been divided, its methods ineffective, and its political goals unrealized. As noted above, labor's political activities during the past century have been limited and intermittent, except for brief periods, such as during Franklin D. Roosevelt's administrations. Perhaps the high point of labor's political action during this period was the formation of the CIO's Political Action Committee in the early 1940s. PAC went in for practical politics in vigorous fashion. It concentrated on getting union members registered to vote, on ringing doorbells, on getting union people and their friends to the polls. PAC seemed to meet considerable success in 1944 and 1948, in the elections of Roosevelt and Truman. It seemed far less successful in the "off-year" congressional elections, when majorities were elected to Congress composed of "anti-labor" Republicans and southern Democrats. The significant feature of labor's political action, however, was the fact that it had modernized but not abandoned Gompers' simple old tactic of "helping labor's friends and defeating labor's enemies." Despite urgings from some unionists and despite various experiments in other directions, as noted below, labor was on the whole content to approach politics on a piecemeal, pragmatic basis, operating through the existing two-party system and supporting or opposing individual Democratic or Republican candidates on the basis of their various records or promises.

Following merger of the AFL and CIO, a new political action organization was formed, the Committee on Political Education, soon dubbed COPE. That COPE would represent no radical new departure in the basic political strategy of labor was made clear by George Meany, first president of AFL-CIO. Meany declared:

> The Gompers policy is very simple. You examine the candidates for public office, and on the basis of their records you decide whether they are friendly or aren't friendly . . . and you act accordingly. The failure of the Gompers policy to give us more results was in the application of the policy. . . .
> There's only one difference between what we're doing now and what was carried on for many years with regard to Gompers' policy. There's no difference in regard to partisanship or nonpartisanship. We absolutely refuse to allow ourselves to be an appendage of the Democratic Party or any other party. We are absolutely nonpartisan. But what we're doing now that wasn't done before is that we're going into localities, right down to the precinct level, with our organization, and we're doing it on an educational basis.

This general approach governed the political tactics of AFL-CIO in 1956, at the time of the merged organization's first presidential election. The Executive Council endorsed Adlai E. Stevenson, the Democratic candidate, over President Eisenhower, but two heads of powerful unions broke away and openly supported the President. The AFL-CIO sponsored get-out-the-vote rallies on a closed circuit program financed by union dues. It distributed pamphlets, posters, clipsheets, stickers, buttons, and organization manuals. It supported favored candidates in newspapers and over the radio. It publicized the records of congressional candidates and supported or opposed thousands of candidates at the state and local levels. The results were mixed. Eisenhower was re-elected, but with a Democratic Congress. However, many of the Democrats were, according to AFL-CIO, "anti-labor," and the AFL-CIO won in only nine of thirty-six congressional districts marked for special effort. Organized labor actively supported John F. Kennedy in 1960, but its contribution was not so crucial that Kennedy could say "Labor did it," as Harry Truman is reported to have exclaimed after his victory in 1948. And labor helped mobilize millions of votes for Johnson in 1964—but doubtless Johnson would have won anyway.

How great is organized labor's political power? A definitive answer is impossible, because its strength varies from place to place and from year to year. Certainly, labor as a whole has wielded far more political influence in the past generation than it has generally in the past century. But that influence is also very much subject to national moods and public opinion trends. For example, in a period of change and reform, such as the mid-1930s, labor had great power in Washington, despite organizational splits and weaknesses, while during the mid-1940s the national reaction against labor power gravely limited it, although in many respects its political action methods were greatly improved.

Labor's political strength is even more spotty geographically. At one end of the spectrum, it has reached peak effectiveness recently in the state of Michigan, where the auto workers are numerous and well organized. In Michigan labor has effectively entered into the Democratic party, taking control of a number of district Democratic conventions and even a state-wide one. A coalition of unionists, Reform Democrats, and a few other elements, according to a careful study, "was able to bring marked changes into the life of the Michigan Democratic party. It filled Democratic primary and convention slates. It entered liberal planks in the state Democratic platform and made the platform more binding. It governed the selection of party officers. It ejected the conservative Old Guard. It used its influence to appoint liberals to policy-determining patronage jobs and used routine patronage to strengthen its coalition. . . ."[16] Not only did labor thus show its influence, but it helped the Democrats win victory after victory, culminating in a clean sweep of statewide officers in elections in 1957. But the strength of labor in Michigan is exceptional.

At the center of the spectrum of labor's political power, a far more typical—and far different—example of labor in politics was in Elmira, New York. This city's politics and voting were studied shortly after the 1948 election by a group of social scientists. Elmira was chosen because it was a semi-industrial, rather small city, with considerable diversity in its industries and in the size and structure of its unions. One might have expected that in such a city labor would have been fairly strong in 1948, the year that the unions hoped to counterattack the forces responsible for the Taft-Hartley Act. On the contrary, the investigators found that the collective union efforts were ineffective, and individual unions took part in political activity only perfunctorily. Among the reasons for such limited forceful political activity, it was discovered, were divisions among the labor leaders themselves, no articulate rank-and-file expression favoring political activity, jurisdictional conflicts, political inexperience of the leaders, and labor's tradition of political individualism.[17]

At the other end of the spectrum of labor power are areas in the South

---

[16] Fay Calkins, *The CIO and the Democratic Party* (Chicago: The University of Chicago Press, 1952), p. 145.

[17] Bernard R. Berelson, Paul F. Lazarsfeld, and William N. McPhee, *Voting* (Chicago: The University of Chicago Press, 1954), p. 53.

and other rural sections where organized labor is small in numbers, faced with strong hostile elements in the community, and divided in policies and methods. Here the political power of organized labor itself is almost nil.

MAKING AND ADMINISTERING
LABOR POLICY

The making and administering of labor policy comes into focus in the nation's capital. Yet this focus is not a narrow one. A great many persons, groups, and agencies "get into the act" in labor policy-making, just as in all other important areas of national policy and politics. This section treats some of the main continuing groups and agencies that shape policy, but it should be kept in mind that sudden and unexpected forces can always affect policy-making. For example, a special committee set up to investigate "Improper Activities in the Labor and Management Fields" in 1957 had probably a much greater impact on public opinion and future policy-making than Labor Department officials or even the regular congressional committees dealing with problems of labor.

Labor Lobbies

Like all other important economic interests, organized labor maintains a formidable array of lobbyists in Washington. In a recent year, the AFL-CIO, and six of its constituent unions, reported spending $720,000 to influence legislation.[18] Most of the larger unions have established their headquarters in Washington; the AFL-CIO recently built its own office building a block from the White House, and some of the national unions such as the Teamsters and the Miners have spacious headquarters. The "legislative" or lobbying divisions in these headquarters are perhaps the most important activity. The head of AFL-CIO's lobbying recently has been an experienced former legislator who, as an ex-congressman, has enjoyed the right to enter the chamber of the House of Representatives and consult its members on the floor.

Usually directing the work of the lobbyists are committees on legislation that meet regularly in the various union headquarters. What does organized labor want? Individual labor unions are of course especially concerned with policies directly relating to their own industries and their role in it; for example, the Miners press for strengthened safety standards, the sailors' unions for better working conditions on the sea and for greater subsidies to the merchant marine, the government employees' unions for higher federal wages and salaries, and so on. The more general demands of

---

[18] *Congress and the Nation* (Washington, D.C.: Congressional Quarterly Service, 1965), p. 1590.

organized labor as a whole are well represented in the resolutions adopted in the merger convention of the AFL and CIO in 1955, and suggest how much of labor's demands have been met in the past decade. They may be divided into four general categories, as follows:[19]

1. *Legislation directly affecting workers and their unions.* Removal of provisions in the Taft-Hartley Act that seriously restrict the right to strike, that strengthen the labor injunction, that restrict the kinds of union security agreements that unions can negotiate, that sanction "union busting" under the guise of strengthening the free speech of employers; extension of the coverage of the Fair Labor Standards Act, increasing the minimum wage to at least $1.25 an hour, and the elimination of exemptions for learners; improved occupational safety standards; broadening of the social security program; a program of national health insurance.

2. *General economic and social policy.* Assumption by government of responsibility for helping maintain full employment through public works, housing, fiscal policies, and the like; adoption of tax policies that help maintain stable economic conditions and are "fair" to the middle and low income groups; full development of natural resources with governmental participation as a yardstick for measuring the effectiveness of development by private interests; federal encouragement of a well staffed, well housed, and well equipped educational system through substantial federal aid to the states; promotion of child welfare through adequate support for government agencies concerned with this.

3. *Civil liberties and civil rights.* Condemnation of actions dangerous to civil liberties, including procedures by certain congressional committees; establishing of a citizens' commission to recommend programs for protecting national security without depriving individuals of their rightful liberties; making illegal wiretapping a criminal offense; effective and enforceable fair employment practice laws at all levels of government; policing by unions of federal contracts to prevent discrimination; utilization of the full powers of the federal government "to frustrate and punish unlawful attempts to block implementation" of the Supreme Court's non-segregation decree in public schools (see Chapter 11); adoption of an anti-lynching law and invalidation of poll taxes as prerequisites to voting.

4. *International policy.* To maintain the armed strength of the United States at a level consistent with a tough-minded evaluation of communist capacity for aggression; to strengthen the economic and military capacities of the free world to resist communist aggression; to invigorate the United Nations as a major instrument for achieving world peace and security; support of such specific policies as Point Four, a liberal trade policy, the use of America's influence against colonialism.

Federal Policy-Making and Administration

The most important, but by no means the only, agency for labor policy-making and administration is the Department of Labor. This department was a culmination of many years of labor agitation for direct representation in federal administration resulting in the establishment of a Federal

---

[19] Drawn from Goldberg, *AFL-CIO: Labor United*, pp. 203–11.

Bureau of Labor, then the Department of Commerce and Labor in 1903, and finally the single Department of Labor in 1913.[20] For many years the Department was headed by a man directly from the leadership of organized labor, and the agency inevitably came to be, in fact as well as law, a place for expressing labor's voice in the councils of government. Partly because of its role as representing labor, the Department has had a rather checkered history, with important functions being moved out of it on the grounds that a "pro-labor" agency should not administer them. With about 9000 employees it is the smallest executive department (compared, for example, with the 56,000 employees in the Department of Commerce).

Among the most important units of the Department of Labor are the *Office of International Labor Affairs*, which advises on the labor aspects of foreign policy, has primary responsibility for directing United States participation in the International Labor Organization, and helps direct the work of the State Department's labor attachés in United States embassies abroad; the *Bureau of Apprenticeship and Training*, which, in cooperation with national advisory committees appointed by the Secretary, develops standards of apprenticeship for training of skilled workers in industry; the *Bureau of Labor Statistics*, a famed fact-finding agency with a staff of over 1600 that compiles data on employment, manpower, productivity, wages, prices, cost of living, and the like; the *Wage and Hour and Public Contracts Divisions*, which administer the wage and hour and Walsh-Healey Acts described above; and the *Women's Bureau*, which does not administer any law but formulates standards and policies for promoting the welfare of wage-earning women and advancing their opportunities for employment.

An agency outside the Department of Labor that probably outrivals it in impact on employer-employee relations is the National Labor Relations Board, which, as we have seen, administers the Wagner Act, Taft-Hartley Act, and related legislation. The Board has about 2100 employees, almost half of whom work in its twenty-two regional and seven subregional offices. Also outside the Department is the National Mediation Board (which includes the National Railroad Adjustment Board), and the Federal Mediation and Conciliation Service. Many other agencies that relate in an important way to labor are housed in other departments, such as the Bureau of Mines in the Interior Department.

All these agencies operate under legislation passed by Congress, or with funds appropriated by it, so that labor is ultimately concerned with the course of legislation on Capitol Hill. Both houses of Congress have committees specializing in labor legislation—the Committee on Education and Labor in the House and the Committee on Labor and Public Welfare in the Senate. It is difficult to generalize about the make-up of these

---

[20] For a detailed account of this period, see John Lombardi, *Labor's Voice in the Cabinet* (New York: Columbia University Press, 1942).

committees, but it can be said that they are usually composed of a substantial number of representatives of strong labor districts. On the other hand, southern Democrats, hostile or at least cool to union labor, often hold the balance of power in these committees between Republicans and northern Democrats. An example of the results of such a situation was the formulation of the wages and hours act in 1937–38, when southern congressmen repeatedly thwarted passage of the legislation despite President Roosevelt's strong support of it. Southerners also tend to become chairmen or ranking members of the committee because of their greater seniority.

The two labor committees are not the only committees affecting labor's interest. The appropriations committees in each house are important because they can limit or augment funds for administering laws supported by labor, such as the wages and hours act. Other substantive committees may often legislate in areas closely affecting labor matters. Finally, special investigating committees may uncover practices that affect public opinion in a direction favorable or hostile to labor's interests. For example, a House committee that investigated the National Labor Relations Board in 1940 held that its administration of the Wagner Act was biased, and this investigation undoubtedly helped create the public opinion behind the Taft-Hartley Act a few years later.

PROSPECTS—POLICY AND POLITICAL ALTERNATIVES

The future of government labor policy will turn on the outcome of a host of basic developments and tendencies. A crisis, such as a war or severe depression, would obviously produce a sharp impact on labor policy. The coming to power of a strongly left-wing or strongly right-wing government would mean a sharp change in the essentially middle-of-the-road policies of the last twenty years. Less spectacular but deep-seated forces might, in the long run, produce more significant changes than the possibilities above. For example, mechanization and automation are altering the techniques and psychology of work in such a way as to have a profound social impact on the attitudes of employees toward their work, their employers, and unions. And workers can no more than other groups escape the influence of social forces such as television, the "slick" magazines, and other of the mass media.

Indeed, even without trying to forecast the social and economic world in which labor will live, prediction of labor's role and of government labor policy turns on an estimate of its place in the quasi-competitive, quasi-regulated economy and the mixed society in which we live. To illustrate, two keen students of labor have come up with very different forecasts of the impact of labor on its economic environment. One believes that organized labor involves an inherent tendency toward monopoly, and that mass unionization means greater government intervention, increased tendency toward controlling and limiting competition, further restrictions on the powers of management, and ultimately the weakening of the competitive price system to the disadvantage of consumers (including union members themselves).[21] The other holds that the implications of labor's role in society are functionally conservative because it has served and will continue to satisfy labor's need for moral status in society, and that, instead of destroying each other, "the corporation and the union will ultimately merge in common ownership and cease to be a house divided."[22]

It is clearly impossible here to do justice either to the complex developments that will both affect and be affected by labor, or to the varying views of students of labor. The possible combinations and permutations would require many volumes. This concluding section will seek merely to describe the various alternatives in major fields of government labor policy for the years immediately ahead, and then to describe alternatives and problems in two areas that intimately affect the course of labor policy, namely: the political methods labor uses to attain its policy goals, and the problem of labor's internal government and the relation thereto of government policy.

Choices of Government

The key governmental policies relating to the most controversial aspect of labor will continue to be the Wagner Act as amended by the Taft-Hartley Act. Although parts of this act have received considerable approval from large sectors of the public, including labor and management, other sections remain highly controversial. It is likely that within the foreseeable future, government policy on labor-management relations will remain at—or reach—a point of compromise somewhere between the demands of organized labor and those of organized business.

Section 14(b)—the provision allowing the states to ban the union shop—has become both the crucial substantive issue in management-relations, and a symbol of the political differences between labor and management. Repeal of the "right to work" provision has been at the head of labor's list of legislative goals during recent years, and as other labor-backed bills have passed, such as minimum wage extension and consumer protection, Section 14(b) will doubtless take on even more symbolic importance. Union leaders strongly support a bill that would nullify all

---

[21] C. E. Lindblom, *Unions and Capitalism* (New Haven: Yale University Press, 1949).

[22] Frank Tannenbaum, *A Philosophy of Labor* (New York: Alfred A. Knopf, Inc., 1952), p. 199. Such brief mention cannot, of course, do justice to the thoughtful views and keen insights of either of the two volumes just cited.

nineteen presently existing state "right to work" laws, would forbid the future enactment of such laws, and thus would make the union shop permissible throughout the country. Labor has lobbied intensively on Capitol Hill for repeal, but has been thwarted by filibusters and other devices employed mainly by congressmen representing states with "right to work" laws.

Most organized business interests have been equally adamant *against* repeal of Section 14(b). A National Right to Work Committee, formed in 1955, has continued to lobby against repeal in Congress and the state capitols. Representing about 18,000 members, of which 8000 were claimed to be individual workers and the remaining small businessmen, the committee has been spending from $500,000 to $750,000 a year in its lobbying efforts—a figure not very disproportionate to the cost of labor's lobbying. The committee argued that the measure had not impeded proper union organization, that "right to work" laws were not simply anti-union devices, that the union shop often brought excessive dues that were used in turn as political slush funds for union leaders, and that—above all—the right of an individual *not* to join a union must be safeguarded.[23] Business interests have not been completely united in support of 14(b), of course. Their stakes differ depending on their size, location, relations with unions, and other factors. In states that have no "right to work" law repeal of 14(b) would have no effect on unions or management; indeed, repeal might help businesses that now must compete with firms located in states where unions are weak. Still, major business interests continue to oppose repeal of 14(b), and prospects of repeal diminished in the congressional elections of 1966, which saw a goodly number of "pro-labor" Democratic Congressmen lose their seats in the House of Representatives to Republicans with a more "pro-business" orientation.

What are the alternatives of government labor policy in areas outside those covered by the Wagner and Taft Hartley Acts? The likely tendencies in some areas are more predictable than in others. It seems probable that the present minimum wage will continue to be raised, especially if the cost of living continues to rise. Although some unions are pressing for contracts that establish work weeks less than forty hours, it also seems unlikely that the "hours" provisions of the Fair Labor Standards Act will soon be lowered. It does seem probable that a serious military crisis would bring about economic stabilization programs, probably with the usual machinery of tripartite representation of labor, management, and the public.

Another important policy question involves whether the federal government should police or control labor-management disputes to a far greater degree than it does now under the Taft-Hartley Act—the question, in short, of compulsory arbitration. Proponents of the notion that the

---

[23] For a useful review of the political forces for and against repeal, see *Congressional Quarterly*. Weekly Report No. 42, Oct. 15, 1965, pp. 2085–88.

government should settle emergency strikes, just as it decides other great issues between citizens or groups of citizens, contend that otherwise we leave this one area of conflict in a condition of anarchy. They can point to many strikes or lockouts that have impaired national production and to the millions of man-days of work lost every year as a result of strikes, large and small. They mention the National War Labor Board during World War II as an example of successful employment of what was in effect compulsory government arbitration of disputes. It seems doubtful, however, that there will be any trend toward compulsory arbitration in the years directly ahead. Successful collective bargaining, informal conciliation and mediation by national, state, and local agencies, and perhaps the Taft-Hartley Act's procedures for delays and "second thoughts" in severe disputes have greatly limited the severe effects of industrial conflict. Both labor and management fear, moreover, that whatever temporary advantage one side might gain would be more than offset by the likelihood that the other side would gain influence over the arbitration officials and exploit compulsory arbitration for its own ends.

Labor's Choice of Political Tactics

Whether or not the pendulum of policy swings toward or away from union preferences will depend in part on the political influence that the unions can mobilize in government. In the early 1960s, after the great majority of union leaders had twice backed the losing presidential candidate and achieved only mixed success in Congress, the new united labor movement was busy assessing alternative political tactics in the light of experience in recent decades.

One alternative was the repudiation of political methods and a total reliance on "tried and true" methods of economic action, such as the strike. But hardly a voice in labor's ranks was raised for such a course. It was clear to all unionists by the mid-twentieth century that economic action was not enough, that it had to be supplemented by political action to bring pressure on the "big government" in Washington that had such influence over unionism, including its economic weapons. The issue was not *whether* unions should use political methods, but what kind, and how much of labor's strength should be expended in this activity.

On the opposite side of the fence are the "labor militants" who call for the establishment of a separate labor party operated and manned by millions of union members and their families. Both the Republican and Democratic parties are too conservative, they argue, to give labor its due; the Republicans are dominated by employer, middle-class, and conservative elements, and the Democrats unduly influenced by their southern wing. The proponents of a labor party point to the success of the Labor Party in

Great Britain; they also point to the many labor parties that have been established in this country over the last century and a half.[24] Yet it seems doubtful that this appeal will attract many unionists or their leaders. The experience of labor parties has often been to isolate union membership in a separate enclave and actually to lower its influence in politics. Some labor parties have met limited success in state politics but never on a national scale.

A third political alternative is for organized labor to enter the Democratic party in force and become a highly influential if not dominant element in its composition and policies. Indeed, in a rough, unplanned sort of way, this is what labor has done in the last quarter-century, and the real question is whether this should become labor's consistent and purposeful tactic. Trade unionists who oppose this alternative hold that participation in the Democratic party means weakening labor's strength and program because of the many other elements, including some hostile to labor, that make up the Democratic party, especially in the South. Those favoring it point to the pro-labor legislation, such as the Wagner Act, won by labor in the past as a result of its support of the Democratic party and its candidates, and they contend that pushing this tactic harder and more steadfastly would lead to even greater legislative victories.

A final alternative is simply continuation of labor's traditional policy of "helping our friends and defeating our enemies," as described on page 275. Such a policy will leave labor free of commitment to either of the major parties, and able, indeed, to work with third parties or independent state or local political groups as the situation requires. The great advantage of this approach is its flexibility; since American politics varies enormously from region to region, labor can adapt its specific techniques to the given political situation in any locality. It can work closely with the Democratic party where the party is strongly pro-labor, but where the party is more conservative, as in the South, labor can support the Republicans or independent parties or groups.

It seems likely that organized labor will pursue the last of the tactics described along with a tendency in some areas to become part of the Democratic party and seek to maximize influence in it. Even so, it is doubtful that labor in any area will make a full commitment to the Democratic party. Actually it has a choice of relationships with that party—it can serve in simply an *advisory* role, offering advice on party nominations, platforms, and the like; it can seek to *supplement* the efforts of the party by giving it money, votes, and workers; it can seek to establish a *balance of power* within the party, so that it can isolate and outmaneuver other interest groups within the party; or finally, it can try flatly to take

---

[24] For a thoughtful consideration of factors attracting labor toward a third party, see Marc Karson, "Contemporary American Labor and Politics," *The Chicago Jewish Forum* (Winter, 1956).

over control of the party by outvoting the non-union elements in it.[25] Labor will employ each of these tactics depending on the local political situation.

Is it possible that in the long run, labor will tend to lose interest in political action provided it meets its economic goals? More specifically, if union members become more "middle class" in the economic sense, will they become conservative or lethargic politically? A recent study suggests that the answer is probably in the negative. After analyzing labor voting in the Detroit area, the investigators concluded that "it is highly probable that improved socio-economic conditions and other influences will make for increasing political *interests*. . . . Both our findings and our speculative analysis lead to the conclusions that it is quite possible for wage earners to experience great social and economic gains and yet remain definitely pro-labor."[26]

Problems of Union Self-Government

As unions have increased in size and functions, popular interest has turned more and more to the question of how fairly, efficiently, and honestly unions manage their internal affairs. This matter involves government policy in at least two ways: since unions are in effect charged with a "public interest," serious failures in internal affairs will inevitably arouse public concern and lead to attempts to reform through government action; and the attitudes toward unions on the part both of members and the general public significantly influence the unity, prestige, and organizational strength of labor and hence its impact on public policy.

The spotlight has been turned on the unions' internal affairs in recent years as a result of disclosures of serious wrongdoing on the part of a number of union leaders. Handling of union welfare funds—that is, funds designed to provide life insurance, sickness pay, hospitalization, and the like—was an especially disturbing source of corruption. It was discovered that through fee-splitting arrangements, shakedowns, and kickbacks, union officials and racketeers had siphoned off millions of dollars in excessive commissions and service charges. Union officials had used welfare funds for their own profit and pleasure, had funneled insurance contracts through wives and other relatives, had steered welfare business to particular agents in return for "consultant" retainers of several hundred dollars a week. An equally grave—though perhaps less publicized—situation was the lack of

---

[25] Each of these various relationships is drawn from the political experience of labor in recent elections, as ably described in Fay Calkins, *The CIO and the Democratic Party* (Chicago: The University of Chicago Press, 1952).

[26] Arthur Kornhauser, Harold L. Sheppard, and Albert J. Mayer, *When Labor Votes* (New York: University Books, 1956). It should be kept in mind that this study involves a particular labor union (the Auto Workers) and area, and the conclusion is suggestive rather than necessarily true of organized labors as a whole.

democracy in some unions. Elections were held only rarely, real alternatives were seldom presented to the rank-and-file, union publicity was used for the aggrandizement of the existing leadership, and freedom of debate and dissent was stifled in one way or the other.

To be sure, the great majority of unions were largely guiltless of such failings. According to a careful study, the typical union was the scene of active and vigorous political life, of considerable compromise among competitive factions, of frequent contests among secondary officials if not for the top positions, of the right of appeal by individual members to appeals committees, of fairly modest salaries for officers. Too, most unions had responsible accounting and auditing procedures for the protection of union treasuries.[27] Still, the flagrant excesses of some union leaders inevitably arouse serious and legitimate public concern as to whether reforms should be instituted.

The main question was whether the unions would clean out their own houses or whether reforms would have to come from the outside through new government policies. This question cannot be answered yet, but it is significant that soon after some of the most serious revelations of union abuse in 1957, the AFL-CIO took drastic steps to prevent financial malpractices and to require democratic processes. In the spring of 1957 the AFL-CIO Executive Council approved a code of ethics previously drawn up by a committee of union secretary-treasurers. Among its provisions were requirements that unions keep detailed and accurate records of accounts, approve all spending through proper authorities, make at least semi-annual detailed financial reports, have the books audited at least once a year by an outside certified public accountant, and outlaw "kickbacks" to union officers. Forbidden practices included contracts bringing personal profit to union officials, personal loans to officers or members of their families to finance their private business, and investment in, or loans to, any business with which the union bargains collectively.

Equally sweeping was a "code of democratic processes" adopted by the AFL-CIO Council also in the spring of 1957. Among its provisions were that each union member should have the right to "full and free participation in union self-government," including the right to vote, to run for office, and to express his views; that each union member should have the right to fair and uniform application of union rules and laws, including such essential elements of due process as notice, hearing, and judgment on the basis of the evidence; that conventions should be held at least once every four years; that elections should be fairly and frequently conducted at all levels; that local membership meetings should be held regularly; that terms of union officials should not exceed four years; and that conventions should be open to the public as far as possible.

---

[27] Philip Taft, *The Structure and Government of Labor Unions* (Cambridge, Mass.: Harvard University Press, 1954), pp. 239–46.

How successful were these codes? Clearly they had done some good, but the clamor on the part of union members as well as employers for legislation such as the Landrum-Griffin Act suggested that self-policing was necessary but not adequate to do the job. Some students of labor believe that full democracy in unions is unattainable. "The conditions that currently characterize unions—the complexity of their organization, the increasing tendency to assume functions complementary to that of management, the status and salary gap existing between leaders and members, not to mention the psychological compulsion of the leaders to retain power, and the members' expectation that their union is primarily a service institution rather than a way of life—do not provide the soil in which the democratic process can operate."[28] Others believe that while full democracy may be visionary, in the long run Americans must place their main hopes for the maintenance of democratic processes on the union members themselves rather than on the long arm of the law. To the extent that this latter view wins out, we will see again one of the most important government policies mentioned above—the *absence* of government policy.

BIBLIOGRAPHICAL NOTE

An extensive treatment of labor in general, with special emphasis on trade union history, internal union government and politics, and union economic and political practices, is Harry A. Millis and Royal E. Montgomery, *Organized Labor*, 1945. Robert R. R. Brooks, *When Labor Organizes*, 1937, describes graphically the problem of union organization from the vantage point of the 1930s. *The American Federationist*, journal of the AFL, provides insights into labor's viewpoints over several decades, and virtually all the larger international unions have journals and newspapers. Harold W. Davey, *Contemporary Collective Bargaining*, 1951, is an extensive treatment of the subject with an especially useful chapter on the impact of public policy on collective bargaining. A readable and pioneering study of the psychology of union leadership is Eli Ginzberg, *The Labor Leader*, 1948. For a recent and authoritative statement of current labor attitudes and problems from labor's viewpoint, see Arthur J. Goldberg, *AFL-CIO: Labor United*, 1956. A study of labor in politics in an industrial area but under varying political conditions is Fay Calkins, *The CIO and the Democratic Party*, 1952. C. E. Lindblom, *Unions and Capitalism*, 1949, and Frank Tannenbaum, *A Philosophy of Labor*, 1952, both offer arresting views on the future of labor in American society, although from very different vantage points. Martin S. Estey, Philip Taft, and Martin Wagner, eds., *Regulating Union Government*, 1964, is a

---

[28] C. P. MacGrath, "Democracy in Overalls: The Futile Quest for Union Democracy," *Industrial and Labor Relations Review*, July, 1959, p. 524.

collection of authoritative essays on this subject. Indispensable sources of views and information are the hearings before the labor committees of the two houses of Congress. For a comprehensive, penetrating treatment, see Herbert R. Northrup and Gordon F. Bloom, *Government and Labor,* 1963.

wars on poverty
and disease:
welfare, health, housing

J. W. PELTASON

This chapter will highlight the long-range problems that have given rise to demands for public action, and indicate some of the continuing conflicts in the fields of welfare, health, and housing. We group these three areas together primarily for reasons of convenience, but they do have some common features: welfare, housing to an extent, and public health in lesser part are designed to benefit in the first instance the less fortunate members of the community; all have ancient origins but their scope and significance have been expanded tremendously since the Great Depression; all are examples of what has become known as the "welfare state."

GOVERNMENT AND WELFARE

Everything our governments do is supposed to promote the national welfare. But the term "welfare" is used in a more restrictive sense to refer to assistance to those who are in need and to programs that protect us against the economic hazards flowing from old age, disability, and unemployment.

What, if anything, should be done to help those who are too old, too ill, or too young to provide for themselves? What if a man can find no job? What if he lacks the moral and mental discipline to take care of himself and his family? We could do nothing—allow them to die. This is the policy in some societies. Not so many years ago in some parts of India there was a grim but efficient solution to the problem of poor widows and orphans. A widow was expected to throw herself on her husband's funeral pyre and her children were given to relatives.

In the United States no one has ever advocated such a drastic policy, but there have been some who argue that the wisest policy is to let the poor perish—or at least shift for themselves. However the policy of "let them starve" is no longer, if it ever was, an alternative for the American people. There is widespread agreement that something should be done. The questions are what should be done, for whom should it be done, and who should do it?

The Elizabethan Poor Law System

American welfare activities are an outgrowth of and, at least until the Great Depression, very much reflect the practices of Elizabethan England.[1] In 1601 the famous statute of the Queen established the basic public welfare system for both England and the United States which lasted with only minor alterations for the next 300 years. Under this system, public assistance was made a duty of the local units of government—the parish in England and the township or county in the United States—financed by a poor-tax collected and administered by the overseers of the poor. Each parish or township or county was responsible for all indigents born in the area or who had established residence there. (Residence requirements for relief are still common.) No person was entitled to relief unless his parents or children were unable to help—the principle of family responsibility.

Poverty was assumed to be a sign of moral and character deficiencies and paupers were treated as sinful persons. Relief was given grudgingly, and its acceptance was made sufficiently onerous that only those in desperate circumstances were inclined to seek help. Paupers had to take an "oath," their names were placed on the "poor rolls," published in the local newspapers, and exhibited in the city along with amounts received. (In 1951 the Social Security Act was amended to allow states to publicize the names of persons who were receiving federally supported relief.)

The Poor Laws divided the needy into three categories and treated them accordingly. The *able-bodied poor*, sometimes called sturdy beggars or unworthy poor—what we now call the unemployed—were sent to workhouses maintained by the parish or county. The *impotent* or *worthy poor* —those we now call "unemployables," the old, insane, feeble-minded, widows, and so on—were placed in the almshouse. Frequently the almshouse and the workhouse were merely different quarters in the same

---

[1] The first English law concerned with the poor was passed in 1349 after the "Black Death" killed two-thirds of the people. Issued by Edward III, this statute came not from compassion for the poor but from the pressures of the landed gentry who needed workers. Edward made it a criminal offense, subject to branding or mutilation, for any able-bodied worker to refuse to accept employment from any master. In the United States the Thirteenth Amendment stands in the way of such compulsory labor, but like Edward some still consider vagrancy to be a crime.

dilapidated building. Into these "human scrapheaps" often operated by unqualified persons were thrown the sick, the old, the mentally ill, petty criminals, orphans, and other destitutes without homes or friends to care for them. *Small children* were, if possible, "farmed out" to foster homes. After they reached eight, the boys were indentured to a master until they became twenty-four, and the girls did domestic work until they married or became twenty-one.

In England primary reliance was placed on "indoor," or institutional, relief; but in some parishes—and more commonly in the United States— "outdoor relief," payments in money or food and clothes, were given, especially to those who needed help to tide them over an emergency. Financial aid was carefully measured so that no person on relief received as much as could be earned by the lowest paid person not on relief. (This practice, called the principle of less-eligibility, is a feature of many present-day welfare programs.)

What was the life of a poor person like under this system? Here is how Charles Dickens in a fictional, but substantially accurate account, described the early days of Oliver Twist, who was born in a workhouse and left an orphan at birth:

> [The] parish authorities magnanimously and humanely resolved, that Oliver should be 'farmed,' or, in other words, that he should be despatched to a branch-workhouse some three miles off, where twenty or thirty other juvenile offenders against the poor-laws, rolled about the floor all day, without the inconvenience of too much food or too much clothing, under the parental superintendence of an elderly female, who received the culprits at and for the consideration of sevenpence-halfpenny per small head per week. . . . The elderly female was a woman of wisdom and experience; she knew what was good for children; and she had a very accurate perception of what was good for herself. So, she appropriated the greater part of the weekly stipend to her own use, and consigned the rising parochial generation to even a shorter allowance than was originally provided for them. . . . [At] the very moment when a child had contrived to exist upon the smallest possible portion of the weakest possible food, it did perversely happen in eight and a half cases out of ten, either that it sickened from want and cold, or fell into the fire from neglect, or got half-smothered by accident. . . .[2]

Oliver, who was made of hardy stuff, managed to survive and at the age of seven was returned to the workhouse.

> The members of this board [of overseers] were very sage, deep, philosophical men; and when they came to turn their attention to the workhouse, they found out at once, what ordinary folks would never have discovered—the poor people liked it. . . . So, they established the rule,

---

[2] Charles Dickens, *The Adventures of Oliver Twist* or *The Parish Boy's Progress*, first published as a serial in the pages of "Bentley's Miscellany" from January, 1837, to March, 1839; quotations here taken from National Library Company edition, Vol. V, pp. 5–6.

that all poor people should have the alternative (for they would compel nobody, not they), of being starved by a gradual process in the house, or by a quick one out of it. [Here Dickens is poking fun at the principle of less-eligibility.] With this view, they contracted with the water-works to lay on an unlimited supply of water; and with a corn-factor to supply periodically small quantities of oatmeal; and issued three meals of thin gruel a day, with an onion twice a week, and a half a roll on Sundays. They made a great many other wise and humane regulations. . . . It was rather expensive at first, in consequence of the increase in the undertaker's bill, and the necessity of taking in the clothes of all the paupers. . . . But the number of work-house inmates got thin as well as the paupers; and the board were in ecstasies. [Here Dickens was attacking the "reformers" who measure public programs solely by the yardstick of "efficiency and economy." They had secured the adoption of legislation in 1834 which reduced poor relief costs by one-third.][3]

Inadequate as poor relief was, some thought that the poor were treated too generously. For example, Francis Wayland, an influential early nineteenth-century American economist urged abolition of the poor laws because they were "destructive of the right of property . . . they must proceed upon the concession that the rich are under obligation to the poor."[4] Others drew upon the writings of English classical economists such as T. R. Malthus who argued that poverty is unavoidable and poor relief unwise. Malthus had it figured out that population increases at a faster rate than do food supplies. Therefore, it is impossible to raise the standard of living of the great mass of the people. To feed the poor merely keeps more of them alive, wrote Malthus, and since there would be no substantial increase in the amount of food, no one would be better off than before. Furthermore, he argued, persons who are unable to provide for themselves are not fit to survive. Instead of the government taking care of the poor, he wrote, the poor should be taught "that they are themselves the causes of their own poverty; that the means of redress are in their own hands, and in the hands of no other person whatever; that the society in which they live and the government which presides over it, are without any direct power in this respect."[5]

In the last half of the nineteenth century, Herbert Spencer, a popular sociologist, was a leading opponent of the poor laws. Although he felt that limited private charity to reduce "superfluous suffering" was permissible, he opposed public assistance because it interfered with the natural laws of selection. If the government did not interfere, Spencer wrote, these natural laws would wipe out of existence the unemployed who were "simply good-

---

[3] *Ibid.*, pp. 14–15.

[4] Francis Wayland, *The Elements of Political Economy*, 3rd ed. (Boston: Leavitt, Lord & Co., 1840), p. 15; quoted by Sidney Fine, *Laissez Faire and the General Welfare State* (Ann Arbor, The University of Michigan Press, 1956), p. 7.

[5] T. R. Malthus, *An Essay on the Principle of Population*, 6th ed. (London, 1826), II, pp. 287–88; quoted by Fine, *op. cit.*, p. 7.

for-nothings, who . . . live on the good-for-somethings—vagrants and sots, criminals and those who are on the way to crime. . . ."[6]

During the decades following the Civil War, industrialization brought large numbers to the cities where they were exposed to the hazards of an industrial society in which illness, injury, or unemployment forced entire families on relief. Many had to live in slums, which set off a vicious circle—living in slums led to disease, and disease in turn caused poverty that forced people to continue to live in slums.

For a time the Spencerian attitude toward relief became embedded in our constitutional interpretation, but despite the writings of many eminent men and the opposition of some courts, as the century proceeded there was a gradual expansion of state and local welfare functions. The essential features of the Elizabethan system were retained but there were some tentative attempts to deal with the causes of poverty.

Some reformers thought that alcoholism was the major cause of pauperism, and in many states they were successful in making the manufacture and sale of alcoholic beverages illegal. In this reform movement, they were joined by employers who felt that consumption of liquor reduced their employees' efficiency. Many employers, however, opposed legislation to forbid child labor, to establish minimum wages, to protect workers against industrial accidents, to establish workmen's compensation, and to protect the right of workers to form trade unions. But despite employer opposition and hostility of the courts, by the twentieth century such laws were gradually being enacted and strengthened in many of the industrialized states.

Any survey of predepression welfare programs would be deficient if it did not note the important role of the big city political organizations. The precinct captain was ready at any time of the night or day to lend a helping hand, find a job for Mr. Murphy, help Mr. Green secure a license for his pushcart, give coal to the Greenbergs, find warm clothing for the Smith family. Where there was a fire, the precinct captain was always ready to aid the distressed. These politicians had no long forms to be filled out and they asked no embarrassing questions. They gave help without making the recipient feel inferior or apologetic. True, it was a costly welfare system. The city organizations voted into office by the many grateful recipients of their favor received their *quid pro quo* in the form of graft. The politicians were unconcerned about rehabilitation or basic reforms, but they did keep people from freezing or starving to death.

What of the national government? It had an extensive program for needy veterans, a limited program for needy Indians, and specialized programs for merchant seamen, but the prevailing belief was that there was no legitimate national interest in welfare and that the national government

---

[6] Herbert Spencer, "The Coming Slavery," *The Man versus the State* (London: Williams & Norgate, 1892), pp. 18–19; quoted by Fine, *op. cit.*, p. 38.

had no constitutional authority to provide assistance. Then came the depression.

The Impact of the Depression

The central fact about the Depression is that suddenly there were lots of poor people. Poverty became something experienced rather than something merely read about; thousands who previously had considered relief as the recourse of the unworthy discovered that they had no choice but to join the breadlines. No longer did they argue that unemployment was produced by the individual's own failings. But whatever the theorizing, there were millions without money to buy food, clothes, or shelter.

The traditional relief structure caved in under the pressures. Local units had no machinery to process the thousands of applicants; even more critical, they did not have the money. State governments began to take emergency action, but by 1932 when even more persons were without jobs the states too were running out of money. Many state governors, especially those of the large industrial states, made frantic appeals to the national government.

At first the national government refused to act, except to urge employers to continue production and the rich to make larger contributions to charity. President Hoover was strongly opposed to federal relief. He was convinced, at first, that the depression was a temporary setback. He believed that relief was the responsibility of the local governments and he was fearful that if the national government acted, it would establish what was to him a dangerous precedent. He also believed that if the federal government gave aid to the unemployed it would deprive them of their self-reliance. However, as conditions continued to get worse and prosperity did not come around the corner, the President reluctantly approved a limited federal relief program, first in the form of loans and then gifts to the states for welfare purposes.

When Roosevelt—who did not share his predecessor's opposition to vigorous federal action—became President he sponsored a large-scale relief program administered through a variety of agencies. The initial emphasis was on getting the money as fast as possible to those in need. But in time the "dole" was replaced by putting men to work on public projects. Recipients of public employment, it was hoped, would be less likely to lose their self-reliance since they would be earning their assistance. In turn society gained through the schools, dams, highways, postoffices, and irrigation projects they were building.

In time these emergency programs were abandoned, but the precedent that Hoover feared had been established—primary responsibility is still vested in the states and local governments. But since 1932 the national government has had a vast welfare program. Perhaps of even greater significance, since the Great Depression the Elizabethan system has been supplemented by social insurance.

Social Insurance

Insurance, unlike assistance, is not charity. There is no need to demonstrate poverty, that is no "means tests," and payments are not handouts from the taxpayers. Rather social insurance gives covered individuals a legal right to certain payments in the event of specified events that cause loss or reduction of income, for example, retirement, disability, unemployment. The insurance is financed by regular deductions from earnings, directly or indirectly. Social insurance is based on the same principle as private insurance—sharing risks, and setting money aside for rainy days. But there are important differences between most social insurance programs and private insurance. Social insurance is compulsory, persons have no contractual rights to benefits but are entitled only to those which the law at the moment allows, and benefits paid out are not necessarily restricted to total funds paid into the system because additional contributions may come from the public treasury.

Social insurance has become accepted as a more systematic, less expensive, and more equitable way to meet the inevitable costs which grow out of old-age, unemployment, and disability. Old-age insurance, for example, compels people to make some provision during their working days for the time when they will retire, and as more people secure this protection the percentage of the aged who have to seek public assistance should decline. Furthermore, beneficiaries of an insurance program do not suffer the loss of dignity often associated with receiving charity. Finally, there is much less opportunity for favoritism or unfair treatment, since there is no necessity to determine each applicant's need, which is so hard to define.

In 1935 Congress enacted the Social Security Act, which strengthened federal participation in public assistance programs and inaugurated federally operated social insurance. Today, except for railroad workers and some government employees who have their own systems, almost all working persons in the United States are covered by federal old age, survivors, disability and medical insurance. Each employee pays a payroll tax of 4.4 per cent of his first $6600 of earnings and his employer pays a like amount. Self-employed persons pay 6.4 per cent at the same time they pay their income taxes. (These rates are scheduled to rise gradually until they reach 5.65 for each employee and employer, and 7.8 for self-employed persons in 1987.)

These contributions, along with some help from the general treasury, provide retirement, survivors, disability, and medical benefits.

Retirement Benefits. The main reason for loss or reduction of income is old age. Less than half the men and only one out of ten women over sixty-five are at work. A man of sixty-five may expect to live on the average twelve years longer, his wife of that age for fourteen. After a man ceases work he must maintain himself and his dependents on the resources he has been able to set aside during his working years. It takes $17,000 to provide an annuity income of $100 a month for himself and his wife. Often his children help, for as the late Professor Sumner Slichter pointed out, "The usual method by which men have provided for their old age has never been thrift—it has been by having plenty of children and expecting the children to help the parents."[7] When large families were common, families with their built-in social security were able to take care of the older members without too much difficulty. Families still provide most of our protection against the hazards of old age, but the income of most "senior citizens" is now also supplemented through social security retirement benefits.

At sixty-two a worker may retire and draw 80 per cent of his benefits; full benefits begin at sixty-five. A person over sixty-five who continues to work receives reduced retirement benefits. After seventy-two there are no restrictions on the amount that may be earned while drawing full benefits. At no time does additional income from investments or private insurance, which the worker has saved for his old age, reduce his old-age insurance payments. Payments vary depending on the age of the wife and the amount paid into the system. Payments are not handsome—the maximum monthly payment to a worker without dependents who retires at sixty-five is $168 a month, or for a retired worker and wife over sixty-five the maximum payments are around $252 a month—but combined with other resources they often make it possible for people to live in their own homes.

Survivors Benefits. If a worker covered by social security insurance dies before retirement, his family receives a lump-sum benefit plus monthly payments that vary according to his contributions and number of dependents. The maximum monthly payment to a widow under sixty-two with two children is $368.

Disability Benefits. After a six-months waiting period an insured worker who suffers from a physical or mental disability expected to last for twelve or more months and of such an extent that he can no longer engage in any substantial gainful activity is eligible for disability benefits. Some benefits also accrue to the permanently disabled child of a deceased or retired person covered by social security.

Almost every year Congress improves the social security system. In 1965 major amendments provided for medical benefits to be discussed later.

Support for social security seems so strong that there is little possibility of the program being seriously restricted. Nevertheless, there are some who object to the national government's compelling people to participate. They

---

[7] Sumner H. Slichter, "The Pressing Problem of Old-Age Security," *The New York Times Magazine* (October 16, 1949), p. 9.

charge that contributors have no guarantee of receiving benefits since these are subject to change by law at any time. They argue that future benefits will be paid in inflated dollars and beneficiaries will not receive as much in actual spending power as they have contributed.

Defenders insist that the government can be trusted to make good its obligations. Benefits are not likely to be changed to the disadvantage of the seventy million citizens in the system who make a voting block large enough to scare any President or Congressman. The possibility of inflation is an inherent risk in any insurance scheme and is an argument not against insurance but against inflation.

Some critics would introduce a means test, which would change the essential nature of the program from insurance to assistance. A more likely possibility, but not probability, is to do away with all the elaborate and expensive keeping of individual records and to pay a pension out of general tax funds to all retired persons. Since payments would not as directly and obviously be related to contributions, the political consequences of such a change and a person's attitude toward his pension might be altered.

Unemployment Insurance

Even during prosperous times, production cutbacks, shifts in plant locations, and changes in technology cause some workers to lose their jobs. In the relatively prosperous 1960s there are still over four million unemployed workers. Prior to the establishment of unemployed insurance, after savings had been exhausted, the only public source of help was the "dole." The dismissal of a few men in one industry frequently set off a chain reaction. Those out of work could no longer buy things they needed, so other men lost their jobs because their employers could no longer sell so much.

Before 1935 a few states, most notably Wisconsin, tried to establish unemployment insurance. But each state hesitated to act, for fear that the additional costs would place its own industries in an economically disadvantageous position with competitors in other states. To deprive industries in states without unemployment insurance of this advantage and to induce all states to establish programs, Congress in 1935 levied a 3 per cent tax on most employers of eight or more (now four) on the first $3000 paid to each employee. However, if an employer is paying a tax to a state unemployment insurance scheme that meets federal standards, he may credit all he pays to the state to cover up to 90 per cent of his federal liability. Hence, a state tax of 2.7 per cent does not increase the employer's total tax payments.

State funds are deposited in the national treasury where they are available to be used by the state to make unemployment payments. The national government gives the states the money to cover administrative costs, and national officials check to be sure federal standards are being followed, but each state has considerable freedom in shaping its own program. Unemployed workers must report in person to the state employment agency to show that they are able to work, and they must be willing to do a reasonable amount of traveling to secure work. Eligible workers unable to find employment are entitled to weekly benefits that vary from state to state, from a high of $70 in Alaska to a low of $32 in Oklahoma. The maximum number of weeks for which unemployment benefits may be drawn in most states is twenty-six weeks. During recent recessions Congress has provided temporary financial help to states wishing to extend unemployment benefits after state funds have been exhausted.

Public Assistance

Social insurance supplements but does not replace assistance: persons not entitled to unemployment compensation or not old enough for retirement benefits (or so destitute that social insurance is not sufficient) may be eligible for public assistance.

Federal support is provided for a variety of what are known as *categorical assistance* programs. In other words, states may secure matching federal funds to be used to help persons who are in need because of certain kinds of disabilities, or as Sargent Shriver, Director of the Office of Economic Opportunity, has said: "Our welfare payments . . . are a list of excuses for being poor which we middle-class Americans consider acceptable excuses and therefore reimbursable."[8] The most significant federally supported programs are for needy aged, dependent children, needy blind and disabled.

Almost two and a half million *needy* aged are now receiving old-age assistance. Old-age assistance, unlike old-age insurance, is administered by state and local welfare officials; the national government's role is, however, most important. The national government supplies about half the money and as a condition of receiving these grants the states must 1) match some of the federal funds; 2) administer or supervise the program through a single state agency; 3) adopt an acceptable merit system for the employees who administer the program; 4) provide a hearing before a state agency for all individuals whose claims for assistance are denied; 5) consider the applicant's income and other resources in establishing standards of eligibility; and 6) impose no conditions more restrictive than certain federal specifications.

It is frequently alleged that "national bureaucrats" have too much control over state and local officials, but the occasions in which they have denied funds to a state because of violation of conditions are extremely rare. United States Senators can be depended upon to defend their respec-

---

[8] R. Sargent Shriver, Jr., "New Weapons in Fighting Poverty," *Journal of the American Public Welfare Association.* XXIV (January, 1966), 10.

tive states against "federal encroachment," and officials in the Social Security Administration (Department of Health, Education, and Welfare) are very sensitive to demands of Senators and Congressmen who appropriate the money.

Each state may grant assistance beyond the limits supported by the national government and may establish its own standards as long as they do not conflict with federal rules. Although federal money is distributed by a formula which gives more to the poorest states, these states with a large percentage of aged on relief give each of their applicants less than do the wealthy states. Among the states, there are also marked differences in the political influence of the aged, and this is reflected in the size of old-age payments. Hence, amounts and conditions of assistance and the details of the administration vary from state to state.

All states have residence requirements, some refuse aid to aliens, and some refuse to help persons convicted of a felony within the last ten years or who have failed to support their children. States have different standards to determine "need" and different procedures to recover from the estates of deceased recipients of assistance. Some states make a serious attempt to recover by making first claims on the estates after federal taxes, if any, have been paid, while others let creditors receive first with the state taking its share if there is anything left.

Applicants for relief apply first at the local welfare office where a worker investigates—perhaps emergency aid will be given—the applicant's resources and tries to locate children or other relatives. If local officials rule that the applicant is not eligible for relief, he is entitled to appeal to a state commission or board, frequently called the department of social welfare.

On a nationwide average, states pay the needy aged about $80 a month, but this varies from an average payment of $110 in California and Wisconsin to $39 in Mississippi. These payments, although small, permit many individuals to remain at home, and with the money they receive, unrestricted as to use, they can live their own lives. This is frequently less expensive to the taxpayers than it would be to provide for them in an institution.

For those who are so poor, so alone, or so ill that money is not enough, there are only the almshouses, which are now generally being turned into nursing homes for the aged and chronically ill. Considerable progress has been made in improving these institutions. Buildings have been modernized and trained personnel have been put in charge. In many areas several counties have pooled resources in order to operate one good nursing home rather than each running an inadequate one. Those who can pay do so; those without families or their own financial resources are given tax-supported care. Although persons living in tax-supported institutions normally are not eligible for federally supported assistance, they may do so if they are receiving medical care in a nursing home. This money can be used to help defray their expenses; an additional incentive for counties to turn almshouses into nursing homes.

Of all who are in need, perhaps it is the children who make the strongest appeal to our charity. Even those most stoutly opposed to public assistance find it hard to argue that children are responsible for their own misfortunes and should be left without care. Nowadays the national and state governments have extensive welfare programs to promote the well-being of children, and except for the aged, more money is spent on these welfare activities than any other.

Social security insurance provides some protection, since children of a person covered by this insurance are entitled to survivors' benefits. But for the most part, needy dependent children are cared for through assistance rather than insurance. If a child has no parents or relatives and it is impossible to secure new parents by adoption or to place him in a foster home, the only choice is an orphanage. These institutions supported by private and public sources are on the whole well-operated institutions. But however well run the institution, most students of child welfare believe that if it is at all possible children should be kept in private homes. Even if the family is broken through death, desertion, or incapacity of a parent, a mother, brother, sister, grandparent, or some other close relative can give the child more special attention and love than is possible in even the finest institution. In order to make this more likely, all states make federally supported assistance payments to dependent children.

A dependent child, defined by federal law, is one under eighteen who has been deprived of parental support but who is living with the other parent or close relative. In 1961 Congress permitted states to divert these funds for a short period to aid families of unemployed workers with children under eighteen. (Only eighteen states have taken advantage of these provisions.) Over a million families receive support, the national average payment being around $141 per family ($34 per person) with average payments per family ranging from $39 in Mississippi to $212 in Illinois. Recently some states have started to restrict aid given to dependent children of unwed mothers on the grounds that their homes are "undesirable," but others have refused to do so because it penalizes the child more than the parents. In 1961 Congress directed that federal funds should be denied to any state that refused relief to children on the grounds that their homes were "unsuitable," but made no provision for removing the children from such homes. Aid to dependent children is administered through the same procedures as old-age assistance and is primarily intended to supplement the incomes of persons suffering adversity. But people in want, especially children, sometimes need advice, training, medical care, and other forms of social service. This is the responsibility of the Children's Bureau, a unit of the Welfare Administration.

The Children's Bureau, first established in 1912 as part of the Department of Labor, but now within the Department of Health, Education, and Welfare, is charged to investigate and report "upon all matters pertaining to the welfare of children and child life among all classes of people" and has the additional responsibility of administering three federal grants to the states—to extend and improve health services for mothers and children, to support state crippled children's programs, and to assist states in improving and expanding child welfare services. In the child welfare program, specialists counsel parents and children, develop community programs, and give special attention to problems of mentally retarded, emotionally disturbed, and neglected children. Some state and local welfare programs are responsible for supervision of foster care of dependent children and operate institutions for delinquent or handicapped children.

In administering the maternal and child health and crippled children programs, the Children's Bureau works with local public health officials. Among other things these grants support health supervision for expectant mothers, public nursing services after delivery, vaccination of school children for smallpox, immunization for diphtheria, and protection against poliomyelitis. The object of the crippled children's program is to locate children who require care and provide therapy and rehabilitation.

In 1921 when Congress first made grants to help states reduce the then very high maternal and infant mortality rates, public health officials—national, state, and local—argued that it was wrong to create a separate public health program for mothers and children and that its administration should be given to the Public Health Service. But the many spirited feminists, joined by spokesmen for organized labor, insisted that health officers were too conservative and unimaginative and that all federal programs concerned with children should be vested in a single agency. Since it has been in existence, the Children's Bureau, staffed primarily by women, has energetically and boldly pursued its objectives. As an eminent public health authority reports, the Children's Bureau—if not rudely, at least abruptly—shattered the "smugness that existed in many state health organizations."[9]

The Disabled

During the course of any single working day about sixty-two workers will be killed, 350 will suffer some permanent impairment, and 7600 more will suffer injuries which will keep them from work for an average of about

9 Harry S. Mustard, *Government in Public Health* (New York: The Commonwealth Fund, 1945), p. 76.

eighteen days.[10] Occupational injuries cause more casualties than war, and even more are injured away from their jobs. When the breadwinner is injured not only is there an increased need for money to pay doctors and hospitals, but at the same time there is a decrease in earnings. If the accident results in a major injury, there may be months, perhaps years, of medical care and rehabilitation before the worker can be returned to productive employment.

As noted, social security provides some protection for disabled workers and each of our states has a system of workmen's compensation that provides some protection for those injured on the job (see page 269). Veterans with service connected disabilities are entitled to a pension. For some of those not covered by these programs, the federal government supports state assistance programs for the needy disabled and the needy blind. These programs supplement the incomes of those in need with monthly grants, a national average of $80 a month in the case of the permanently disabled and $85 a month for the needy blind.

Instead of making cash payments for the rest of the disabled person's life, it is less expensive for society and more satisfactory for the individual, if it is at all possible, to rehabilitate a man so that he can earn his own living and no longer be dependent on relief. For this reason there has been a gradual expansion of vocational rehabilitation. The Veterans Administration has a well-established program. The states provided more limited services for civilians, but recently the federal government has increased its financial grants to the states to encourage them to improve and expand these activities. After a disability has become stabilized, persons who can become self-sufficient through surgical and medical care and training are eligible for a free examination. Those who can afford it are expected to pay for the necessary medical treatment, as well as for the required vocational training, but those who are unable to do so are given these services free. The costs to the taxpayer of restoring a disabled person to the wage-earning category are returned many times over in the form of his tax contributions and freedom from dependence on assistance payments.

The Politics and Administration of Welfare

The whole field of welfare services is characterized by segmented programs and overlapping administrative organizations. In the area of disability insurance and assistance, state labor departments enforce industrial safety and occupational disease regulations, workmen's compensation is adminis-

---

[10] Herman Miles Somers and Anne Ramsay Somers, *Workmen's Compensation* (New York: John Wiley & Sons, Inc., 1954), p. 1; most of the information in this section on workmen's compensation was taken from this excellent and comprehensive account.

tered by one state agency, vocational rehabilitation by another, and in some states aid to the blind by still another. Local health officials and local welfare agencies are involved. At the national level the Public Health Service and several bureaus of the Social Security Administration as well as units of the Department of Labor administer grants having to do with some aspect of disability. Moreover, the extent of individual protection varies. In some industries, trade unions have been able to bargain for generous welfare, disability, and old-age programs, but in others there is no such protection.

Today welfare expenditures of state and local governments are among the largest, ranking only behind education and highways. Most of this expansion has taken place in recent decades, much of it in response to programs initiated by the national government. The pattern of groups supporting welfare programs is formidable. Both major political parties claim to be pioneers and champions of social security. The trade unions, which in the past were not enthusiastic about social security but preferred to rely on their own bargaining power, have become staunch supporters. Many employers have ceased to oppose. Some companies have agreed to pay their employees old-age pensions that are tied into social security insurance. The larger the benefit under social security, the less the company must pay. Hence, these employers now favor social security. Small employers who are unable to finance the welfare funds created by large unions and large employers now find that securing protection for their workers through public insurance programs presents an attractive alternative. Added to these pressures are growing proportions of older people who press their demands with considerable vigor. (Some observers have suggested that the projected increase in proportion of aged persons and the coincident increase in number of children are going to force the middle-age wage earners to choose between larger expenditures to care for their parents or larger expenditures to educate their children.) There are still a significant number of Americans who are apprehensive that the burden of supporting these welfare services is becoming too great, and who fear that these programs will undermine our sense of initiative and willingness to take risks, but the political forces now supporting these programs appear to be so considerable that they have in their grand outlines almost ceased to be items of political controversy.

However, there are still significant differences among the various groups over the details of the programs, their future development and expansion. Trade unions, employers' organizations, insurance companies, medical associations, bar associations, and organizations of welfare and health workers often have different ideas of what policies should be adopted. Each tends to be concerned with special aspects, each tends to emphasize special dangers; each is true to the national interest, in its own fashion.

Special Problems of Minorities

One person out of nineteen in the United States receives some form of public relief. Many of these recipients are members of minority groups who are discriminated against in education, who are forced into substandard housing, and who find it difficult to secure jobs. Traditionally, the most recently arrived immigrant groups have been subjected to this discrimination, and as a result they constituted a large portion of persons needing public relief. As soon as they became integrated into the mainstream of American society and were permitted to participate in the productive life of the economy, and perhaps even more important, as soon as they were allowed to reap the rewards of their own ability, they had less need for public assistance. Today the Negroes are given the fewest opportunities, and as a result they constitute the largest percentage of those in need.

Some persons justify discrimination because they argue that the relatively large numbers of Negroes on relief shows that they lack the initiative and self-reliance to take care of themselves. Obviously this confuses cause with effect. Discrimination leads to lack of education and opportunity, and it is opportunity that produces initiative and independence. Why should a man sacrifice to secure a college education if when he graduates the only jobs open to him are as a day laborer? As long as Negroes are denied equal opportunities, not only do they suffer, but the entire community pays in the form of high cost of relief, and we are all denied the full productive and cultural contributions of those discriminated against.

The New War on Poverty

After almost thirty years of social insurance and more than a century of welfare assistance, thirty-three million Americans live in families with a combined income of less than $3000. Moreover, many government programs presumably designed to help the less fortunate are doing little to relieve poverty: farmers receive support but the poorest farmers receive almost nothing; the employment services do little for those who are too sick or too illiterate to hold a job; unemployment compensation is not available to the chronically unemployed; old age insurance benefits do not accrue for those who have no work.

Revelations about the extent and persistence of poverty in the midst of national affluence came as something of a surprise. Most people appeared to assume that our expanding economy was gradually eliminating poverty and that in the meantime welfare programs were taking care of those in need.

By the late 1950s some were expressing concern about automation and the creation of technological unemployment, and the national government directed assistance to areas of persistent unemployment, but the poverty issue was of little political significance. Critics of the welfare programs complained about their costs, and some championed tighter enforcement to prevent diversions of tax funds to the poor. In some states the question of whether public funds should be used to promote birth control generated political heat, but there was not much sustained interest.

Then suddenly—or so it seemed—poverty became a major issue of domestic politics in 1963–64. And in 1964 Congress enacted into law the Economic Opportunity Act and formally declared War on poverty. The Anti-Poverty Program has antecedents in earlier programs dating back to the 1930s. In fact little new has been added. What is new is the coordination of efforts, the commitment of billions, and the focusing of national attention on the challenge of eliminating poverty.

Why did the issue come to the front in 1963–64? There was no economic disaster, no upsurge in popular demand, no major social crisis, no organized compaign or extended political agitation. The Civil Rights Revolution of 1963 did dramatize the interconnections between discrimination and poverty, and it did furnish some political ammunition for the war on poverty. But it was only after the War had been declared that it became merged with the civil rights movement. Perhaps to a greater extent than any other major piece of social legislation, the Anti-Poverty Program stemmed from the investigations of scholars, the writings of social critics, and the minds of two Presidents—Kennedy and Johnson. The "times were ripe," but the Economic Opportunity Act of 1964 is one of the few examples of leadership producing a new policy not in response to a social crisis.

During his 1960 presidential campaign in West Virginia, President Kennedy found an entire area suffering from extensive economic blight and benefiting very little from national prosperity. He pledged massive economic aid for Appalachia. His Council of Economic Advisers sponsored major analytic studies. Social critics such as Michael Harrington through his widely read, *The Other America,* focused attention on the extent to which poverty persisted in the most prosperous nation in the world.

Three days before he was assassinated, President Kennedy urged Walter Heller, Chairman of the Council of Economic Advisers, to bring federal agencies together behind a series of new initiatives. In January of 1964 President Johnson in his State of the Union Message provided the dramatic label when he announced "an unconditional war on poverty in America." A Presidential Task Force went to work and by that fall, Congress enacted the Economic Opportunity Act of 1964.

Alternative-Strategies

That the national government should do something about the persistence of poverty in the United States is not a much debated issue, but what it should do is. And there is no agreement about the dimensions of the problem, how many poor exist, who are they, and why they are poor.

The Council of Economic Advisers counted 35 million Americans as poor, defined as persons living in families with incomes of less than $3000. A more refined study by the Social Security Administration that takes into account noncash income and size of family sets the figure at thirty-four million. Twenty-three million are poor enough to qualify for public assistance. By whatever measure, it is clear that the poor are a large enough group to count as a major political force, although one that heretofore has been politically inert.

One-third of the poor are from families where the breadwinner has been without a job for a long time. Some are headed by a wage earner but one whose skills are so meager that his earnings keep his family in the ranks of the very poor. A large portion of the poor live in families headed by a person over sixty-five years of age or with an education of eight years or less, or by a woman. One-fourth of all poor families are nonwhites.

Some economists have insisted that poverty can be most efficiently dealt with by stimulating economic growth to eliminate unemployment. Others of both liberal and conservative persuasions have argued that the best strategy would be some form of income maintenance, that is either by a negative income tax or by direct payments. (Many persons who earn less than $3000 a year still pay income taxes.) They argue that it would be less expensive and more consistent with the maintenance of personal freedom just to divert a greater share of our national wealth to the very poor. No elaborate governmental organizations would be needed and no one would be compelled to submit to the requirements of a welfare worker in order to receive assistance.

The Economic Opportunity Act of 1964 and its companion measures, however, are built on the assumption that the causes of poverty are many and call for multiple strategies. Merely to provide cash benefits to the poor, it is argued, is not sufficient. Poverty is more than an economic condition, it is a way of life. As Michael Harrington has written, "There is . . . a language of the poor, a psychology of the poor, a world view of the poor. To be impoverished is to be an internal alien, to grow up in a culture that is radically different from one that dominates the society."[11] What are needed are programs that help the poor break through the cycle of poverty, a long, difficult, tedious, heartbreaking process.

---

[11] Michael Harrington, *The Other America* (Baltimore: Penguin Books, 1963), pp. 23–24.

Nor will economic growth alone, however important, be sufficient to overcome poverty. A larger percentage of the poor have some kind of job, but they lack sufficient skills to yield a decent living. The task is to equip them with knowledge, skills, and health. As Walter Heller, then Chairman of the Council of Economic Advisers told the Congress, economic growth opens exits, "But open exits mean little to those who cannot move—to the millions who are caught in the web of poverty through illiteracy, lack of skills, racial discrimination, broken homes, and ill health—conditions which are hardly touched by prosperity and growth."[12] To merely increase the flow of wealth will do little for the many who will just watch it flow by. In fact, economic progress may add to their difficulties, for as our society becomes more technological, those who get an education will move up; those who miss out at the start will be at an even greater disadvantage.

The Multi-Facet Approach

The Economic Opportunity Act of 1964, the basic anti-poverty legislation, is supplemented by other important legislation: the Elementary and Secondary School Act of 1964 that directs most of its funds into projects designed to improve educational opportunities for the poor; the Civil Rights Act of 1964 that puts the authority of the national government behind the drive to open educational, employment, housing, and other opportunities to all; the Manpower Development and Training Act that attempts to help workers overcome job skill obsolescence; the Area Redevelopment Act, and the Appalachia Act that provide funds to improve the basic economic and social resources of areas of persistent poverty; the Social Security Act, and many others.

Because so many federal agencies participated in some phase of the war on poverty, the 1964 Act created the Office of Economic Opportunity within the Executive Office of the President as a kind of coordinating or command post. OEO, headed by a director with the usual kinds of advisory committees, distributes federal funds to other agencies, and through its own staff operates a variety of programs.

The war on poverty consists of a bundle of different programs, each aimed at a specific poverty-creating condition or at a special clientele group. The main thrust is to provide educational and job opportunities for the young. It is often too late to do much more for older people than take care of their most urgent needs—to hospitalize, to provide food and shelter, perhaps to give them some basic skills. By "zeroing" in on the children, it may be possible not merely to treat the symptoms of poverty but to cure its causes, to overcome the handicaps of those who have in the

---

[12] Quoted by Charles E. Silberman, "The Mixed-Up War on Poverty," *Fortune Magazine*, LXXII (August 1965), p. 226.

terms of Senator Abraham Ribicoff lost in the "lotteries of parenthood, skin pigmentation, and birthplace."[13]

Among the programs aimed at the young are the following:

Operation Headstart. There is considerable evidence that children whose parents are uneducated and who lack stimulating experiences at home are so handicapped by the time they reach the ripe age of five or six and go to school that they are already far behind in their ability to learn. These children have seen so little, heard such a restricted vocabulary, and lack even such elementary skills as how to hold a pencil that they have lost out in the "race of life" before they even get started. By the third or fourth grade they are sidetracked into schools and classes for slow learners. In short, cultural deprivation at an early age has a permanently crippling impact. But if these children can be given special attention while still at the preschool age and exposed to language, arts, sounds, and sights that are ordinarily supplied in the homes of those with more economic and cultural benefits, then they may have a chance to secure the education they will need.

In hundreds of communities thousands of children are being given such attention. As a by-product of Operation Headstart, physical handicaps of thousands of children have been identified and treated. In the first year alone, more than 100,000 children were discovered who needed glasses.

Neighbor Youth Corps. This program is designed for teenagers who have just dropped out of school or who are in danger of doing so. It provides work experiences after school hours and during the summer, special counseling, and guidance. The Corps is operated by the Department of Labor with 90 per cent of the cost paid by the federal government. It is designed to prevent teenagers from drifting into society prior to achieving the education and the skills that they will need to earn their own living.

Job Corps. This is a high cost, last-ditch effort to try to save as many as possible young "drop-outs from society." The OEC through contracts with industrial firms and educational institutions provides camps for young men and women who have dropped out of school and who are unable to find and hold adequate jobs. These camps, some located on public lands as conservation groups, others in cities, give Corps members a change of environment, a chance to prepare for jobs capable of providing an adequate living, and special counseling. While in the Job Corps they are given room, board, medical and dental care, and a small allowance. In addition, funds are accumulated to their credit and made available when they leave.

The Economic Opportunity Act provides a variety of other programs for older people: basic education, work experience, manpower development, rural family loans, legal aid, and small business development, for example. OEC also operates a domestic peace corps—Volunteers in Service

---

[13] Quoted in *Time*, May 13, 1966, p. 26.

to America (VISTA)—of volunteers from eighteen to eighty who work with poor Indians, in slums, in migrant labor camps, in depressed areas on a variety of projects. Finally, there is the ambitious, at least so far the most controversial, Community Action Programs.

Community Action Programs. The drafters of the 1964 Act attempted to overcome what they considered the basic weakness of prior welfare programs: fragmentation and middle-class bias. Welfare departments, schools, employment agencies, urban renewal, training programs, and many others deal with one aspect of poverty-creating conditions, and sometimes at cross purposes with each other. These programs administered by middle-class professionals have sometimes reinforced the very sense of the dependence that they should be trying to eliminate.

> "This message [of dependency] is communicated in many different ways: by the old, unscrubbed buildings in which programs are housed; by the interminable waiting on hard benches; the indifference or rudeness of the people who are supposed to be helping, the thoughtless rules and the unconscious slights and snubs that drive home to the poor the fact that they are receiving charity."[14]

In some cities welfare workers stage midnight raids of apartments of those receiving aid for dependent children to be sure that no able-bodied man is present.

To overcome the purported deficiencies of fragmentation and middle-class bias, the Community Action Program conditions its grants of federal funds—up to 90 per cent of the cost—on local communities planning and operating coordinate programs that are "developed, coordinated, and administered with the maximum feasible participation of the residents of the areas and members of the group for whose benefit the Act was passed." In other words, the poor themselves are to participate, and communities are to deal with poverty as a series of interlocking problems.

The Politics of Poverty

A federal program pouring billions into the economy, and operating through a variety of federal, state, and local officials, has created a whole host of political issues. Among these are the following:

1. Charges that funds are being squandered, a charge associated with almost every major federal program, and usually involving a debate about what is meant by "squandering."
2. Charges that those running anti-poverty programs are being paid exorbitant salaries. With hundreds of new programs in thousands of communities, there has been an upsurge in demand for experienced welfare workers. As a result salaries are being bid up. Although salaries paid are

---

[14] Silberman, *The Mixed-Up War on Poverty*, p. 218.

not unusually high for professionally trained persons, the fact that the first impact of the anti-poverty program has been to raise the salaries of the welfare workers has created an obvious political issue.

3. Youth Corps programs by their very design are for young people in trouble. The placing of large congregations of such persons into communities, many of whom are Negroes, has sometimes aroused fear and hostility. Charges that the federal government is sponsoring rest camps for "hoodlums" and headlines directing attention to any difficulties experienced by these Youth Corps camps, are not infrequent.

Beyond these relatively minor issues—perhaps inevitable in the start-up phase of any such extensive program—and of greater significance have been the conflicts over what appears to be a threatened alteration in what is coming to be known in the popular parlance as the "power structure."

City officials, especially mayors of large cities, are both skeptical and fearful about the participation of the poor. They argue that programs must be designed by professionals who have a trained and sophisticated knowledge of what should be done to correct the conditions of poverty, and that such programs involving the expenditures of thousands of dollars of public funds should be administered by public officials who are accountable to the electorate. As an official in New York commented, "You can't go to a street corner with a pad and pencil and tell the poor to write you a poverty program."[15] Mayor Daley of Chicago told reporters that to put poor people in charge "would be like telling the fellow who cleans up to be a city editor of a newspaper."[16]

City officials are fearful that local community action programs will create a new base of political power in their own backyards. The traditional welfare apparatus has been incorporated into the standard political system. Mayors are in control. The placing of thousands of dollars of anti-poverty funds directly from Washington into hands of agencies dominated by persons and organizations not dependent on the local authorities threatens an alteration in the political system.

At the other extreme are those who charge that the anti-poverty program does not involve sufficient participation by the poor. Saul Alinsky, for example, the controversial leader of a self-help movement in Chicago, argues that only the poor can help themselves and only through their own organizational and political ability to fight City Hall. He is skeptical that OEC can withstand the political pressures that are generated when OEC funds are used to fight the local political leaders.

Whatever and however the poor are involved this much seems clear: the poor are becoming a more active segment of our politics. Acute poverty

---

15 Quoted by Silberman, *The Mixed-Up War on Poverty*, p. 158. See also, Barbara Carter, "Sargent Shriver and the Role of the Poor," *The Reporter*, XXXIV (May 1966), 17–20.

16 Silberman, *op. cit.*

is not conducive to political action, but the anti-poverty programs by providing a little help and by making the poor aware of their comparative disadvantages means that the poor are not likely to return to their former quiescent political role. Whatever the success of the anti-poverty programs, they are not likely to move quickly enough or massively enough from the perspective of the poor. As one congressional aide commented, "We've funded a monster in community action. The programs are a bunch of Boston Tea Parties all around the country. They're creating a third force."[17]

TO PROTECT THE
PUBLIC HEALTH

When we think of government and protection of health we usually think of public health departments, but this is only part of the story. Government action to protect our health is not limited to the things that public health departments do. Welfare assistance and social insurance give people the money to buy food, clothing, and shelter which they need to protect their health. Highway safety officials attack one of the major hazards. Housing agencies attempt to create better environments for the care and feeding of children. In this section, however, the focus is on programs that deal more directly with threats to health caused by illness, both physical and mental in origin.

There are some highly contentious public health issues: for example, should fluorine be added to our drinking water? But for the most part public health programs are routine. They seldom excite the general public, make the headlines, or cause governors and Congressmen to lose sleep. Life is precious and precarious and threatened by factors that can be dealt with only by systematic social action. Only through government can we take the necessary action to prevent disease, prolong life, and promote health. There is little opposition to public regulation to provide safe water supplies and adequate sanitation facilities, to control communicable and infectious diseases, to care for the mentally ill, and to provide medical and hospital services for indigents and such special groups as veterans.

Patterns of
Public Health—Background

Epidemics and foul-smelling refuse promoted the first local health ordinances. By the beginning of the nineteenth century, city public health departments were common, but neither the state of medical knowledge

---

[17] Quoted in *Time*, May 13, 1966, p. 29.

nor the art of government had progressed sufficiently for effective programs. High death rates from plagues and childbirth and among infants were considered normal hazards beyond human control. The public became aroused only during an epidemic and interest subsided after the death rate came down.

Dr. Stephen Smith, the first President of the American Public Health Asssociation, relates how just before the Civil War he discovered a tenement house in which there were over 100 typhus cases. "The doors and windows were broken, the cellar was filled with sewage, every room was occupied by families of Irish immigrants who had but little furniture and slept on straw scattered on the floor."[18] The city government had no authority to act and the landlord refused to correct the situation. The Board of Health, an ex-officio board of aldermen, seldom met, and when the Doctor asked the Mayor to call the Board to deal with the epidemic the Mayor replied, "I will not call the Board, for I consider it more dangerous to the city than typhus."[19] Nor were the "Health Wardens" any better. Most of them were saloonkeepers who did little more than have sulphur burned in houses if contagious diseases were called to their attention.

By the end of the nineteenth century considerable progress had been made. Medical science was making spectacular advances in understanding the causes of communicable diseases and developing vaccines and antitoxins to immunize against them. After the Civil War, state health departments were established and the American Public Health Association provided the leadership of medical men and other specialists to put pressure on city councils, state legislators, and Congressmen to establish professionalized public health services.

State Health Departments

Nowadays within a single state there may be as many as eighteen different state agencies concerned in some way with some aspect of public health. But all states have a public health department, usually headed by a board, often with an executive officer in charge of administration. State health departments supervise local programs, distribute the sizeable federal grants to the local health departments, operate laboratories to service local departments, provide health services in areas where there are not local health facilities, and in many states are responsible for the operation of mental and tuberculosis hospitals.

---

[18] Stephen Smith, "The History of Public Health, 1871–1921," *A Half Century of Public Health*, ed. Mazyck P. Ravenel (New York: American Public Health Association, 1921), pp. 4–5.

[19] *Ibid.*, p. 7.

Local Health Departments

Local health officers provide most of the services directly for the public. City health departments, although subject to state supervision, normally function as self-contained and practically autonomous units. In rural areas, public health is usually a county function, but public health officials have successfully sponsored the establishment of public health districts consisting of several counties containing a sufficiently large population to support a more adequate health program than each county could afford. In order to be eligible for federal grants, public health employees must operate under a merit system. Heads of the departments are almost always medical men, and where available are specialists in the public health field.

Protection of water and milk supply is another well established public health duty. Milk, so vital to the physical development of children, is a potentially dangerous drink. Health regulations, backed by vigorous inspection of the production and distribution of milk from cow to consumer, have largely licked this menace. Likewise we drink water with assurance that the health department has guaranteed its safety for human consumption. Although drinking water has been made safe and sanitary, water pollution is still a vexing problem. Polluted water annually destroys thousands of dollars' worth of wildlife, creates offensive odors, and defaces the landscape.

Recently public health officers have become concerned with air pollution which aggravates respiratory conditions, may cause or contribute to lung cancer, and may even lead to fatal poisoning. Some cities—Philadelphia, Pittsburgh, and St. Louis, for example—have been able to improve the air their citizens breathe by requiring residential and industrial fuel users to burn only certain kinds of fuels and to use purifying devices. Although there are some unsolved technical problems (such as filtering exhaust from automobile engines), the knowledge is now available to reduce drastically the pollution of the atmosphere. However, in many cities there is insufficient political pressure to secure adoption of the sometimes costly remedies.

Public health departments concentrate on the prevention of disease and, except in special circumstances, leave to private practitioners the major responsibility for treatment. In line with this tradition, in forty-seven states health officials have been persuaded by medical and dental science that we could reduce substantially the number of dental cavities if controlled amounts of fluorine were added to drinking water. Although over 1000 communities have acted on this advice, the question has lead to many intense community political battles.

Certain groups object to fluoridation because of religious reasons, and their opposition was not unexpected. In view of the long accepted and standard practice of adding chlorine to our drinking water, the intensity and violence of the objections of others, however, was both unexpected and difficult to explain. Opponents of fluoridation have argued that the statistics of health officials are incomplete and misleading. They caution that it is too soon to determine the harmful effects of adding fluorine, a poison, to drinking water, even if it is added in small amounts. Some have argued that fluoridation smacks of socialism and undermines individual liberty. Some have even accused the sponsors of these proposals, usually the local dental and medical associations and public health officials, of wanting to weaken the population so that the Communists can more readily take over. In many cities so intense have been the battles between the pro- and anti-fluoridation groups that they have made the regular partisan campaigns between Democrats and Republicans look tame.

The Federal Government and Public Health

The central, but not the only, public health agency of the national government is the Public Health Service headed by the Surgeon General, now a constituent part of the Department of Health, Education, and Welfare. One of the oldest federal agencies, it was created in 1798 as the Marine Hospital Service to provide prepaid medical and hospital care for American merchant seamen.

The service now *provides medical services and operates hospitals* where seamen employed on American vessels, Coast Guard personnel, and certain other groups receive free hospitalization, medical, and dental care and preventive health services. It also administers medical and hospital facilities for Indians and supervises Freedmen's Hospital in the District of Columbia, a general hospital for the treatment of serious conditions, which also furnishes teaching facilities for medical students of Howard University. It is responsible for the medical services for persons in federal penal institutions and operates hospitals for drug addicts.

The service enforces foreign *quarantine regulations*, inspects sea, land, and air traffic, and *conducts medical examinations of immigrants*. It also has the authority to prevent the spread of diseases through interstate commerce but rarely exercises this power and routinely advises and assists the state health authorities in these matters.

The service *licenses the manufacture and interstate sale of biological products* such as serums, toxins, and vaccines, to guarantee their potency and freedom from dangerous extraneous ingredients. (However, the inspection of food and drugs sold in interstate commerce is the duty of the Food and Drug Administration, now also housed in the Department of Health, Education, and Welfare, which also enforces the federal labeling laws. Food and Drug officials attempt to prevent the sale of impure food and dangerous drugs, and enforce the laws against making false claims for drug products. Still another agency, the Federal Trade Commission, regulates the interstate advertising of these products to prevent misleading and false statements. And still another agency, the Bureau of Narcotics in the Treasury Department, enforces federal tax regulations against illegal sale of narcotics.)

The Public Health Service *engages in and sponsors research* through its National Institutes of Health. These institutions operate their own research hospitals and administer grant programs to other scientists searching for ways to treat and cure cancer, heart disease, mental illness, and other specified diseases.

The Public Health Service also administers *grants to the states* to aid them in improving their general services along with special grants to improve particular programs. Among the larger of these is the federal aid program to promote the construction of hospitals, nursing homes, diagnostic centers, and rehabilitation and other medical facilities.

The Special Problems of the Mentally Ill

Over half of all hospital beds in the United States are occupied by the mentally ill. Persons physically sick are treated with compassion and consideration, but until recently those suffering from mental illness were chained and treated as a public danger. Even today concern for the mentally ill, especially if the illness causes antisocial behavior, is colored by implications of moral condemnation not placed upon those suffering from other disabilities.

Governments have always assumed a much greater role in providing direct medical and hospital services for the mentally ill than for those suffering from physically based illness for the following reasons: 1) The original purpose of public action was to protect the society from what were then thought to be dangerous evil spirits. Just as government incarcerated criminals, so it chained up the mentally sick. 2) The high cost of medical and hospital care, which often takes months or even years, is beyond the means of all except the very well to do. Hence, tax-supported institutions have become the general pattern.

State governments operate mental hospitals, although a few states continue to use county institutions. State policy in the administration and operation of these institutions defies classification. In some states, each hospital is administered independently by its own board and officers; in others, the state mental health departments run all hospitals; in some, the state public health department operates them; in others it is the department of welfare; and in others, a single department of public institutions operates mental hospitals, prisons, and reformatories.

Some states offer minimal services, others have a more liberal program.

Dr. George S. Stevenson, noted authority in this field, has classified the scope of state programs as follows:

> "The state may intend: 1) To hospitalize the patient if he is a danger to himself or others—a police function. 2) To hospitalize the indigent—essentially a welfare function. 3) To offer hospital service to all who need it, charging according to financial capacity. 4) To provide all types of psychiatric service in the community as well as in the hospital for all who need it."[20]

The quality of treatment also varies from those states that provide little more than a hospital bed to those that make a serious attempt to treat patients. It is doubtful if any state hospital has the financial support or staff to give its patients the best treatment that medical and psychiatric knowledge makes possible. Despite major increases in financial support, the states still spend from a third to a fifth as much per mental patient as the best federal or private hospitals. More than half of the patients in state hospitals receive no active treatment of any kind to improve their condition.[21]

Legislators, governors, and others who must slice up the state's expenditures respond to the demands of the electorate. Groups interested in better schools, better highways, and better welfare have more political power than do those interested in improving the care for the mentally ill. Hence, appropriations for these hospitals tend to be what is left after the other more powerful political demands have been assuaged. Mental institutions are often geographically and socially isolated from the rest of the community. Despite the fact that about one in every seventeen Americans is suffering from some form of mental illness, there is an apparent reluctance on the part of the electorate to recognize that mental hospitals may be of service to them or their families.

But even if the hospitals had more money, they would still have difficulty in providing the best possible medical service because of a shortage of attendants, nurses, and doctors. Although advances in developing cures for mental diseases have lagged behind some other medical developments, even with the existing knowledge, more cures could be produced if resources, finances, and manpower, were devoted to the effort.

By and large public health officers have been slow in developing preventive mental health programs. Mental hygiene is relatively less developed scientifically than is hygiene for organically based diseases, but part of the explanation for its lack of attention is that public health personnel are primarily trained in the nonpsychiatric phases of medicine. However, after World War II with the encouragement of the Public Health Serv-

---

[20] George S. Stevenson, *Mental Health Planning for Social Action* (New York: McGraw-Hill Book Company, 1956), pp. 50–51.

[21] Digest of Final Report of Joint Commission on Mental Illness and Health, *Action for Mental Health*, reprinted *The Modern Hospital*, March, 1961.

ices, state and local departments have started preventive programs. Perhaps the most important action has been the establishment, often in cooperation with local volunteer groups, of community mental health clinics. These clinics provide psychiatric services either free or at a price that most people can afford, and through these clinics it is hoped that potentially dangerous cases can be identified and, if treated in their early stages, arrested before hospitalization is required.

The national government operates a large number of mental hospitals. Nearly 10 per cent of the hospitalized psychiatric patients in the United States are in Veterans Administration hospitals. The Public Health Service also provides psychiatric care in its hospitals, which—although limited in terms of numbers treated—have had a disproportionate significance, their high quality service having set standards for the rest of the nation. The federal government through the National Institute of Mental Health furnishes almost 60 per cent of the financial support for research in this area.

How to Pay the Bills?

The adoption of Medicare amendments to Social Security in 1965 brought to a close the first phase in what has been for thirty years a hotly debated political issue. To oversimplify, on one side Democratic Presidents, northern Democrats, labor and liberal organizations have long argued that some kind of public insurance is the best way to cover the financial burden of sustained illness. Private health insurance, they argue, does not protect the lowest income families who cannot afford it. And private insurance covers only a select portion of the population so that its per-person cost is higher than if all were covered and there were a wider sharing of risks. Advocates of public insurance have insisted that such a program would provide the least expensive and most sensible way to meet the inevitable costs of illness and spread the benefits of medical science to the largest number of people. They deny that it is or would lead to "socialized medicine."

On the other side, southern Democrats, Republican congressional leaders, and the American Medical Association have long argued that supporters of compulsory health insurance exaggerate the existing needs. Most people, they contend, are willing and able to finance their own medical and hospital costs. Three-fourths of the civilian population is already protected by voluntary health insurance, 15 per cent are covered by public plans, and only 12 per cent have no protection. Public insurance, they have argued, would lead to regimentation since the government would fix the doctors' fees, require them to fill out elaborate forms, and police them in their practice. They also insist that since persons would no longer be restrained by the immediate costs of medical care, many would rush to the doctors on the slightest provocation and would so swamp the medical profession and the hospitals that the whole quality of American medical practice would be endangered.

In 1943 the Wagner-Murray-Dingell bill was introduced in Congress proposing a payroll tax to finance national health insurance. In 1945 President Truman supported unsuccessfully a comprehensive, prepaid medical insurance for all persons of all ages to be financed by raising the social security tax. President Eisenhower was opposed to compulsory health insurance, but he gave mild endorsement to a scheme of government reinsurance of private insurance companies to permit low cost insurance against unusually heavy medical bills.

In 1957 proponents of federal health insurance limited their immediate goal to providing hospital insurance for those over sixty-five, the group with the largest number of medical problems and the least extensive financial resources. Opponents "countered" by securing in 1960 the adoption of the Kerr-Mills Bill, which provides federal grants to states to help pay for medical care for persons sixty-five and over who are not poor enough to qualify for public assistance but too poor to pay medical bills. This program varies from state to state since each state determines its own eligibility requirements and determines benefits. Opponents of federal insurance argued that after Kerr-Mills no additional federal legislation was needed: those who could afford to cover their own bills or private insurance need no federal help; those who need help could secure it through the Kerr-Mills program.

Proponents of what was by the early 1960s coming to be known as "Medicare" continued to press their case: Kerr-Mills, they argued, helped only the most destitute and only those who lived in states with adequate programs. President Kennedy made Medicare a major issue in his campaign, and his Administration secured its adoption in the Senate, but it failed to secure approval of the House.

On November 3, 1964 the political picture was radically changed. Medicare had been cleanly and clearly endorsed by President Johnson and the overwhelming victory of the Democrats was taken as a mandate for a Medicare program. President Johnson told congressional leaders that he wanted them to give top priority to medical care legislation, Cabinet members were instructed to use their full authority in its behalf, and the Department of Health, Education and Welfare was instructed to have a new bill ready for consideration by the Congress when it convened.

The House Ways and Means Committee from which Medicare legislation had to emerge had long been a major obstacle. But in the 1964 elections three Republican members of the Committee who had opposed the legislation were defeated. The Democratic Chairman, Wilbur Mills of Arkansas, who had fought Medicare for fear that it would endanger the Social Security System, indicated that he was softening his stand. But to be sure, the Democrats increased the Democratic-Republican ratio on the

Ways and Means Committee and carefully appointed strong proponents of Medicare to the newly created positions.

Certain changes were made to pacify Chairman Mills—for example, deductions for Medicare are separately listed from those that support other parts of social security insurance. Finally, after extended debate and additional amendments to strengthen the other features of the basic social security law, including significant increase in federal support for medical assistance to those in need, President Johnson journeyed to Independence, Missouri to sign Medicare into law on July 23, 1966 in the presence of former President Truman.

Medicare is a complicated program. It is divided into two basic parts: the Basic or Hospital Insurance Plan, and the Voluntary or Doctor's Bill Plan.

The Basic or Hospital Insurance Plan provides for hospital care and for post-hospital care in a nursing facility or at home, after a $40 deductible amount is paid by the individual. It covers all persons sixty-five and over who are eligible for retirement benefits under social security. Persons not eligible may nonetheless become eligible for Medicare Benefits if they reach sixty-five by the end of 1967 or if they have some minimum stipulated payments into the system. The Basic Plan is financed primarily by payroll deductions with an assist from general revenues.

The Voluntary or Doctor's Bills Plan reimburses most of the costs of doctors' bills. There is a $50 deductible provision and the insured must pay for at least 20 per cent of his bills. The Voluntary Plan is available to all persons over sixty-five who sign up for it. It is paid for by a contribution of $3 a month from each person enrolled and matching amounts from the general tax revenues.

As a result of Medicare, about the only important financial medical risk not covered for persons over sixty-five will be for private-duty nursing, prescription drugs and medicines used outside of a hospital or nursing home, hospitalization that continues beyond ninety days, and medical expenses incurred outside the United States.

Medicare does not mark the end of the political battles. Will it work and how well will it work? Should it be extended to those under sixty-five? These are questions that are going to be debated in the years ahead.

HOUSING

Americans live in better houses than do most other people. Human "needs," however, are measured by what is available. If all live in mud huts, those without bathtubs are not likely to be considered wanting in the necessities of life; but in a nation as rich as the United States, a family of four or five living in two or three rooms without decent sanitation needs better housing. And despite our wealth, we have slums. The 1960 census classified 8.4 million housing units as deteriorating and 4 million as dilapidated—out of a total of fifty-eight million units. One-third of our urban dwellings are over thirty years old, and many people live in blighted areas. Dirty, crowded tenement houses and rural shanties are evident to any who would make a casual investigation.

Inadequate housing is more acute in some portions of the nation and for some groups than for others. In one southern state, 50 per cent of the total dwellings are dilapidated or lack running water. Negroes in most places, Latin Americans, Puerto Ricans, and Orientals in some areas have difficulty in finding clean and modern living quarters. Many Negroes who have the least opportunities for education and remunerative employment cannot afford to buy or rent good homes. But even when they can afford to do so, they are forced to live in "Jim Crow" areas which, to say the least, are not located in the most desirable parts of the city and do not contain the nicest homes. In the rural areas, some tenant farmers and migratory workers are crowded together in work camps or forced to live in shanties that have no heat or electricity. Other Americans live much better. They have invested their savings in good homes, and they hope to preserve the value of their property. They want to be sure that the apartments they rent or the houses they buy are safe and the neighborhoods they live in are conducive to the "good life."

Our governments are involved in helping all of us enjoy better housing. Government housing programs may be characterized as falling into three general categories: 1) programs, such as building and zoning regulations, that preserve property values, protect health and safety, and guide community development; 2) programs, such as insured mortgages, that indirectly create a demand for homes and supply a market for private builders; 3) programs, such as public housing, slum clearance, and urban redevelopment, that directly increase the supply of houses and make it possible for low income groups to have better homes.

Building Codes, Zoning, and City Planning

In the country a person can do almost whatever he wishes with the land he owns. He may build almost any kind of structure on his land. But when he moves to the city, where his actions affect the health and well-being of others, he discovers a host of regulations restricting his use of his own property. Building codes, electrical codes, plumbing codes, and fire codes establish minimum standards for construction, lighting, ventilation, sanitation, and fire protection. These codes apply to new construction of all kinds, and in the case of public buildings and those that accommodate the public—apartment houses, stores, theaters—there are periodic checks to insure compliance with the standards.

Building codes are supposed to protect the public against buildings falling or burning. Their actual writing reflects the combined pressures of manufacturers of building materials, builders, real estate people, insurance companies, apartment owners, and building-trade unions. It has been alleged that some of these codes keep up the cost of construction and give special advantages to builders and workers. Some were written years ago and do not allow the use of modern and economic means of building such as prefabrication and dry-wall construction. Some prevent the use of new labor-saving techniques. On the other hand, others have alleged that building codes are not stringent enough to protect the public. Most complaints are directed at enforcement. Often inspectors are untrained patronage appointees. Only after a disastrous fire in which flammable materials and blocked exits cause unnecessary deaths or after a building collapses does the general public become aroused. But the subject is so technical that sensible public discussion is difficult.

Most cities have elaborate regulations requiring landlords to maintain their properties and keep their buildings in safe and sanitary condition. But in the decaying parts of some of our cities these regulations are not vigorously enforced. Tenants lack the knowledge or are afraid of eviction, and there are not enough city inspectors to go around. By crowding many families into small space and by spending no money to keep the buildings in repair, these slums return rich rewards. A few cities—for example, Milwaukee and Baltimore—however, have adopted ordinances which permit the city to repair properties if the owner fails to do so after he has been properly warned, and the costs are then assessed against the property.

Many subdividers have moved outside the city to escape building codes. Others who could not afford to build a house that would meet city standards went to the surrounding country. Some of these hastily built tract homes and cheaply constructed buildings may deteriorate so rapidly that in the not too distant future slums may no longer be limited to the central core of the city.

Most American cities, especially those over 25,000, also have zoning restrictions concerning the use of buildings, their height, and their location on lots. The city is divided into zones—for example, a single family zone, a light-industry zone, a heavy-industry zone, and so on. There are also regulations requiring structures to be set back so many feet from the street, and specified distances must be maintained between adjoining lots.

Comprehensive zoning ordinances date from the end of World War I and were not imposed until after the uses of the land and the location of the buildings had already been determined through the dictates of the market and the desires of each individual owner. In most states, the courts would object to retroactive application of zoning requirements so all that the regulations can do is prevent future unplanned development. However, ordinances which give thirty or forty years advance notice for the termination of noncomplying uses are permissible.

Zoning boards are subject to intense pressures to make exceptions. This "spot zoning"—the classification of a single lot or a few lots to permit a grocery store or filling station in a residential area means, as Charles Adrian has pointed out, "a loss in the total value of the community. Because this loss is socialized among many persons who individually have less incentive to pressure the council than does the single profiteer, such practices take place with considerable regularity in some cities."[22] Once an exception is made for one store it is hard, perhaps illegal, to hold the line against others.

Unless the county has introduced zoning outside of the city limits, the only protection property owners have against having a factory located next door is if there are deed restrictions covering the entire area. To enforce these provisions it is necessary to bring a civil action against the violator, an expensive and time-consuming practice. Hence many city fringe developments are still largely uncontrolled as to land use.

Building codes and zoning ordinances are techniques to bring about ordered development of living areas. In order to use these techniques to achieve desired goals there must be a plan. Today all our large cities have some kind of planning agency, usually consisting of from five to seven members, some city officials and some private citizens, and aided by a professional staff. The planning board is responsible for considering all the human and material resources and developing long range and integrated programs covering parks, housing, slum clearance, traffic, parking, public health, utilities, zoning, building codes, and other elements that make up city life.

After a comprehensive plan has been adopted, and constantly revised, it is supposed to guide the various decision-making agencies. However, frequently the plan is adopted by the city council as a statement of policy, only to have everyone proceed as before without much consideration of the beautiful maps and glowing descriptions of the future. Furthermore, planning is complicated by the fact that many of our metropolitan urban areas consist of a dozen or so cities, unincorporated areas, and a mixture of special districts. These suburban governments are not bound by the planning programs of the central city. To overcome this, metropolitan planning commissions consisting of representatives of all the governments in the area have drawn up advisory plans to coordinate programs. So far these plans have had little impact upon city development. The federal government has tried to strengthen city planning by making matching grants to help cities of less than 25,000 as well as large metropolitan areas

---

22 Charles R. Adrian, *Governing Urban America* (New York: McGraw-Hill Book Company, 1955), p. 413.

to develop their planning programs. It is too early to determine if these grants-in-aid will have any major effect.

Indirect Governmental Action to Increase the Demand for Houses

Although the cumulative costs for all the automobiles that each American feels he must buy during the course of his life may exceed all other expenditures, for most people buying a home is the single largest purchase. Until the Depression only those with enough money to make a substantial down payment and good enough credit to borrow the rest were able to build or buy a home. Today the national government through the Department of Housing and Urban Development, and the Veterans Administration has made it possible for middle-income groups to buy their own homes.

The Federal Housing Administration in the Department of Housing and Urban Development insures lending institutions that in the event the home buyer defaults and the lender suffers a loss the FHA will make it good. Thus private lenders are encouraged to lend at a lower rate and for longer periods of time than would be the case if the creditor had to assume the entire risk. FHA insurance is financed by collecting a small premium from each person who has an FHA insured mortgage. FHA also insures loans to allow repair and improvement of homes and insures loans to builders to permit them to borrow the capital to construct rental units.

The Veterans Administration guarantees rather than insures mortgages, which gives lenders slightly more protection, but the effect is the same as the FHA program. Would-be home owners still must find a lender willing to lend the money at the rates allowed by the laws. The homes purchased must meet standards of the VA or FHA.

The Voluntary Home Mortgage Credit Program was created to assist members of minority groups who are often discriminated against in securing mortgages, as well as persons living in remote areas and small communities where lending institutions are scarce. This is a joint industry-government program in which applicants who have made at least two unsuccessful attempts to obtain FHA-insured or VA-guaranteed loans may apply. The VHMCP brings these applicants together with life insurance companies, and if they are qualified and their homes meet standards, they may thus obtain benefits on FHA and VA home mortgage credits.

The national government also increases the supply of home-buying credit through chartering savings and loan institutions and insuring those who place their savings on deposit with these institutions that they will suffer no loss. (Each account is insured up to $15,000.) Thus many private individuals are encouraged to make their savings available to supply credit for those who wish to build or buy homes. The national government further encourages the flow of credit for homes through the Federal National Mortgage Association—popularly known as "Fanny May"— which by purchasing mortgages creates a secondary market for these investments and introduces a liquidity into the market and increases the supply of mortgage money. Thus even persons who do not use FHA or VA mortgages and buy their homes with what are called conventional mortgages benefit from the federal government's credit-supplying activities.

Public Housing, Urban Redevelopment and Renewal

It is the ambition of most Americans to own a home out where there are grass yards, playgrounds, and sunshine. Whenever they can afford to do so, they rush to the periphery. The central core of the city is allowed to run down. Decay sets in and old homes are turned into apartments. Into these low-rent quarters move those who cannot afford anything better. Large numbers are crowded into small apartments and little is spent to keep them in repair, only what the city health and sanitation officials insist on. Before long, the area becomes a slum.

Since the end of World War II, this trend toward urban decay has been compounded by a growing racial imbalance of poor Negroes moving into the city and a flight of middle-income white families to the suburbs. Unlike their predecessors the newer arrivals in the city have encountered additional obstacles of prejudice and discrimination that have "trapped" them into ghettos "just as surely as barbed wire."[23] City officials are faced with increasing demands for better social services, while at the same time the economic capacity of the city to provide these services is being undermined. These officials have turned to the federal government for help.

The federal government launched a public housing program in 1937 with the creation of the Public Housing Administration. The program was just getting started when it was interrupted by World War II. Public housing has always been hotly opposed by the building industry, and it has been criticized for stifling the ambition of occupants. Those who raise their incomes beyond prevailing limits are forced to move out. There have been charges that public housing authorities have supported segregation, that vast building projects provide an inhospitable human environment. None theless, there are now 900 local authorities administering 40,000 units in which 1,500,000 persons live. An important, and controversial, new development is the authorization by Congress of rent subsidies. This program permits local housing authorities to subsidize the rent for some families eligible for public housing so that the families do not have to move into

---

[23] Robert C. Weaver, "Poverty in America—The Role of Urban Renewal," *Poverty in America*, ed. Margaret S. Gordon (San Francisco: Chandler Publishing Co., 1965), p. 324.

public housing projects. The family must pay 25 per cent of its income for rent; the federal subsidy covers the difference to provide a fair rental charge for a house of modest design and cost.

As is true of many first steps in a "reform movement," many persons expected too much from public housing. They failed to realize that merely to relocate the impoverished into new quarters in the midst of a slum area would not by itself "solve" the problem of poverty.

To attack the problem on a more drastic scale and at the same time to overcome the opposition of some private builders, in 1949 Congress launched a comprehensive program of urban renewal and rehabilitation. This program makes federal funds available to cities for the acquisition and clearance of slum properties and the resale of the cleared land to private builders, who agree to redevelop such land according to an approved plan. Congress has also provided for low interest federal loans to cities to improve water, gas, oil, sewage plants, and mass transportation systems, provided cities have adequate plans.

In its early years urban renewal projects in some cities got a bad name. "Urban Renewal Means Negro Removal," it was charged. The worst slums were torn down and replaced with desirable commercial and housing units, but the poor who had lived in the slums had no place to go. These charges were exaggerated, for the fact is that most persons displaced by urban renewal programs were helped to find better housing;[24] but to avoid any possibility that urban renewal will work to the detriment of the poor, Congress amended the program to be sure that displaced families are properly relocated. Federal subsidies are now available to help cover the rent of those who are displaced so that they may be located in adequate housing. In addition, Congress had directed federal authorities to give more attention to the rehabilitation of decaying neighborhoods to prevent them from becoming slums.

A Department of Housing and Urban Development

Forty-two per cent of our people live in the 676 largest cities. Frequently these people and those in charge of their municipal affairs find that they secure a more sympathetic hearing in their efforts to deal with problems of mass transportation, slum clearance, and housing from federal officials than they do from those in charge of their state governments. And in recent decades the conflict between state and city governments has grown more intense.

State governments are sometimes controlled by rural groups and by those who although they may live in cities are, nonetheless, fearful of the liberal tendencies of city voters. On the other hand, the political con-

---

[24] Robert P. Groberg, "Urban Renewal Realistically Reappraised." *Law and Contemporary Problems*, XXX (Winter 1965), 218–20.

stituency of the President is very similar to that of the mayors of our large metropolitan centers. Therefore, faced with difficult problems city officials have tended to turn more and more to Washington to find help.

At the national level and outside of the South, the Democratic Party tends to have the center of its strength in the core cities of our large metropolitan complexes. For the cities today, as always, include a large proportion of low-income persons seeking new opportunities. In the past these were the most recent arrivals from Europe; lately they are Negroes, rural whites, and Puerto Ricans. It is not surprising, therefore, that President Kennedy urged the establishment of a new cabinet department to deal with urban affairs and housing. Opponents of this department, consisting of governors of states with predominantly rural populations, conservatives, and spokesmen for the private housing industry, argued that a new department would weaken the relationship between the states and their cities, focus increased pressure on Congress for new federal aid programs, and splinter existing programs, such as highway construction and housing.

In the background of the controversy was the fact that Robert C. Weaver, Administrator of the Housing and Home Finance Agency and a Negro, was a leading possibility for becoming the secretary if a new cabinet officer were created. Opponents were able to delay approval. However, the increased urbanization of the nation, the growing political power of Negro voters, and the active support of President Johnson led finally to congressional approval for a Department of Housing and Urban Development.

Congress insisted that the Federal Housing Administration be retained as a separate identity under a separate Commissioner, who is also an assistant secretary to handle matters relating to the private mortgage industry. The new department also consists of the Housing and Home Finance Agency, the Public Housing Administration, and the Federal National Mortgage Association. In addition to the Secretary, Congress provided for an undersecretary and five assistant secretaries. After some delay President Johnson appointed Robert C. Weaver as Secretary.

BIBLIOGRAPHICAL NOTE

A standard text on social welfare can provide detailed references to materials in this area. There is a growing literature relating to the War on Poverty. The most influential book has been Michael Harrington, *The Other America*, 1962. Burton A. Weisbrod, *The Economics of Poverty*, 1965 contains readings and basic documents as well as an excellent bibliography. Margaret S. Gordon has edited the Proceedings of a National

Conference held at the University of California, Berkeley, February 26–28, 1965 under the title *Poverty in America*, 1965, a bibliography is also included.

There is a large literature on housing. Martin Anderson's *The Federal Bulldozer*, 1964, presents the opinions against a public program. For a response see, Robert P. Grosbery, "Urban Renewal Realistically Reappraised," *Law and Contemporary Problems*, XXX (Winter, 1965), 212–29. David R. Hunter, *The Slums: Challenge and Response*, The Free Press, 1964 is very useful and contains an excellent bibliography.

Charles E. Gilbert, "Policy-Making in Public Welfare: the 1962 Amendments," *Political Science Quarterly*, LXXXI, 2 (June 1966), is a sophisticated case study in the legislative and administrative politics of welfare.

government
and
education

LAWRENCE J. R. HERSON
and
R. Roger Majak

In 1957 the Soviet Union astounded a world seemingly inured to surprise by shooting a satellite into space. And although this Russian victory over gravity represented a military and diplomatic gain of the greatest magnitude, it also demonstrated in the most tangible terms the rewards that are to reaped by a nation that places its educational system in the service of the state. In little more than forty-five years, Russian science and technology had leaped from the backwardness of the nineteenth century to the vanguard of the twentieth.

In the United States, military and scientific reaction to Soviet space success has been profound and far-reaching; equally far-reaching has been the debate over American education touched off by Russian rocketry. More accurately, the Russian space shot helped lift an already intensive debate over education to new levels of anxiety and consequent public action. What had begun in the postwar years as a debate confined largely to educational circles and the more learned journals, moved in the early 1950s to newspapers and magazines of mass circulation, and from there has now come to haunt our legislative chambers.

Our schools, we are told with considerable frequency, are in crisis; and government must act to resolve that crisis. Some aspects of this crisis, of course, are more or less "mechanical"; and accordingly are relatively easy to solve.[1] A rising birthrate along with a mobile population has created a mounting shortage of schools and schoolrooms; but that shortage, in all probabil-

---

[1] The concept of mechanical, as opposed to other attributes of the school crisis, is taken from Mortimer Smith, *The Public Schools in Crisis*, Introduction (Chicago: Henry Regnery Co., 1956).

ity, can be resolved through greater public expenditures upon school construction. Other aspects of the school crisis are both mechanical and a cultural. A rising school population has created a significant shortage of
teachers. (One estimate sees a need for considerably more than one quarter
million new teachers by 1970!)[2] An increase in teacher salaries may help
recruit college graduates into teaching but (say the critics of our school
system) we shall not really overcome the shortage until our social values
change sufficiently to make teaching an increasingly attractive occupation.

And still other aspects of the school crisis cut so deeply into our culture
that resolution, if it comes at all, will have the profoundest effects upon
the future of our society. For example, our present system of education,
reflecting a basic social commitment to equality, has tended to emphasize
mass education at the expense (we are told) of educational excellence. In
the interest of academic excellence shall we "segregate" our brightest
children in special schools and perhaps close our colleges to all but
graduates of those schools? Or, in the interest of national survival, shall
we ensure an adequate future supply of scientists (or humanists or computer experts), by curricula control that begins in the primary grades and
extends through the colleges?

Stated so baldly, these questions can do no justice to the complex and
important reasoning that lies on all sides of the argument. And, in fact, the
very form of these questions is somewhat misleading, for they imply that
government action on these problems will be decisive and direct, whereas
the tradition of American government is that of a piecemeal and
compromise-laden solution to public problems. Moreover, any solution to
public problems is affected by the pressure group activity that surrounds
them as well as by the governmental structures that encase them. Thus,
our present school system is built, essentially, into the framework of
American local government. (There are roughly some 27,000 local school
boards in the U.S.) And any attempt at reforming our schools may require
that we move responsibility for our schools upward, from the local to the
state level, and quite possibly into the hands of the federal government.

But at this point, our discussion falls dangerously close to the admonition that Americans would rather debate education than describe it.
Accordingly, and in keeping with the purposes of the present chapter, we
shall attempt a more systematic canvass of government's role in education
by examining: 1) the basic educational policy that forms the backdrop for
both educational politics and present-day movements for reform, 2) the
institutional structure that is today responsible for our school system, 3)
the range of pressure group activity that, in its turn, is tied to the level of
government that controls our schools, and 4) some of the problems that
have created political debate over education, including one of the great
political issues of our day: federal aid to education.

---

[2] U.S. President's Commission on Higher Education, *Second Report* (Washington, D.C.: Government Printing Office, 1957).

THE POLICIES OF EDUCATION:
A NINETEENTH CENTURY LEGACY

Basic Patterns

Although current debate over education reflects the crises of our time, the foundations of this debate are built deep in Western history. From the time of the Ancient Greeks, social philosophers have pointed to the intimate connection between government and education, teaching, in fact, that "education is the foundation of the state": For it is through education that there can be instilled in the citizenry loyalty to the regime and the skills necessary for the technology that brings material wealth and military strength. The Soviet Union has long understood this relationship between education and polity and almost from the first months of the communist regime education has been utilized as an instrument of governmental purpose: to create loyal Soviets and to transport Russian society from the feudalism of the eighteenth century to the technology of the twentieth.

In the United States, too, this relationship between education and polity has been understood from our earliest days as a nation. But as a society whose immediate roots are in the soil of eighteenth-century liberalism—with its concern for elevating the individual *over* the state—we have built an educational system that seeks to benefit the individual every bit as much as the state. In fact, as our system is often viewed, it is built to serve the individual primarily; and only through him, the state. The language of the Ordinance of 1787 is instructive here, for it reads in part that "religion, morality and knowledge, being necessary for good government and the happiness of mankind, schools and the means of education shall be forever encouraged." And if by this language the individual is not clearly elevated over the state, he is at very least made an equal beneficiary of the services of education.

Given this tradition of individualism, it should hardly be surprising that our first great debates over education in the early and middle nineteenth century centered on the question of publicly supported schools and compulsory school attendance. While few men disagreed with the ideas of the Ordinance, not all were agreed that government should encourage education to the point of making it mandatory or by assuming its costs. In an age of *laissez faire*, there was considerable support for the proposition that the individual should be coerced by government in as few areas of life as possible, and further that education should remain a private enterprise, falling to those who could afford it, or at least, to those who were willing to pay for it.

In due time, of course, the debates were resolved to create the pattern that we know today: compulsory attendance (of the school-age child) either at tuition-free, publicly supported schools or at approved, privately operated schools. And though subsequent generations have revived the debate to question (and then increase) the number of years of mandatory schooling, the basic pattern has remained intact, and essentially has removed itself from the area of public policy dispute.

But if the basic resolution of the nineteenth-century debate continues to lie quietly in the twentieth century, the same cannot be said for a number of other issues that accompanied the "great debate." More explicitly, the question of establishing a basic pattern for our schools also involved a series of other questions such as: What agency within the state shall assume the actual management of the schools? What shall be the relation of government schools to private ones? And what, if anything, shall be the place of religious instruction within the public schools? But to explain these issues more fully, and, at the same time, to demonstrate the way in which the hand of the past continues to stir the present, it is necessary to consider the constitutional and social context of the great debate.

Constitutional Patterns

To begin with the Constitution, it may be necessary to state the obvious: When the balance of federalism was being struck for the nineteenth century, the weight of major governmental action was presumed to lie with the states. The central government was said to be one of enumerated powers only; and nowhere in the Constitution's enumeration of federal powers was mention made of education. Moreover, by the spirit of the Constitution (and by the wording of the 10th Amendment) the states were made the inheritors of the English concept of the *police power*—government's responsibility for regulating the network of social relations, that is, man's relationship to his fellow men—and for undertaking what in today's parlance would be called social welfare functions. Thus, education was seen as being the sole responsibility of the several states.

Beyond this view, and given a governmental philosophy that looked to as much decentralization (that is, local government) as possible, the task of the states was seen essentially as that of making the basic decisions concerning education; then, turning responsibility for operating the schools (in accordance with state law) over to local governments within the states. And finally, in a frontier age, with local governments differing markedly in their capacity for performing such service functions as education, there was marked variation between the states regarding: 1) the time when educational structures were established, and 2) the elaborateness of the educational enterprise. Roughly speaking, the drive for establishing the "common" (public) school began in the East in the 1830s and did not reach the Mississippi River until the 1850s. The drive for compulsory education began in Massachusetts in 1852 but did not become universal until 1918 when Mississippi at last came under the attendance umbrella.

To the student of politics, the significance of these constitutional patterns is many fold: First, they help explain how an early assumption by the states of responsibility for education has created a political tradition that severely tends to resist attempts to bring education within the purview of the federal government. (As the cement of political tradition hardens, it becomes increasingly difficult to break.) Second, there is explanation here of the decentralized pattern of school control; of friction generated in recent decades as the state governments have attempted to wrest power from local school boards; and of the kind of shared powers (between state and local governments) that have emerged as a compromise from the attempts at centralizing education within the states. Third, there is explanation here of the diversity of educational practices from state to state: a diversity that often leads to arguments in favor of federal control and subsequent educational uniformity. And finally, there is not so much explanation as there is challenge in these constitutional patterns: Given a tradition of state independence regarding education, how does it happen that there is variation between the educational systems of the fifty states but not utter dissimilarity?

Two levels of answers suggest themselves: On one, there is the "borrowing" practice of our states, whereby the social legislation of one state, if successful, is often copied by other states. (Here, there comes to mind the celebrated metaphor that our states are "insulated chambers of experimentation.") And on the other level, there is the political practice within our states of turning over to selected professions responsibility for policing those professions. Thus, lawyers' guilds write bar examinations, and doctors' associations control the process whereby aspiring doctors are educated and eventually admitted to practice. Teachers' associations and teachers' colleges in similar fashion, have done much to impose commonly held professional views upon our legislatures, and in this fashion (considering the potential for chaos) they have brought considerable uniformity to the American education system. Our later discussion will again lead us into considering the importance of guild controls for the politics of education; but to pick up the main threads of the present discussion, we turn now to the social and political context of the nineteenth-century debate.

Social and Political Patterns

From the election of Thomas Jefferson in 1800 to the administration of Jackson and beyond, the great issue of American politics was that of expanding the majoritarian aspects of our governmental system. From the

Presidency of George Washington, when approximately only one male in seven was permitted to vote, the suffrage underwent steady expansion, culminating finally in the Jacksonian philosophy that attempted not only universal, white, male suffrage, but a system of government that sought to make as many offices as possible elective offices and that viewed every citizen as being capable of filling any public office. That famous slogan of Jacksonian politics, "To the victor belongs the spoils" was more than a demand that public office be given Jackson's deserving Democrats. It was also a demand that public office should no longer remain a monopoly of the rich, the wellborn, and above all, of the elegantly educated.

The impact of Jacksonian politics upon our school system has been profound. To that political theory we can trace the present-day practice of filling school board membership by local election; and to that practice, in turn, we can trace the pattern of some of the pressure-group politics that surround local school administration. To Jacksonian beliefs we can also trace the equalitarian aspects of our public schools: that all are to be educated alike; and that equal education for all is to be preferred to a system which emphasizes special educational opportunities for the talented student.

Because of this Jacksonian tradition, we have never developed the kind of school system operating in other democracies (in Great Britain, France, Denmark, Sweden, for example) whereby those marked for college are sent to special, academically oriented high schools that stress high standards and scholarly excellence—while all others are sent to "folk schools" that emphasize such practical matters as commerce and vocation.[3] This Jacksonian commitment (as opposed to what is sometimes called a Jeffersonian view: of high standards and higher education only for the talented) has lain in our education system like a time bomb, ticking quietly for a hundred years, and threatening now to explode upon a society worried about the scholarly standards of its school system and worried even more about the ability of the school system to produce the educated leadership necessary for national survival.

But perhaps most important of all, the *school system* with which we are here concerned can be traced to Jacksonian politics. For as the suffrage expanded in the 1830s and 1840s, putting control of our governments into the hands of an ever widening circle of the citizenry, it became increasingly clear that democratic government, if it was to survive, would require that it be supported by an educated citizenry. For how, except by literacy and learning, would the majority be able to understand the issues confronting government, to exchange views concerning them, and to make the choices upon which democratic government ultimately depends? That an educated

---

[3] Or, as in the "modern school" of Britain, the high school offering terminal education may concentrate upon widening the student's fund of "general and useful" knowledge.

citizenry is a requisite of democracy was a truism that loomed large in the legislative debates eventually leading to the establishment of our public school system.[4]

But over and above the Jacksonian imprint, our schools bear other marks as well. Again, as part of the setting for the nineteenth-century debate, there was a rising tide of immigration that was to culminate in one of the most remarkable population movements in history: from the period of about 1890 to the First World War, a million immigrants a year came to establish themselves as Americans. And as early as the 1840s there was considerable popular concern over the effects of these immigrants upon the character of the American life. "Shall these adopted citizens become a part of the body politic, and firm supporters of liberal institutions, or will they prove to our republic what the Goths and Huns were to the Roman Empire?"[5] This was a question asked by the President of Middlebury College in 1849, and the fact that his fears were not realized is a tribute to a school system built, in part, to accomplish one of history's most remarkable jobs of acculturation.

Literacy helped make these immigrants and their children responsible members of the political process; and also (as part of acculturation within the schools) our educational process was given over to fostering general sentiments of patriotism and loyalty to our style of government. Thus, the present-day arguments about whether the schools shall attempt to inculcate a patriotism appropriate to the twentieth century is a direct legacy of the nineteenth century. Unfortunately, the "making of Americans" out of immigrants was less ideologically clouded than the problems of fostering patriotism today. A goal remaining, supported by considerable popular sentiment, is for the schools to teach love of country. But is that goal to be reached by teaching suspicion of the United Nations? Or by teaching students to oppose the welfare state (whose institutions, for some appear as the moral equivalent of a communist regime)? For present purposes it is sufficient to say that this expectation of patriotic instruction provides the grist for some of the warmest controversy of our own time.

Secularism and the Schools

To bring this discussion of our nineteenth-century school legacy to a temporary conclusion, there are two more items requiring at least brief mention. Both of these relate to the place of religion in the schools. First,

---

[4] In parallel fashion, when the British suffrage was extended through the Reform Bill of 1867, Robert Lowe—contemplating the power that was to be placed in the hands of the populace—is said to have remarked: "Now we must educate our masters."

[5] From Lawrence A. Cremin, "The Future of the American Common School," in George Z. F. Bereday and Luigi Volpicelli, *Public Education in America* (New York: Harper and Row, Publishers, 1958), p. 37.

given a society that in Colonial times had seen government enter into religious persecution, and given, too, the eighteenth-century Deism fashionable among the educated classes, it is hardly surprising that the public schools should be established as secular schools. Banishing religious instruction from them was in keeping with nineteenth-century views concerning the "wall of separation" between church and state established in both the federal and state constitutions. And it was also in keeping with a more general American view "that churches should be free from control by the state and that the state should be free from political influence or control by ecclesiastical authorities."[6]

But if public opinion favored secularism in the public schools, that same opinion did not seek to drive out private schools, even when those private schools made religious instruction the core of their curriculum. The laissez-faire philosophy of the nineteenth century had no room in it for establishing a government monopoly of education; nor did the wall of separation preclude the existence of private, sectarian schools.

From these decisions have come two further issues for present-day school politics: First, out of a growing concern for the moral fabric of our society, there have been increasing attempts in recent years to pierce the secularism of the schools by introducing such forms of religious instruction as Bible reading and communal prayer. And second, to help sectarian schools meet rising costs, government has considered supporting them with public funds. Both these activities have met with criticism and mounting rounds of constitutional litigation. However, we shall save recounting these, and other political battles, until some further ground has been covered. For that, we leave our nineteenth-century legacy and move now to an examination of contemporary patterns of school administration.

THE FIFTY STATES:
THE SCHOOLS AND THEIR POLITICS

With each of the fifty states largely free to set its own educational policy, there is considerable diversity in the American school system (or rather, in the American school *systems*). But there is, at the same time, a remarkable continuity between these systems: Each is built around a system of local controls over education coupled to an increasing measure of state supervision. Each system achieves integration between local independence and state supervision in a twofold fashion: by means of laws and legal penalties and by means of a pattern of cooperation between school officials at the state and local levels. Each system traces a considerable portion of this pattern of cooperation to the common concerns of educator-

---

[6] From R. Freeman Betts, "Basic Features of American Education" in Bereday and Volpicelli, *ibid.*, p. 10.

administrators, who often look past the government employing them to the education colleges that trained them and to the professional conferences and journals that help equip them with a philosophy of education and a system of shared values and purposes.

The existence of a guild outlook within the bureaucracy is fairly common to all levels of American government. Also fairly common to our government structure is a pattern of friction between the policies of the elected policy-makers and those of the guild-oriented civil servants. This guild perspective, however, reaches an unusually high development within our school system; and accordingly, so does the recurring tension between school boards, and school administrators. How one views this tension depends, of course, upon one's own perspectives. School boards and state legislators often complain about the ways in which their policies are frustrated (or rendered inoperative) by the bureaucrats. More disinterested citizens, while troubled by the implications of bureaucratic intransigence for a theory of democratic responsibility, often see the guild orientation of, say, the school superintendent as a way of freeing local school policies from the narrowed outlook of the local school board.

But to construct a backdrop against which this friction may be more profitably considered, it is now necessary to discuss the allocation of educational responsibility between state and local governments.

State Controls Over Education

Similar to the general who commands an army but never takes the field, our state governments command the school systems, but never operate them directly. Essentially, the state governments, by legislative action, create the enabling legislation that gives authority to local school boards and prescribes the ways in which the schools shall be run. Thus, the state law brings into being the school districts within the state and creates the school boards that will govern them. State law provides for the means of choosing school boards (almost everywhere, by popular election); and authorizes these boards to lay and collect the taxes that will operate the schools, to engage in necessary school construction, to hire (and fire) necessary personnel; and to lay down a broad range of local school policy.

In fact, in every state, the state law governing schools is detailed and voluminous. It ranges over such matters as the number of days per year that schools shall remain open; the number of years of compulsory school attendance for each child; the types of schools that may (or must) be operated by local boards; the manner in which school children are to be grouped for purposes of instruction (generally, in grades one through eight; and from nine through twelve); and the rules under which teachers shall be hired, fired, and paid. Over and above these things, every state possesses legislation under whose terms state money is apportioned among the local school districts.

Most state legislatures also attempt to fix, in some fashion, the content of the curricula. Most often, such forays into educational content are confined to prescribing the type of course to be required (for example, that all high school students shall be required to receive instruction in "The American System of Government"), leaving it to school agencies to create the details of such courses; but in a few instances—and most especially, when the legislature is responding to a persistent public demand—the legislature may attempt to fix course content in greater detail. For example, Tennessee's one-time attempt to "repeal" the laws of evolution by forbidding the teaching of Darwinian theory.

An Increasing Centralization

From one perspective, the state's role in education might be viewed as that of creating, through statutes, the broad foundations upon which local school agencies will build and operate. And though this perspective is essentially correct, it is also somewhat misleading: for state control over education goes far beyond enabling legislation. In the field of education, as in nearly every other aspect of government, the drift of power has been upwards, in terms of centralized direction and control. Thus, where state governments, say, forty years ago, were content to limit their controls over education to the kind of statutory enactments noted above, state governments today are busily engaged in the process of pulling tighter the reins of educational controls—and, in this fashion, circumscribing the freedom of local school boards.

Stated somewhat differently, state governments today are increasing their control over education by turning over to state administrative structures responsibility for augmenting and detailing broadly sketched legislative enactments. Where the filling-in of legislative details was once placed in the hands of local school boards, that task is increasingly being placed in the hands of state boards of education (or state superintendents of public instruction). Where local school boards were once kept to the line of the law only by threat of court action (at best, a very ineffective device for securing compliance) the state maintains its controls today largely by offering fiscal grants-in-aid of education: grants that can be withheld should the local school district deviate from state standards or otherwise violate state regulations.

Devices of state aid and control. These two devices—a centralized administrative structure and the use of fiscal grants-in-aid—are commonly used by both state and federal governments in the service of centralization. In the context of education, however, a few further words about each may be in order.

To begin with the administrative structure, it might be first noted that today every state has an administrative agency charged with general supervision of public schools below the college level. In most states, this agency consists of a State Board of Education; in a few states, the agency is built around a State Superintendent of Public Instruction. Again, in most states the chief officer of these agencies is appointed by the governor; and the agency itself forms part of the executive branch of state government. In a few states, however, the chief officer (the Superintendent of Public Instruction) is an independently elected executive; and in still other states, the education-agency is controlled by a board whose appointment may be lodged with the Governor, but whose term of office exceeds that of the Governor who appoints them.

For the student of politics, there is considerable significance in the manner in which these agencies are staffed. For a Superintendent of Public Instruction who is independently elected is, in certain respects, a political rival of both the governor and the legislature. A Superintendent who, by the terms of his appointment, forms part of the governor's "cabinet" becomes a pawn in any political struggle between the legislature and governor. A board of education deliberately made bipartisan and otherwise independent of the governor, often becomes the trusted agent of the legislature, and the recipient of a considerable measure of delegated power. All of this, however, may be an awkward way of expressing a simple political fact: the political and administrative environment often determines the amount of policy-making and supervisory power allocated to the state education agency.

Despite the variations in power given these agencies, one trend is common to all the states: state boards of education (or their equivalent) are increasingly being used to centralize the state's control over education. It was not so many years ago (take 1925 as a convenient benchmark) that state boards of education, if they existed at all, were employed largely for such routinely administrative tasks as auditing the accounts of local school districts and "certifying" new teachers. School policy was largely made in the local school districts, presumably in conformity with the large outlines of legislative statutes. Today, however, the hand of the state agency is very much evident in the local school district. Course outlines are sometimes prepared by the central agency; the textbook is often prescribed; and teaching methods are suggested. The central agency is given responsibility for countless matters that were once within the province of the local school board; but perhaps most important of all, as a tool of centralization, is the state agency's responsibility for administering the state educational grants.

Every state now uses these grants to local school districts in one form or another; and although the program (commonly called the school foundation program) varies from state to state, certain features are common to all. First, nearly every state has viewed these grants as a means whereby the superior taxing powers of the state may be made available to local government structures. The states have at their command a variety of tax devices; most local governments—and school districts in particular—are bound to that most inflexible of all taxes, the property tax. Second, and closely coupled to the idea of a system of state-raised, locally spent taxes, are the equalitarian purposes of a school foundation program. The program is viewed as a means whereby the wealthier sections of the state (which, as a matter of course, fall most heavily under the tax) will contribute to the educational needs of the poorer sections. Third, and also equalitarian in character, by giving local school districts funds to undertake programs that might lie beyond the resources of the local tax base, the states have been assured of a fairly equal system of education in rich and poor districts, alike. Or, perhaps more properly put, every school district, no matter how poor, is assured of being able to perform at some state-set, minimal standard. And fourth, by threatening to withhold school grants from districts that "misbehave," the states can place a stout stick in the hands of those state officials who are charged with supervising local school districts.

Federal overtones. Viewed in this fashion, the school foundation programs exhibit two of the issues, centralization and equalization, that figure prominently in contemporary discussion of federal aid to education. Many observers, in fact, see the foundation programs as "microcosms" of (or "rehearsals" for) a system of federal aid; and the experiences within the states become grist for the mill of congressional discussion.

Two aspects, especially, of the foundation program have caught the congressional eye. One of these involves a perennial feature of state legislative politics: the unresolved rivalry between the rural and urban sections of the state. This rivalry becomes especially intense in legislation calling for the distribution of state funds to local governments; and with state legislatures essentially under the control of rural America it should hardly be surprising that many rural legislators view the foundation program as a convenient method for letting the people of the cities pay for the education of the ruralities. In nearly every state, the foundation program is based on a very complicated formula that—instead of merely allocating a fixed sum for every child in school—takes into account the value of taxable property within the school district. Under the usual formula, the city school district (with its rich stands of industrial property) receives far less per school child than does the rural school district. And though these formulae have an equalitarian cast, there is no mistaking their rural bias. Thus, Congressmen, especially those from the larger urban areas, are concerned lest this same rural advantage be smuggled into federally supported programs for the schools. And, as will be later noted, this concern for disproportionate rural advantage has led Congress toward giving special attention to urban areas by providing funds for the improvement of education in pockets of urban poverty.

Of course, it may happen, given the re-apportionment revolution now sweeping the fifty states, that rural control over the state legislatures will be sharply curtailed. One consequence may be adjustment of the school foundation programs in the direction of greater equalitarianism. An opposite and perhaps more likely consequence may be revision of the school foundation programs to favor the nation's urban areas.

The other aspect of foundation programs that has caught the congressional eye concerns the suspension of funds from districts that violate state laws. Here, as suggested earlier, the foundation program becomes a stick and a carrot; used to induce school districts to undertake state-conceived programs and also used to "persuade" these districts to adhere to the *entire* body of state law, lest their state funds be cut off.

Every Congressman, of course, knows that grant-in-aid money is both persuader and policeman, an effective instrument of centralization. Every Congressman also knows that centralization—especially by way of a grant-in-aid program—contributes to the size of the bureaucratic structure. The idea of a burgeoning bureaucracy touches one of the perennially raw nerves of Congress (as well as the body politic), but few things stir congressional wrath so much as the idea that a centralizing bureaucracy will also use its powers to thwart the wishes of elected policy-makers. And here, we return to a theme upon which the present discussion began, the guild-perspective within educational administration. Many Congressmen have received complaints from school board members of alleged collusion between the local school superintendent and the state education agency. In disputes over policy, the school board members say: "We vote one way, but the superintendent suggests another course of action, saying that the state board will never approve of our spending money the way we propose. We give in; but in our hearts we have a sneaking suspicion that the superintendent has already called his cronies up at the state capital, and they have agreed to back up his point of view by disallowing our expenditures, if and when we decide to carry through our proposals."

Despite the tone of the foregoing exchange, the school board is far from being bureaucratic putty; and one of the common occurrences of American school politics is the superintendent sent packing by an angered school board. But to see school politics at still closer range, we turn now to the school board itself. With that canvass we shall have at least identified the three major instruments of state school administration: the legislature, the state board of education, and the local school board.

The Local School District

To understand the working of today's school boards, a few historical observations are in order. First, as part of the decentralization of nineteenth century government, every state divided its school system into a series of highly localized administrative units (school districts) whose boundaries sometimes coincided with a unit of local government (the town, the township, and so on) and, in other instances, represented nothing more than the area served by a single school: the four-mile-square district of rural America. Second, and again reflecting our nineteenth-century legacy, control over these school districts was vested in an elected commission—the local school board, with membership running anywhere from three to eleven, or more. And third, but this time reflecting a somewhat different aspect of American political belief, that schools be "kept out of politics," these school districts were not made a part of the general local government of their area. They were formed as special districts, whose officers were often elected in special elections, on a different "calendar" than the more ordinary government officials.

Thus, the school district comes down to us today as a special unit of government, commission-controlled and highly localized in jurisdiction. It is not, however, insulated from politics; but, as we shall presently see, very much enmeshed in a special style of politics that reflects its localism and its commission-form. Nor is the present-day school district as geographically small as it once was. School districts, too, have fallen under the wheels of centralization; for they have been combining their boundaries in a consolidation movement that has been moving with increasing vigor since the First World War. In 1932, for example, there was a total of 127,531 school districts in the forty-eight states. By 1962 the fifty states were operating with only 35,676 school districts, and it is estimated that only about 24,400 districts were in operation in 1965–66.[7]

The school consolidation movement, like many other attempts at changing governmental structure, is a product of technological, cultural, and political clash: The coming of the motor bus that could transport children to more distant schools made consolidation physically possible. Rising educational standards and legislative prescriptions for a more complex curriculum made it impossible for the one room, one school district to meet these demands. The offer of federal grants (The Smith-Hughes Act of 1917) to high schools that would offer training in home economics and agriculture brought public pressure upon legislatures and school boards to consolidate school districts to the point where the school population and the tax resources could support a more variegated curriculum and employ more and specially trained teachers. More important than these pressures for consolidation were counter pressures: from school boards having no

---

[7] There were an estimated 2400 additional nonoperating districts, which operated no school facilities but rather transferred their students to other school districts. Sources: U.S. Department of Health, Education and Welfare, *School District Reorganization*, Special Series No. 5 (Washington, D.C.: Government Printing Office, 1957), p. 8; also National Education Association, Research Report 1965–R17, *Estimates of School Statistics 1965–66* (Washington, D.C.: National Education Association, December, 1965), p. 6.

wish to vote themselves out of existence; from taxpayers not wishing to be taxed to build and maintain new and larger schools; and from a local populace wishing to keep the schools more directly under local control.

The school consolidation movement has far from run its course; and one citizens' study group has recently recommended that the total number of school districts be reduced to about 10,000 if this nation is to have a school system "that is to operate effectively and efficiently."[8] That recommendation, however, takes us into the realm of unsolved school issues. We shall postpone those issues for the moment in order to return to our present theme: the powers of the local school board.

The local school board. To speak now of the powers of the local school board we might first note, despite the centralization of educational controls, that the local school board remains the pivot of the state school system. The legislature and the state school agency may lay down policy in fairly detailed fashion and it may supervise and control expenditures; but it is the local school board that fills in the final details and in so doing makes the ultimate policy decisions.

It is, of course, impossible to detail in short space the many areas of school board action. A few examples may illustrate and further the explanation. Thus, the architects of the state agency may be required to approve the local board's plans for building a new school; but far more important is the fact that it is the local board that decides if a new school is to be built at all, and if so, which side of town will get it. Or, as another aspect of local independence in policy: the state agency may send down general directives concerning the need to build a school system that is free from class (or racial) bias; but the local school board can make certain that the children of the well-to-do mingle only with their own class by the simple expedient of maintaining schools in sufficient number so that each of these schools is attended only by children living within the confines of a single geographic (and socially or racially homogeneous) area.

To take another example: the state agency may require that twelfth graders undergo a literature course in which a number of "great American novels" are read. But the school board might very well decide that a book that is "controversial" or critical of American institutions does not qualify as a great novel. Accordingly, students who read only the works of Hawthorne or Cooper will receive a far different education from students in a school district where, say, Dos Passos' *U.S.A.* is standard fare.

As a final example, the state agency may certify teachers for the school system, but it is the local board which performs the actual hiring. It is here that the board has fairly free choice in recruiting teachers who will either reflect and reinforce the prejudices and social outlook of their students, or

---

[8] Committee for Economic Development (CED), *Paying for Better Schools*, 1960, pp. 59 ff.

who in contrast may help them alter their fundamental social views. Certain school boards, especially those in rural areas, are notorious for their exclusionary hiring practices: refusing to hire members of locally disliked ethnic or religious groups or even teachers who have received their training in the allegely "radical" colleges of the big city. The local school board may argue of course that its hiring practices democratically reflect the community's will; and though here we will not unravel the threads of that argument, the example does serve to illustrate another of the ways in which the local school board can indelibly stamp the educational process.

To speak, however, of school board policies reflecting the community will is to raise again the connection between policy-making and politics. To follow that lead, and thus complete our canvass of states, schools, and politics, we turn now to a closer examination of the political context in which the school boards operate.

School board politics. In the school board we discover the American predilection for tempering centralization with devolution. The school board is an agent of the state. It derives its legal authority from the state and therefore is legally responsible to the state. As an arm of the state, it is subject to state legislative statutes, the rules and sanctions of state boards of education, and the legal interpretations of state attorneys general and the state courts.

At the same time, almost everywhere the school board is locally elected. (In some jurisdictions, notably in large cities, school boards are appointed by the mayor.) It is an agent of the state by virtue of constitutional establishment; but by virtue of the power of the polling place, it is also an agent of its local constituency. The school board is thus deeply embedded in local political processes. In some communities, where school board members maintain close affiliation with the "regular" party organization, the school itself may become one of the prizes of political patronage. Thus, in cities with a tradition of bosses and machines, the school board is often merely another facet of local political jobbery: utilizing its powers of school construction, of purchases of supplies and the like, as an instrument of political brokerage and personal gain. In most communities, however, the school board is both part of the ordinary political structure; and, at the same time, set somewhat apart from that structure. School board politics, it is often said, has a "style and flavor" all its own.

Contributing to this special political style are both political traditions and the legal arrangements under which the school boards operate. Thus, the American belief that "schools should be kept out of politics" is not taken fully and literally anywhere; but this belief, nonetheless, is capable of rousing the public to heights of considerable anger when gross corruption within the schools is revealed: for example, the recent revelation that a large eastern city had permitted its schools to fall into disrepair because of bribery within its school renovation contracts.

A second contributing factor is the tradition of voluntary service on school boards. School board members nearly everywhere serve without pay; and consequently, the office has tended to become the special preserve of that group within our society which has best developed the tradition of civic service: the fairly well-to-do, small businessman. To risk a gross generalization, school board members, reflecting the views of the business community to which they belong, tend also to believe in a low tax rate, limited government expenditures, and "small government." As a result, there is within nearly every school system a predisposition to friction and argument: between the school board and its hired superintendent, who as a professional educator tends to promote the virtues of an expanding curriculum and fuller integration with the state school structure.

A third factor of political style is the tradition that school boards hold open meetings, at which past decisions are defended, new policies sometimes made, and townspeople given opportunity to speak their minds and vent their emotions. Tempers often run high at such meetings; and they offer special invitation to pressure groups to pack the audience and attempt a policy stampede.

Still another factor is the school board constituency. Everywhere local, and, except in the larger cities, small enough to convey a sense of intimate contact between school officials and the community, the school board members do not possess the shield of distance of the state legislator or Congressman. Nor can the school board member often take advantage of the size and heterogeneity of his constituency (as does, say, a state legislator) to play the demands of one social class against another, and thus retain for himself a measure of pressure group independence. Recent studies of community power structures support the proposition that school board members usually are closely aligned with influential groups within the community. Furthermore, school board recruitment processes, both formal and informal, tend to emphasize the adherence of prospective candidates to dominant values considered consistent with community stability.[9]

And finally, there is the factor of money. School taxes are circumscribed by legislative statute everywhere. Tax increases—and bond issues floated for school construction—generally must be approved by the district's taxpayers. Perhaps the most universal rule of political thumb can be expressed: nothing so invites controversy as the suggestion that taxpayers be asked to vote themselves a tax increase.

These factors, singly and especially in combination, work to involve the

---

[9] School board politics are presently being studied by political scientists as an arena of community power. The theoretical underpinnings for this approach are presented in an interesting collection of essays in Robert S. Cahill and Stephen Hencley, eds., *The Politics of Education* (Danville, Ill.: Interstate Printers and Publishers, Inc., 1964). The contributions by Luvern L. Cunningham ("Community Power: Implications for Education," pp. 27–50) and David Minar ("Community Characteristics, Conflict, and Power Structures," pp. 125–44) are especially relevant.

community directly in school politics; equally important, they open the floodgates of pressure group agitation.

The roster of pressure groups participating in school politics will, of course, vary with the issue. But certain groups are fairly regular participants in the struggle to control the schools. Such groups as property owners' associations, business associations, parent-teacher groups, and patriotic organizations tend to be particularly vocal in local school board politics. Five hundred school board members in New England, for example, were asked to list the individuals and groups that had made demands of them in their respective positions as school board members. The most frequently mentioned pressure group was "parents and PTA" (74 per cent said they had been exposed to parental or PTA pressure). Forty-four per cent said they had been pressured by teachers, 38 per cent by taxpayers' associations, and 29 per cent by local politicians. Other groups mentioned included "economic influentials," "old-line families," business and commercial organizations, the press, church and religious groups, service clubs, and veterans' organizations. Labor unions and chambers of commerce each were mentioned by only 5 per cent of the school board members, and farm and welfare organizations were mentioned by only 4 per cent and 1 per cent respectively.[10]

Collectively, these pressure groups concern themselves with a wide range of specific issues growing out of the substance and methods of education in the local schools. Individual groups, however, often limit their attention to a particular issue. Thus, patriotic organizations tend to be concerned lest the schools be negligent in fostering Americanism, or equally negligent in rooting "subversives" from the teaching staff. Property owners' associations are traditionally dedicated to trying to prevent increases in school tax rates, and businessmen's organizations focus particularly on matters concerning school construction contracts and school board purchases of goods and services.

While we cannot here catalog all the issues that engage school boards, several basic issues seem to attract the attention of interest groups and the general public in nearly every school district. The New England school board members cited "school taxes, revenues, and bond proposals" as the issue that most frequently stimulates the public to articulate political interests and demands. Issues centering on athletic programs, services for pupils, range and substance of courses offered, teaching methods, and views expressed by specific teachers were also listed as frequent subjects of political controversy and conflict.[11] A survey of 15,000 teachers and other educators by the National Education Association in 1966 revealed a considerable increase in the amount of group pressure reported and the

---

[10] Neal Gross, *Who Runs Our Schools?* (New York: John Wiley & Sons, Inc., 1958), p. 50.

[11] *Ibid.*, p. 49.

proportion of that pressure judged "destructive" by the educators as compared to findings of a similar study by the Association in 1962. Particular increases were noted in community pressure involving proposals to censor or ban books used in the schools on "patriotic" or "moral" grounds.[12]

To the degree that each of these issues represents a threat to the established values of the community, it is a potential contributor to the volatility that seems so often to characterize school board politics. Thus, the issue of integration in the South and the mob violence that has sometimes spilled into the streets as a result of a school board's decision to desegregate a school. To shift locale to an outstate, rural community of dwindling population and a declining economy, tempers will flare in the face of a superintendent's program for an expanded, college-oriented curriculum; for the school board's concern is that of reducing school expenditures and, at the same time, of retaining a farm oriented curriculum preaching the virtues of rural life while perhaps helping to stem the outward migration of the area's young. And, as a final example, the battle between old settlers and newcomers in the suburban fringe. Charles Adrian describes that battle neatly:[13]

> As an area on the fringe of a city comes under the eye of land-development companies and gives up its bucolic existence, it is characteristically overrun by children, for those who move into new developments are predominantly young couples. The newcomers find the established governmental structure in the hands of farmers and small town merchants who have a low-tax attitude. The newcomers demand expanded urban services—beginning with the schools. Generally the first battles between the newcomers and the old timers center around the questions of issuing bonds to expand the school system and replacing the farm-oriented curriculum with one designed to prepare suburban children for college—for a degree is a cherished goal established by suburban parents for their children. The battles are often furious, but the newcomers practically always win through sheer force of numbers and a common purpose.

If it is sometimes difficult for school boards to reconcile divergent interests within their districts, it is no less difficult for them to reconcile the interests of their districts with requirements imposed from above by the state. Thus, the political dilemma of the school board is compounded: being responsive to its *formal* master, the state, while at the same time fulfilling the expectations of its *informal* master, the local community. State requirements reflect the aggregate interests of the entire state as expressed by the state legislature, as well as the preferences of state educational "experts" and bureaucrats whose views are often suspect in

---

[12] See *The New York Times*, "Pressure Grows on Public Schools," January 18, 1966, p. 38.

[13] Charles R. Adrian, *State and Local Governments* (New York: McGraw-Hill Book Company, Inc., 1960), p. 146.

communities where grass-root values and common sense decision-making have traditionally taken precedence over the sometimes alien ideas born of expertise. Malapportioned state legislatures weighted in favor of rural interests produce policies which urban citizens frequently find ill-suited to the educational needs of their youngsters. Even in reapportioned states where legislatures are more realistically representative of the urban-rural split, educational policies emanating from state capitols rarely meet approval from all school districts.

For a "school board to become a board of education" and to "take an independent stand about curricular matters and high academic standards" (as Mortimer Smith[14] phrases the problem) produces a political process couched in a dilemma that probably cannot totally be resolved. Too often, the outcome of this strained political battle is more heat than light.

But here we have reached a watershed in our exposition; we have thus far attempted, in the fashion of the political scientist, to suggest a range of reciprocal relations that interconnect political traditions, political structures, and political processes. Now we shall examine some issues that are not readily resolved by present traditions and institutional patterns and that as a result may rise to break those patterns.

A BUDGET OF
EDUCATION ISSUES

Statistics on the Rise

No discussion of contemporary school problems can stray very far from the expanding scope of the educational enterprise.

To begin, public school enrollments are on the rise everywhere; a consequence of a birthrate that began soaring in 1940 and accelerated still further in 1946. Public school enrollments *increased* by more than one-half million *per year* from 1946 to 1951 and by over one million per year from 1951 to 1959. In terms of absolute numbers, public school enrollments have gone from about twenty-four million in 1944 to about forty-two million as of 1965. The enrollment curve is still on the rise, for it is estimated that by 1975 total enrollment in public schools (from kindergarten to grade twelve) will exceed 47.4 million, with an additional eight million in private schools.[15]

---

[14] A *Citizen's Manual for Public Schools* (Boston: Little Brown & Co., 1965), p. 56.

[15] Sources: CED, *Paying for Better Schools*, Chapter 2; U.S. Department of Health, Education, and Welfare, Health, Education, and Welfare Trends (Washington, D.C.: U.S. Government Printing Office, 1964), p. 41; NEA Research Report 1965–R17, p. 5.

Of course, not all of this remarkable increase can be traced to birth rates alone. Some part of this increase is also attributable to a changing public expectation as to the amount of schooling that constitutes a "proper" education. Thus rising educational standards (reinforced by compulsory school attendance laws) have brought a considerable increase in the number of days in the "school year" and in the number of students who remain to complete a high school education. Consequently, since 1900 the length of the school year has grown from as little as four months (in some parts of the rural South) to today's nearly universal requirement of the (roughly) nine month school year. And in 1890 some one-half million students were enrolled in public high schools, representing only 8 per cent of the youth of high school age. By 1947 nearly six million were attending high school (some 70 per cent of the youth of high school age) while today, our public high schools contain upwards of 15.5 million students, representing over 93 per cent of those of high school age.[16]

Educational standards have been on the rise in other ways. Most significant perhaps is the growing demand that elementary school teachers possess at very least a bachelor's degree. In 1947, for example, only fifteen states required that degree for teacher certification; in 1965 a total of forty-six states (including the District of Columbia) made that degree the minimum requirement for certification.[17]

Thus, rising enrollment and rising educational standards combine to put at least two additional problems upon the schools: First, where shall we find teachers in sufficient supply to educate the rising school population? One estimate has it that we shall need some 340,000 new teachers by 1970. Will the present group of teacher's colleges be capable of turning out teachers in sufficient number to meet this demand? And, will teaching prove itself a sufficiently attractive profession to recruit new teachers in the numbers needed? Many factors, of course, determine the flow of recruits into any profession. Financial rewards, while not controlling, are sufficiently important to warrant this comment: In 1959, 18 per cent of the nation's classroom teachers received less than $3500 salary per year; and the average salary for classroom teachers (in 1965) was about $6250 (elementary $6000; secondary $6500).[18]

And second, where shall we house our increasing school population? From 1949 through 1957 approximately one half million classrooms were

[16] CED, *Paying for Better Schools*; U.S. Office of Education, *Statistical Summary* (Washington, D.C.: U.S. Government Printing Office, 1957); and U.S. Office of Education, *Digest of Educational Statistics* (Washington, D.C.: U.S. Government Printing Office, 1965).

[17] National Commission on Teacher Education and Professional Standards, *A Manual on Certification Requirements for School Personnel in the United States, 1964* (Washington, D.C.: The Commission, 1964), p. 4.

[18] National Education Association, Research Report 1965-R7, *Economic Status of Teachers in 1964–65* (Washington, D.C.: NEA, 1965), p. 5.

built in the United States. More recently, production has been stepped up to about 70,000 classrooms a year. Classrooms, however, continue to be in short supply (and they will become increasingly so): Even in 1965—and despite the construction of over 350,000 classrooms in the preceding five years—the U.S. Office of Education estimated that a shortage still existed of 104,000 classrooms.[19]

As a result, a burgeoning school population is increasingly faced with a shortage of both teachers and classroom space; and though it is tempting to suggest that these problems can be met simply by requiring that government spend more upon its schools, the thought is cut short by one of the most trenchant of contemporary political clichés: Where will the money come from?

Paying for Public Schools

To approach the school-cost problem by way of a brief excursion into statistics: In the school year 1929–30, public school expenditures were $2.3 billion. In 1958–59 public school expenditures had reached $14.4 billion and when the 1966 expenditures are tabulated they will run to about $25.8 billion for elementary and secondary schools alone—up 136 per cent over the index year 1955–56. In addition, at least $13 billion will be spent for public and private higher education, bringing the total to nearly $40 billion.[20]

Whether one regards these expenditures as "extravagant," or "unwise" depends, of course, upon one's views about the wisdom of publicly supported education. But before concluding that Americans are staggering under the weight of a growing school burden, consider this data: If the cost of schools is computed against the general wealth of the society, using the economists' standard index of Gross National Product (GNP: the sum total of all goods and services produced in any year) then the 1929–30 expenditures represented 3.1 per cent of the GNP; and the 1964 figures about 6.3 per cent of the GNP. Or, laid upon a much cruder line, compare the present public educational expenditure of $40 billion with the yearly amounts spent in this country for recreation ($23.8 billion) and that spent yearly for whiskey and cigarettes ($19.2 billion).[21]

But given the American commitment to a system of public education, there seems little doubt that the system will be maintained and quite likely

---

[19] Sources: U.S. Office of Education, *Conditions of Public School Plants, 1964–65* (Washington, D.C.: U.S. Government Printing Office, 1965); also U.S. Office of Education, *Digest*, p. 48.

[20] Figures include interest and capital outlay as well as current expenditures. Sources: U.S. Office of Education, *Digest*, pp. 58, 134; NEA Research Report 1965–R17, p. 19.

[21] U.S. Office of Education, *Digest*, p. 136; also *Statistical Abstract of the United States* (Washington, D.C.: U.S. Government Printing Office, 1965), p. 326.

improved—even in the face of spiraling costs. Thus another question presents itself: How successful will school districts and states be in meeting these mounting costs?

Obviously, the burden of the schools will vary between the states and even from district to district within a single state. Areas of industrial wealth will support schools more easily (and probably more willingly) than rural areas, or those chronically depressed. Areas of declining population will be less pressed by spiraling enrollments than areas of population boom. The drift of population—about thirty-four million people change locale every year—to the North and West will place special burdens upon those areas. The continuing migration to the suburbs will probably make their school districts the most costly of all to maintain. (By 1975 it is estimated that eighty million people will live in the suburbs that ring our central cities.) [22]

The problem of school support does not belong simply to the future. Future population changes may exacerbate the problem; but the burden of the schools lies very heavily upon state and local governments today. Everywhere, states (and their school districts) are concerned over the ability of school districts to meet education costs; over the adequacy of the state's share of the school foundation program; and over the wide variation of that share from state to state. Equally important, public opinion on the national level is increasingly concerned with a problem whose roots extend back into our nineteenth-century school legacy: the unequal support given education among the fifty states.

Again a few statistics may be useful. It is estimated that in 1965–66, 7.8 per cent of school revenues in the United States will come from Federal sources (as compared to 1.8 per cent in 1940 and 4.6 per cent in 1956), 39.1 per cent from state sources, and 53.1 per cent from local sources. Since 1940, the level of state contributions has remained about constant, while revenue from local taxes has declined slightly. But the balance between local support and state support varies widely from state to state. In Nebraska, for example, local districts assume nearly 90 per cent of the cost of education, while in Delaware the local districts provide only 20 per cent of education revenues and the state contributes the other 80 per cent. By comparison, in Minnesota local districts pay about 56 per cent; in New York the local share is about 50 per cent; in Ohio about 67 per cent; and local districts in Mississippi pay only about 29 per cent. [23] There is no direct connection between, say, urbanism and state contribution. The pattern in each state is probably a consequence of factors such as: the

[22] See Catherine Wurster, "Framework for an Urban Society," in *Goals for Americans*, The American Assembly, Columbia University, New York (Englewood Cliffs, N.J.: Prentice-Hall, Inc., 1960).

[23] National Education Association, Research Report 1966–R1, *Ranking of the States 1966* (Washington, D.C.: NEA, 1966), pp. 37, 43; also U.S. Office of Education, *Digest*, p. 57.

strength of the tradition of local controls; urban-rural rivalry in the legislature; and the disparity among local districts regarding their abilities to support schools.

Between the states, the variations in school support are marked and wide. Here, the wealth of the state is very obviously a key and controlling factor. New York, in 1965–66, for example, ranked highest among the states with an expenditure on education averaging $869 per pupil, while at the other extreme Mississippi spent only $318 per pupil. Considering educational expenditures as a per cent of state personal income, however, Mississippi ranked twelfth among the states. On the average, the states spend $533 per pupil—about 3.8 per cent of the average state personal income. By way of further comparison, expenditure per pupil was $603 in California (eighth among the states), while in South Carolina it was $350—in Alabama $356.[24]

Although state school expenditures do not control the problems of illiteracy, they affect it in very large measure. Wealthier states generally weave the tightest net of compulsory education laws. Poorer states, in contrast, require fewer years of school attendance. Their standards for teacher certification are, likewise, lower; they generally afford fewer opportunities for individualized instruction. In short, the poorer the state, the greater the outcroppings of illiteracy. And lest it be thought—in the present discussion of future school needs—that illiteracy is no longer a problem in the United States, consider Louisiana, where as of 1960 nearly 6.3 per cent of the population fourteen years of age or older was unable to read and write, South Carolina with a 5.5 per cent illiteracy rate, or Hawaii with an illiteracy rate of 5 per cent.[25]

Thus, the problem of supporting education cuts in several directions. It brings forth continuing debate within the states over state government's "proper" share of educational costs. And increasingly, within the society at large, it brings argument as to whether the costs of education should be assumed by the federal government so that: 1) the burden of education will fall upon the entire society, and 2) all children within the society will receive an education made at least equal in terms of the money that supports it. From this perspective, the question of where the money will come from becomes more politically realistic by changing its form to: which level of government will assume the costs of education? Because an increasing share of taxes will be diverted to support education, we may also expect an increased concern for another question: *how* will the money be spent? The argument over curricula, already a heated one, will probably become more intense with the coming years.

---

[24] National Education Association, *Research Bulletin*, XLIV, 1 (February, 1966), 13. Figures based on number of pupils in "average daily attendance."

[25] NEA Research Report 1966–R1, p. 29.

The Great Curriculum Debate

Although today nearly every phase of education falls under public scrutiny and consequent criticism, there seems to be fairly widespread agreement that the curriculum of the primary schools is aimed at the proper goals: giving the primary-school child a mastery over the fundamentals of writing, reading, arithmetic, and of imparting to him a fund of general knowledge. There is, however, considerable criticism of matters such as the technique by which those fundamentals are taught, of the child's rate of progress, and of the degree of competitiveness that enters into the learning process. Symptomatic both of this criticism and of the public's eagerness to join the curriculum debate is a book that appeared a few years ago, *Why Johnny Can't Read*, a scathing denunciation of a widely used technique for teaching reading that raced to the top of the "best sellers" list.[26]

Whether Johnny really can read, or do sums, or write with literacy are questions without offhand answers, simply because any judgment requires the use of some yardstick against which the answers can be measured; and because the yardstick itself invokes subjective judgment. (Shall we measure reading accomplishment by comparing, say, a sixth-grade American textbook with its French counterpart? And if we did, would we be examining reading skills, or perhaps some aspect of cultural difference?)

Of special interest in this debate for the student of politics is the assertion by several educator's associations: the attack on the primary school curriculum is not produced by concern for the curriculum alone, and in many specific instances (as when the town turns on the school board, demanding the dismissal of its superintendent) that curriculum is really only a convenient basin into which all manner of grievances and frustrations can be poured. Thus, the property owner angered by a rising tax rate, the patriotic organizations fearful of subversive teaching, the Jeremiahs who may bemoan the decline of manners, or morals, or initiative in today's young people—all of these can make common camp under the banner of curriculum-attack and they will be joined there by a citizenry seemingly anxious to join any curriculum fight.

Whether this picture is over or under drawn is difficult to say; but to the student of politics it has perspectives of probability for he knows that symbolic battles and psychological displacement are the elements common to the political process everywhere.

---

[26] Rudolf Flesch, *Why Johnny Can't Read* (New York: Harper & Row, Publishers, 1955). Present public concern and not infrequent parental resentment over the introduction of the "New Math" to the primary grades illustrates: 1) the public propensity to join the curriculum debate, 2) the unseen hand of centralization exercised by the "educational guild."

But if arguments over the primary school curriculum are flecked with shadow and confusion, a number of the high school issues seem almost painfully clear; for they involve nothing less than the social structure of our future society. As the Rockefeller Report suggests, "We have been extraordinarily tolerant . . . in the matter of electives in the high school. In the great 'democracy of subject matters' which we have allowed to develop, it is only moderate exaggeration to say that beyond the prescribed subjects (which take about half the student's time) any subject has been considered to be as important as any other."[27]

Thus, a considerable portion of the discussion centers on the system of high school electives, a system that includes such "frills and fads" (to use the now popular terms of derision) as instruction in baton-twirling, automobile driving, social dancing, and repair of home appliances. Courses such as these, say many of today's critics, not only compete for funds with the traditional (and academically oriented courses) but they also depress standards of scholarship by drawing off the talents and time of the better students and by permitting the lazy and the indifferent student to turn education into a time-filling, frivolous experience. And this at a time of technological and national crisis, when our society stands in increasing need of a citizenry well trained in the liberal arts and above all, in the sciences.

To quote again from the Rockefeller Report:

> The heart of the matter is that we are moving with headlong speed into a new phase in man's long struggle to control his environment, a phase beside which the industrial revolution may appear a modest alteration of human affairs. Nuclear energy, exploration of outer space, revolutionary studies of brain functioning, important new work on the living cell—all point to changes in our lives so startling as to test to the utmost our adaptive capacities, our stability and our wisdom.
> The immediate applications for education may be briefly stated. We need an ample supply of high calibre scientists, mathematicians, and engineers . . . [and we must also bring] balance in education between the sciences, the social sciences and the humanities. Each has a vital part to play . . .[28]

In pursuit of academic excellence, there are many who suggest that we "train the best and abandon the rest." They counsel creating a dual high school system with the brightest students in separated schools, earnestly preparing for college and for professional training beyond, and with all others in vocationally oriented schools where they will learn both practical subjects, and (inasmuch as this is to be a terminal education) a fairly broad range of general knowledge.

Such counsel, however, has thus far met with cold reception, for the

---

[27] Rockefeller Brothers Fund, Special Project, Report V, *The Pursuit of Excellence*, 1958, p. 26.

[28] *Ibid.*, p. 28.

hard truth is that our society wants many things from its high schools, academic excellence being only one of them. For example, in our schools we continue to retain a large portion of our eighteenth-century liberal heritage, and though we do not fully put into practice the belief that "all men are created equal," we demonstrate a firm reluctance to foster a class society by segregating and giving special education to our brightest students—even though any resulting elite would be one in the Jeffersonian sense, an aristocracy not of wealth or birth but of talents. Our educational system, we argue, must serve the individual as well as the society; and if we are to develop the talents of the least as well as the most able students, we must rely upon the presence of the gifted students to leaven the mass (itself an unegalitarian term!) and to create a social system of each contact between all groups within the society.

More than this, our society gives evidence of wanting its school system to offer more than traditional academic training: We expect our schools to offer forms of mass entertainment (football and basketball games and the like), to function as a courtship arena and marriage market, to instill (and instruct in) social graces, and to equip our students to deal with problems of "everyday living," not the least of which—given the slaughter on the highways—is management of the automobile. Even beyond these things, we also seem to want the schools to act as custodians of those teenagers who have no interest in education, but who we feel are too young to work and too old to roam the streets unsupervised.

As a result, demands on the schools are many. More to the point, they are often conflicting. Accordingly, the curriculum debate continues; and though the truncated version given here runs the risk of being caricature rather than portrait, the essential point is this: The current arguments over primary and secondary education—and indeed, over our colleges—is political debate of the greatest importance; for it spills beyond mere argument as to what the schools will teach, or what will be the cost, into argument over the very nature of our society.

Higher Education

Although the major concerns of this essay are with the politics and problems of primary and secondary education, any rounded discussion calls for at least brief mention of these items at the level of the publicly supported college. Essentially, the problems and politics of the colleges and the lower schools are cut from much the same cloth. Publicly supported colleges are, by and large, the product and responsibility of the states; the growing curricula and expanding college enrollments reflect the same forces that are working to expand the primary and the secondary school enterprise.

In one aspect of this expansion, however, the colleges reflect with even greater clarity the affinity of the democratic government for the welfare state. With government—that supreme secular social institution—in the hands of the greatest number, one consequence of this popular control has been for the majority to use government as a tool for acquiring a range of social services and products which the individual might not be able to afford for himself. Old age assistance and insurance against unemployment are two recent examples of this affinity; a far older example—but one that is operating with growing vigor—is the use of governmental power to provide college education for an increasing sector of our society.

Thus in 1900 less than 92,000 persons were enrolled in public colleges and universities as opposed to 146,000 enrolled in private colleges. In 1947, the balance was almost swung around, for 422,000 were enrolled in public colleges as opposed to 455,000 in private colleges. By 1965 there were an estimated 5.5 million college students in the United States, nearly 3.5 million of whom were attending publicly supported schools. And by 1970 some estimates foresee nearly seven million college students, of whom perhaps five million will be in the public schools.[29]

Public education at the higher levels is being squeezed by the same vectors at work upon primary and secondary schools: rising costs, shortages of classroom space (and most especially of teaching laboratories), and a lessening pupil to faculty ratio. If anything, these problems may be even more acute at the college and university levels, if only because the cost of education mounts proportionately with the grade level and because of the greater complexity and longer time needed for educating for the Ph.D.

Again, and very much in the pattern of the high schools, our colleges today are an extremely mixed enterprise, serving the society's demands that the young be taught "social living" as well as being educated. Beyond this, there is more than a considerable measure of vocationalism in the college curricula! Courses of study and degrees, that in other countries are solved by vocational schools and technical institutes, are part of the college enterprise, so that, for example, housewifery, photography, dramatic acting, and mortuary science are all part of the mills that grind our degrees.

Americans, seemingly, will not have it otherwise; for increasingly (and perhaps unhappily) there is growing recognition in our society that social mobility is slowing down. The poor boy rarely rises nowadays from office boy to corporation president. The poor boy may make that ascent, but with increasing invariance he does it not so much with Horatio Alger's pluck and moral fiber as with the aid of a college degree. For Americans the escalator of financial and social success for their children has become, increasingly, a college education. Understandably, they wish to put as

---

[29] Sources: U.S. President's Commission on Higher Education, *Second Report*, CED, *Paying for Better Schools*; and U.S. Office of Education, *Digest*, p. 74.

many as possible on that escalator: by widening the curricula to include all manner of vocational training, and often by blocking attempts to make academic excellence the heart of the collegiate enterprise—witness, for example, the laws of nearly half our states requiring that any high school graduate, no matter how poor his training or his grade record, be admitted to the state university.

To use our colleges to broaden the base of social equality and to widen avenues of social mobility is very much in keeping with our egalitarian goals; and while this perspective accommodates (and even creates) the growing college population, it does not help us solve the problem of academic excellence. Nor does it equip our schools to educate in sufficient numbers either the specialist or the broadly educated citizen capable of coping with a world convulsed by technological, social, and political revolutions.

This problem of stimulating excellence while increasing enrollment opportunities is being attacked on several fronts. After a brief decline early in the 1950s, the number of junior colleges supported (with federal assistance) by cities, counties, and special local districts has for the past decade climbed steadily. There are now more than 450 junior colleges, some with enrollments as high as 20,000.[30] These institutions offer an opportunity for college instruction to students who might otherwise seek admission to already overcrowded state and private universities. In addition, they offer an opportunity to attend college for those unable to meet the higher costs and tighter admissions requirements of the larger universities. By offering a wide range of technical-professional courses in addition to more traditional fare, these colleges are able to attract and hold students with a wide variety of interests and levels of capability. Similarly, many of the state universities are increasing the number and size of their branch campuses to handle spiraling admissions demands and to relieve crowded conditions on their main campuses.

These measures may not necessarily lower prevailing levels of academic excellence, but there is little evidence to suggest that they do much to upgrade it. That task is left chiefly to the established public and private universities, several of which are experimenting with honors colleges and other kinds of accelerated programs open only to undergraduates with the best credentials.

In considering ways of stimulating academic excellence, no one device or formula suffices. To argue that the money spent on public colleges must be used to train for quality instead of quantity, or that our colleges must

---

[30] From *People, Purposes, Programs: Annual Report of the American Association of Junior Colleges,* 1965, reprinted in the hearings on the Higher Education Act of 1965, Subcommittee on Education of the Committee on Labor and Public Welfare, United States Senate, 89th Congress, III, pp. 1130–32.

create engineers instead of football players is, of course, to miss the point. For any adjustment in curriculum would require a corresponding change in beliefs that are basic to our society. The "fallout" from Sputnik jarred those beliefs, but it did not destroy them. Thus, there is growing recognition that our educational system, with its egalitarian and individualistic base, may be an inefficient instrument for achieving the scientific and cultural leadership that we now seek. There is also recognition of the fact that we are in the presence of a familiar political conflict: between individualism and collective social purpose. But we seek to do in education what we have done in other fields touched by this conflict—preserve our traditional patterns, while attempting at the same time to change them sufficiently to meet the problems that chew at them most insistently. Thus, for the present, we seek to preserve our basic educational patterns (and are consequently trying to find funds to do so) but at the same time we are concerned with finding techniques for mitigating mediocrity and lack of national purpose that many see as a consequence of bulk education.

One such technique (and source of funds) may be federal aid to education. We shall complete the present essay by examining some recent proposals for that aid, pausing first, however, to canvass one further problem that is often cited as an impediment to federal aid: that of Religion and the Schools.

Religion and the Schools

What often passes as the problem of "Religion and the Schools," more accurately is a compound of two distinct, but related issues: the issue of religious instruction in the public schools, and the issue of public funds being used to support sectarian schools. Both however are interconnected by a provision in Amendment One of the Federal Constitution (and by similar provisions in state constitutions), which reads that government "shall make no law respecting an establishment of religion or prohibiting the free exercise thereof." From this phrase which the Fourteenth Amendment applies to state governments and their local units has come our traditional view that a wall shall be erected between church and state; and out of both phrase and tradition have come our expectation that in this, as in other matters of constitutional interpretation, our courts shall be the final voice of public policy.

Like many other problems of constitutional politics, these issues of church and school are clouded by a variety of plausible constitutional interpretations. One interpretation is that the language of the Constitution has established a complete and absolute separation between church and state, a separation that forbids any and all commingling—whether it be religious instruction in public schools, public aid to religious schools, or the requirement that public oaths be affirmed upon the Bible or by reference to God.

An opposing view has it that there is no support in the wording of the Constitution for a concept of intervening wall between church and state; and that the constitutional phraseology (especially when interpreted against the experiences of the framers) signifies nothing more than an injunction against government decreeing a national religion comparable to the state-supported Church of England. This argument thus denies the absoluteness of separation between church and state; and, in the specific context of education, it suggests that religious instruction may be given in the public schools and that public funds may be used to support church schools—providing only that government does not use its powers to favor one religion over any others.

In setting forth public policy on the separation issue the Supreme Court has poised itself somewhere *between* the foregoing arguments, favoring in the most recent decisions (since 1960) the former rather than the latter. Thus, regarding the religious instruction issue the Court has constructed a somewhat permeable wall. In 1948, the Court struck down a practice of the public schools in Champagne County, Illinois, whereby students were released to receive instruction in the religion of their choice for thirty minutes a week. In giving its decision, the Court noted that religious classes were held in tax supported buildings, that instructors were subjected to the scrutiny and control of the county superintendent of schools so that "the States' compulsory education system thus assists—the program of religious instruction carried on by separate religious sects." Accordingly, said the Court, the program falls "under the ban of the First Amendment (made applicable to the States by the Fourteenth)."[31]

But in 1952 the Court did not feel that the ban extended to a system whereby the students were released from a portion of the school day in order to receive religious instruction off the school grounds. Dissenters on the Court argued that the program functioned under the supervision of the schools, that teachers were required to take attendance and report truants; but the majority of the Court argued that "We are a religious people whose institutions presuppose a supreme being" and accordingly, the First Amendment does not accommodate "a philosophy of hostility to religion."[32]

This decision obviously did not satisfy those who believe in an impermeable wall; and it was even less satisfying to those who regard the First and Fourteenth Amendments as guarantees of freedom of conscience for those whose fundamental philosophy is one of atheism. But under the protection of the 1952 ruling, several states and school districts moved more boldly into the realm of religious instruction. Three of these moves were challenged in the courts and settled in a pair of Supreme Court decisions that have become known as the "prayer decisions."

---

31 *McCollum v. Board of Education* (*of Champagne Co.*), 333 U.S. 203 (1948).
32 *Zorach v. Clauson*, 343 U.S. 306.

The first decision, made by the Court in 1962, concerned a New York law that required that an official state prayer be recited in the New York public school system at the beginning of each school day. Even though the prayer was "denominationally neutral" and provisions were made in the law to permit pupils to be excused from reciting it, the Court ruled (6–1) that official state sanctioning of religious utterances constitute an unconstitutional tendency to "establish religion." The majority opinion emphasized the "indirect coercive pressure" likely to be exerted by the statute upon religious minorities.[33]

This concern for minorities was repeated in a second school prayer decision involving two separate cases. Both of the laws in question, one a state and the other a local statute, required a daily religious exercise in the public schools. The state law (Pennsylvania) required at least ten verses from the Holy Bible to be read each school morning without comment, and provided (under the original terms of the law) that teachers who refused to participate in such readings were subject to dismissal from the school system. The law was challenged by a father of three school children, a Unitarian, who argued that the content of the doctrines being taught (for example, the divinity of Christ, and of the Trinity) were contrary to the religious beliefs that he wished to impart to his children. While Pennsylvania was appealing a district court ruling that the law violated both the First and Fourteenth amendments, the state legislature changed the terms of the law by deleting provisions for firing noncooperative teachers and permitting children to be excused from the readings upon written request of a parent or guardian. It was this revised version of the law upon which the Supreme Court agreed (in 1961) to rule.[34]

The second case involved a Baltimore Board of School Commissioners rule requiring the city's schools to begin each day by reading (without comment) a chapter in the Holy Bible or the Lord's Prayer. The plaintiff, a professed atheist whose son attended a school in which the Lord's Prayer was read each morning over the intercommunications system, contended that the rule threatened her and her son's religious liberty by "placing a premium on belief as against nonbelief," and that it subjected their "freedom of conscience to the rule of the majority."[35]

On June 18, 1963—nearly two years after the Pennsylvania case was submitted—the Court handed down its decision. Both laws, it ruled (8–1), were unconstitutional. The majority opinion, written by Justice Clark, focused on the feeling of the Court that the Free Exercise Clause "has never meant that a majority could use the machinery of the state to practice its beliefs." That, it said, was the effect of the laws in question, and to adhere to the elusive line separating the secular from the sectarian

---

[33] *Engle v. Vitale,* 370 U.S. 421 (1962).

[34] *Abington Township School District v. Schemp,* 373 U.S. 203 (1963).

[35] *Murray v. Curlett,* 373 U.S. 203 (1963).

in American life, the state must be "firmly committed to a position of neutrality."

Public reaction to the 1963 ruling was vociferous. The ruling was, after all, a "defeat" for the Christian majority who might be expected to favor Bible readings and prayer in the schools. Evangelist Billy Graham, a staunch member of that majority, asked perhaps rhetorically "Why should the majority be so severely penalized by the protests of a handful?"[36]

If the Prayer Decisions did not fully answer that question, they nevertheless continue to loom large in educational policy-making. For the present at least, they have shifted the balance of legal opinion back toward a relatively strict separation of Church and state. Furthermore, they have insulated more thoroughly than before the minority groups (Unitarians, Jews, Moslems, atheists, and others) who are concerned lest religious instruction be tantamount to indoctrination in the religious beliefs of the dominant Christian groups within our society. Finally, for Congress, in its considerations of federal aid to education, the decisions erected a barrier to using federal funds to support sectarian schools.

On the issue of public support for sectarian schools, the Supreme Court has tendered two decisions, which, when compared, offer two conflicting views of the permissible relations between government and church schools. One case, decided in 1947 (and which by its age may no longer represent the views of the present Court personnel) held it legal for the State of New Jersey to reimburse parents whose children attended parochial schools for the cost of transportation to and from those schools. In handing down its decision, the Court spoke of respecting the argument whereby government may not favor one religious group over others, but it suggested that in the immediate case the payments went in support of the school child and not his church.[37]

A more recent case, however, has upheld the ruling of the Vermont Supreme Court that state tuition payments to a church school violate the Federal Constitution. The case arose from a Vermont law requiring every school district either to maintain a high school or, if it does not, to pay tuition costs to private schools. In consequence, one school district that had no high school enrolled its students at Roman Catholic schools and paid the necessary tuition. And even though children being supported by public funds at these schools were excused from religious instruction there, the court held that here was commingling beyond the bounds of the Constitution.[38]

Taken together, these decisions give Congress an uneven wall against which to lean: they might give Congress incentive to provide loans to

---

[36] Quoted in *Congressional Quarterly Weekly Report*, No. 25, June 21, 1963, p. 1002.

[37] *Everson v. Board of Education (of Ewing Township)*, 330 U.S. 1 (1947).

[38] *Anderson v. Swart* (# 856) 366 U.S. 925 (1961).

parochial schools on grounds that such support aids the child not the school. Or, contrariwise, they might stay the hand of Congress on grounds that any support is essentially church support. But to see these matters in fuller perspective, we turn now to the issue of federal aid to education.

Federal Aid to Education

Patterns of federal aid.   Although it is common to speak of federal aid to education as an issue for present and future legislation, commonplace speech here is deceiving; for the federal government has long been engaged in this very form of educational aid. Its first forms extend back before the present Constitution was ratified; and one of its benchmarks in the nineteenth century was the Morrill Act of 1862 under whose terms the states were encouraged to establish colleges whose leading object "shall be, without excluding other scientific and classical studies . . . to teach such branches of learning as are related to agriculture and the mechanic arts."

In the present century, federal aid has broadened enormously to include such things as: grants to aid vocational and home economics training in the high schools, loans to colleges for building dormitories and for the purchase of equipment to improve the teaching of science and mathematics, grants to the states for the purchase of food for school-lunch programs, and the "GI Bills" of World War II, the Korean War, and the Vietnam conflict, under whose terms (or those of related laws) well over eight million veterans have or will receive some form of educational training.

Clearly, the federal government is no stranger to the educational enterprise; and if we persist in referring to federal aid as a contemporaneously explosive issue it is because the aid that is currently being administered or contemplated by the federal government is of such scope and touches all levels of public education so directly that the traditional state monopoly over education is severely challenged.

Federal aid is thus embroiled in a traditionally sensitive area of American politics, *states rights*; and in attempting to deaden that sensitivity, it is understandable that contemporary legislation attempts to build upon fairly traditional ideas and techniques. In passing such legislation, Congress follows a familiar path: achieving radical ends by employing familiar (and thus "conservative") forms.

The most basic of these familiar forms is the use of a system of grants-in-aid, comparable to the foundation programs of the states, under which the federal government fulfills the traditional function of the higher level of government: that of using its superior wealth and fund-raising powers to underwrite the educational costs of lower government levels. In the fashion of foundation programs, federal aid has been aimed at ensuring a uniform and minimum level of education throughout the country by requiring (in essence) that the wealthier sections of the country help support the poorer. To justify this redistributive function, the argument used with mounting frequency is that government support of education is an investment in the individual for the benefit of the entire nation, and not merely for those who live in a particular local area or region.

Again, in the realm of the familiar, recent federal aid legislation has stepped up the pattern (set, for example, by the Smith-Hughes Act) of using the persuasive power of money to help solve a series of specific problems related, directly or indirectly, to the educational process. Thus, since 1940, school aid has been directed at "impacted areas" where tax-exempt federal installations have placed burdens on the local school systems. To ease the teacher shortage, the federal government offers scholarships and loans to college students who are considering teaching careers in a variety of (needed) fields. Most recently, the "discovery" of poverty amidst affluence in the United States has offered a justification and problem-oriented goal for the allocation of federal funds to states and local districts. Beyond a mere justification, however, "poverty" has also provided the basis for a distribution formula that has eased the resentment of wealthy urban areas at the prospect of becoming the mainstay of rural education by enabling these urban centers themselves to qualify for large amounts of federal funds.

Finally, to complete this checklist of the familiar, recently approved programs of federal aid have brought renewed attention to the question of support for parochial schools and a new sounding of the wall of separation between church and state.

To turn from generalizations concerning palimpsest to palimpsest itself, we will conclude this essay by scanning in greater detail the development of federal aid legislation from 1961 to 1965—a period during which major trends in the scope and style of federal participation in education were firmly, if not irreversibly, set.

The education proposals of 1961–1963. When the education bill of 1961 was breathed into life by a special presidential message to Congress, many saw it as the mold from which all future education bills would be cast. In that message, President Kennedy—attempting to redeem a portion of his campaign pledges of the previous year—spoke of twin national goals: "A new standard of excellence in education and the availability of such excellence to all who are willing and able to pursue it." To achieve these goals, the President called first for an extension of federal programs now aiding our colleges: scholarships to deserving students, and loans for classroom and dormitory construction. Second, and far more controversial, he proposed a program of massive federal aid to primary and secondary education. Under the terms of his proposal, Congress was being asked to appropriate $2.3 billion (over a three-year period) to be used by the states for boosting teacher's salaries and for classroom construction. This money was to be apportioned among the states in grants to equal at least $15 per school child, and in addition—in an attempt to equalize education throughout the nation—states were to receive additional sums on the basis of per capita income within the state. Poorest states were to receive the greatest aid; wealthier states proportionately less. Thus, under the equalization formula, Mississippi would receive $29.67 per pupil, while Illinois and New York (at the other end of the scale) would receive only $15.00 per pupil.

As might be expected, these proposals touched off considerable controversy both inside and outside the Congress. Four issues, however, came to the forefront of the controversy and remained there to harass the proposals on their journey through the legislature.

First, came renewed expression of congressional fear that disbursement of federal funds would result in expanding the powers of the federal bureaucracy, most especially of the Department of Health, Education and Welfare; and that expanded policy-making powers of federal officers would constitute another in a long line of invasions into state control over public policy.

Second, came objection to the payment of teachers' salaries on grounds that such payment might eventually lead to a system of national "thought control," or, if not that, at least congressional meddling into what it is that teachers may do and say in the classroom.

Third, came the concerns of southern Congressmen that northern liberals would attempt to build into the program requirements that only desegregated schools could receive federal funds. Southern Congressmen wanted no additional leverage to be used against them in their fight to maintain school segregation; and they foresaw just such leverage as the bill went into the House Education Committee headed by Harlem Congressman Adam Powell.

And fourth, came objections that were to prove most lethal of all, those that took the President's proposals to task because they contained no provision for aid to church schools. The President's message had, in fact, considered and rejected aid to parochial schools, saying that any payment of parochial school salaries or grants for parochial school construction would clearly violate the prohibitions of the Constitution. For a variety of politically potent reasons, however, the President's argument was not sufficient to still the church-school controversy:

First, although federal aid to sectarian schools would, in principle, be open to all religious groups, far and away the largest benefits would fall to the schools of the Roman Catholic Church—for they account for over 90 per cent of all sectarian schools and have an enrollment of about six million. Second, Roman Catholics are by far the largest religious minority in the country (if it be permissible to label a church with upwards of forty-five million members a minority). From their numbers and from the hierarchical organization of their Church, Catholics possess considerable political power in Congress—a power that is further enhanced by the concentration of Catholics in the northern urban areas of the country and the subsequent existence of congressional constituencies (especially in the lower house) that are overwhelmingly Catholic in population. Thus, the Catholic viewpoint is not easily smothered in Congress; and even before the President's message was delivered, Catholic sentiment was being marshalled and laid before the nation.

Francis Cardinal Spellman, Archbishop of New York, called for the inclusion of parochial and private schools in any federal aid for education, saying, in part, "I am still opposed to any program of federal aid that would penalize a multitude of America's children because their parents choose to exercise their constitutional right to educate them in accordance with their beliefs."[39] Other Catholic spokesmen reiterated the theme of aiding the child and not the school; and still others suggested that the wall of separation was, in reality, only a crude political club: for Congress, when it so wished, had given aid to sectarian schools in a great variety of programs, from loans for college dormitory construction, to school lunch programs, to tuition payments for veterans attending schools under the "G.I." bills.

Thus, the President's proposals moved into the legislative chambers, saddled with a variety of potent objections.

In the Senate, after beating back civil rights riders (that would have withdrawn federal aid to segregated school systems) the bill was passed much in accordance with the substance of the President's proposal. Out of deference to states rights, however, provision was made for a guarantee that, in administering the program, no federal agency or employee "may exercise any direction, supervision, or control over the policy determination, personnel, curriculum, program of instruction, of administration, or operation of any school or school system." And in the debate over equalization, the Senate altered the formula to provide that the lowest income state would receive three times as much per school child as the highest income state.

In the House, however, the bill's passage was far more tempestuous. As reported out by the House Committee on Education and as placed on the calendar of the Rules Committee, the House bill again followed the substance of Presidential recommendations, arriving, however, at an equalization formula somewhat different than the Senate's and setting the minimum state allotment at $12 per school child.

But even as the bill was moving through the House, its opponents were combining forces and strategies to defeat it. Supporters of parochial aid had introduced a measure designed to authorize low interest construction

---

[39] The Cardinal's statement was carried in *The New York Times* for January 18, 1961.

loans to church schools; and Southern Democrats issued warnings that the Kennedy Administration, by its actions elsewhere, had demonstrated that it would use federal aid to control education and force desegregation upon the public schools.

The House Rules Committee, though it had the bill on calendar, refused to release it for the debate that precedes any passage. Two members of the Rules Committee (Delaney of Queens, New York, and O'Neil of Massachusetts) were frank in their support of aid to parochial education, and withheld their votes for release until the education bill might be paired with a bill authorizing church school loans and sent in tandem with that bill to the House floor. Southerners on the committee also withheld their votes, reflecting the views of the Committee's Chairman (Smith of Virginia) who had already made his opposition to the bill known through a broadside letter dispatched to one hundred or so southern newspapers.[40]

Thus, the House waited for Rules to act; talk was heard of the House invoking special proceedings to pull the bill from the Rules Committee, but there was insufficient support for such procedure. Time ticked on; and the bill eventually died, stillborn in the Rules Committee.

The 1962 congressional school aid fight was essentially a repeat of 1961. With bitterness still running high from the 1961 battle, neither the administration nor the Congress was anxious to push very hard for passage of a program. As a result, nearly all the Administration's bills, including requests for grants to provide for public school construction and teachers' salaries (left over from the ill-fated 1961 bill), died again in the House Rules Committee. Despite this obvious unwillingness of the Congress to act on his education proposals, President Kennedy continued to send a steady stream of new proposals to the Hill (including 1962 requests for grants to improve the quality of teaching, to combat adult illiteracy, and to provide special training for handicapped children), which prompted some Congressmen to complain that the Administration was flooding them with bills among which there were no established priorities.

In an attempt to revamp and consolidate his education proposals, the President drafted the National Education Improvement Act of 1963. While the Congress refused to act on the bill as a single omnibus package, by the end of 1963 it had effected a major about-face by passing nineteen out of forty-seven specific proposals authorizing more than $2 billion for federal aid to education. In addition, it approved the Higher Education Facilities Act of 1963 which authorized a five-year program of federal grants and loans totalling almost $1.2 billion for construction and improvement of public and private higher education facilities.

In contrast to these major concessions, however, the "Education Congress of 1963" (as President Johnson later referred to it) still refused to

---

40 See *The New York Times* for June 16, 1961.

pass the heart of Kennedy's program—general federal aid to elementary and secondary schools. This part of the program, which included a request that the Congress authorize $1.5 billion to aid the states in supplying urgently needed improvements in the public schools and to increase teachers' salaries, continued to be plagued by the church-state controversy.

The education programs of 1964–65. Keyed to President Johnson's early policy of pressing for passage of President Kennedy's unfinished programs, the Congress in 1964 enacted several education measures—an extension of the National Defense Education Act (supplying grants and loans for graduate study), a one-year extension of school aid programs to federally impacted areas, and enactment of a library services bill. All these measures had been requested by President Kennedy as part of his 1963 omnibus bill. Thus, at its own deliberate pace, Congress was moving steadily toward the broad program of federal aid to education originally envisaged by Kennedy in 1961. At the same time, general aid proposals continued to meet strong opposition based upon the same issues and arguments that had undermined the 1961 program. Despite increased congressional appropriations for highly specific kinds of assistance to education, little change had occurred by the end of 1964 to realign the forces opposed to general school aid.

It was this alignment of forces and arguments on the stumbling-block issues that had weakened Kennedy's programs in 1961 and 1963 that was apparently uppermost in President Johnson's mind, and the collective mind of his staff, in the drafting of his Elementary and Secondary Education Act of 1965. To circumvent these areas of dispute and bring about a favorable realignment of forces, the President tied his program to the problem of poverty, to the concept of "impacted areas" (perennially popular in Congress since the first "impacted areas bill" in 1940), and to the idea of aiding *students,* not *schools.* Instead of taking a stand on the "aid to parochial schools" issue (as Kennedy had done in a 1961 Justice Department legal brief which concluded that existing court decisions would prohibit such aid), Johnson largely avoided the issue. It was left to the states to decide (subject to broad regulations set by the U.S. Commissioner of Education) the extent to which aid would be used to benefit private school children. Money requested for the construction of educational service facilities was earmarked for special community educational centers and facilities to which parochial students, as citizens of the community, could have access outside their parochial school classrooms.

By focusing on aid to students instead of aid to schools, the President effectively undercut many of the arguments on both sides of the church-state dispute. To enhance the palatability of his program for congressional consumption, he reversed the precedent set by Eisenhower and Kennedy's unsuccessful attempts to reduce school aid to areas "impacted" by large numbers of children of workers at federal installations. Instead, he expanded the very concept of the "impacted area" to include states and school districts "impacted" by large numbers of low income families. This strategy offered the additional advantages of increasing the number of Congressmen whose districts would benefit from the program, and of complying with congressional insistence that school aid be aimed at a specific national problem beyond better education for its own sake. Coupled with the concept of aid to the student, the "poverty" orientation presented education as a problem that affects not only isolated individuals and school districts, but also the entire nation, its economy, and its security.

In effect, passage of the 1965 program broke the last barrier to general federal aid to education by authorizing grants to about 95 per cent of the nation's counties. Over a billion dollars of the $1.3 billion cost of the program in its first year was earmarked for school districts with large numbers of children from families on public relief or with annual incomes under $2000. These funds could be used in any way local districts would decide to use them (subject to approval by state and federal educational agencies). In addition, funds were provided in the program for textbooks, library materials, and community-wide educational centers and services.

The major role allocated to the states in the 1965 program is significant. Not only are grants made to the states, leaving with state agencies the responsibility for making allocation decisions; additional funds also are provided to strengthen the state educational agencies themselves. Because of its position at the nexus of local and national perspectives, the state continues to be the principal contribution and controller of education in terms both of money and ideas. The role of the Federal government is to suggest national standards "at least to the extent of guidelines" but not to the point of "uniform policy direction."[41]

Thus, massive federal aid to education has come to the American polity under terms of an emerging federal-state educational partnership. But the partnership remains both flexible and uncertain. The potential use of economic sanctions by the federal government to exert its influence on state policies promises to be the critical factor in future educational politics. Already, threats have been issued to suspend federal funds to numerous school districts in the South, as well as in several northern cities, where satisfactory plans for desegregation of public schools have not been submitted to the federal government (as required by the 1964 Civil Rights Act) or where accusations of *de facto* racial segregation have cast doubt upon compliance with the law that school districts receiving federal funds not practice racial segregation.

---

[41] The prescription of the "role of the states" panel of the 1965 White House Conference on Education (the first such conference held since 1955), as expressed by Chairman Terry Sanford (former Democratic Governor of North Carolina), quoted in the *Congressional Quarterly*, 33, August 13, 1965, p. 1613.

Finally, the federal formula for the allocation of funds to the states, and the *amounts* of funds themselves, are subject to annual congressional review and revision. So, while it appears that the federal interest in education is firmly legitimized and that federal aid to education is here to stay, the political struggle continues. With the federal government firmly committed to providing extensive general aid to American students, the political struggle focuses increasingly upon refinements in that policy.

BIBLIOGRAPHICAL NOTE

General surveys of American education, its features and problems are to be found in: George Z. F. Bereday and Luigi Volpicelli, *Public Education in America*, 1958; I. L. Kandel, *American Education in the Twentieth Century*, 1957; Martin Mayer, *The Schools*, 1961.

Critical reflections of the professor who is not himself part of the teacher's college enterprise are found in: Jacques Barzun, *Teacher in America*, 1945; Max Lerner, *America as a Civilization*, 1957, "The Higher and Lower Learning"; David Riesman, *Constraint and Variety in American Education*, 1956.

For the substance and flavor of the controversy over schools see: John Keats, *Schools Without Scholars*, 1958; Mortimer Smith, *The Public Schools in Crisis*, 1956; Arthur Bestor, *The Retreat from Learning in Our Public Schools*, 1955.

On the goals for and challenges to American Education: Rockefeller Brothers Fund, Special Project, Report V, *The Pursuit of Excellence*, 1958; The President's Commission of National Goals, *Goals for Americans*, 1960; The President's Commission on Higher Education, *Second Report to the President*, 1957; James B. Conant, *Education in a Divided World*, 1948. For a well-documented summary of the arguments in defense of the need for massive federal intervention in education by a former U.S. Commissioner of Education see Francis Keppel, *The Necessary Revolution in American Education*, 1966.

On school board politics, pressure group activity, censorship in the schools, etc., see: Ernest O. Melby, *American Education under Fire*, 1951; Ernest O. Melby and Morton Pruner, *Freedom and Public Education*, 1953; David Hubbard, *This Happened in Pasadena*, 1951; Neal Gross, *Who Runs Our Schools?*, 1958; Keith Goldhammer, *The School Board*, 1964; Robert S. Cahill and Stephen Hencley, eds., *The Politics of Education*, 1964.

For descriptions of schools and their politics in specific social settings see: Robert C. Wood, *Suburbia*, 1959; and Arthur Vidich and Joseph Bensman, *Small Town in Mass Society*, 1960 (Anchor). Joseph Pois, *School Board Crisis: A Chicago Case Study*, 1964.

For specific issues and problems see: The American Assembly of Columbia University, *The Federal Government and Higher Education*,

1960; The Committee for Economic Development, *Paying for Better Public Schools*, 1960; and a wealth of research publications issued by the U.S. Office of Education: for example, *Local Boards of Education*, Bulletin 13, 1957; *School District Reorganization*, Special Series No. 5, 1957; *The State and Education*, Misc. No. 23, 1958. Recent research includes the American Association of School Administrators, *School District Organization: Journey That Must Not End*, 1962; Archie R. Dykes, *School Board and Superintendent: Their Effective Working Relationships*, 1965; and Mortimer Smith, *A Citizen's Manual for Public Schools*, 1965.

government
and
civil rights

LAWRENCE J. R. HERSON
and
R. Roger Majak

Civil rights in America blends the legacy of history with the politics of today.[1] Constitutional framers, legislators, judges, policemen, and private citizens have all helped shape our liberties and freedoms. Accordingly, the present chapter will attempt to view the impact of these groups upon civil rights by examining: 1) the relationship of civil rights to democracy itself, 2) the connection between civil rights and the pattern of American constitutions, 3) the impact upon civil rights of legislative, judicial and police processes of government, and 4) the consequences for civil rights of a range of contemporary political issues. In essence, this chapter will move from constitutional theory to contemporary politics; and to set the stage for discussion, we begin by examining the *dual nature* of civil rights within our system of government.

CIVIL RIGHTS AND DEMOCRACY

Similar to the other subjects considered in this book, civil rights can be viewed as a product of the governmental process, an outcome of the governmental will. Thus, when the legisla-

---

[1] Civil rights will be used here as a general term, denoting those rights also called civil liberties. More technically speaking, civil liberties generally refers to such rights as are included in the first three amendments to the Federal Constitution (freedom of speech, press, etc.), while civil rights generally refers to the equality requirements of the Thirteenth, Fourteenth and Fifteenth Amendments and to "fair trial" requirements such as those contained in Amendments Four to Eight.

ture passes a law forbidding discrimination in public housing, the ensuing right emerges as a product of government and is subject, therefore, to all the pressures, conflict, and politics inherent in any governmental decision. But civil rights are more than a product of government. They are also an essential characteristic of democracy and in this sense they are an *attribute of democracy*, one of its identifying hallmarks.

To make this attributive aspect of civil rights clearer, it would be useful to stretch our imagination to a time when government is not much concerned with things such as old age pensions, housing, economic regulation and the like. Such, indeed, approximates the actual state of governmental affairs in the United States not more than three or four decades ago. And yet, if we assume that democracy, roughly put, is a system of government that acts upon the demands of the greatest portion of society; and if we further assume that society is not much concerned with social security or housing, then it is perfectly valid to conclude that lack of government action in these areas is perfectly consistent with democracy. Or, conversely put, a democratic government need not concern itself with housing, pensions, and the like.

Now take by way of contrast this matter of civil rights. Let us suppose an instance in which the government, again responding to the wishes of its citizens, decides to repress freedom of speech. There would be in many minds grave doubts as to the democratic qualities of that government, for in those minds free speech is an essential characteristic of democracy. Without free speech, it can well be argued, democracy is no more.

It may be, of course, that repression of one right or freedom might not constitute sufficient grounds for reading a government out of the democratic ranks. But, at the same time, there is little doubt that if a government proceeded systematically to destroy all freedoms, then that government would cease to operate as a democracy. Thus the point to be made here is simply that civil rights constitute both a *product* of democratic government and also one of its *essential characteristics*. Accordingly, our first concern in making this canvass will be with the attributive phase of the civil-rights duality: the relationship between these rights and democracy itself.

THE COMPONENTS OF DEMOCRACY

Metaphorically speaking, it is almost as easy to kill an elephant with a slingshot as it is to define democracy with a single sentence. Lincoln, perhaps, came closest to accomplishing this feat in the sonorous closing line of his Gettysburg Address. But even there, the idea of a "government of the people, by the people and for the people" does not so much define democracy as it sums up its underlying ideas and calls attention to the fact that, in the last say, democracy involves a *process*, a method of governmental action.

Process, of course, invokes activity and operation, and when we look to the center of the democratic operation, we find that its motive force is provided by a single social commitment: that the activities of government shall reflect the wishes and desires of the greatest number in the society. But for government to reflect and carry out these wishes there must also exist some device for determining what these wishes are and for determining what constitutes the greatest number in the society. And at this point, we become aware of two very remarkable social inventions that constitute the vital linkages of democracy. The first of these inventions is the *election*, for it is the show of hands and the counting of ballots that give the society a device for scheduling and measuring the preferences of its members. And the second of these inventions is a formula for ascertaining with some precision the wishes of the greatest number. This formula is expressed in terms of the *majority* (one half plus one, of the total number voting); and with these parts in place it thus becomes possible to speak of democracy as a system of government operating according to the principle of majority rule.

However democracy involves ingredients other than majority rule and their presence serves not only to thicken the democratic broth but to complicate the definitional process. Briefly put, civil rights are these other ingredients of democracy and to explain their importance to democracy it is necessary to look to the purposes of majority rule.

The Purposes of
Majority Rule

It might first be noted that majority rule is not an end in itself, but merely a device for achieving more important purposes: that of permitting the members of a democratic society to control their government, to bend governmental power to their demands, to create governmental decisions in their own image. In a word, majority rule is a technique through which the members of a society decide what government is to do about each one of a never-ending series of social questions and problems. As each new problem is solved, as each new social demand is met, it is majority rule that determines the form of the solution, and consequently, the majority rules, not once, but through a never ending series of vote tallies. In these terms, there is not one majority and its rule, but a new majority created for every vote taken and for every problem to be solved. Thus, democracy might be described as a system of majorities in flux, and it is in the protection of the process by which new majorities are constructed that civil rights assume their true importance.

To understand this importance, it is necessary to speak briefly about the ideas and premises that underlie majority rule itself. For a society to commit itself to rule by the greatest number implies, first of all, that the society has faith in the collective wisdom of its members. This faith, in turn, rests upon the idea that men will have knowledge of the issues before them. And if men are to have this knowledge, upon which they will base their judgment and eventually their vote, then it is necessary that they have access to information about those issues.

Second, if majority rule is to prevail, it must be understood that all men have equal access to the voting out of which a majority will be tallied. Anything other than equality of voting will produce rule by less than the majority (that is, by a *minority*) thus breaking the system, even before it begins.

And third, if men are to participate equally in voting and if they are to bring their best judgment to bear upon the issue at hand, they must be protected against being punished for their vote or for expressing their ideas upon the issue with which they are concerned.

Now, when we reassemble this chain of premises we find that civil rights constitute its welding force. For men to acquire the knowledge upon which their vote will rest, it is necessary that all men have the right to communicate freely about the problems that confront the society. Free speech, free press, free conscience—these are the liberties that the individual must enjoy if majority rule is to achieve its own ultimate purposes. For men to have equal access to the vote, it is necessary that liberty of the ballot be guaranteed; and for the individual to be free from the threat of punishment for his voting and communicating, it is necessary that the government's powers of punishment be carefully confined to acts outside the realm of political participation. And for this purpose, it is necessary that there be established a code of law and justice specifying most carefully the nature of crime, punishment, and the process by which guilt is established. For if this code is not established, it then becomes possible to stretch the meaning of crime, to increase the degree of punishment, and to relax the standards of establishing guilt in a fashion so as to intimidate those who join in the process of unseating old majorities and bringing new ones in to rule.

Thus, it is civil rights that provide the motive force behind democracy's basic process of majority rule. They make it possible for the society to remedy an unsolved problem or a previously solved problem for which a new majority creates a new solution. In essence, these *remedial rights* make it possible for majority rule to continue operation. Without them, continuing majority rule (a system of majorities in flux) would simply not be possible. As a consequence, our definition of democracy must now be broadened to denote a system that provides for *both* civil rights and majority rule. And at this point, we have reinforced our original contention that civil rights constitute a significant characteristic, or attribute, of democracy. Before we can lay to rest our definition, there is one further problem that needs to be explored. It concerns still another aspect of the relationship between majority rule and civil rights; and out of this relationship, in fact, has come the constitutional structure that we are soon to examine.

THE CONFLICT BETWEEN MAJORITY RULE AND CIVIL RIGHTS

Although civil rights and majority rule are the building blocks of democracy, these elements are not easily bound within a single system. In logic and practice, these principles are not harmonious, and every democratic system exhibits the stresses and strains that result from fusing these elements into a single whole.

Majority Rule as an Example

To illustrate this disharmony, take the principle that governmental power is to rest in the hands of the majority. Suppose, for example, that the majority were to decide that the "best interests of the nation" required that advocacy of vegetarianism be punished as a criminal act and that persons accused of this advocacy be denied the right to public trial. Those affected by this majority ruling (call them for the moment, a minority) would accordingly be stripped of two of democracy's fundamental freedoms: the right to communicate freely concerning beliefs that they espouse, and the right to trial procedures within the meaning of "due process of law." At this moment, and for this minority, democracy would cease to exist.

Picture, by way of contrast, another ending to this conflict between majority demands and minority rights. Suppose the hand of the majority were stayed from action and the rights of the minority were upheld. At this moment, the minority would triumph over the demands of the majority, resulting in a situation of rule by the minority—presumably, and once again, the antithesis of democratic government.

Examples of this conflict of principles stud the history of our government; they include the sedition acts of 1798, the sedition and criminal-anarchy statutes passed both by Congress and several state legislatures during World War I, and the more recent anti-communist laws, which (among other things) make it a crime to advocate knowingly the overthrow of government by force or violence, or to aid any organization engaged in such advocacy.

Included in these examples of conflicting principles is the bundling off to concentration camps during World War II of some 112,000 Japanese of whom 70,000 were American citizens. These people were accused of no crime and were guilty of nothing other than the fact that their heritage constituted a supposed threat to the nation's wartime safety. Also included in the examples are the various acts of local majorities in our southern states whose total effect has been to deny Negroes access to the ballot box.

In each of these instances (and the list is merely illustrative, not exhaustive) majority demands have been pressed home and civil rights (minority rights) have been lost. And yet however one may disagree with these majority demands, it is difficult to deny that the problem the majority was attempting to solve was, in the majority's eyes, a crucial one. The survival of a nation, of a culture, a way of life, is the justification that threads these acts together, and those who side with the majority must realize that however justified, each of these acts buries democracy by burying its civil rights principle.

Those who oppose the majority, however, are also in difficult straits, for they lay themselves open to a series of sharp challenges: Is majority rule that smothers civil rights never justified? If it is justified in instances involving the survival of the community, who is better qualified than the majority to define the steps necessary for that survival? Is it better to "protect a right" or to lose the system? And, if the answer is, "lose the system," should not the majority be the judge of so momentous a question?

No easy answer can be given these questions, for any answer reveals that when majority-rule and civil rights conflict, one of democracy's basic principles must be elevated to a position of superiority over the other. Ideally, of course, the way to avoid this elevation is to prevent any clash between these principles. But sooner or later, given a truly significant issue and given the disharmony of these principles, conflict is bound to arise.

Majoritarians Versus Libertarians

To help our society thread its way through such conflict, a series of writers have dissected and sought solutions to this basic problem. In situations of conflict, one group of political theorists (the majoritarians) would have us abide by the wishes of the majority; for these writers generally argue that the ultimate function of a government is to solve society's problems and that in a democracy any resulting action must accord with the preferences of the majority. These writers recognize the importance of civil rights and they further recognize that the healthier the democracy, the greater its concern for those rights. But, say these writers, the majority must be supreme and the freedoms accorded the individual must be regarded not as rights that are immune from majority control, but rather as privileges that the majority bestows upon the members of the society, in order to further the goals of the society—as the majority defines those goals.

An opposing group (the libertarians) generally recognizes that in the history of democracy, determined majorities nearly always get their way. Such success, however, does not clothe majority action with moral correctness; for the defenders of civil rights argue that though the function of government is to act, the highest duty of democratic government is to preserve democracy. If necessary, non-action is preferable to government action, for democracy cannot be preserved when basic freedoms are suppressed. Moreover, if democracy is to be true to its principles, such freedoms must be regarded as rights and not as privileges that can be bestowed or destroyed by majority action.

But however much these writers divide on their solution, each camp links itself to our constitutional tradition, for the American constitutions, both federal and state, were created in large measure to solve this very problem of clashing democratic principles. What the constitution framers did, in fact, was to recognize the necessity for majority rule; but in order to prevent that rule from smothering liberty and freedom, they weighted the scales of government in favor of civil rights. Basically, majorities were to be permitted to rule, but only within a set of barriers that afforded special protections for civil rights. By building these special protections into our constitutions, the framers hoped to solve the problem of clashing principles; and in so doing, they established civil rights as a basic fixture (an attribute) of our governmental system.

CIVIL RIGHTS AND THE AMERICAN CONSTITUTIONS

Although the fifty-one American constitutions are complex documents, their over-all purpose is fairly simple to define; for their basic goal is to place permanent limitations upon the powers of government. And, since government in the American system belongs to whatever majority can capture it, our constitutions may be defined as a system of permanent limitations upon majority action, a hobble affixed to majority rule.

Basically, these constitutions construct their network of limitations on two levels. On the first level, through outright prohibition, they attempt to place a great range of affairs forever beyond majority reach. For example, in the national constitution, state governments (that is, state majorities) are denied the power to raise armies, to lay and collect import duties, and so on. More important to this discussion is the list of prohibitions upon the national government pertaining to civil rights: Congress shall pass no law abridging free speech, press, and so forth.

On the second level, the limitations upon majorities are not direct, but indirect; for the limitations upon majority rule are constructed out of the groups into which the constitutions divide the body politic. Through the twin principles of separation of power and check and balance, groups are set apart, and played off, each against the others. In order to catch hold of governmental power, these divided, separated groups must overcome their division and fuse into a majority. Such fusion generally involves caution, compromise, and bargaining between interested groups. As a result, majority-sway over contentious issues is made difficult, and in this fashion additional safeguards are built around such protected areas as civil rights. But to see more clearly these civil rights protections, it is now necessary to treat more fully these two levels of constitutional limitations.

Civil Rights and Constitutional Prohibitions

Fortunately for the student of American politics, the broad pattern of both state and federal government is much the same. In part, this sameness arises our of the shared belief system of the American people, and in part this sameness can be traced to the similarity of the fifty-one American constitutions. Each constitution is built around the principle of separation of powers, and each constitution has a similar declaration of civil rights. Thus, for simplicity's sake, the following analysis will be drawn largely from the Federal Constitution.

In providing for civil rights, the fifty-one constitutions have sought to wall out the majority by building an injunctive fence around each of a series of liberties and freedoms. But where most state constitutions set their prohibitions upon majority action *within* the body of the constitution, the Federal Constitution is distinguished by the fact that most of its civil rights protections are contained in the *amendments* to the original document. One explanation for this placement is that the framers of the Constitution thought they were building a government of specified, enumerated powers; and since the Constitution did not authorize the central government to abridge civil rights, no further statement of protections for these rights was thought to be needed. Opposition to the omission of these protections was so great, however, that they were appended to the Constitution within two years of its ratification. This appended statement of civil rights comprises the first ten Amendments to the Constitution, the national government's Bill of Rights. In these ten amendments, in five others (Thirteenth, Fourteenth, Fifteenth, Nineteenth, and Twenty-fourth Amendments), and in a few short sentences in the original document, are contained the basic constitutional prohibitions against an abridgement of civil rights.

These prohibitions group themselves into the categories of democracy's essential freedoms: freedom of thought and communication, equal access to the ballot box, and the freedoms gained through a rigidly defined code of justice. Basically, the Constitution's prohibitions take the form of a denial of power to the chief instrument of majority rule, Congress, constitutionally the architect of public policy. Thus, in the First Amendment, whose very priority is an indication of its essentiality, comes the denial to government of the power to make any law "respecting an establishment of religion, or prohibiting the free exercise thereof; or abridging the freedom of speech, or of the press, or the right of the people peaceably to assemble, and to petition the Government for a redress of grievances."

In the Fourth through the Eighth Amendments requirements for a system of justice are delineated. The Fourth Amendment forbids "unreasonable searches and seizures" and speaks of the "right of the people to be secure in their persons, house, papers and effects." The Fifth Amendment lays down the rights that shall be accorded those accused of crime: no call to trial without a prior indictment by a Grand Jury, no "double jeopardy," no denial of the traditional procedures of the law ("due process of law"), and no self-incrimination. The Sixth Amendment extends these rights to a "speedy and public trial, by an impartial jury" and gives the accused the right to know the charges being brought against him, the right to confront the witnesses against him, and the right to "a compulsory process for obtaining witnesses in his favor." The Eighth Amendment states that "Excessive bail shall not be required, nor excessive fines imposed, nor cruel and unusual punishments inflicted." And the foregoing rights are augmented by two provisions in the original Constitution (Article III, Section 9) that forbid the suspension of the Writ of Habeas Corpus, except in circumstances of rebellion or invasion; and that forbid legislatures (both national and state) to take on the powers and duties of a court, or to punish vengefully. ("No bill of attainder or ex post facto law shall be passed.")

In the Thirteenth, Fourteenth, Fifteenth, Nineteenth and Twenty-fourth Amendments are stated constitutional injunctions against inequality: the Thirteenth Amendment abolishes slavery and other forms of peonage; the Fourteenth Amendment removes from states ("sectional majorities") the power to abridge citizenship or any of the "privileges and immunities of citizens of the United States," including the right to "life, liberty and property" and "equal protection of the laws"; the Fifteenth Amendment forbids any abridgement of voting rights on account of "race, color or previous condition of servitude"; the Nineteenth Amendment extends the vote to women; and the Twenty-fourth Amendment rounds out these injunctions against inequality by banning the payment of poll taxes as a "qualification" for voting in Federal elections.

Thus, through these enjoinders, the Constitution attempts to keep from the majority the power to abridge democracy's essential freedoms.

Civil Rights and the Dilution of the Majority

Although the American constitutions attempt to guarantee civil rights by wrapping majorities in a net of prohibitions, these guarantees are also reinforced by the structure of government that these constitutions create. In all fifty-one constitutions, the governmental process revolves around the principle of separation of powers. Governmental power is apportioned among the executive, legislative, and judicial branches in order to guard against the possibility that any branch will take onto itself power of such magnitude as to become tyrannical. Concern for the possible tyranny of one branch of government is thus one purpose of separation of powers and its attendant principle of check and balance. A concern for the tyranny of the majority is a second such purpose; for as a result of separation of powers, majority action is discouraged and made difficult. As a consequence, the likelihood is lessened that a majority will overstep the bounds of civil rights enumerated in the Constitution.

This relationship between separated powers and majority restraints proceeds in at least two ways. First, as a result of the separation of powers, the body politic is divided into a patchwork of electing bodies—constituencies—each of which has a representative who answers to the majority within that constituency. Thus, in the national government, the constituency of the President is the country as a whole. (Technically speaking, because of the electoral college, his constituency is a composite of fifty state constituencies, and the majority to whom he must eventually answer is fused out of the majority within each state.) The people of his state are the constituency of each Senator, and that of the Representative a still smaller unit, the congressional district. Each of these constituencies, varying as it does in size, economic activity, traditions, party affiliation, and population characteristics, tends to demand different things of its representative. These demands, in fact, are made still more diffuse by the varying times in which they are put forward, for each "class" of representative seeks his mandate at a different calendar interval: the President every four years, the Senator every six years, and the Representative every two years. Thus, the Constitution breaks the society up into a series of separated and often competing "majorities." It permits not one majority, but only a patchwork of groups competing for political power.

The essential connection between the protection of civil rights and this atomization of power is simply this: for public policy to get made, representatives of these competing groups must fuse themselves into an effective whole. Enough of them must band together in common cause to constitute a majority, the requisite for a capture of governmental power. But for these representatives to weld themselves into a majority, they must compromise and mediate their conflicting demands and, in fact, search out the area of greatest common agreement. This area of greatest agreements is not always readily found, or, more precisely, it is generally found only by watering down a program of action, sometimes to a point of inoffensiveness. In this fashion, majority rule is blunted; and given the concern of a great part of our society for the rights spelled out in the Constitution, and given further their concern not to offend against these rights, a stout yoke is thus fastened upon any potential majority that seeks to destroy these rights.

Checks and Balances

The force of the majority is yoked, however, by more than the creation of competing constituencies. For the constitutions (once again, through the device of separation of powers) do not permit any sort of *direct* majority rule on the part of the society's political representatives. That is, governmental policy is not created merely by forging a majority out of the total and combined membership of the House, Senate, and the Presidency. Instead, as is well known, Senators, Representatives, and the Presidency are grouped into fixed institutions; and for public policy to be made, a majority *within* each of these institutions must concur with a majority within each of the other two. (The President, so to speak, in himself constitutes a majority within his office.) And because each institution has its own traditions, its own outlook, and its own view of what is useful and wise for our society, the resulting inability of these institutions to agree readily upon a course of governmental action constitutes another check against encroachments upon civil rights. And should majorities within these institutions find an area of common agreement, there is still the Supreme Court to be reckoned with. For the constituency of the Court, like that of the President, is the nation as a whole. But unlike the President, its responsibility to the nation is not defined through elections, but (given the life tenure of the justices) through the conscience of the judge. Thus the power of the Court to disallow legislation through judicial review constitutes still another check upon majority rule, and it takes its place as one of a series of institutional hurdles over which any encroachment of civil rights must pass.

To sum up, separation of powers—as a separation of constituencies and institutions—creates a series of barriers that stand between any majority and the abridgement of civil rights. In fashioning these barriers, our constitutions work to establish civil rights as an essential element of our governmental system. And thus, having reinforced the proposition that civil rights are an attribute of our governmental system, our discussion may now move to its second phase, that of viewing these rights as a *product* of that system. But before moving to this discussion, some last comments need to be made about the relative success of separation of powers as a device for protecting civil rights.

A Final Perspective

Separation of powers, to state the obvious, is no sure formula for the suppression of majority tyranny. One test of this proposition is the varying performance of this formula from the federal to the state governments and among the states themselves. For in viewing the incidence of affronts to civil rights in this country, it is difficult not to conclude that the traditional enemy of these rights has been, not the federal government, but the states. Witness the disabling and punitive statutes directed at Orientals by the western states, the legal jostling of the Hispano in the Southwest, the treatment of evangelical religious sects in states such as West Virginia, and, of course, the treatment afforded Negroes in the South.

Majority tyranny that rests upon prejudice is a complex problem, not easily analyzed. But in terms of the present discussion, it seems significant to note first, the obvious conclusion that constitutional patterns have been incapable of blunting the thrusts of determined state majorities; and second, a suggestive hypothesis: that the creation, through separation of powers, of separated constituencies within the state governments does not create the same degree of check and balance as is found in the federal system, perhaps because such check and balance works best when the separated constituencies are marked by a wide measure of heterogeneity. Heterogeneity, in short, creates the competing demands that result in compromise and restraint. In the states, given their limited geographic area, heterogeneity does not exist so markedly as it does in the federal system. And, in fact, the states that are characterized by the majority tyranny referred to above may be the very ones that are generally the most homogeneous.

Of course, the ability of state and local majorities to act as individual decision-makers on a broad range of public affairs is one of the hallmarks of our federal system. And the "grass-roots" democracy entailed in this system of local action is highly valued by our society. But every gain, as Emerson once suggested, has its debit side; and though our society sees positive gain in permitting local majorities to solve local problems, the society is also concerned when these same majorities act to smother civil rights. Thus, there is growing sentiment in this country for removing responsibility for civil rights protection from local to national majorities (from state to federal control); and it is this sentiment that provides—as we shall shortly see—the backdrop for some of the most significant political controversy of our time.

CIVIL RIGHTS AS A
PRODUCT OF GOVERNMENT

Having examined civil rights in relation to the pattern of American constitutions, we turn now to a second important relationship, that between civil rights and the policy-making and policy-enforcing organs of government. Here, we view civil rights as a product of government, for the specific content of these rights is created by legislatures, courts, and executive agencies (especially local police departments). Metaphorically speaking, the constitutions provide a foundation for civil rights, but the usable edifice of these rights is created by the political organs of government. Thus, what we will do here is examine the ways in which the operating branches of government build civil rights upon constitutional foundations; more specifically, our concern is with three basic activities that shape civil rights: first, the ways in which government agencies attempt to give precise meaning to the general constitutional provisions for civil rights; second, the ways in which these agencies extend civil rights clearly beyond those provided for in a constitution; and third, the ways in which government agencies clothe with civil rights the individual members of our society.

Defining Civil Rights

Although nearly every constitution is constructed out of the most precise words available to its framers, every constitution, nevertheless, is a bundle of ambiguities. Words have a way of defying precision of meaning—more accurately put, men will differ in the meaning that they impute to words—and hence one of the most common characteristics of the American system of governments is a never ending debate over the meaning (and therefore, power) of the various provisions of the several constitutions.

For those who assign meaning to constitutions, the range of definitions is almost as broad as man's skill in manipulating words. Certain constitutional provisions, more than others, attract intense argument over meaning. Generally speaking, these are provisions that cut to the heart of the political process and affect the way in which the government is to be carried on or the control that government is to have over its citizenry. Debate upon such matters is sharp, for the groups that win such debate do more than read their own meaning into the Constitution: They ultimately come to bend governmental power to their own ends.

As might be expected, civil rights fall within this category of the controversial provision, and to illustrate the range of definitions available to those who interpret constitutions—mainly, legislatures and courts—let us take the First Amendment to the national Constitution, which reads in part that Congress shall make no law abridging the freedom of speech. Here is forthright expression, and yet even to the casual reader certain difficulties of definition come forward. What things are included in the word speech, and what is meant by "abridging"? To take a simple example: Are the words used in radio broadcasting a form of speech? If so, may radio messages be sent without regulation? Logically, both these questions might be answered in the affirmative; but as Congress and the courts have defined speech, their definition has not included speech that is sent out over the airwaves. No man may build and operate a radio station without express governmental consent, and once that consent is given, he is severely restricted as to what he may say over the air. Thus, as Congress and the courts have dealt with radio broadcasting, they have defined one aspect of speech and one aspect of "abridgement"; accordingly, they have turned general constitutional language into a more precise statement of rights and privileges.

Broadly speaking, the opportunities for choice in defining constitutional terms proceed on two levels. On the first level exists the opportunity for expanding or contracting the coverage of constitutional words. Thus, in the radio illustration used above, Congress might have expanded the category of speech to include radio broadcasting. As it happened, Congress shrank the category to exclude that particular form of communication, and in so doing, was able to subject that communication to rigorous control. To take another example of categorical manipulation, what is meant by the federal Constitution's protection against "unreasonable searches and seizures"? Does a tape recording of a telephone conversation made without the speakers' knowledge constitute an unreasonable search and seizure? Should the recording be admitted as evidence in criminal prosecution? More than this (and here we move to another constitutional concept) would use of the recording constitute a situation in which the accused is being compelled to give testimony against himself?

For the most part, federal courts have expanded these categories of unreasonable search and seizure and evidence against oneself so as to preclude the use of "wire-tapped" evidence in criminal trials. This posture at the national level has been increasingly imposed by the courts on the states, breaking some earlier state tendencies to define these categories so as to admit wire-tapped conversations as valid trial evidence.

Now, the second level of choice-through-definition is woven out of an American tradition of constitutional interpretation which holds that no provision of a constitution stands completely free. Any statement of a right or power must harmonize with other sections of a constitution. Thus, in legislating on radio transmission, Congress felt free to regulate to the point of extinction, because the Federal Constitution also provides that Congress may regulate interstate commerce. By expanding its definition of commerce to include electronic transmission, Congress was thus able to regulate radio messages on grounds other than the privileges of speech. What occurred here was a bringing of two constitutional provisions (commerce and speech) into a kind of harmony. More pointedly, by expanding one category of constitutional provision, Congress was able to deflate a rival category.

In most instances of fixing meaning to civil rights the rivalry of categories is not so specific. All constitutions, either by direct statement or by inference (that is, by interpretation) require that the government provide for the safety, health, and welfare of its citizens. These provisions constitute categories of governmental power susceptible to the broadest sort of expansion: For what, after all, may not be attempted in the interest of public safety? By regarding these categories as rivals of constitutional provisions for civil rights, and by expanding these categories, legislatures and courts have often squeezed to the wall and deflated the scope of civil rights. Through this process, for example, the right to free speech in wartime has been curtailed in the interests of national survival. Again, in the interests of public safety and morals, southern legislatures and courts have required the segregation of the races.

But the process of controlling civil rights through competing categories can also work in the other direction. Categories of public safety and morals have also been deflated to expand the scope of civil rights. In recent years, for example, the Supreme Court has been setting aside arguments that protection of public morals and safety require a segregation of races, and segregated schools have been declared to be a violation of the Fourteenth Amendment's requirement of equality before the law. The significance of competing categories is thus not that they inevitably curtail civil rights, but that in conjunction with defining constitutional terms, they afford vast discretion to the arms of government that decide upon the precise meaning and coverage of civil rights.

Thus, to sum up, constitutional provisions for the protection of civil rights are flasks into which legislatures and courts pour definitional content. In doing so, two further characteristics are given these rights. First, because of the legislative role in defining civil rights, these rights are affected by majority action within legislative bodies, and accordingly, they are tied back once again into the problem of majority-minority relations and the attendant problem of possible majority tyranny. Second, given the number of courts and legislatures in our federal system and given the principle of check and balance by which these bodies are often pitted one against the others, civil rights are in constant flux, always awaiting some newer legislation or court decision that will, for the moment, redefine those rights, and accordingly, tell the citizen the precise nature of his freedoms.

Extending Civil Rights

Although the greatest portion of civil rights is cut directly from constitutional cloth, another portion has come into existence out of *legislative* supplements to our constitutions. Constitutional provisions for civil rights, it will be recalled, are cast largely in the form of prohibitions upon government action. But there is generally thought to be no provision in any American constitution that prevents the legislature from extending the scope of liberty and freedom. Thus what has happened in this country, largely since the turn of the present century, is the growth of an additional body of guarantees, concerned mainly with rights in the *social* and *economic* realms.

Some of these supplemental rights border, of course, upon the provision of the Fourteenth Amendment that no person be denied equal protection of the law nor any of the privileges and immunities of citizens of the United States. Though these clauses might be construed as forbidding racial discrimination in public transportation, in hotel accommodations, and so on, the Supreme Court, for several decades, refused to enter the realm where private ownership and the "public utility" converged. But in the 1940s the Court began expanding the coverage of the amendment, first forbidding discrimination on public carriers moving in interstate commerce, and then on those moving/intrastate. More recently still, the Court has shown signs of broadening the amendment to cover an increasing number of businesses "clothed with the public interest."

An example of rights that are more clearly supplemental to the Constitution consists of the Fair Employment Practices Acts now in effect in several of the states. Under the terms of this legislation, employers, labor unions, and employment agencies are generally forbidden to discriminate against employees as regards race, creed, or national origin.

Supplemental civil rights may be an inapt phrase for these outward extensions, for many persons regard them as requisites to the enjoyment of the more ordinary (politically oriented) civil rights: How may a man participate, such persons ask, in the process of politics, make meaningful decisions with his ballot, or even retain the legal counsel necessary for fullest trial protections if he can find no employment because of his race or social background? And again, of what use is political equality if a man be treated as a second class citizen in the ordinary affairs of life? And finally, how free is free speech if those who hold unpopular views are punished for their ideas by finding the doors of employment closed?

But while our legislatures show an increasing concern for the creation of social and economic rights, legislation in this realm is filled with noteworthy difficulties. First, establishing rights in this realm constitutes a marked departure from the quality and style of the more ordinary civil rights. Those rights, it will be recalled, are established by building around the citizen a wall of protection against the government. Such civil rights are hence maintained by forbidding governmental action, but in this realm of supplemental rights, the protections are afforded the citizen against his *fellow citizens*. As opposed to the more ordinary style of rights, government here is not to be inactive; instead it must act in positive fashion. This positivistic feature in itself invokes caution on the part of legislatures, for positivistic government not only involves complex problems of enforcement, but also a problem as to whether freedom shall be used to nullify freedom.

What is meant by this last problem is simply this: shall one man's freedom be guaranteed by foreclosing another man's freedom to act? Shall an employer lose his right to hire and fire whom he chooses in order to guarantee equal access to employment for all? Shall persons of one racial, religious, or ethnic group be forced to admit to their neighborhood persons with whom they do not desire to associate in order that all men may have equal access to opportunities for housing? Shall a man who professes disturbing ideas be forced upon unwilling coworkers in order that freedom of conscience be given its fullest extent?

These questions admit of no simple answer, for the issue of freedom, in some measure, lies on both sides of the argument. There is a clash here—as there is in nearly all arguments over civil rights—of one meritorious principle versus another. We have seen one aspect of this clash in our discussion of majority rule versus minority rights; and have alluded to another in terms of local decision-making versus the nationalization of protection for civil rights. And here in the matter of freedom versus freedom, we are in the presence of still another clash; as much as our society may prize economic and social equality, it also values another principle, that of freedom of association.

The abrasive quality of this clash between freedoms is well illustrated by the Fair Housing legislation now being considered by Congress and several state legislatures. Having migrated northward, the Negro has settled in Negro sections of many northern cities. These urban areas, economically depressed and already overcrowded, have swelled with the influx of migrants to the point where they have degenerated from urban slums to so-called Negro ghettos. As Negroes have spilled into adjacent neighborhoods, these areas too have become segregated. The whites have not merely admitted Negroes to their neighborhoods, they have fled en masse to new bastions of all-white living—the suburbs. Indeed, the rush of the whites to the suburbs is such that one problem now confronting many Northern cities is the prospect of soon becoming all-Negro centers.

As new urban areas open for Negro settlement, some of the pressure for achieving living space and improved housing is relaxed. But to the Negro seeking equality based on integration with the white community, mere physical expansion of all-Negro areas falls far short of equalitarian goals. As a consequence, pressure continues to mount for legislation that would put an end to separation of races with respect to geographic living areas. Proposed (and, in a few states, accomplished) legislation seeks to outlaw racial discrimination in the renting of housing units, in the selling of residential property, and in the financing of home ownership. Tersely summarized from the viewpoint of the legislation's proponents, the all-white neighborhood (and the all-Negro neighborhood) is to be a thing of the past.

For the urban North, this drive for "open housing" legislation is one of the most dramatic and tension-laden aspects of the process of extending civil rights. The issue will be touched again in later sections dealing with civil rights enforcement and the role of Congress in nationalizing civil rights; but for the moment, let us return to the theme of clashing principles: free association *versus* forced association; freedom of physical movement and the "open access" that characterizes democratic society *versus* the freedom of association that also characterizes democratic enterprise.

As long ago as 1835 a talented French observer of our society, Alexis de Tocqueville, suggested that the ability of American democracy to preserve itself against majority tyranny lay in the presence in our society of self-contained and differing social groups. These, he said, were the pockets of diversity that help thwart the conformity of thought upon which majority tyranny feeds. Traditionally, the forge of this group diversity in American society has been the right of free association and the attendant right to exclude from one's associates (formal or informal) whomever one might choose to exclude. But when that right impinges upon the equally important right to equality and personal dignity, as it does when the right of association is exercised using race as the basis of group cleavage, then compromise and adjustment become necessary.

Compromise and adjustment bring to the fore an obvious point: that the business of civil rights is always unfinished business, and each generation makes necessary adjustments in terms of past experience and ascendant values. In the mid-1960s, the balance is being struck increasingly in favor of those principles that represent an open society; and freedom of association has yielded in the scale of American values to ascendant demands for social equality. The balance, however, has tipped against freedom of association *not* to the point of threatening its role as the foundation of the group basis of American politics, but only to the extent that freedom of association is synonymous with racial separation.

Enforcing Civil Rights

Basically, the *enforcement* of civil rights is a transaction in the realities of political life. For no matter how broad the scope of legislative and court protections, these rights amount to nothing if officers of law enforcement are unwilling to act within the spirit of the law. When police are lax, when jurors are prejudiced, when prosecuting attorneys fear to protect the unpopular, the guarantees of civil rights are lost, for they are simply not enforceable.

Civil rights are created by the democratic society as a buffer that protects the citizen from the jostlings of his government and, to a degree, from the abuse of his fellow men. Paradoxically, enforcement of these rights rests with officers of that government; equally important, enforcement rests largely with *elected* officials, who by virtue of their office are especially sensitive to the currents of community pressure. Thus, the basic problem of civil rights enforcement is how shall respect for civil rights be forced upon those who, in turn, enforce these rights? As Seneca once asked: "Who guards the guardians?"

Ideally, it ought to be community sentiment—alert to the importance of civil rights—that imposes respect for these rights upon law enforcement officers. But for a variety of reasons, such sentiment is never easily marshaled; most often it is never forthcoming. For example, in the ordinary day-to-day processes of law enforcement, public opinion gives only scant attention to the processes of police arrest and prisoner interrogation. Understandably perhaps, the community is more concerned with the prevention and solution of crime than with the civil rights of those arrested. And yet, arrested persons do have civil rights, none being more important than those that prohibit the accused from being forced to testify against himself (the guarantee against self-incrimination).

Our courts have not hesitated in dismissing charges brought as a result of *established* police coercion even though such brutality is difficult to determine. (Who will be witness against the police since they alone are present during prisoner interrogation?) But between proven coercion and the act of simple questioning, there is an area of undefined police activity. The Supreme Court, for example, after hearing a case that involved the forced pumping of a prisoner's stomach (in search for evidence of heroin possession) dismissed that case as being a "shocking" affront to standards of justice and "constitutionally obnoxious."[2] But it condoned, in another case, the drawing of blood from an unconscious suspect in order to obtain proof of drunkenness.[3] To take still other examples, what shall be done regarding a suspect who confesses to crime after being threatened with torture? Or with one who confesses after several days of grilling by police working in relays around the clock so as to wear away his resistance—and quite possibly his ability to differentiate fact from fancy?

---

[2] *Rochin v. Calif.*, 342 U.S. 165 (1952).

[3] *Breithaupt v. Abram*, 352 U.S. 432 (1957).

In the stomach pumping case the Supreme Court spoke of striking down coerced confessions which offend the "community's sense of fair play and decency." While it would be reassuring to report that this community sense is generally sufficient to guide and restrain police action, it is difficult not to conclude that the public is largely indifferent to those rights that lie in the juncture at which police and private citizens meet. As a result, our legal processes have long been overshadowed by a question of important dimensions: what type of police interrogation constitutes permissible crime detection, and at what point, and under what circumstances, does this interrogation become an unconstitutional attempt to force self-incrimination? To clarify this question (and quite likely also because it had despaired of marshaling the community's sense of fair play), the Supreme Court has now moved more fully into the process of defining permissible police practices.

The guarantee against self-incrimination has never been so strictly interpreted as to preclude police questioning of persons suspected of crime. Such interrogation is generally regarded as a necessary part of crime detection and an equally necessary first step in the process of criminal prosecution. But two recent Supreme Court decisions have set severe restraints on police questioning procedures—so severe, some critics argue, that it may become all but impossible for police to elicit confessions or to obtain evidence for the prosecution by questioning suspects.

The first decision ruled inadmissible any evidence against a suspected criminal obtained after having refused him access to legal counsel, or after having failed to tell him of his right to remain silent.[4] This entry of the Court into the back-rooms of police station civil rights raised more questions than it answered, as local police officials struggled to infer from the new ruling some positive indication of how the Court expected them to proceed so that evidence obtained in questioning would be admissible in the courts.

With local police looking increasingly to the nine justices (instead of the public) for *prescriptions*, the Court handed down a second ruling in which it stipulated that the criminal suspect must be informed *before* interrogation of his right to silence and of his right to have legal counsel during interrogation. Finally, the Court prescribed, police must stop questioning any suspect who "indicates in any manner" that he does not want to be interrogated.[5] Thus, the Court has moved boldly into an area of civil rights in which interpretation has long been left to police officials operating frequently behind the closed doors of local precinct stations.

With crime rates reaching all-time high levels in the postwar period, much of the limited public sentiment that is articulated on the subject

---

[4] *Escobedo* v. *Illinois,* 378 U.S. 478 (1964).

[5] *Miranda* v. *Arizona,* 382 U.S. 925 (1966).

tends to give higher priority to obtaining convictions than to protecting the rights of suspects. So, inevitably, the new rulings have come under strong criticism, with sharp division of opinions reflected not only in the narrowness of the Court's decisions (5–4 in both cases), but also in the uncertainty of the experts over what the effects of the rulings will be.

Defenders of the Court's action look to police ingenuity in perfecting new techniques to supplant interrogation as a means of obtaining incriminating evidence. The Federal Bureau of Investigation, they point out, has long operated under self-imposed regulations similar to those prescribed by the Court rulings, depending largely on carefully perfected techniques other than interrogation to achieve its record of successful convictions.

Among the critics, perhaps the most outspoken are local and state prosecutors who fear that the rulings will render impossible the task of obtaining confessions, leaving officials further handicapped in trying to protect the public against crime rates that will climb ever higher. Among the first available bits of concrete evidence on the effects of the new rulings, however, is a study by the District Attorney of Los Angeles County, himself an early critic of the decisions. Of all felony charges brought over a sample three-week period in his county (which bears the largest criminal case load in the country), the study shows, confessions proved essential to successful prosecution in less than 10 per cent of the cases. Furthermore, nearly 55 per cent of the defendants, having been treated in accord with *Miranda* prescriptions and informed of their rights to silence and counsel, confessed anyway.[6] Should the findings of this study be reinforced by other studies showing similar conclusions, the position of the critics will be severely weakened. Otherwise, courts and legislatures will begin exploring further means of adjusting the balance between the pre-trial rights of the accused and the demands of society for protection against criminal acts.

Civil Rights and Mass Action

If public opinion on issues involving the civil rights of isolated individuals (such as individuals accused of a crime) has tended to lag, it has been far from indifferent to situations involving organized groups. And this is especially true for groups that seek to lay claim to civil rights in the teeth of prevailing community custom. Thus, in the present day South, protesters seeking equal accommodation for Negroes in public places (lunch counters, theaters, bus terminals, and the like) have attempted to force that accommodation by means of picketing, sit-in strikes, and deliberate

---

[6] See Sidney Zion, "So They Don't Talk," *The New York Times,* August 21, 1966, p. E–13.

mass-violation of local segregation laws in an attempt to force federal court determination of the validity of those laws.

In addition to these endeavors to accomplish by direct mass action what has not come through the legislative and judicial processes, the protestors have also launched educational and voter registration drives aimed at increasing the efficacy, participation, and influence of Negroes in established political channels. In Montgomery, Ala., Cambridge, Md., Jackson, Miss., and many other northern and southern cities, mass action has bolstered Negro influence and forced a long list of concessions: desegregation of buses and lunch counters, employment of Negroes on all-white construction crews and police forces, admission of Negroes to previously all-white schools and universities, and increases in Negro voter registration (in some areas, with the help of federal registrars and expanded registration facilities, from less than 1 per cent to more than 50 per cent of eligible Negroes).

These forms of mass and direct action have not only brought the Negro tangible gains, they have been viewed with considerable favor by equalitarians within the white populace. In marked contrast, however, are those incidents of direct action characterized by rioting, death, and extensive property destruction that have erupted in the Negro ghettos of Northern cities. Rioting, by its very nature, is the antithesis of the remedial processes of democracy. Thus, another serious problem rises to haunt us: Where is the line to be drawn between acceptable and unacceptable forms of direct action?

Action that is nonviolent may stretch—but presumably does not break —the bounds of acceptable remedial recourse. Violence, however, goes beyond the pale. But aside from the tidiness of these boundaries in logic, how in practice is the protest demonstration to be kept from swelling to riot proportions? More importantly, what is to be the long range effect upon our political culture of acceding to demands lodged *outside* the ordinary processes of government? It is difficult not to conclude that, however justified the demands, mob violence cannot be condoned; for violence tears the essential fabric of any democratic system, reducing to absurdity all the provisions within the democratic framework for orderly change through orderly redress of grievances.

Specific causes and protests, of course, change with time; but the more general problem of securing civil rights remains. When, for example, civil rights are lost through failure to observe the requirements of a fair trial, a remedy may be found in the provisions society has made for court appeals. When community prejudice conspires to deprive a racial or ethnic minority of its rights, the remedy may be found by lifting responsibility for the enforcement of those rights to another level of government. By lifting the responsibility from county to state or from state to federal government, it is sometimes possible to dilute the prejudices of local majorities through the infusion of a larger, more heterogeneous, more distant, and hence more dispassionate majority.

But in many instances of faulty civil rights enforcement, no such remedies are available. A sheriff who abandons his prisoner to the brutality of a lynch mob violates the guarantees of a fair trial in a final, irremediable act. A police officer who yanks a nettlesome speaker from his soapbox, rather than defending his right to speak, may someday let him return to his rostrum. By that time, however, the occasion for speaking may have slipped by and nothing will serve to right that particular wrong.

The problem of enforcing civil rights is thus a recurring one, intimately connected with the daily enforcement of our laws and the day-to-day practices of our government officers. Courts and legislatures may provide those officers with guidelines for conduct and with correctives for errors of past judgment. In the final analysis, however, there is no surer protection of these rights than a citizenry sufficiently concerned to engage in a twofold plan of action: to resist for themselves the temptation to engage in violent extra-legal remedial action, and to demand from the officers of government scrupulous attention to the civil rights of others.

CIVIL RIGHTS IN TRANSITION

To this point, we have strung our lines of inquiry so as to capture some idea of the forces that mold civil rights and some idea of the general pattern of these rights. But general patterns by themselves cannot fully convey the dynamics of civil rights formation, nor can they indicate in detail the directions in which these rights are now being carried. Fuller understanding of our subject requires an examination of civil rights issues set within the context of historical development. Therefore, as a final task we will convass two of the most important issues of present-day civil rights: the reconciliation of the Fourteenth and Fifteenth Amendments with the treatment afforded Negroes, and the confronting of free speech with the requirements of national security.

The Issue of Racial Equality

With the possible exception of the American Indian, no group in this country has suffered more at the hands of the majority than the Negro. Despite the requirements of the Fifteenth Amendment that race constitute no bar to suffrage and despite the requirements of the Fourteenth Amendment that no state deprive any person of due process of law or equal protection of the law, the American Negro has enjoyed far less than a full measure of basic civil rights. He has been forced to live in segregated housing in nearly all areas of the United States, but his deprivations have been especially acute in the South. There, he has been forced to attend segregated schools, ride segregated conveyances, use segregated facilities in public buildings, and more, he has been denied both access to the ballot box and the full guarantees of fair trial.

As little as three decades ago the Negro seemed frozen in his status as a "second-class citizen," and the lack of civil rights that attended that status was a source of despair both to the Negro and to all who took seriously democracy's basic premise of equality. But even during this period of discouragement, beneath the surface of events, there were forces at work that were eventually to thaw the civil rights glacier. For one thing, the increasing migrations of Negroes to the North, following the industrial demands of World War I, made the Negro an important element in northern politics, and his congressional representatives began demanding federal intervention in behalf of civil rights. For another thing, the increasing concentration of Negroes in the great northern cities, coupled with the importance of those cities to presidential elections, has made the "Negro vote" an important factor in presidential politics and has worked to make the presidential office especially sensitive to Negro demands. For a third thing, the growing power of labor unions, accompanied by an increasing Negro membership in many of those unions—as for example, the United Auto Workers—has given the Negroes an important set of non-Negro, pressure group spokesmen. And fourth, an era of economic prosperity has enabled the Negro to divert an increasing portion of his earnings in support of pressure groups directly concerned with his welfare. The National Association for the Advancement of Colored People (NAACP) is one such organization, and among its many activities has been the underwriting of litigation designed to force the courts into reconsidering their approval of such state laws as those which require segregated schools and segregation of passengers in public conveyances.

Challenging the constitutional validity of such laws is generally a costly process. To carry a case through successive judicial levels until at last the Supreme Court is reached requires that lawyers be hired, that witnesses be found, that court reporters be retained and that legal briefs be printed. Successful litigation is expensive, and especially so if it is part of a program of recurring challenges to the validity of not one law but a whole series of laws in each of several states. Litigation of widespread proportions has been one of the programs of the NAACP, and as its membership and its treasury have swelled, its courtroom activities have likewise increased.

But parties, pressure groups, and litigation are not the only factors working to thaw the glacial barriers to Negro rights. This country's struggle against totalitarianism in World War II and the Korean War and our clash with international communism after each of these wars have made our society increasingly conscious of democracy's basic precepts. Reacting to this awareness, a growing sector of the citizenry has found it increasingly difficult to reconcile the treatment afforded Negroes with the second paragraph of the Declaration of Independence.

Thus, even before the end of World War II, the tides of change were running. In 1941 President Roosevelt, by virtue of his wartime-emergency powers, ordered all federal agencies to include in their war production contracts a requirement forbidding discrimination against persons of any race, color, or creed in the matter of employment; and even though Congress refused to enact this requirement into peacetime law, several of the states carried forward this wartime policy and enacted the fair employment practices legislation referred to earlier in this chapter. In 1946 the Supreme Court ordered an end to segregation on motor vehicle carriers moving in interstate commerce, and in 1950 the Court forbade the railroads to segregate dining accommodations on interstate trains.[7] In 1948 President Truman took the first of a series of steps designed to end segregation in the armed forces, and in that same year the Supreme Court declared nonenforceable all real-estate contracts designed to prevent Negroes from acquiring property in so-called restricted (for example, all-white) communities.[8]

Still other examples might be cited of this changing pattern of civil rights, but because the most dramatic of these changes are in the areas of segregated schools and equal access to the ballot, it is to these that we now turn.

The Demise of
Segregated Education

Although the school segregation issue may be reduced to a single question, packed within that question are nearly all of civil rights' many dimensions. Basically, this issue asks whether it is constitutionally valid that Negro and white children be required to attend separate public schools. But within this question come the issues which formed our earlier discussion: the potential disharmony between majority rule and civil rights; the utility of constitutional limitations; the possibility that the federal government, reflecting larger majorities, may dilute the tyranny of local majorities; and the need to pour definitional content into constitutional clauses. In these terms, the segregation issue is macrocosmic, and to see its several dimensions, some historic perspective is now necessary.

The Fourteenth Amendment, it will be recalled, requires (among other

---

[7] *Morgan v. Virginia*, 328 U.S. 373, and *Henderson v. United States*, 339 U.S. 816.

[8] *Shelley v. Kramer*, 334 U.S. 1.

things) that no state shall deprive any person of the equal protection of the laws nor any of the privileges and immunities belonging to a citizen of the United States. Adopted in 1868, this amendment was designed to afford the newly freed Negro a legal status equal to that of white citizens, but despite the wording and intent of the Amendment, the states of the South later put upon their statute books laws requiring a segregation of race in places of public gathering, in public conveyances, and most important for this discussion, in the public schools.[9]

For about fifty years, the validity of these statutes—particularly as they applied to school segregation—was upheld by the United States Supreme Court, following a line of reasoning made famous in the case of *Plessy* v. *Ferguson* (1896).[10] In that case, the issue turned around the legality of enforcing segregated railroad accommodations upon Negro and white passengers and the Supreme Court decided that a separation of races did not violate the requirements of the Fourteenth Amendment if *equal accommodations* were provided for both races. "Separate but equal" thus became the judicial formula that put the stamp of constitutionality upon segregation, and it was not until late in the 1930s, in the instance of school segregation, that this formula was successfully challenged.

In 1938, the State of Missouri, having no law school for Negroes, and having rejected a Negro's application for admission to the law school of the state university, offered to pay the applicant's expenses at any of the law schools in neighboring states that were open to Negroes. But the rejected applicant, not satisfied at going elsewhere for legal training, appealed to the Supreme Court to force his admission to the University of Missouri. The Supreme Court accepted the applicant's argument that the doctrine of separate but equal facilities was violated by Missouri's failure to provide a law school for Negroes, and the Court went on to say that the state's offer to send the student elsewhere did not overcome this violation. In this case, the "separate but equal" formula was held to be constitutional, but under the terms of the Court's ruling, the student could not be "separated" beyond the borders of the state. The Court had thus begun the first of a

---

[9] "The South" is a geographic, political, and social term, not a legal one. As such, it does not have precise meaning, but is often spoken of as "a state of mind" common to those states that are marked by allegiance to the Democratic party, a discriminatory treatment of the Negro, and a high concentration of Negroes whose presence makes especially acute the problems arising out of such discrimination.

Here, we use the term "Solid South" to include the eleven states that seceded from the Union to form the Confederacy: Alabama, Arkansas, Florida, Georgia, Louisiana, Mississippi, North Carolina, South Carolina, Tennessee, Texas, and Virginia. More generally speaking, the South also includes the "border states" of Kentucky, Oklahoma, Missouri, Maryland, and Delaware.

On this problem of definition see V. O. Key, Jr., *Southern Politics* (New York: Alfred A. Knopf, Inc., 1950), chap. 1; and Austin Ranney and Willmore Kendall, *Democracy and the American Party System* (New York: Harcourt, Brace, and World, Inc., 1956), chap. 8.

[10] 163 U.S. 537.

long series of steps leading to the contraction of a constitutional category.[11]

Then, in 1950 came another important case also dealing with separated legal education. In *Sweatt* v. *Painter*, the Supreme Court refused to admit that a newly established law school for Negroes could satisfy the demands of the equal protection clause.[12] Sweatt had come before the Court asking that the State of Texas be forced to admit him to the University of Texas Law School. Prior to appealing to the Supreme Court, he had petitioned the courts of Texas to enter him at the University of Texas but the answer of Texas judiciary had been to require the state to establish a law school for Negroes inasmuch as none was then in existence. Sweatt, however, refused to enter the newly created school, claiming that its establishment had created separation *without* equality, inasmuch as the Negro law school was a small college with few faculty and a minimal library, in contrast to the law school of the state university which was built around an excellent library and a faculty of renown.

The members of the Supreme Court, as lawyers and former law teachers themselves, accepted the merits of Sweatt's argument and stressed the idea that the quality of legal training is determined not merely by courses of instruction, but by such intangible factors as a university's intellectual climate, its traditions, prestige, and the social status of its alumni. Segregation in the law schools of Texas was thus declared to be a violation of the equal protection clause of the Fourteenth Amendment and in handing down this decision, the Supreme Court served notice that it had begun to look at the *realities* that lay behind the "separate but equal" doctrine.

On the same day as the Sweatt case was decided, came another inquiry into these realities. In *McLaurin* v. *Oklahoma,* the Court decided that educational equality was violated in the instance of a Negro graduate student, newly admitted to the University of Oklahoma, who was forced to sit in a special section in his classroom, use a segregated desk in the library, and eat at a special table in the university dining hall. These restrictions, said the Court, impaired the student's "ability to study, to engage in discussions and exchange views with other students," and generally handicapped him in his pursuit of education. As a result, said the Court, his educational opportunities were separated from, but hardly equal to those afforded white students.[13]

In the three cases cited above, the Supreme Court had looked at segregated education on the college level and had found it wanting in equality, but the Court had not as yet disturbed segregation in the *primary* and *secondary public school systems*. However, the pattern of the Court's

---

[11] *Missouri ex rel. Gains* v. *Canada,* 305 U.S. 337.

[12] 339 U.S. 629.

[13] *McLaurin* v. *Oklahoma State Regents,* 339 U.S. 637.

approach to segregation was becoming increasingly clear, and for many southerners the consequences were profoundly disturbing. In the words of many southern leaders, racial segregation of the young was so completely the basis of the South's social structure that they were prepared to defend this segregation no matter what the cost nor how great the sacrifice.

But the Supreme Court, if it heard these angry words, did not depart from its pattern of subjecting segregation to an ever closer scrutiny, and in 1954 the capstone of this pattern was firmly set in place: for in that year the Court handed down a decision, declaring primary and secondary school segregation to be a violation of the Fourteenth Amendment; and in so declaring, the Court ordered an end to segregation in public schools.[14]

To arrive at its decision, the Court chose to go once again behind the existence of two school systems (one for Negroes and one for whites) to inquire into the effects of segregation upon the learning process. In looking to these effects, the Court took its lead from a carefully prepared brief drawn up by lawyers for the NAACP. In that brief were set down sociological and psychological evidence as to the effects of segregation upon learning and social adjustment; and stress was placed upon the psychic sufferings of Negro children who were forced by segregation to wear the badges of a "second-class citizenship." School segregation, this brief argued, by its very nature creates a condition of inequality, and in so doing, violates the meaning and intent of the Fourteenth Amendment.

With these arguments the Supreme Court concurred; and it placed in the hands of the various federal district judges responsibility for enforcing desegregation upon the school systems of the several states.

Within two years of the Court's decision, desegregation had taken place quite readily in those states just north of the Mason-Dixon line (in school districts of southern Illinois, for example). The northern tier of Southern states has also accomplished desegregation largely without untoward incident, but in some parts of the deeper South desegregation has met with outraged protest and open violence.

In 1956 for example, in Little Rock, Arkansas, public disorder grew so great that President Eisenhower ordered federal troops to a newly integrated school: to protect Negro students who sought to enter there, to quell rioting, and in effect, to support the orders of a federal court after local police and the state-controlled national guard were used to thwart those orders. In 1966 as another example, in New Orleans, Louisiana, protesting parents maintained picket lines for several weeks around a school marked for integration, jeering and stoning those who tried to pass through the pickets.

But legal maneuver, rather than mass action, has been the South's strongest weapon in its battle against integration. Southern legislatures

---

[14] *Brown* v. *Board of Education*, 347 U.S. 483, and *Bolling* v. *Sharp*, 347 U.S. 497

have conceived legislative programs of "massive resistance" whose aim is that of bewebbing the process of integration in a hopeless tangle of litigation, counter-litigation, and wearying delay. And though these statutory programs vary from state to state, certain aspects are common to all, for they seek to exploit two of the fundamental aspects of the integration controversy. First, while federal courts may force integration, general responsibility and financial support for education continues to lie with the states. And second, school integration, though public policy of the highest order, has been made by the Supreme Court and not by Congress. Accordingly, southern strategy seems to be that of 1) providing (through continuous litigation) opportunity for the Supreme Court to change its mind about pushing single-handedly so vast a program of social change, and 2) forcing the courts to decide "hard cases" that is, cases involving choice between two generally acceptable and important legal principles. Thus, Virginia, among other states, requires the closing of any school ordered integrated. A federal judge handing down any such order is consequently aware of the fact that his decision may deprive large numbers of children, both Negro and white, of educational opportunities. Other states provide for the immediate dismissal of school officials carrying out integration orders; and, in some cases, make those officials guilty of violating state law. Confronted by such laws, a federal judge ordering integration is faced with the unpleasant task of exposing local officials to state prosecution, of leaving a community without school officials, and of beginning an extended process of injunction hearings by which school officials may be *forced* to remain in jobs that they seek to resign and by which state law enforcement officers may be prevented from carrying out their state-assigned duties.

Such situations make for "hard law"; but harder still are cases that involve respected and traditional educational policies. Thus, Alabama, among others, has enacted pupil placement laws that permit local school boards to assign pupils to schools on the basis of educational achievement, intelligence, and the like. Even though such laws are in fairly common use in school systems across the nation, their use by southern school boards has largely been that of assigning Negro students to all-Negro schools. Understandably, federal courts have been reluctant to strike down these laws wholesale, and the result may be to require a separate court hearing for each student who feels he has been given his school assignment upon the basis of race, rather than academic qualification.

Ultimately, the goal of massive resistance laws seems to be that of creating an endless chain of litigation in *each* of the school districts of the South (nearly 3000), in hopes that the integration program will break under the weight of such protracted court controversy. Great numbers of Southerners remain convinced that commingling of the races is morally wrong, and their moral conviction, bolstered by legal defenses, has slowed integration. Ten years after the 1954 Supreme Court decision outlawing segregation in the schools the Civil Rights Commission reported no evidence that resistance to integration in the South was dissipating. In 1964, of the nearly 3000 school districts in the eleven states of the "deep South," only about 600 had been desegregated, and only about 2.25 per cent of all Negro students in those states were going to school with whites. In the seventeen southern and border states, the number of Negroes attending school with whites rose only from 6 per cent in 1960 to 10.8 per cent in 1965.[15]

EXTENDING NEGRO SUFFRAGE

Much like the issues of segregation, the problem of Negro suffrage has revolved largely around the Constitution's Civil War Amendments and the attempts of the southern states to thwart those amendments. Legal and extra-legal barriers have long blocked the path of Negro voting, and it is only in recent years that the federal government, through courts and Congress, has made serious attempts to haul the barricades down. Negro suffrage, in fact, is almost a twice-told tale; for as we shall presently see, the drama of Negro voting has unfolded in a fashion similar to that of segregation.

Suffrage and the Courts

In the aftermath of the Civil War, with control of Congress firmly in the hands of abolitionist and antisouthern groups, the national legislature in 1870 and 1871 passed a series of laws designed to ensure Negro suffrage by placing congressional elections directly under federal supervision and by providing severe penalties for any persons found guilty of intimidating or using force against any voter. On the surface, these laws would appear to have been constitutional inasmuch as the Fourteenth and Fifteenth Amendments provide Congress with the power to enforce the rights of citizenship "by appropriate legislation," while the Fifteenth Amendment directly states that "The right of citizens . . . to vote shall not be denied or abridged . . . by any state on account of race, color, or previous condition of servitude." But the Supreme Court, in *United States* v. *Reese* (1876) and in *United States* v. *Harris* (1883), destroyed the force of the congressional voting acts by declaring 1) that neither the Fourteenth nor the Fifteenth Amendment was designed to take from the states their control over elections, and 2) that these amendments forbade only state

---

[15] Sources: Southern Education Reporting Service, December, 1964; also U.S. Office of Education, Report of Compliance with Title VI of the Civil Rights Act of 1964, September 1, 1965, as reported in the Congressional Quarterly Service, *Federal Role in Education*, Washington, D.C., 1965.

action, not the action of private individuals such as those who might bar the Negro from approaching the polling place.[16]

With these decisions, control over elections was returned to state hands, but seemingly on condition that the state governments take no discriminatory action against the Negro voter. Negroes, of course, might be kept from the polls by mob action (for the Court forbade only *state* interference with voting, not interference by private individuals) but neither violence nor public disorder was to the liking of most southerners. As a consequence, they began a search for legal devices that would bar the Negro from voting but remain, at the same time, within the Court's admonition that the *state governments* practice no discrimination. Eventually, three such devices were found, and they were adopted almost universally by the eleven states constituting the former Confederacy, and in part by several of the states bordering the "Solid South."

Voting Barriers

The poll tax. The first of these devices, the poll tax, required the payment of an individual voting fee (generally $1 or $2 per year) as a prerequisite for admission to the voting rolls. To cloak this tax with constitutionality and thus smuggle it past the courts, it was made applicable to whites and Negroes alike. The logic of the tax was, however, that it would discourage the poorer citizen from voting. But given the greater incidence of poverty among Negroes, it would cut most heavily against that race. Logic and practice, however, do not always go hand in hand, for as the Negro has been disenfranchised by other devices, the poll tax has fallen upon those who do succeed in voting—the white citizenry. Perhaps for that reason, the Supreme Court, in a recent ruling that struck down the use of poll taxes in any public election, avoided characterizing the tax as discriminatory against Negroes. Rather, it based its ruling on the frankly equalitarian proposition that "wealth, like race, creed, or color, is not germane to one's ability to participate intelligently in the electoral process."[17] That ruling, coupled with the ban on the use of poll taxes in Federal elections imposed by the 24th Amendment to the Constitution, spells the demise of the poll tax in American politics.

The literacy test. The second of these devices for disenfranchising the Negro also cuts both ways—at least in the logic required to obtain court approval. In principle, the literacy test is no more than a device for assuring that those who participate in the elective process can understand the purpose and importance of their vote.[18] Under the terms of such tests the

---

[16] 924 U.S. 214, and 106 U.S. 629.

[17] *Harper* v. *Virginia State Board of Elections,* 383 U.S. 663, 1966.

[18] Not a Southern invention, the literacy test has been used in the North to keep the newly arrived immigrant from the polls and (in New York, for example) to keep him from being exploited for purposes of the political machine.

prospective voter is generally required to give to voting officials evidence of his capacity to read and write and understand the general terms of his state's constitution. In principle, the literacy test should cut against the illiterate voter, both Negro and white. But in practice, the test has been rarely applied to whites, whereas the standards of literacy applied to Negroes have been such that few, no matter how well educated, have been able to pass these tests. As one careful student of southern politics has phrased it: "No matter from what direction one looks at it, the southern literacy test is a fraud and nothing more."[19]

While the literacy test has remained relatively free from judicial interference, the legislative branch has moved to impose conditions on its use that have largely curbed its effectiveness as a discriminatory tool. Congress, in the Voting Rights Title of the Civil Rights Act of 1964, stipulated that standards in registering voters, including devices like literacy tests, must be uniformly administered, and that all tests must be given in writing unless provided otherwise by agreement between local authorities and the United States attorney general. To discourage further use of the literacy test, the law provides that any person who has completed a sixth grade education in an English-speaking school must be presumed literate enough to vote unless proved otherwise. Finally, as a swift and devastating follow-up to this legislative assault on the literacy test, Congress approved a provision in the Voting Rights Act of 1965 suspending the literacy test as a condition for voter registration in any state or county where less than 50 per cent of the voting-age population were registered as of November 1, 1964.

The longevity of the poll tax and literacy tests as more or less effective voting barriers may now be compared to the third of these devices, the *white primary*. So important has this device been for disenfranchising the Negro that its disallowance by the Supreme Court in 1944 is marked as a major turning point in the extension of Negro civil rights.

Briefly put, the significance of the white primary lies in the fact that the politics of the deeper South have been one-party politics. Partly out of resentment against the Republican party which prosecuted the Civil War against the South and governed it in the Reconstruction era, the South, since those times, has been firmly committed to the Democratic party. As a result of the citizenry's allegiance to this party, nearly all who secure its nomination for office are assured of being elected to that office in the general elections. With election thus assured to the Democratic party's nominees, the truly important political contests in the South have been those that choose the various candidates to be the party's standard bearers in the general elections. In short, *effective* political participation is confined to the primary elections within the Democratic party, and to keep the Negro from that participation it has been necessary only to exclude him from participation in the primaries.

---

[19] V. O. Key, Jr., *Southern Politics*, p. 576.

End of the White Primary

As might be expected, the course of the white primary has left a great deal of litigation in its wake. In the 1920s and 1930s these elections were given Supreme Court sanction on the grounds that the choice of party candidates was not an election within the *meaning* of the Fourteenth and Fifteenth Amendments. Briefly put, the argument accepted by the Court was that political parties were *private* associations and not agents of the state. As such, elections *within* parties (as opposed to elections between parties) involved no state action, and any resulting racial discrimination did not, therefore, violate the terms of the suffrage amendments, which spoke not of private discrimination but only a discrimination by the state government.

But in the 1940s, following its general pattern of looking into the realities of Negro rights, the Supreme Court came to recognize that primary elections were tantamount to ultimate elections, and thus part of the general election machinery of the states. In 1944, in the case of *Smith v. Allwright*, the Supreme Court declared that the choosing of party candidates, whether by primary elections or by party convention was part of the state-controlled election process.[20] As such, it lay within the meaning of the suffrage amendments and could not, therefore, be closed to Negro voters.

With the outlawing of the white primary a long-standing bastion against Negro suffrage was destroyed; and several sections of the South then moved to other mechanisms of defense, including the intimidation of Negroes seeking to vote, and the creation of labyrinthian processes of voter registration. For example, Negroes seeking to register as voters were often refused registration on grounds that necessary records had been lost. In other instances, and without giving public notice, registration boards altered their meeting times, or in equally arbitrary fashion, moved the registration office from place to place. In some communities, registration boards opened their "rolls" for only one or two hours a month, and by administering a lengthy literacy test (requiring, say, that the applicant copy longhand the U.S. Constitution) they limited the processing of new (Negro) voters to one or two a month. And in still other communities, common practice had it that if too many Negroes demanded registration, the board of registrars would resign, with no provision being made for the appointment of new registrars.[21]

Evasions such as these enabled the South to hold the color line of suffrage; but in so doing, the South stirred an increasing measure of national concern and resentment. Consequently, attempts were made to

---

[20] 321 U.S. 649.

[21] *The New Yorker* for June 10, 1961 contains a fascinating account of registration tactics and disenfranchisement schemes in Tuskegee, Alabama.

lift control over voting from the state to the national level and out of this struggle to "nationalize" suffrage have come recent federal Civil Rights Acts and the Voting Rights Act of 1965.[22]

The Civil Rights Acts of 1957, 1960, 1964;
The Voting Rights Act of 1965

When viewed in historical perspective, the Civil Rights Acts of 1957, 1960, and 1964 suggest that remedial channels for protecting civil rights are extending at a quickening pace. These acts indicate clearly that the remedial technique lies chiefly in lifting responsibility for civil rights from local to national control. Even more importantly, they suggest that in this process of nationalizing responsibility for civil rights there has occurred a concomitant nationalizing of the public conscience with respect to righting "civil wrongs."

The 1957 Act. Recent legislative policy-making on civil rights began in earnest with the creation of a bipartisan commission in the 1957 Civil Rights Act to investigate alleged civil rights violations and to suggest alternatives for corrective legislation. Because the commission found itself unable to procure election records from recalcitrant election officials, the 1960 law further enlarged the commission's powers by requiring that registration records and federal voting tallies be preserved by local officials for at least twenty-two months and that they be turned over to the Attorney General upon demand.

The 1957 Act, by creating a special civil rights section in the Justice Department, augments the number of federal attorneys who will be active in civil rights' enforcement; and the Act also permits federal judges to enforce suffrage rights through the use of restraining orders (injunctions) against obstructive election officials. Prior to the Act, those denied voting rights might bring suit to punish for past action. Such suits, however, were of little value: 1) because punishment of election officials for past action did not affect future elections, and 2) because southern white jurors simply would not find election officials guilty of any violations of the law. The 1957 Act, however, looks to present and future elections, not to those past, for it permits federal judges to *enjoin* election officials from *interfering* with Negroes' attempts at registration and subsequent voting.

One difficulty, however, inheres in these provisions. For judges to use tellingly their powers of restraint and injunction, they must also be permitted to punish for defiance of those injunctions (for "contempt of court"). Under the terms of the 1957 Act, a judge may impose only short-term jail sentences and fines; any punishment over forty-five days in jail

---

[22] Helping to mold the public opinion that lay behind these acts were two widely read reports by government commissions: The Report of the President's Committee, *To Secure These Rights* (Washington, D.C., U.S. Government Printing Office, 1947), and The Federal Civil Rights Commission, *With Liberty and Justice For All* (U.S. Government Printing Office, 1959).

and involving more than $300 in fines requires conviction by a local jury. Accordingly, it is not surprising that federal judges made few inroads upon the pattern of voting in the South; and it was in partial response to the limited success of the 1957 law that the Act of 1960 came into being.

The 1960 Act. Like the law that it augments, the 1960 Act is also one of limited federal expansion into voting rights. Under this law, federal attorneys may bring suit to protect an individual Negro's right to vote; and if the suit is won, the government attorneys may then ask the court to determine if a general pattern of discrimination prevails in the area. If the court subsequently finds discrimination to be in general practice, then any Negro in the area can apply for a court order qualifying him to vote providing: 1) he meets the general (state) voting requirements, and 2) he has already exhausted the remedies available to him under local law and election procedures.

Admittedly, the provisions of this act are cumbersome and time consuming; and the process of exhausting administrative remedies on the local level seemingly invites further litigation and evasion—a cumbersomeness that clearly marked this act as a part-way congressional measure. But any attempt at greater federal control would probably have caused the Act to die in Congress; for Congress moves with caution on all matters involving "states' rights" and with the greatest caution on matters concerning state control over the political process.

As is usual with any major piece of legislation, the laws of 1957 and 1960 represent a compromise on many sides; but here, the greatest compromise has been between the northern Congressmen and their opponents from the South. Given the South's previous intransigence on civil rights legislation,[23] and given the power bestowed on the South by the filibuster threat, its yielding in 1957 and 1960 raises an intriguing question: How did these bills survive? The answer, in part, may lie in the threat offered by northern senators of both parties to move for the abolition of those rules that make the filibuster possible, thus stripping the South of its protections against future legislation. The answer may be that some southern congressmen as Democrats wished to aid their party colleagues from the North in wooing the Negro vote. When the Democrats are a majority in Congress, southern Congressmen, by virtue of seniority, take over a large share of committee chairmanships. But in order for the Democratic party to gain that majority, the party's northern wing must capture a sizable portion of the northern Negro vote. Thus, southern Congressmen may have been willing to see a civil rights bill pass Congress, to help assure their party's future control over Congress.

The 1964 Act. The 1964 Civil Rights Act, while also a product of

---

[23] The 1957 Act marks the first civil rights legislation to have passed Congress in more than eighty-five years.

compromise, is heralded as the strongest, most far-reaching legislative action on civil rights since the Reconstruction. The Act strengthens the voting guarantees of the 1957 and 1960 bills, but also extends guarantees of equal access to public accommodations, employment, and education. It prohibits discrimination or intimidation of persons seeking accommodations in restaurants, gasoline stations, concert halls, theaters, sports arenas, motels, and lodging houses. Private dwellings renting less than five rooms, private clubs, barber shops, and small amusements are either not explicitly covered, or are specifically exempted, but the effect of the public accommodations provisions is to outlaw discrimination in a large majority of public places that can be shown to service interstate travelers or to deal with goods or services that move in interstate commerce. Congressional jurisdiction over interstate commerce also provided the basis for Title VII of the Act which outlaws discrimination in hiring, union membership, and treatment of employees.

Early versions of the bill would have permitted the Attorney General nearly unrestricted powers to file suit against individuals or firms for noncompliance; but to gain wider support for the bill, particularly among Republicans, compromises were made which provided for greater use of the carrot to urge adherence to the letter and spirit of the law before resorting to the stick. The U.S. Office of Education, for example, is authorized to provide special technical and financial assistance to any local public school system planning or executing desegregation. A Community Relations Service was established (under the Department of Commerce) to aid communities in resolving at the local level disputes and issues involving alleged discriminatory incidents. Similarly, the Act established an Equal Employment Opportunity Commission (EEOC), authorized to furnish technical assistance and conciliatory services to public and private groups wrestling with problems arising out of the nondiscriminatory requirements of the law.

In the event these "soft" enforcement provisions fail, the bill provides for strong sanctions. Both the EEOC and the Community Relations Service are given power to refer to the Attorney General for legal action all cases that cannot be solved by local conciliation and negotiation. In the area of education, the Attorney General is empowered to file suit against any public school or college upon receipt of a signed accusation of segregation in which the complainant has been unable to initiate or maintain legal proceedings. Finally, the Act gives legislative legitimacy to the policy of cutting off federal funds and payments to any organization, business, or group engaging in discriminatory practices.[24]

It is difficult to measure the significance of the threat of loss of federal

---

[24] A major exception is that this provision cannot be used to force changes in employment practices. Cases in which federal funds are cut off for alleged discriminatory practices are subject to judicial review.

funds as compared to the lawsuit as devices for encouraging desegregation. National civil rights legislation has widened the conditions under which lawsuits may be filed, as well as the powers of the Attorney General to sue to force compliance with legal desegregation requirements. Federal funds have been suspended in several cases and explicit threats of imminent suspension have been issued in others, but how many organizations have desegregated because of the cut-off provision that might otherwise have resisted desegregation cannot easily be determined. Almost certainly, however, the cut-off provision provides the federal government with a weapon equal to if not more powerful than the lawsuit in deterring resistance to desegregation, even if it is applicable to a much narrower range of circumstances than the wide variety of situations in which the lawsuit may be employed.

The Voting Rights Act of 1965. In the area of voting, the provisions of the 1964 Civil Rights Act largely set the stage for the stronger provisions of the Voting Rights Act of 1965. The 1964 Act increased incrementally the ways in which control over voting rights can be transferred from local to federal jurisdiction by providing, for example, that suits by the Attorney General against alleged "patterns and practices" of discrimination can be heard by a three-judge federal court. But it remained for the 1965 Voting Rights Act to authorize direct federal intervention in the voter registration process in areas where less than 50 per cent of voting age residents were registered to vote on November 1, 1964 or actually voted in the 1964 Presidential election. States or local political units that trigger this formula are subject to 1) replacement of state or local voting registrars and examiners by federal voting examiners, and 2) suspension of literacy tests and similar devices for five years or until a three-judge federal court sitting in the District of Columbia finds the political unit in compliance with all orders of the federal voting examiners and no reasonable cause to suspect resumption of voter registration denials.

Not only did the provisions of the 1964 Civil Rights Act and the 1965 Voting Rights Act break new ground in legislating Civil Rights, the political processes that forged the Acts also were marked by significant innovation. In action on the 1964 bill, for the first time in the history of civil rights legislation, Senate proponents were able to muster the two-thirds majority vote needed to cloture filibustering opponents of the bill. The healthy majorities both bills received reflected an unprecedented degree of support for civil rights legislation. This increased support can be traced in large part to the greater effectiveness of organized interest groups in urging indifferent and uncommitted legislators—particularly those from nonurban northern and western states who had little reason to take a strong position on civil rights—to support cloture and passage of the bills. Interest group effectiveness, in turn, can be traced to the fact that the established, predominantly Negro civil rights organizations (such as the

NAACP, CORE, and the National Urban League) were joined in their efforts to get the bills passed by numerous more broadly based groups, including Protestant, Catholic, and Jewish religious organizations, labor unions, and political action groups. The Leadership Conference on Civil Rights, which had coordinated the lobby activities of some fifty groups in support of the 1957 and 1960 civil rights bills, had the support of more than eighty groups in 1964 and 1965. This increased interest groups participation was indicative of a greater public awareness and concern over the problems and plight of the Negro in American society, stirred in part at least by the long chain of civil rights "incidents," demonstrations, and protestations that culminated in a massive "Civil Rights March for Jobs and Freedom" that drew more than 200,000 whites and Negroes from all over the nation to the Capitol in the summer of 1963.

If it accomplished nothing else, the March on Washington illustrated clearly that the problem of racial equality had been transformed from one of predominantly sectional, southern concern to a position of national salience. Public opinion polls showed from about 1960 to 1964 that a majority of Americans considered "civil rights" the most pressing problem facing the nation (overshadowed after 1964 only by concern over U.S. involvement in the Vietnam war). Thus, the 1964 Act constituted a national commitment to seek a solution to long-standing racial antagonisms and inequalities. The key to this commitment was the nearly complete nationalization of voting rights achieved by the combined voting provisions of the 1957, 1960, and 1964 Civil Rights Acts, and the 1965 Voting Rights Act.

Suffrage and Beyond

The extension of Negro suffrage in the South promises to have telling effects upon the entire pattern of civil rights in that section of the country. For, as the Negro—protected by national legislation and impelled to register by sweeping voter registration campaigns—gains the vote, officeholders are increasingly compelled to compete for his vote. In seeking that vote, they are forced to promise the Negro whatever it is that government can do to improve his status. Accordingly, the ballot box promises to become an engine of change, providing motive force for other aspects of Negro civil rights: extended school integration; open access to places of private accommodation; and law enforcement processes that are blind to color.

The list of areas in which government will be pressed to help the Negro will extend beyond the South into the North and especially into northern cities and the troubled areas of Negro slums. The quickening of national conscience that lay behind the most recent civil rights legislation has moved Congress to consider accepting—as a national concern—responsibility for open housing to quiet the conditions that, in recent years, have led to outbreaks of urban disorder.

In 1966, legislation passed the Lower House which would have increased Negro representation on state court juries, strengthened federal criminal statutes applicable to racially motivated acts of violence, and most importantly, prevented owners of property who sell or rent three or more houses or apartments a year from discriminating on the basis of race in their sales. When it reached the Senate (in late summer, 1966) the bill faced a filibuster for which not enough votes could be mustered to invoke cloture. And the bill, in effect, died as the Senate turned its attention to other legislative concerns.

The death of the bill was a consequence of many factors, all operating in concert. For many Senators, perhaps the equation of national conscience and federal action had reached a balance. New legislation might need to wait for a further burgeoning of that conscience. Many voiced concern that open housing legislation, coming on the heels of mass action that in several cities took violent form, would appear to condone a political pattern that moved outside the acceptable channels of remedial recourse. And still other Senators feared the ballot box retaliation (the white backlash) of urban white homeowners faced with compulsory neighborhood integration.

Thus, the 1966 legislation died, not out of congressional indifference but out of cautionary concerns. It seems a safe prediction that socio-economic extensions of civil rights will be revived in future Congresses. Successful extension of these rights will depend upon many factors, not the least of which will be the deepening of a national commitment to the solution of civil rights problems and the behavior of those seeking social change to contain their actions within the acceptable channels of political remedy.

NATIONAL SECURITY AND THE FIRST AMENDMENT

In the issues that center on national security, we come again to a problem of familiar dimensions. Basically, the problem springs from majority determination to protect our government from communist subversion even if the price of protection is an undercutting of democracy's requirement of free speech and conscience. Where the ultimate principles of democracy might require (in the words of Oliver Wendell Holmes) that we protect even those "opinions that we loathe and believe to be fraught with death," we have stopped short of ultimate principles and have chosen, instead, to deny free speech to those who would carry us into communism.

In the recurring tension between majority rule and civil rights, the majority here has won.

But to state the problem so baldly is to strip it of the complexities and justification that have determined the course of majority action. For one thing, those who advocate communism are no ordinary political minority who, having once achieved control of government, would be content to be *displaced* by a succeeding political majority. With the accession of communists to power, the remedial processes of democracy might be forever closed. And for another thing, the speech that the majority now seeks to suppress is no ordinary political advocacy: strong evidence supports the fact that communist groups intermingle ordinary political agitation with plans to overthrow the government by force and violence. Thus, the choice for government has been a hard one, and because a majority in Congress has not thought it possible to reconcile the demands of unfettered speech with those of national security, Congress has opted for security.

Congress and National Security

Briefly, the most important federal legislation upon this subject is contained in three laws. The first of these is the Smith Act of 1940, which forbids any person to advocate the violent overthrow of the government, to organize or be associated with any group having that intent, or to teach or encourage such violence. The second of these laws is the Internal Security Act of 1950 (the McCarran Act), which provides, among other things: fine and punishment for anyone who contributes substantially to the "establishment within the United States of a totalitarian dictatorship, the direction and control of which is to be vested in . . . any foreign government, foreign organization, or foreign individual." And beyond these provisions, the McCarran Act attempts to cripple communist activity generally by forbidding communists to secure passports, to work in defense plants, or to hold nonelective federal offices, and by further requiring every communist organization to register with the Attorney General and to reveal to his office the names of all members and the source and disposition of the organization's finances.

And third, the Communist Control Act of 1954 declares the Communist Party of the United States to constitute a "conspiracy to overthrow the government of the United States" and that "its role as the agency of a hostile power" makes it a danger to the security of the United States. Accordingly, the Act denies to the Communist Party all the rights and privileges generally possessed by political parties under federal and state law. Beyond this, the Act declares any willful or knowing member of that party to be subject to the punishments and penalties of the McCarran Act.

From the language of these laws, it is clear that their basic purpose is not that of punishing sabotage, espionage, or an armed uprising against the government. Such acts are clearly within the category of the criminal endeavor and Congress has provided other laws for their suppression. Instead, the three laws cited above are concerned first, with preventing the accession of communists to political office even through ordinary, legal channels (for example, elections), and second, these laws seek to crush communist activity in general, on the grounds that such activity can lay the basis of later acts of violence, sabotage, and espionage. The argument here is that in an age of atomic warfare, for government to wait until the first blows are struck before bringing the offenders to justice is to openly invite disaster. Thus, these laws look more to the prevention of communist successes than to punishment for achieved success. But in seeking these goals, they have crowded the requirements of the First Amendment.

The Place of the
First Amendment

The First Amendment, it will be recalled, requires among other things that Congress shall make no law "abridging the freedom of speech, or of the press, or the right of the people peaceably to assemble, and to petition the Government for a redress of grievances." Under the terms of these anti-subversion laws, communist groups are forbidden such peaceful assembly; moreover, by outlawing the communists as a political party, their right to petition for redress of grievances is also abridged; and further, by making a crime out of the *advocacy* and *teaching* of communist doctrines (such as those that call for overthrow of government) these laws have spelled an end to free-speech in certain areas of discussion.

Taken as a group, these laws do not rest easily among the liberties of the First Amendment, but to understand their present relationship to that amendment, it is necessary to recall the object of an earlier discussion, namely: that few, if any, of the Constitution's clauses are self-defining; and that, as a consequence, constitutional requirements are in a state of constant transition, evolving in accordance with the meanings poured into that document by the political and judicial organs of government. Accordingly, as Congress has come to apply the First Amendment to the treatment accorded communist groups, the congressional position, broadly put, is that liberties are never absolute, that free speech and freedom of political association are always subject to governmental control in the interests of a secure and orderly society, and that the communist presence requires precisely such control.

Thus, to reduce the communist threat, Congress has deflated certain of the First Amendment's liberties, and though there are few who would question the need for suppressing communism, there are many who rest uneasy at the thought of defining to the point of extinction any aspect either of free speech or freedom of political association.

Congress, of course, does not bear sole responsibility for giving meaning to the Constitution. The definitional process is also the responsibility of both the President and the courts, and the Supreme Court, especially, is the linchpin in this endeavor. Like Congress and the President, the Court has its own bag of formulas for defining the Constitution and for testing statutes against the requirements of that document. But in many ways, it is the Court that is the chief conveyor of changing meaning, for in each successive piece of litigation, the Court has an opportunity not only to redefine the Constitution, but to determine the meaning (and scope) of the relevant congressional statutes. As a result, even though Congress has defined (and constricted) First Amendment liberties as they apply to communist action, the Supreme Court has begun a definitional spiral of its own: moving, at times, toward the congressional pattern; more recently, moving away from it.

When the appeal of eleven communist leaders, convicted under the Smith Act, came before the Court in 1951 (*Dennis* v. *United States*), the Court agreed with Congress that freedom of speech and association were never so absolute as to be exempt from regulation.[25] Our society, said the Court, is confronted with "an apparatus designed and dedicated to the overthrow of the government, in the context of world crisis after crisis." In the face of such grave and probable danger, speech is permissibly constricted, and accordingly, the Court upheld the conviction of the communist leaders and sustained the constitutionality of the Smith Act as well.

But in making these decisions, the Court aroused criticism, both inside the judicial chambers and out. Justice Frankfurter, although supporting the Court's majority, warned that "in sustaining the conviction before us we can hardly escape restriction on the interchange of ideas . . . without open minds there can be no open society." And Justice Black, dissenting from the majority, labelled the Smith Act "unconstitutional on its face," and the conviction "a virulent form of prior censorship of speech and press which . . . the First Amendment forbids."

Outside the Court as well there was criticism of the formula that had been used to sustain both the conviction and the Smith Act. Prior to this case, the Clear and Present Danger Rule had long been regarded as a bulwark in the cause of free speech. This phrase (coined by Mr. Justice Holmes in *Schenk* v. *United States*, 1919) admits that speech is never

---

[25] 341 U.S. 494.

absolutely free, but seeks to determine the need for curtailing speech by proposing that it may be fettered only when words "are of such a nature as to create a clear and present danger that they will bring about . . . substantive evils."[26] And in an extension at the hands of Mr. Justice Brandeis (*Whitney* v. *California*, 1927) the Rule was said to require that "no danger flowing from speech can be deemed clear and present unless the incidence of the evil is so imminent that it may befall before there is opportunity for full discussion."[27] Thus, as employed by Holmes and Brandeis, the Clear and Present Danger Rule required that danger or evil be imminent, that cause and effect be clearly seen before speech could be curtailed.

But in the Dennis case, the Court was no longer concerned with clear and present danger. The communist leaders, in fact, had not been indicted on a charge of actually conspiring to overthrow the government by force or violence, but merely on a charge that they had conspired to form groups advocating such overthrow and had conspired to form groups that taught this same overthrow. In these terms, the test of clear and present danger did not apply to their actions; therefore, in sustaining their conviction the Court invoked another formula, that of grave and probable danger. Technically speaking, the Court continued to invoke the clear and present danger formula, expanding it however, so that its meaning became practically coterminus with that of grave and probable danger. To understand this expansion, the reader must further understand that courts often inflate and deflate the formulas used in interpreting constitutional passages, in much the same fashion as constitutional categories themselves are expanded and contracted. As a test of speech that may be restrained, the grave and probable danger formula is far looser than a test of clear and present danger, for under the Grave Danger Rule, speech may be forbidden even though its effects are beyond the horizon. As a result, there were many critics in 1951 who felt that the Court had collapsed the First Amendment beyond the point called for by the communist threat.

But change and adjustment are the hallmarks of the Supreme Court's operation. New justices bring to the Court a new outlook as to the needs of society and the formulas that can be used to fill those needs. Accordingly, in the summer of 1957, when the Court re-examined the Smith Act, it *overturned* the conviction of another group of communist leaders.[28] In this case, the Court showed itself to be returning to the clear and present danger rule, for it stated that in order for advocacy of communism to be a crime, "those to whom the advocacy is addressed must be urged to do something now or in the future, rather than merely to believe in something." In short, the Court has *modified the Smith Act* so that its penalties

---

[26] 249 U.S. 47.

[27] 247 U.S. 357.

[28] *Scales* v. *U.S.* (#1, Oct. Term 1960; Decided 5 June, 1961).

will not apply to those who engage merely in "abstract preaching" or "advocacy in the realm of ideas," but only to those who advocate a concrete course of illegal action.

This modification was given further content and clarity in 1961 (with some veering, once again, toward the bad-tendency doctrine when the Court affirmed the conviction of a communist party leader by noting that the crime punishable by the Smith Act extends to those who are active, and not passive, within the Communist Party and who have a specific and personal intent to overthrow the government.[29]

But if the Court has worked to shorten the reaches of the Smith Act, it has been slightly more supportive of the thrust of the McCarran Act. In 1961 the Court upheld those provisions of the Act that require that the Communist Party U.S.A. register as an agent of world communism, and make complete disclosures of the party's membership and financial resources and expenditures. Such registration may expose the members of the party to punishments provided for in both the Smith and McCarran Acts, and consequently, the Court's decision was seen by many libertarians as cutting against such freedoms as that of free association, and the guarantee against self-incrimination. But a later (1964) decision ruled unconstitutional the section of the McCarran Act that disqualified Communist Party organization members from passport privileges on grounds the provision violated the "due process" clause of the Fifth Amendment. Thus, the Court seemed anxious to judge each section of the Act on its own merits. After stating in the earlier decision, with language rich in majoritarian overtones, that "the legislative judgment . . . is not to be set aside merely because the judgment of judges would . . . have chosen other methods (of combatting communism)," it nevertheless undertook selective pruning of the Act in its second ruling.[30]

Thus the problem remains to vex us: individual freedom versus national security. Libertarians may object when the Court rules in favor of restrictive congressional policy; and majoritarians become unhappy when legislative judgment is struck down by the courts. Nearly all, however, would agree that in cutting civil liberties, no matter how good the cause, we risk slashing the very jugular of democracy.

---

[29] *Communist Party, U.S.A. v. Subversive Activities Control Board* (#12, Oct. Term 1960; Decided 5 June, 1961).

[30] *Communist Party, U.S.A. v. Subversive Activities Control Board* (#12, October Term, 1960; decided 5 June, 1961); and *Aptheker v. Secretary of State*, 378 U.S. 500 (decided 22 June, 1964).

BIBLIOGRAPHICAL NOTE

On the general dimensions of American democracy see: Robert M. MacIver, *The Ramparts We Guard*, 1950, Carl L. Becker, *Freedom and Responsibility in the American Way of Life*, 2nd ed., 1955, and Robert A. Dahl, *A Preface to Democratic Theory*, 1956.

For a universal argument on behalf of civil rights (for example, liberty) see John Stuart Mill, *On Liberty*, 1859 (in several subsequent editions), and for an examination of the difficulties involved in protecting those rights see David Spitz, *Democracy and the Challenge of Power*, 1958.

On the relationship between American constitutional patterns and civil rights, *The Federalist*, 1787–1788 (in several editions) remains a basic exposition, especially papers numbered 9, 10, 31, 35, 51. On the (constitutional) interpretive powers of the courts see Edward Levi, *An Introduction to Legal Reasoning*, 1948; on the interpretive powers of the President, see Edward S. Corwin, *The President*, 1948, Chapter IV.

Useful surveys of the present state of civil rights in America are found in: U.S. President's Committee, *To Secure These Rights*, 1947, U.S. Civil Rights Commission, *With Liberty and Justice for All*, 1959, and Alan P. Grimes, *Equality in America: Religion, Race and the Urban Majority*, 1964. For a summary of civil rights provisions in the fifty states see Richard Marnett, and Joseph Garai, *Where the States Stand on Civil Rights*, 1962.

Specific civil rights issues are treated in the following. On dissent, nonconformity, and the holding of unpopular views: Henry S. Commager, *Freedom, Loyalty, Dissent*, 1954; Sidney Hook, *Conspiracy, Yes—Heresy, No*, 1953; Morton Grodzins, *The Loyal and the Disloyal*, 1956. On the Japanese Evacuation: Morton Grodzins, *Americans Betrayed*, 1949. On the legal aspects of desegregation: Albert Blaustein, and Clarence Ferguson, Jr., *Desegregation and the Law*, 1957; Joseph Tussman, ed., *The Supreme Court on Racial Discrimination*, 1963. From among the flood of recent books on the Negro civil rights movement the better treatments include Charles Silberman, *Crisis in Black and White*, 1964; Nat Hentoff, *The New Equality*, 1964; and Robert Penn Warren, *Who Speaks for the Negro?*, 1965. On Southern politics and voting practices: V. O. Key, Jr., *Southern Politics*, 1949, especially Part IV. On First Amendment liberties and national security: Harold Chase, *Security and Liberty: The Problem of Native Communists, 1947–1955*, 1955; Thomas Cook, *Democratic Rights versus Communist Activity*, 1954; Walter Millis, *Individual Freedom and the Common Defense*, 1957; Harold Lasswell, *National Security and Individual Freedom*, 1950; and Harry Howe Ransom, *Can American Democracy Survive the Cold War?*, 1964. On police and trial processes: David Fellman, *The Defendant's Rights*, 1958; Jerome A. Skolnick, *Justice Without Trial*, 1966; and Robert M. Cipes, *The Crime War*, forthcoming, 1967. In general, Robert Summers, *Law: Its Nature, Functions, and Limits*, 1965.

some conclusions
on the study of
public policy

LEWIS A. FROMAN, JR.

This book began with a description of the policy-making process as one that reflects the acivities of groups. It is through the efforts of more or less like-minded groups of individuals, in competition with others, that policies are hammered out to deal with the complex questions bound to arise in an ever-changing world. The following chapters then discussed, in considerable detail, the significant features of the most important of these questions, with a view to giving the reader a firm grasp of the historical and contemporary efforts of government to provide answers to these questions.

On the basis of what we now know about both domestic and foreign policies of the United States, can we draw some generalizations that will help us to understand the direction in which public policies seem to be headed and the intricate political processes that produce them? This final chapter is designed to provide a framework for just such an effort. But one caveat should immediately be entered. The advantages of generalizing from the specific and concrete are numerous, including summarizing a large amount of material and relating it to other important questions. But the effort of generalization is not without dangers. It is up to each individual student of politics to take a cold and detached look at the conclusions of others, for generalization also means simplification and simplification can be inaccurate and misleading.

SOME HISTORICAL PATTERNS
OF PUBLIC POLICY

The following generalizations concern some major aspects of public policy that are meant to apply over a long period of time. It would be useful for the reader to check these generalizations against each of the discussions of specific policies in the previous chapters. Although in some cases examples will illustrate what is meant by the generalization, it must be remembered that statements meant to encompass long time periods and large numbers of policies cannot be proved, or disproved, by single examples. Each of these generalizations should be read in the context of "for the most part," "by and large," or "more often than not." These generalizations should also be considered as tentative attempts to summarize a large body of literature and not as absolute truths. If they are used as departures for discussion, they will have served a useful purpose.

1. Governmental activities have increased in number and in scope.

This conclusion seems to follow naturally from the previous chapters. As a society becomes larger and more complex, as technological innovation increases, and as specialization of labor takes place, it becomes increasingly likely that the activities of one group will touch upon and perhaps interfere with the activities of others. As the members of a society become more interdependent, it means that a problem at one point in the system is likely to have consequences elsewhere in the system. As long as people are self-sufficient, providing themselves and their families with food, clothing, and shelter, they will be unaffected by many events happening elsewhere. But as soon as they let others take the major responsibility for growing their food, making their clothes, and building their houses, they are to some extent at one another's mercy.

It is largely because interdependencies have increased so remarkably in the last century that governmental activities have also increased. And most people, being so dependent upon others for so many things, probably would not have it otherwise. Governmental activity provides us with protection against other people's whims.

2. The role of the federal government has increased.

In one sense this conclusion simply follows from the previous one. Governmental activities in general have increased, and the federal government has participated in this over-all rise. But more is implied in this second conclusion than merely that. The federal government has entered into more and more activities that were at one time almost exclusively state and/or local functions, or private functions.

The reasons for this are many. The fact that the federal government has better sources of revenue than do most state and local governments, the fact that those who govern the states for one reason or another have been reluctant to enter into certain areas of public policy, and the fact that many current problems are more truly national problems requiring national responses are undoubtedly all significant factors. States and localities vary significantly in their willingness and abilities to undertake and pay for many functions now being demanded by citizens. These demands come from rich and poor, Negro and white, blue-collar and white-collar. The transportation of goods and people, for example, as our society becomes increasingly more mobile, transcends state boundaries. Our culture is increasingly becoming a national one through the influence of the mass communication industry (radio, television, newspapers and magazines, movies, and so on). Although state and local governments are also being called upon to step up their activities, a larger increase of functions is occurring within the federal government.

3. The role of the President and the Executive Branch has increased, at the expense of legislative bodies.

This generalization must be viewed as a tentative hypothesis, for some would argue that Presidential-congressional conflict shows a cyclical pattern, with periods of congressional ascendancy followed by periods when the President is predominant.

The explanation of the initial hypothesis has many facets, the major one being that modern policy questions require tremendous amounts of knowledge and technical expertise that busy and overworked Congressmen and Senators simply do not have time to assimilate. The Executive Branch, including the tremendous bureaucratic structure that provides for specialization of labor, is better equipped to process information and formulate public policy.

Congress, as a result, has become a body that amends and ratifies policy, but is not likely to be a body that initiates or provides new directions to policy.

The altered role of Congress reflects a current trend in many other countries. Part of the reason lies in the increased attention to foreign affairs, in which the Executive is normally constitutionally empowered to act independently. But whatever the reasons, Congress is now called upon to examine and approve or disapprove, with changes if Congress can agree, administrative programs that are, by and large, initiated and drawn up in the Executive Branch.

4. Except during periods of crisis, changes in public policy are incremental.

What is being suggested by this generalization is that, except when the normal pattern of life breaks down and war or depression intervenes, new policy will develop by small changes in old policy. Looking at policy changes in twenty- or thirty-year intervals may give the impression that policy changes are radical departures from the past. If one carefully examines the intervening years one will find, however, that the beginning and terminal points are directly related by small changes.

This is even true over shorter periods. The Federal Reserve Board, for example, may over the course of several years raise or reduce the rediscount rate by as much as two percentage points. Such a change, however, is likely to take place in steps of ½ per cent each.

The same is true with other programs. What looks like a major step, twenty years later will turn out, on close inspection, to be a series of smaller steps.

Examining the previous chapters will lend a good deal of credence to this generalization. In almost every policy area, whether it is education, housing, agriculture, labor, or whatnot, the year by year changes have been slight modifications of previous years. The differences in policies over longer time periods may appear to be quite large. But these larger shifts hide a serial process of incremental changes.

The major exceptions to this generalization are, of course, periods of crisis. Wars and depressions often require immediate radical departures from past programs. The Civil War and its aftermath, and the Great Depression are two notable examples of extensive policy changes. What these periods of crisis reflect is a rapid change in the environment. Old policies are no longer applicable to the changed conditions. Small changes will not do the trick; major departures from policy are required. When the crisis no longer is threatening, the incremental approach again comes into play, but this time from the new base. This is why, for example, it is impossible to begin at the point where one left off before a crisis occurred. It would require a radical change to go back, and such changes require a new crisis.

One of the interesting implications of this is that "new" programs that are being proposed by various governmental officials or interest groups are likely not to be new at all but merely modifications of present policies. The "War on Poverty," for example, is not a radical departure from previous policy. In fact, most of the money allocated for the antipoverty program has been given to ongoing agencies of government to increase their current activities. The reasons for billing it as a new program are somewhat complex, but they have more to do with "images" that office-holders and parties may attempt to create and the emphasis that certain programs will have in the administration than with the content of the program itself.

A second interesting implication is that incremental changes in past policy may contribute to the development of crisis situations. One of our first responses to change is to continue doing what we succeeded in doing before, only to a greater degree. Such incremental change in the same direction may not be an appropriate response to a new situation. Increasing the rediscount rate of money in the Federal Reserve System, for example, may help check inflation but it may also help to produce a recession or worse. Learning new responses to new situations is always difficult, whether one is speaking of government or individuals.

5. There is a time lag between the initial public discussion of a public policy and its final acceptance and implementation.

The American political system, as we shall see, is a highly decentralized one. Normally the acceptance and implementation of a public policy requires agreement among a large number of people and the approval of a large number of political institutions. In order to gain wide acceptance, most public policies go through what might be described as a "hazing" period, not unlike fraternity and sorority initiations.

The initiation of a public policy is often the product of a relatively small group of people. They recognize a problem, and after much discussion among themselves and with interested outsiders, prepare a policy to take care of it. This, however, is just the beginning. The task of convincing others of the utility of this proposal has just begun. Through negotiations and public discussion, the arena of political action is increased. The attempt is made to get office-holders and important interest groups in the political system to endorse the proposal. Sometimes the price of such endorsement is some change in the original policy.

Many ideas, like many fraternity and sorority rushees, drop out of competition. For one reason or another they are unable to make the final stages. Primarily the "dropouts" are proposals that have simply been unable to gain sufficient support among important groups in the society.

Those proposals that do make the grade are then ready for the intricate and complex stage of securing endorsement of the program by a political party and the institutions of government, primarily the President and Congress, but also the department that will administer the programs and agencies like the Bureau of the Budget.

Even when endorsements have been secured, honest men can differ with each other, and the negotiations continue among those who want a "strong" program, a "weak" program, or no program at all. Perhaps the first time the program goes to Congress it fails (as did, for example, medical care for the aged and federal aid to primary and secondary schools, and more than once). Given the high degree of decentralization of our political institutions it is possible that the legislation will gain Presidential approval and perhaps even pass the Senate, but fail in the House, or *vice versa*. After an initial failure the sponsors of the legislation may then retrench and try again, or they may give up entirely. Perhaps some entirely different program, going through the same process, can gain support. Perhaps they will come back next year to try again.

It is certain, however, that if and when the program finally receives congressional and presidential approval, a successful program will probably be quite different from the first proposal, made as many as ten or fifteen years earlier. Getting support for policies is a long and drawn-out business, and it is not an activity for the weak and fainthearted. It requires much hard work, and much negotiation.

Even after the program has been accepted, there are opportunities to change it or even to scuttle it—through court action or through its administration. Public policies are continuous, ongoing programs and are always subject to change and even cancellation.

The important point, however, is that proposals for public policy must compete in the marketplace with other proposals for acceptance by the institutions of government. The initial proposal, and its sponsors, must be flexible and patient enough to endure many changes and many delays. Those who will be most directly affected by the policy must be convinced of its merits, and those who may initially be reluctant must at least be convinced not to put obstacles in the way. There is a long period of time between the proposal and final action, and this time is charged with opportunities for failures as well as success. The political skills required to negotiate the obstacle course successfully are difficult to define, but certainly they would include hard work, patience, flexibility, ability to convince others, knowledge of how the American political system operates, the ability to anticipate trouble spots, and the ability to gain support from many different people and groups.

POLICY-MAKING IS A POLITICAL PROCESS

Some people argue that policy-making is too important an enterprise to be left to politicians. Billions of dollars are at stake each year, and the lives of many people may be in the balance. Given the important nature of the questions that policy attempts to answer, why shouldn't some rational allocation of resources be devised in making public policy rather than leaving policy-making to the idiosyncrasies of the political process? Going further along this line of thought, many have argued that what is needed is the introduction of rationality or rational decision-making into the political process. Basically the argument is as follows:

What one needs to do in order to make policy is to think out very clearly what the goals of that policy are to be. When this is completed one must then think of all of the possible alternative ways of achieving these goals, calculate the consequences of choosing one alternative as opposed to another, and then choose the alternative most likely to accomplish the goals. If public policy-making were only put on this basis, so runs the argument, we could avoid the many mistakes likely to result from leaving such decisions to the random forces of political interest.

There are two ways to answer this argument. We could point out the difficulties inherent in the rational method, and we could show the advantages of political decision-making. In fact, we will do both.

The Pitfalls of
Rational Planning[1]

The first exercise called for under rational decision-making is to "think out very clearly what the goals of the policy are to be." This may in fact be a useful injunction for individual decision-making, but *societies* are likely to be populated by individuals and groups who do not share the same goals. From this heterogeneity of preferences springs the necessity of some form of political negotiation.

The fact that people differ in their goals need not be documented here. Randomly select a Republican and randomly select a Democrat and one has the basis for an all-night bull-session over the goals of public policy. One could even randomly select two Democrats or two Republicans and come up with significant differences between the two.

So, when the rational decision-making method calls for a clear specification of the goals of public policy, it presumes there will be agreement on those goals. Such a happy event rarely exists even in families, let alone nations.

The second step in the rational method is to "think of all the possible alternative ways of achieving the goals." Undoubtedly there is a finite number of such alternatives, but the total is likely to be large indeed. And in the absence of trying them out, there will be considerable controversy as to which items should be on the list. There will also be controversy as to the acceptability of certain means to ends, since people will differ just as strongly on how something is done, as they will about whether it should be done at all. The interesting thing about means is that they are likely to raise other value questions apart from the goals they are designed to achieve. Military action may be a means to achieving peace, but all may not support such an alternative in the face of the possibility of achieving the same goal through other means.

Third, rational decision-makers are called upon to "calculate the consequences of choosing one alternative as opposed to another." This injunction raises two problems. The first is calculating the probability that the alternative proposal will accomplish the desired ends. What are the chances, for example, that if we step-up our pressures against Communist China, we will weaken this governing regime? What is the probability that World War III might ignite as a consequence? These are indeed difficult probabilities to calculate. Decision-makers must guess, on the basis of the information (often incomplete) at their disposal. To calculate these

---

[1] See David Braybrooke and Charles E. Lindblom, *A Strategy of Decision* (New York: Free Press of Glencoe, Inc., 1963), especially chapters 1–6.

probabilities in advance would require knowledge that few of us are ever likely to achieve.

The second problem in calculating consequences is that very often the choices we make have side effects of which we may be unaware. Even in the more exact science of medicine, new drugs must be tested in advance for their possible consequences that physicians may not discover until too late. In the political world, where testing is much more difficult, political careers, not to mention the lives and fortunes of millions of people, can rest on an unanticipated consequence of a decision.

To calculate in any precise manner the probabilities of alternatives, and to unearth all the consequences of even a single alternative, intended or unintended, is indeed to expect a level of knowledge that most men do not possess.

The last requirement of the rational method is to "choose the alternative that has the best chance of accomplishing the goals." On the basis of what we have said so far I think it is now clear how impossible this demand is. The "best" alternative will depend upon what goals are to be satisfied, and whether people can agree that they are the goals to be satisfied, what means of achieving the goals are available, information as to probabilities of means reaching goals, the unintended effects, and attitudes toward the use of means as well as ends. Given all of these limitations on rational decision-making, is it any wonder that men are accused of "muddling through?"

The Advantages of Political Decision-Making

Given these criticisms of rational decision-making, what are the alternatives to it?

One alternative is politics. Essentially the argument runs as follows.[2] Decisions affecting the lives and fortunes of so many people must be considered in light of the preferences of all those who consider themselves to be affected one way or another. But different people will have different sets of preferences. In that case, provide people with some way they can meet to discuss their differences. The result, assuming a willingness to negotiate, will be a policy that ought to satisfy at least a majority of the participants. If it doesn't, they can come back and try again. As conditions change they can modify their answer, add to it, subtract from it, or perhaps scrap it altogether. Assuming that all people with preferences are allowed to participate, assuming that there are many different kinds of resources that contribute to political power, and assuming that no one set of people has a monopoly on the decision-making apparatus, the outcomes should

<hr>

[2] For a fuller discussion of decision-making as a political process see Lewis A. Froman, Jr., *People and Politics: An Analysis of the American Political System* (Englewood Cliffs, N.J.: Prentice-Hall, Inc., 1962).

provide acceptable answers. And, if in the light of experience the answer is not acceptable, it can always be changed.

Most students will recognize this as the rationale for democratic decision-making. But democratic decision-making is a *political* process. The advantages of such a system of making public policy are that those who want to be heard on a matter of interest to them can be heard. If they can influence enough people to agree with them, their view may prevail. If they cannot, they can come back and try again at some future time.

Another advantage is that it avoids the many problems of rational decision-making we have already discussed. Political decision-making recognizes that people will differ over goals, it recognizes that there are huge information costs in collecting knowledge about all possible alternatives, it recognizes that one cannot always specify in advance the "best" solution. Political decision-making is, in a sense, a trial and error method that builds into the system mechanisms allowing change to take place. As has already been discussed, such changes will very often be incremental in nature, changing the policy somewhat here, deleting some unacceptable provision there. It is a mechanism that allows whole societies to adapt to a constantly changing environment.

SOME FEATURES OF POLICY-MAKING
IN THE UNITED STATES

We have already referred to the fact that the American political process is highly decentralized. This decentralization has a number of very important implications for policy-making in the United States.

1. There are many institutions in the United States that are designed to make policy.

Policy-making is not simply a function left to Congress. Although Congress does, in fact, make a good deal of policy, almost all agencies of government are part of this process also. The judiciary makes policy, and especially the Supreme Court, in that courts are often called upon to settle disputes for which there are no precedents, or if there are precedents, the total environment and political climate has changed sufficiently to warrant a fresh look at the problem. For example, in 1896 the Supreme Court ruled that separate facilities for Negroes does not violate the Constitution. In 1954 the Supreme Court ruled just the reverse, that separate facilities are inherently unequal and hence in violation of constitutional rights. Had the Constitution changed during that sixty-year period? New amendments were added to the Constitution but amendments that were not relevant to this problem. What had changed was the political climate in the country and the members on the Court.

Why did the Supreme Court make the decision? Why didn't Congress make this policy? The reasons are somewhat complex, but Congress, until recent times, has usually been reluctant to make policy concerning the civil rights of Negroes. Partially this is due to the influence of southern Congressmen and Senators, in an institution that promotes individuals to positions of influence partially on the basis of how long they have been in Congress and the fact that southern constituencies are essentially one-party districts and states. Partially it is a result of the ability of a relatively small group of Senators to prevent voting to take place through filibusters. The Supreme Court on the other hand is not subject to these kinds of influence. The fact that certain aspects of public policy in this country are constitutional questions and that the Supreme Court is the final authority on the Constitution means that the Court, as well as other agencies of government, can make policy decisions.

The President, of course, also makes public policy. Not only is this true in foreign affairs, where a President can make policy decisions of war and peace with little interference from other agencies, but it is also true in domestic politics as well. The President, by executive order, can make policy in many fields, and can influence policy decisions in almost every field simply by lending or not lending the status and resources of his office in support of certain policies.

Administrative agencies also make policy. The day-to-day decisions, which the President neither has the time nor the inclination to make, are sometimes of enormous importance. Decisions are made every day in the Departments of Agriculture, Health, Education and Welfare, Commerce, Labor, and the rest, which influence the lives of millions of people.

The Independent Regulatory Commissions, such as the Interstate Commerce Commission and the Federal Power Commission, are empowered by Congress to make policies affecting everything from the price of oil at the well-head to the number of flights an airline can make from one city to another. The range of such decision-making is enormous. These are but a few examples of the multitude of decision-makers in our government, all of whom, in one way or another, make policy.

2. The existence of these many decision-points means that all groups in the society are likely to find at least one agency of government sympathetic to them.

This does not mean, of course, that all groups can get government to do what they want it to do. It does mean, however, that most groups can at least expect a sympathetic ear and can compete in the governmental marketplace for support and favorable policy decisions. Whether in fact groups will be successful will depend upon a number of factors, such as their ability to gain support among a large number of groups and other governmental decision-makers, including the President. Traditionally, for example, Negro organizations, and especially the National Association for the Advancement of Colored People (NAACP), have gone to the federal courts in their efforts to achieve favorable decisions from government. Recently other Negro organizations have grown up to supplement the activities of the NAACP (such as the Congress on Racial Equality and the Southern Christian Leadership Conference) and have at the same time developed a good deal more support in Congress.

3. The fact that many agencies of government may make policy also means that there will not necessarily be an over-all consistency to public policy in the United States.

The validity of this proposition has been demonstrated time and time again. For example, the Federal Reserve Board is empowered, by Congress, to make certain decisions that have a major impact on monetary policy in this country. In recent years there has been a dispute between those who prefer fiscal policy (expenditures and revenues) as opposed to monetary policy (interest rates, money supply) as the best method for controlling the economy. It is quite possible for those who are in charge of monetary policy (the Federal Reserve Board) and those in charge of fiscal policy to work at cross purposes with one another.

Or, it is quite possible to have a feed-grain surplus and spend millions of dollars a year storing feed-grain and at the same time spend millions of dollars to build dams for the purpose of reclaiming land to grow more feed-grain. One could proliferate examples of this kind almost endlessly.

This is not to be critical of a political process that may produce policy inconsistencies. As has already been mentioned, developing a rational policy even in a smaller area like housing or antitrust appears to be an impossible task. To expect agreement on a rational and consistent over-all policy would be out of the question. We should not be surprised, however, to find inconsistencies in policies, given a political system that decentralizes policy-making to the extent that we do in the United States.

4. Given the decentralized nature of the policy-making function, the importance of staffing policy-making positions looms very large.

Perhaps the best way to win a political battle is to have in positions to make decisions people who agree with your point of view. This is true whether we are speaking of Supreme Court Justices, Agency Heads, Congressmen, Commissioners on Independent Regulatory Commissions, or Presidents. Although we recognize the importance of rule of law rather than of men, we do not blind ourselves to the important contributions men make as individuals or to the fact that men, all men, have certain biases that will influence their judgments. The importance that Western democracies place on elections and appointments to positions of influence testifies to the concern with this element of politics. Many important political battles take place over who will assume what position in government. All this is obvious in the case of the top policy-making positions of the President, Congress, and the Supreme Court. But it is also true in the less visible staff positions, where quiet battles for influential posts can substantially affect policy.

5. Rules and procedures in the political system are not neutral in their effects on policy.

As was emphasized in Chapter 1, this is probably one of the most important, yet least understood, aspects of governmental structures. The rules and procedures by which policy decisions are made are indeed not neutral in their effects. Examples of this generalization abound.

For example, the existence of the seniority rule in Congress, whereby many positions of leadership, but especially committee chairmanships, are given to those members of the majority party with the longest tenure, means that those Congressmen and Senators who come from one-party districts and states are more likely to survive and gain positions of influence. If those areas of one-partyism are not representative of the country at large, then the seniority rule tends to over-represent interests which are located in those states and districts. When the Democrats have controlled Congress this has meant that Southern Democrats, who are on the average more "conservative" than Northern Democrats, have gained a disproportionate share of committee chairmanships, although many Northern Congressmen are achieving seniority these days. When the Republicans are the majority party, the seniority rule tends to promote midwestern rural Republicans into committee chairmanships. In each case, the seniority rule tends to over-represent certain interests and under-represent other interests.

Similarly the recent dispute regarding apportionment of state legislatures also illustrates this point. If state legislatures are apportioned in such a way as to over-represent rural interests and under-represent urban interests, then one can draw the conclusion that the very rules of government themselves lend greater support to certain people than to others.

This, of course, is one of the reasons why some of the fiercest political battles in history are over the "rules of the game." Even seemingly minor questions, such as whether bills coming out of committees in the House of Representatives should or should not go to the Rules Committee in the House, have provoked major and intense argument and have provided some very close voting margins. President Roosevelt's "court-packing" plan in the late 1930s in which President Roosevelt proposed to add additional members to the Supreme Court (because the current membership was unsympathetic to his New Deal legislation) created a furore in Congress and in the country.

It is important, therefore, when proposals are made to change certain rules, to inspect those proposed changes carefully. Sometimes there is a "joker" in the hand being dealt. Given the fact that almost all current rules give advantages to some people, proposals to change those rules are probably designed, at least in part, to take those advantages away. If one is against the interests that currently enjoy an advantage, then the change in the rules may look very attractive. If, on the other hand, the current rules are to one's advantage, then a change in the rules may not seem quite so desirable.

The perennial fight in the Senate to change the filibuster rule is a good example of what is involved. Currently it takes two-thirds of those Senators present and voting to cut off debate in the Senate. What this means is that one-third plus one of the Senators can prevent a vote from taking place, even though a majority of the Senators favor a particular piece of legislation. Clearly this rule has enormous consequences for public policy in this country. By and large a relatively small number of Senators have been able to prevent action on many significant public policy questions, including civil rights, apportionment of state legislatures, and labor legislation. To change the filibuster rule to a majority rather than two-thirds would undoubtedly reduce the ability of minorities in the Senate to prevent legislation from coming to a vote.

6. As a result of this large and complex decision-making structure, matters of public policy require skillful bargaining.

We are not a political system that allows any governmental official to initiate and carry out programs by fiat. Rather, our political system places a good deal of emphasis on insuring that if a public policy is to be implemented it must have a good deal of political support. Congress can refuse to grant funds to carry out Executive programs, the President can veto legislative proposals, the Supreme Court can overturn decisions of Congress and the President; these and many more obstacles are part of the familiar "check and balance" system first initiated by our Founding Fathers and still very much like it was 175 years ago.

Because we are a system that requires agreement, or at least noninterference, among a large number of people and institutions there must be political mechanisms whereby men can attempt to reconcile their differences and work out policies on which they can agree. These political mechanisms are called "bargaining." Without bargaining it is unlikely that a decentralized political structure could reach agreement on anything or could handle the many complex questions with which it is faced every day. A political system that has so many points at which public policy can be effectively blocked must provide some means whereby men can talk to one another to settle their legitimate and honest differences.

There are many different ways in which men may negotiate with one another. We will be concerned with two of the most important and widely discussed. We should keep in mind, however, that in addition to these two, men may also threaten, cajole, plead, force, convince, charm, hustle, bribe, bluff, and engage in any number of other forms of negotiation.

One time-honored way of reaching agreement is compromise. Essentially compromise is a bargain of the form, "you want x, I want z, let's settle on y." Bargaining by compromise is a very useful way of reaching agreement when it is important to make some decisions but when no one proposal gains enough support to win acceptance. It is then possible to "give and take" a little, among all the parties to the controversy, in order to form a coalition around the preferences of at least a majority of those who will be making the decision. Probably most, if not all, of the policies discussed in the previous chapters required for their adoption at least some compromise.

Unfortunately, in many circles, bargaining by compromise has come to mean something to be avoided. Many Americans feel that men should stick up for what they feel is right, regardless of the consequences. "I'd rather be right than President" is an old attitude. The concept of a political figure who is uncompromising, who is a "man of principle" and will not give in on those "principles" is an image widely shared and applauded in American society. It is only "politicians" who compromise; "statesmen" stick to their principles.

There is, of course, an alternative way to describe people who are uncompromising. Adjectives such as inflexible, rigid, unyielding, pig-headed, unbending, easily come to mind. And whether a man is described as pigheaded or a man of principle will often depend upon whether you agree with him or not and whether he is protecting your rights or the rights of those you oppose.

But more importantly, had there been no compromise, had there been no Congressmen and Senators, bureaucrats and judges, Presidents and commissioners who were willing to engage in compromise, it is unlikely that any of the policies discussed in this book would now be public policies of the United States. Such matters can only be decided by men who are willing to negotiate with one another. The attitude of "half a loaf is better than no loaf at all" is the basis upon which compromise may take place.

The second method of bargaining, as widely criticized as it is wide-spread, may be called logrolling. This is a bargain of the form, "you give me what I want, and in return I'll give you what you want." This form of bargaining is especially important when public policies under discussion affect only a small segment of the population (agriculture, veterans, poverty, labor, and specific industries are but a few examples). No government official, no matter what his position, can be as highly interested in all matters of public policy as he is in a few. Congressmen from urban areas, for example, will be much more interested in problems of slum clearance, mass transportation, unemployment, and low-cost housing than will Congressmen from rural areas, who in turn will be more interested in questions of agriculture. In addition, government officials tend to specialize in one or two policies, since they cannot possibly be expected to know everything about every issue that comes along. Congressmen, for example, specialize in policies that are handled by the Committees to which they are assigned, executive personnel concentrate on their agencies' policies, and so on.

Because of this high degree of specialization and because very few policies will interest, equally, all members of the government, bargaining often takes place by logrolling. Rural Congressmen might say to urban Congressmen, "you support our sugar-beet bill and we will support your mass transportation bill."

This form of bargaining has been highly criticized on the grounds that government officials should decide questions of public policy on the merits of the question, not on the basis of "you scratch my back and I'll scratch yours." The difficulty with this criticism, of course, is that no government official could possibly digest the mass of information, some of it highly technical, that comes across his desk on every public policy. Many even find it difficult to keep up with what they are most interested in, the other hundreds of policies of government notwithstanding.

One could argue further that such specialization in fact increases the likelihood that policy will be considered on its merits, since men who are experts, representing all points of view, will be involved, even if the group represents only a small proportion of all of those who will eventually be making the decision.

Compromise and logrolling, then, are two highly used and probably indispensable mechanisms of gaining agreement within and among the highly decentralized policy-making machinery of our government. The advantages of such bargaining should be considered equally with the disadvantages, and the necessity of compromise and logrolling considered in light of the whole complex structure of American government. Certainly it would be easier and quicker to make policy by administrative fiat rather than by bargaining. But administrative fiat smacks of a political system that most Americans would find anathema and, indeed, have expended a good deal of resources in attempting to prevent, both home and abroad.

PUBLIC POLICY AND THE STABILITY
OF THE AMERICAN POLITICAL SYSTEM

Several major implications may be drawn from this summary of public policy and public policy-making in the United States.

First, given the fact that most policy changes take a long time from their initial conception to final enactment, most interested parties will have some opportunity to comment upon and offer suggestions for changing the proposals. This is no mean accomplishment in a country as large and diverse as ours. Adequate time must be available for public comment, for in some measure the stability of a political system will depend upon the degree to which people feel that they have had some say in their government's decisions. To some the process may be viewed as excessively long and drawn out. But it would be a mistake to think the time it takes to have people voice their opinions is wasted. One needs support for public policies if they are to be accepted without force. Time must be available for discussion and dissemination of information so that all interested parties may participate if they choose to do so.

Second, the fact that most changes in public policy are incremental in nature means that a minimum of disturbance to the economy, society, and polity will result from changes in policy. Our political system is not known for its wide swings on matters of public policy. We are known as a society with a high degree of political stability. The relationship between small policy changes and high political stability is too close to be accidental.

Third, given our highly decentralized political system, and the ability of all, or most, citizens to participate in it, we also have a policy-making process that attempts to listen to, and satisfy, legitimate problems. Almost everyone in our society benefits in one way or another from special governmental programs. Veterans, businesses, labor unions, school children, farmers, unemployed persons, Negroes, shipbuilders, old people, and almost any other group that one can mention in one way or another receives such attention. This lends a good deal of stability to our political system. Almost all people have a stake in what government is doing, and they feel that government action is an appropriate remedy for social, economic, and political ills.

There are, of course, some major exceptions to this generalization. Negroes for many years have been badly treated in all parts of our country. The NAACP had been effectively raising the status of Negroes in this country, but many people felt much too slowly. Recent activity by more militant civil rights groups has served to bring the needs of Negroes to the attention of more and more people, and has effectively brought increased governmental action. The American Indian is another good example of a group that has not received its share of what our country has to offer. However, unlike the Negro, the American Indian has not been as effective in bringing his plight to the attention of the government. Part of the problem, obviously, in a system largely responsive to voters, is that Indians simply do not comprise a very big voting bloc. But it would not be unreasonable to suppose that the American Indians, if as a group they could be mobilized, could make their demands more effectively known.

We have, then, at least three major influences tending to contribute to the stability of the American political system: large time intervals between the initiation of public policy and its implementation, incremental changes in public policy, and the attempt to satisfy legitimate claims for help from citizens. Other contributing factors could be mentioned as well. But the important point is that our system pays relatively close attention to the preferences of the governed. Undoubtedly some people's preferences are given more weight than others. Among the many political resources that could be mentioned are wealth, numbers, organization, leadership, skill, diligence, and hard work. There is no reason to suppose that all groups and individuals share equally in these resources. Neither is there any reason to suppose that any one group has a monopoly of all, or even most, of these resources.[3]

The fact that political resources are relatively widely dispersed and that most citizens have an opportunity to share in the making of public policy as well as the benefits of public policy means that intense antagonisms against the government, or severe dissatisfaction with government is not likely to take place.

To maintain a relatively stable political system in a large and diverse country and in a constantly changing environment without excessive use of force is an accomplishment to which few countries can point. The analysis of why stability exists, through a close look at public policies, helps to give a reasonable interpretation of why this should be the case for the United States.

---

[3] See Robert A. Dahl, *Who Governs?* (New Haven: Yale University Press, 1961).